CorelDRAW™ 7
SECRETS®

The IDG Books SECRETS Advantage

The formula for a book in the SECRETS series is simple: Give an expert author a forum to pass on his or her expertise to readers. A SECRETS author, rather than the publishing company, directs the organization, pace, and treatment of the subject matter. SECRETS authors maintain contact with end users through feedback from articles, training sessions, e-mail exchanges, user group participation, and consulting work. Because our authors are not distanced from the reality of daily computer use, our SECRETS books have a strategic advantage: SECRETS authors are directly tied to the readers.

SECRETS authors have the experience to approach a topic in the most efficient manner, and we know that you, the reader, will benefit from a "one-on-one" relationship through the text with the author. Our research shows that readers make computer book purchases because they want an expert's take on a product. Readers want to benefit from the author's experience, and the author's voice is always present in a SECRETS series book. Some have compared the presentation of topics in a SECRETS book to sitting at a coffee break with the author and having the author's full attention.

In addition, the author is free to include or recommend useful software in a SECRETS book. The software that accompanies a SECRETS book is not intended to be casual filler but is linked to the content, theme, or procedures of the book. We know that you will benefit from the included software.

You will find what you need in this book, whether you read it from cover to cover, section by section, or simply one topic at a time. As a computer user, you deserve a comprehensive resource of answers. We at IDG Books Worldwide are proud to deliver that resource with *CorelDRAW 7 SECRETS*.

Brenda McLaughlin
Senior Vice President and Group Publisher
YouTellUs@idgbooks.com

CorelDRAW™ 7 SECRETS®

by William Harrel and Winston Steward

IDG
BOOKS
WORLDWIDE

IDG Books Worldwide, Inc.
An International Data Group Company

Foster City, CA ♦ Chicago, IL ♦ Indianapolis, IN ♦ Southlake, TX

CorelDRAW™ 7 SECRETS®

Published by

IDG Books Worldwide, Inc.

An International Data Group Company
919 E. Hillsdale Blvd., Suite 400
Foster City, CA 94404
www.idgbooks.com (IDG Books Worldwide Web Site)

Copyright © 1997 IDG Books Worldwide, Inc. All rights reserved. No part of this book, including interior design, cover design, and icons, may be reproduced or transmitted in any form, by any means (electronic, photocopying, recording, or otherwise) without the prior written permission of the publisher.

Library of Congress Catalog Card No.: 96-079765

ISBN: 1-7645-3039-9

Printed in the United States of America

10 9 8 7 6 5 4 3 2 1

IB/RT/QS/ZX/FC

Distributed in the United States by IDG Books Worldwide, Inc.

Distributed by Macmillan Canada for Canada; by Contemporanea de Ediciones for Venezuela; by Distribuidora Cuspide for Argentina; by CITEC for Brazil; by Ediciones ZETA S.C.R. Ltda. for Peru; by Editorial Limusa SA for Mexico; by Transworld Publishers Limited in the United Kingdom and Europe; by Academic Bookshop for Egypt; by Levant Distributors S.A.R.L. for Lebanon; by Al Jassim for Saudi Arabia; by Simron Pty. Ltd. for South Africa; by Pustak Mahal for India; by The Computer Bookshop for India; by Toppan Company Ltd. for Japan; by Addison Wesley Publishing Company for Korea; by Longman Singapore Publishers Ltd. for Singapore, Malaysia, Thailand, and Indonesia; by Unalis Corporation for Taiwan; by WS Computer Publishing Company, Inc. for the Philippines; by WoodsLane Pty. Ltd. for Australia; by WoodsLane Enterprises Ltd. for New Zealand. Authorized Sales Agent: Anthony Rudkin Associates for the Middle East and North Africa.

For general information on IDG Books Worldwide's books in the U.S., please call our Consumer Customer Service department at 800-762-2974. For reseller information, including discounts and premium sales, please call our Reseller Customer Service department at 800-434-3422.

For information on where to purchase IDG Books Worldwide's books outside the U.S., please contact our International Sales department at 415-655-3172 or fax 415-655-3295.

For information on foreign language translations, please contact our Foreign & Subsidiary Rights department at 415-655-3021 or fax 415-655-3281.

For sales inquiries and special prices for bulk quantities, please contact our Sales department at 415-655-3200 or write to the address above.

For information on using IDG Books Worldwide's books in the classroom or for ordering examination copies, please contact our Educational Sales department at 800-434-2086 or fax 817-251-8174.

For press review copies, author interviews, or other publicity information, please contact our Public Relations department at 415-655-3000 or fax 415-655-3299.

For authorization to photocopy items for corporate, personal, or educational use, please contact Copyright Clearance Center, 222 Rosewood Drive, Danvers, MA 01923, or fax 508-750-4470.

Fulfillment of coupon offers, if any, is the sole responsibility of the offeror.

is a trademark under exclusive license to IDG Books Worldwide, Inc., from International Data Group, Inc.

ABOUT IDG BOOKS WORLDWIDE

Welcome to the world of IDG Books Worldwide.

IDG Books Worldwide, Inc., is a subsidiary of International Data Group, the world's largest publisher of computer-related information and the leading global provider of information services on information technology. IDG was founded more than 25 years ago and now employs more than 8,500 people worldwide. IDG publishes more than 275 computer publications in over 75 countries (see listing below). More than 60 million people read one or more IDG publications each month.

Launched in 1990, IDG Books Worldwide is today the #1 publisher of best-selling computer books in the United States. We are proud to have received eight awards from the Computer Press Association in recognition of editorial excellence and three from *Computer Currents*' First Annual Readers' Choice Awards. Our best-selling *...For Dummies*® series has more than 30 million copies in print with translations in 30 languages. IDG Books Worldwide, through a joint venture with IDG's Hi-Tech Beijing, became the first U.S. publisher to publish a computer book in the People's Republic of China. In record time, IDG Books Worldwide has become the first choice for millions of readers around the world who want to learn how to better manage their businesses.

Our mission is simple: Every one of our books is designed to bring extra value and skill-building instructions to the reader. Our books are written by experts who understand and care about our readers. The knowledge base of our editorial staff comes from years of experience in publishing, education, and journalism — experience we use to produce books for the '90s. In short, we care about books, so we attract the best people. We devote special attention to details such as audience, interior design, use of icons, and illustrations. And because we use an efficient process of authoring, editing, and desktop publishing our books electronically, we can spend more time ensuring superior content and spend less time on the technicalities of making books.

You can count on our commitment to deliver high-quality books at competitive prices on topics you want to read about. At IDG Books Worldwide, we continue in the IDG tradition of delivering quality for more than 25 years. You'll find no better book on a subject than one from IDG Books Worldwide.

John J. Kilcullen

John Kilcullen
President and CEO
IDG Books Worldwide, Inc.

**Eighth Annual
Computer Press
Awards ≥1992**

**Ninth Annual
Computer Press
Awards ≥1993**

**Tenth Annual
Computer Press
Awards ≥1994**

**Eleventh Annual
Computer Press
Awards ≥1995**

IDG Books Worldwide, Inc., is a subsidiary of International Data Group, the world's largest publisher of computer-related information and the leading global provider of information services on information technology. International Data Group publishes over 275 computer publications in over 75 countries. Sixty million people read one or more International Data Group publications each month. International Data Group's publications include: **ARGENTINA:** Buyer's Guide, Computerworld Argentina, PC World Argentina; **AUSTRALIA:** Australian Macworld, Australian PC World, Australian Reseller News, Computerworld, IT Casebook, Network World, Publish, Webmaster; **AUSTRIA:** Computerwelt Osterreich, Networks Austria, PC Tip Austria; **BANGLADESH:** PC World Bangladesh; **BELARUS:** PC World Belarus; **BELGIUM:** Data News; **BRAZIL:** Annuário de Informática, Computerworld, Connections, Macworld, PC Player, PC World, Publish, Reseller News, Supergamepower; **BULGARIA:** Computerworld Bulgaria, Network World Bulgaria, PC & MacWorld Bulgaria; **CANADA:** CIO Canada, Client/Server World, ComputerWorld Canada, InfoWorld Canada, NetworkWorld Canada, WebWorld; **CHILE:** Computerworld Chile, PC World Chile; **COLOMBIA:** Computerworld Colombia, PC World Colombia; **COSTA RICA:** PC World Centro America; **THE CZECH AND SLOVAK REPUBLICS:** Computerworld Czechoslovakia, Macworld Czech Republic, PC World Czechoslovakia; **DENMARK:** Communications World Danmark, Computerworld Danmark, Macworld Danmark, PC World Danmark, Techworld Denmark; **DOMINICAN REPUBLIC:** PC World Republica Dominicana; **ECUADOR:** PC World Ecuador; **EGYPT:** Computerworld Middle East, PC World Middle East; **EL SALVADOR:** PC World Centro America; **FINLAND:** MikroPC, Tietoverkko, Tietoviikko; **FRANCE:** Distributique, Hebdo, Info PC, Le Monde Informatique, Macworld, Reseaux & Telecoms, WebMaster France; **GERMANY:** Computer Partner, Computerwoche, Computerwoche Extra, Computerwoche FOCUS, Global Online, Macwelt, PC Welt; **GREECE:** Amiga Computing, GamePro Greece, Multimedia World; **GUATEMALA:** PC World Centro America; **HONDURAS:** PC World Centro America; **HONG KONG:** Computerworld Hong Kong, PC World Hong Kong, Publish in Asia; **HUNGARY:** ABCD CD-ROM, Computerworld Szamitastechnika, Internetto online Magazine, PC World Hungary, PC-X Magazin Hungary; **ICELAND:** Tolvuheimur PC World Island; **INDIA:** Information Communications World, Information Systems Computerworld, PC World India, Publish in Asia; **INDONESIA:** InfoKomputer PC World, Komputek Computerworld, Publish in Asia; **IRELAND:** ComputerScope, PC Live!; **ISRAEL:** Macworld Israel, People & Computers/Computerworld; **ITALY:** Computerworld Italia, Macworld Italia, Networking Italia, PC World Italia; **JAPAN:** DTP World, Macworld Japan, Nikkei Personal Computing, OS/2 World Japan, SunWorld Japan, Windows NT World, Windows World Japan; **KENYA:** PC World East African; **KOREA:** Hi-Tech Information, Macworld Korea, PC World Korea; **MACEDONIA:** PC World Macedonia; **MALAYSIA:** Computerworld Malaysia, PC World Malaysia, Publish in Asia; **MALTA:** PC World Malta; **MEXICO:** Computerworld Mexico, PC World Mexico; **MYANMAR:** PC World Myanmar; **NETHERLANDS:** Computer! Totaal, LAN Internetworking Magazine, LAN World Buyers Guide, Macworld Netherlands, Net, WebWereld; **NEW ZEALAND:** Absolute Beginners Guide and Plain & Simple Series, Computer Buyer, Computer Industry Directory, Computerworld New Zealand, MTB, Network World, PC World New Zealand; **NICARAGUA:** PC World Centro America; **NORWAY:** Computerworld Norge, CW Rapport, Datamagasinet, Financial Rapport, Kursguide Norge, Macworld Norge, Multimediaworld Norge, PC World Ekspress Norge, PC World Nettverk, PC World Norge, PC World ProduktGuide Norge; **PAKISTAN:** Computerworld Pakistan; **PANAMA:** PC World Panama; **PEOPLE'S REPUBLIC OF CHINA:** China Computer Users, China Computerworld, China InfoWorld, China Telecom World Weekly, Computer & Communication, Electronic Design China, Electronics Today, Electronics Weekly, Game Software, PC World China, Popular Computer Week, Software Weekly, Software World, Telecom World; **PERU:** Computerworld Peru, PC World Profesional Peru, PC World SoHo Peru; **PHILIPPINES:** Click!, Computerworld Philippines, PC World Philippines, Publish in Asia; **POLAND:** Computerworld Poland, Computerworld Special Report Poland, Cyber, Macworld Poland, Networld Poland, PC World Komputer; **PORTUGAL:** Cerebro/PC World, Computerworld/Correio Informático, Dealer World Portugal, Mac*In/PC*In Portugal, Multimedia World; **PUERTO RICO:** PC World Puerto Rico; **ROMANIA:** Computerworld Romania, PC World Romania, Telecom Romania; **RUSSIA:** Computerworld Russia, Mir PK, Publish, Seti; **SINGAPORE:** Computerworld Singapore, PC World Singapore, Publish in Asia; **SLOVENIA:** Monitor; **SOUTH AFRICA:** Computing SA, Network World SA, Software World SA; **SPAIN:** Communicaciones World España, Computerworld España, Dealer World España, Macworld España, PC World España; **SRI LANKA:** Infolink PC World; **SWEDEN:** CAP&Design, Computer Sweden, Corporate Computing Sweden, Internetworld Sweden, it.branschen, Macworld Sweden, MaxiData Sweden, MikroDatorn, Nätverk & Kommunikation, PC World Sweden, PCaktiv, Windows World Sweden; **SWITZERLAND:** Computerworld Schweiz, Macworld Schweiz, PCtip; **TAIWAN:** Computerworld Taiwan, Macworld Taiwan, NEW ViSiON/Publish, PC World Taiwan, Windows World Taiwan; **THAILAND:** Publish in Asia, Thai Computerworld; **TURKEY:** Computerworld Turkiye, Macworld Turkiye, Network World Turkiye, PC World Turkiye; **UKRAINE:** Computerworld Kiev, Multimedia World Ukraine, PC World Ukraine; **UNITED KINGDOM:** Acorn User UK, Amiga Action UK, Amiga Computing UK, Apple Talk UK, Computing, Macworld, Parents and Computers UK, PC Advisor, PC Home, PSX Pro, The WEB; **UNITED STATES:** Cable in the Classroom, CIO Magazine, Computerworld, DOS World, Federal Computer Week, GamePro Magazine, InfoWorld, I-Way, Macworld, Network World, PC Games, PC World, Publish, Video Event, THE WEB Magazine, and WebMaster; online webzines: JavaWorld, NetscapeWorld, and SunWorld Online; **URUGUAY:** InfoWorld Uruguay; **VENEZUELA:** Computerworld Venezuela, PC World Venezuela; and **VIETNAM:** PC World Vietnam.   10/1/96

This book is dedicated to my wife, Heidi. She didn't really understand what it would be like being married to a computer journalist. Her adjustment has been the result of admirable and endearing patience.

William Harrel

For Barbara, Larisa, Trevor, and Irma.

Winston Steward

Preface

CorelDRAW is an extremely versatile graphics product that has grown more and more powerful with each new release. In addition to being a full-featured graphics application suite, CorelDRAW has continued to provide new features to help the nonartist, middle-management, and small business owner to create professional-looking graphics — without having a lot of artistic know-how. In fact, when one of this book's authors started his desktop publishing firm several years ago, having CorelDRAW in the firm's software arsenal provided an edge. It had the automatic drawing, type manipulation, and special effects features we needed to create graphics that often looked as though they were created by a professional design studio. CorelDRAW still provides those automatic tools today, but on a much larger scale.

In the Macintosh-dominated computer graphics field, CorelDRAW has made graphics in a Windows environment a viable, less-expensive solution. Many Windows draw programs have come and gone, and some others hold on by the skin of their teeth. Meanwhile, CorelDRAW maintains at least a 75 percent market share of the Windows graphics applications.

Part of the reason for this success is Corel's unrelenting commitment to value. With each new version of CorelDRAW, its power and versatility have increased dramatically. In addition to providing some very fine draw, paint, and special effects tools, CorelDRAW 7 comes with everything you need to create spectacular graphics with minimal fuss (including thousands of clip art, stock photography, and 3D model images), hundreds of fonts, and several useful utilities. And now you can use CorelDRAW to create colorful Web pages.

New Features

In reality, we could write an entire book this size dedicated solely to pointing out and explaining the scads of new features in version 7. And some in particular are worth pointing out here. First is the new Property Bar each program in the suite now sports. If you're familiar with PageMaker's Control Palette or QuarkXPress's Measurements Palette, you'll appreciate the Property Bar. It displays context-sensitive controls for virtually all of each program's features, almost eliminating the need to wade through cumbersome menus, dialog boxes, and roll-ups.

In the flagship application, CorelDraw, you'll also find several new interactive tools for creating blends and fills. No longer is it necessary to make obscure settings in dialog boxes to figure out how to place blend steps or fountain fill midpoints. CorelDraw also now provides the capability of creating HTML Web pages from the drawings and publications you create — with just a few mouse clicks.

Corel Photo-Paint also has many enhancements, including the capability of creating the animated GIF files you see all over the World Wide Web. And, it too has a highly useful Property Bar. CorelDream 3D is also greatly enhanced, making it a full-featured and relatively easy-to-use 3D modeling program.

This brief mention of the new features and enhancements in CorelDRAW 7 barely scratches the surface. The entire package seems to run and load faster, and it has fewer quirks than version 6. Our hats are off to Corel. Version 7 is truly a magnificent feat of software engineering.

Who Should Read This Book?

CorelDRAW 7 SECRETS is designed for advanced and intermediate users — people who are already familiar with the basic ins and outs of CorelDRAW. In this book, we emphasize the seldom-used but highly beneficial features and techniques of the program. We use CorelDRAW in our daily work and we know how to get results. With the secrets we provide, you can quickly get the results you need, too.

In addition, as CorelDRAW users, we know that most other users of this highly versatile graphics program usually confine their work to one, sometimes two, applications in the suite, say only CorelDraw, or maybe CorelDraw and Photo-Paint. With this in mind, I've tried to produce a book that helps you use all of the programs and utilities in the suite — even if you usually focus on only two or three. Unlike most other CorelDRAW books, in this one you'll find extensive coverage of Photo-Paint, Dream 3D, and chapters on how to use CorelScan, the templates, clip art, and more. We think this is the most well-rounded and useful book on CorelDRAW available — even if we are just a little biased.

So, even if you are already familiar with CorelDraw (the suite's drawing application), you need this book so you can get the most from the *entire* suite.

How This Book Is Organized

CorelDRAW is so powerful and versatile that it's almost impossible to learn everything about the entire application suite. We use it almost daily and we're still learning. In addition, Corel's yearly update schedule means that you always have new features to contend with.

You can read this book in two ways: from cover to cover, or as needed as a reference. Frankly, we don't know anybody who reads after-market software books from cover to cover, especially one this size. With that in mind, we've arranged the book according to task and application so you can dive in wherever you want and find exactly the information you need. I've divided this book into four parts, as follows:

- **Part I** consists of several chapters covering just CorelDraw, the vector drawing part of the application. Here you'll find numerous tips and secrets for working with type, fills, and special effects, as well as invaluable information on preparing your images for various destinations including the computer screen and prepress. Much of this information is also pertinent to working with Photo-Paint and Dream 3D, so try not to skip it, especially Chapter 7.

- **Part II** concentrates on the other full-featured applications in the suite, namely Photo-Paint and Dream 3D. If you have never used or installed these two quite useful and powerful programs, here's your chance to fire them up. Photo-Paint, of course, enables you to edit and enhance photographs and create Web graphics. Dream 3D lets you create both still and animated 3D models.

- **Part III** deals with the utilities, clip art, clip media, and templates included on the CDs. You'll learn how to scan and trace bitmaps, as well as use OCR-Trace to turn scanned text into editable text. And you'll learn how to use the suite's useful scripting language to automate several aspects of your work.

- **Part IV** brings into focus an all-new forum for computer graphics — the World Wide Web. You'll learn about using Web browser color palettes, creating multimedia events for the Internet, and much more.

Conventions

As I've said, *CorelDRAW 7 SECRETS* is designed to provide in-depth and insightful coverage of the CorelDRAW graphics suite. To help you find information quickly, the text is annotated with the following icons. Use them as navigational aids.

Secret

The **Secret** icon highlights information about CorelDRAW that is not documented well or not widely known.

Design

The **Design** icon highlights information relating to or impacting decisions you make regarding image and document design issues and principles.

Note

The **Note** icon marks additional information about a feature or task, providing more insight on the standard procedure topics. Notes sometimes direct you to other parts of the book or other sources for finding additional information.

Tip

The **Tip** icon points out hints that can help you work easier and faster.

The **Expert Advice** icon marks information, techniques, or preferences from design experts and CorelDRAW experts.

Warning

The **Warning** icon warns you about procedures to which you should pay particular attention. Do yourself a favor — don't skip these.

Remember

The **Remember** icon reminds you about points that are easily over-looked or forgotten.

Finally, to assist you in reading and learning the material in this book, we use the following formatting conventions throughout the text:

- Alternative command paths are formatted in stylized brackets. For example, the command you use to open a dialog box would appear like this: Choose File ⇨ Open [Ctrl+O].
- Text that you are asked to type appears in **bold**.

Another convention we follow throughout the book is to say "CorelDRAW" when referring to the entire suite of applications, and to say "CorelDraw" when referring to the Draw application by itself. Occasionally the distinction is important, but usually the context emphasizes the distinction whenever it really matters.

One more thing. Although two of us wrote this book, we've written each chapter using singular pronouns (I, me) rather than plural. But two of us are really out there!

By now we're sure you're more than ready to learn all you can about CorelDRAW 7. That's what this book is for, so let's get started.

Acknowledgments

Heart-felt thanks go out to the editors at IDG Books Worldwide, Ellen Camm, Ron Hull, Michael Welch, and Bob Campbell. If it were not for their efforts in keeping me focused during this enormous task, there might never have been a *CorelDRAW 7 SECRETS*. And that would have been a shame.

I'd also like to thank Winston Steward for his exhaustive efforts, and my wife Heidi for putting up with the late nights and ill-temper these projects invariably produce. Her help putting together the CD-ROM material for this book was nothing short of spectacular.

William Harrel

I would like to thank Ron Hull and Ellen Camm for superb editorial support and accepting setbacks with good humor and grace. Thanks also to Margot Maley, agent extraordinaire. A special thanks to MegaImage, of Pomona, California, for building a laptop computer that would rise to this significant challenge.

Winston Steward

Contents at a Glance

Table of Contents

Chapter 11: Plug-Ins for Photo-Paint and CorelDraw 377

Chapter 12: Dream 3D...391

Part I

Drawing with CorelDraw

Chapter 1

The CorelDraw Interface

In This Chapter

You'll learn about the interface of the CorelDraw module of the CorelDRAW 7 suite. The topics covered include the following:

▶ Customizing your keyboard, menus, toolbars, roll-ups, and color palette

▶ Touring the new Property Bar

▶ Working more efficiently in CorelDraw

When the folks at Corel created CorelDraw, they designed the program to be as useful as possible for the largest number of users. The problem is that no two users work the same way. Consequently, Corel has made CorelDraw completely customizable. You can create your own menus, add buttons to the toolbar, create your own shortcut keys, and perform all sorts of customization wizardry to make the program's interface fit your needs. In this chapter you'll learn how to make CorelDraw work more like you do.

If you're like most computer program users, you learn one way to perform a task and then use the same method over and over to achieve the same results. If it works, don't fix it, right? Well, no — not necessarily. CorelDraw provides several ways to achieve the same results, and usually one method is faster and more efficient than others. In the last part of this chapter we'll look at some of the program's shortcut features, such as using pop-up menus, dragging and dropping between documents, and so forth. One feature that can really speed up your work is CorelDraw 7's new Property Bar, which we'll also look at in this chapter.

Customizing the Interface

The CorelDraw interface is based on a drawing-table metaphor. Picture yourself sitting at a drawing easel. You arrange your tools — pencils, pens, rulers, and so on — in a manner that best suits the way you work. Working in CorelDraw is the same. You can customize the user interface to adapt the program to the type of work *you* do. For example, you can add, delete, and modify the following:

■ Keyboard shortcuts

■ Menus and menu commands

- Toolbar options
- Colors on the color palette

You can also customize the way roll-up palettes work. You perform each type of customization option in the Customize dialog box, shown in Figure 1-1, which you access by choosing Options ⇨ Customize.

Figure 1-1: Use the Customize dialog box to rearrange interface options.

As you can see in Figure 1-1, the Customize dialog box contains five different sheets: Keyboard, Menu, Toolbars, Roll-Ups, and Color Palette. Click on each one of these tabs to display the associated sheet as we go over the options available on these sheets one at a time.

Changing Default Attributes

In addition to enabling you to customize menu, keyboard, toolbar, and roll-up options, CorelDraw also lets you modify virtually all aspects of the interface, including the default line weight, fill, text size, and typeface. To change these default attributes, you simply make a change without selecting an object. For example, to change the default typeface to, say, Garamond 14-point, *with nothing selected,* simply choose Text ⇨ Format Text. CorelDraw displays a dialog box informing you that you are about to make a change to the default text attributes. The dialog box also gives you the option to assign the new default to artistic text, paragraph text, or both. (If you were working with a line or fill attribute,

CorelDraw would provide a different message, of course.)

When you click OK, the Format Text dialog box appears, enabling you to set text attributes. The changes you make at this point are changes to the default settings. As you can imagine, this is a powerful way to customize CorelDraw to work the way you do. We'll look closer at this feature in the next chapter.

Once you get the settings exactly to your liking, you make the changes permanent with the Settings for New Documents command on the Tools menu. This option reconfigures the default new document settings, including the changes you make to the interface, as you'll do during the remainder of this chapter.

Keyboard shortcuts

Keyboard shortcuts (sometimes called *hotkeys*) are keystrokes that execute commands, often saving you the trouble of opening menus and wading through nested dialog boxes. CorelDraw comes with several keyboard shortcuts already assigned. You can see many of these shortcuts simply by viewing the menus. On the Text menu, for instance, the shortcut that opens the Character Attributes dialog box (Ctrl+T) appears to the right of the Character command.

Secret

You can use CorelDraw's Help system to get a list of shortcuts on each menu. To do so, simply select Help ⇨ Help Topics, and then click on the Find tab in the Help Topics dialog box. Then, in the Type the Word(s) you Want to Find field, type **keyboard,** as shown in Figure 1-2. In the "Click a topic, then click Display" list, scroll until you find the menu you want. Double-click on the topic (such as "Accessing the Customize dialog box") that corresponds to the menu. You can also get a list of all the preassigned function key shortcuts by searching for "function keys in Help" and then double-clicking "Function Keys."

Figure 1-2: To view a list of keyboard shortcuts for a specific menu, type **keyboard** in the top field and then in the bottom field look for a topic related to that topic.

Although you'll find many of the preassigned keyboard shortcuts to be useful, you can speed up your work by modifying the preassigned shortcuts and adding your own. You can add, remove, and change around the keyboard shortcuts using the Keyboard sheet in the Customize dialog box. Choose Tools ⇨ Customize. Then, if it's not already selected, click on the Keyboard tab in the Customize dialog box.

In the list on the left labeled Commands, you'll find an index of CorelDraw menus. To view the list of commands on a menu, click the small plus sign (+) to the left of the menu name (or double-click the name). To add a keyboard shortcut — or to modify or remove an existing shortcut — click on the appropriate command in the Commands list. If the command already has a keystroke shortcut assigned, the key combination shows up in the Current Shortcut Keys field near the center of the dialog box, as shown in Figure 1-3.

Figure 1-3: To see the keyboard shortcut(s) assigned to a command, highlight the command in the Commands list.

To delete a currently assigned shortcut, simply select the keystroke combination in the Current Shortcut Keys field and click on Delete. To add a keystroke shortcut, make sure the appropriate command is selected in the Commands list, move the cursor to the Press New Shortcut Key field, and then press the keystroke combination you want to assign. Keystroke shortcuts can consist of the following kinds of combinations:

- Ctrl+*key* or *function key*
- Ctrl+Shift+*key* or *function key*
- Ctrl+Alt+*key* or *function key*
- Ctrl+Alt+Shift+*key* or *function key*
- Alt+*key* or *function key*
- Alt+Shift+*key* or *function key*

If you choose a keystroke combination already assigned to another command or option, the existing assignment appears in the portion of the dialog box labeled "Currently assigned to." Because the same keyboard shortcut cannot be assigned to two different commands or options, you'll need to either choose a new keystroke combination or change the existing keyboard shortcut that conflicts with the new assignment. (If you check the "Go to conflict on assign" checkbox, CorelDraw automatically takes you to the command with a conflicting keyboard shortcut so you can change that assignment.) To complete the procedure, click the Assign button. You can make as many assignments and changes as you want before leaving this dialog box, but remember to click OK. If you click the Cancel button, you will lose your new keyboard shortcut assignments.

Assigning Keyboard Shortcuts to Styles and Scripts

If you've been using CorelDraw for a while, than you probably already know about the program's powerful style and scripting capabilities. (If not, Chapter 4 discusses text styles, Chapter 5 discusses color styles, and Chapter 19 covers scripting.) *Styles*, of course, enable you to define several attributes (such as typefaces, type styles, point sizes, outlines, and fills), assign them to a style name, and then apply them to an object with a mouse click or two. *Scripts* are macros you can record to execute several commands or functions at once, much like the macro function in word processors.

In addition to assigning commands, you can also assign styles and scripts to shortcut keys. Doing so enables you to apply a style or run a script simply by pressing a key combination. You can do this in the Customize dialog box, as shown in Figure A. To assign a style to a keyboard shortcut, scroll in the Commands list until Apply Styles appears, displaying a list of styles defined for the current template. Now use the same

method described earlier in this section for assigning shortcuts to commands. You assign scripts in the same manner, except you need to use the commands listed in the Apply Styles folder in the Commands list.

Figure A: To assign shortcuts to styles and scripts, open the Apply Styles folder to view a list of available styles and scripts.

Multilayered keyboard shortcuts

If you assign keyboard shortcuts to a lot of commands, styles, and scripts, you could conceivably run out of keystroke combinations — or you might forget which keyboard shortcuts have already been assigned. CorelDraw provides a way to expand the number of combinations and at the same time logically organize your shortcuts. Unlike many other Windows applications, CorelDraw supports *multilayered shortcuts*. In other words, your keystroke combinations can consist of many consecutive keys, up to four levels deep, such as Ctrl+Alt+1,2,3,4. In this example, you would press Ctrl+Alt and then press 1, 2, 3, and 4 in succession.

Multiple layers are especially useful for organizing script and style shortcuts. For example, if you have several styles for headings, subheads, and so on, you might decide to number your heading styles in layers. You could give level-one headings the shortcut Ctrl+Alt+1; level-two headings Ctrl+Alt+1,1; level-three headings Ctrl+Alt+1,1,1; and so forth. With a little ingenuity, you can create multilayered shortcuts that are organized in a way that enables you to work most efficiently.

Multiple keyboard-shortcut layouts

Secret

If you use CorelDraw to create several different types of documents — say, a newsletter one week, a flyer the next, and so on — you might find it useful to create and save two or more keyboard-shortcut layouts. That's right, you can set up a new keyboard-shortcut layout for each type of document you create.

While many word processing programs support multiple keyboard-shortcut layouts, this feature is usually not available in graphics applications. But it can be quite handy, especially if you use CorelDraw to lay out entire documents rather than simply for creating drawings and images.

By default, CorelDraw uses the file CDRDEF.ACL to define the current keyboard shortcut layout. (*ACL* stands for *accelerator* file. Corel calls time-saving keyboard shortcuts *accelerator keys*, and the files in which the shortcuts are defined are called accelerator files.) After assigning your accelerator keys, to save the current configuration to a new file, you simply click Save As, name the file, and that's that. The program automatically adds the .ACL extension. To load a different accelerator file, click the Load button and double-click on the one you need.

Remember

Remember, Windows 95 and Windows NT support long filenames. So give that accelerator file a meaningful name, perhaps something like "Monthly Newsletter Keystrokes."

Menus and menu commands

Okay, so CorelDraw has numerous features that can turn even unartistic people into illustrators. But let's face it, all those features translate into way too many menus and choices. This is especially true of CorelDraw 7, which has even more menus and choices than previous versions. I've been using CorelDraw for years, and I still find all those long menus a bit daunting. With version 7, though, you can get rid of the menu options that you never use.

You might also decide to create custom menu structures for certain kinds of documents that involve similar tasks. For example, if you perform repetitive tasks in a document such as a monthly catalog or brochure, you can create a menu structure for that kind of document with only the commands and scripts you need.

Tip

In addition to letting you add and modify menus, CorelDraw 7 enables you to change the pop-up menus that you access with the right mouse button. These are the menus that pop up when you right-click during certain functions or operations. Figure 1-4 shows an example. In version 7, you can determine which options appear in the different pop-up menus. Neat, huh?

Figure 1-4: CorelDraw 7 makes pop-up menus fully customizable.

You can modify CorelDraw's menus from the Menu sheet of the Customize dialog box, as shown in Figure 1-5. Choose Tools ⇨ Customize ⇨ Menu.

Figure 1-5: Use the Menu portion of the Customize dialog box to modify CorelDraw's menu structure.

From here you can perform the following tasks:

- Add and delete menus on the menu bar
- Change the order of menus on the menu bar
- Add and delete submenus
- Rearrange submenus on a menu
- Add and delete commands on a menu
- Rearrange the commands on a menu
- Move commands or submenus from one menu to another
- Add styles and scripts to menus

Let's take a look at each of these tasks related to customizing the menus.

Adding, deleting, and moving menus

When you open the Customize dialog box and click the Menu tab, CorelDraw displays your current menu structure, as was shown in Figure 1-5. The Commands list on the left displays all of the available functions, including options on many of the roll-ups and any styles or scripts you might have created. This list is where you choose objects for inclusion in your new menu structure. In the Menu list on the right you build new menus and modify existing ones.

When you're customizing the menu bar itself — the row of menus across the top of the screen — make sure that Main Menu is selected in the Menu drop-down list. (The other items in the drop-down list are your pop-up menus, grouped by context.)

To add a menu, click the Add Menu button. This creates a new menu on the list. The space for the menu's name is automatically selected so you can name the menu, as Figure 1-6 shows. Because the menu is brand new, it does not contain any commands or options. You'll see how to add those a little later.

Figure 1-6: When you add a new menu, its name is automatically highlighted so you can customize it.

To delete a menu, simply select it in the Menu list and then click Remove. Keep in mind that deleting a menu removes not only the menu name but also all the commands on it. Those commands will be unavailable while you work (unless they are available in roll-ups or through shortcut key assignments). You can assign the deleted commands and options to other menus.

To change the position of a menu on the menu bar, select it, and then click on the Move Up and Move Down buttons to position the menu where you want it, as shown in Figures 1-7 and 1-8.

Figure 1-7: Use the Move Up and Move Down buttons to position a menu on the menu bar.

Figure 1-8: When you click on the Move Down button enough times, the selected menu moves to the end of the menu bar.

Adding, deleting, and moving submenus

Submenus, also called *flyouts*, are menus within menus. Submenus can add a wide variety of options to a menu. For example, a typical submenu is the Font submenu, in which you can view a list of the typefaces available on your computer. Submenus can hold commands, scripts, and styles. They can also contain other submenus. The procedure for adding, deleting, and moving submenus is similar to adding, deleting, and moving menus, except that the drop-down list on the Menu sheet of the Customize dialog box must display the name of the menu you want to customize.

To add a submenu, double-click on the menu where you want to add the submenu. The name of the menu should appear in the Menu drop-down list. Click on Add Menu and then give the menu a name, just as you do when you add a new menu to the menu bar. (You can add as many submenus as you like, but at some point it becomes counterproductive.)

Delete submenus by selecting them and then clicking Remove. As with menus, when you delete a submenu, all of the commands and options on the menu are also deleted. You can change a submenu's position on a menu by clicking on the Move Up and Move Down buttons.

Adding, deleting, and moving commands, styles, and scripts

When talking about menu entries, Corel calls everything that can be placed on a menu a *command*; these items include styles, scripts, roll-up options, and regular commands. Menu commands can include the styles and scripts you create within a document template as well as predefined options.

You can add menu commands (that is, styles, scripts, commands, and so forth) to either submenus or menus, by following these steps:

STEPS

Adding and Removing Commands on a Menu

Step 1.   In the Menu list, double-click on the menu or submenu where you want to add or remove a command.

Step 2.   In the Commands list on the left, scroll to the command you want to add or remove and then highlight it.

Step 3.   Click on the Add button or Remove button.

Step 4.   To move an item up or down on a menu, use the Move Up or Move Down buttons.

Working with Templates and Styles

Most experienced CorelDraw users are familiar with templates. *Templates* are predefined shells, or blueprints, you can use to create drawings and documents. CorelDraw ships with several predesigned templates for various projects, such as newsletters, brochures, and other documents. Each template contains its own set of predefined text, graphics, and color styles. You can also create and save your own templates for use in repetitive or similar projects.

When you start a new CorelDraw document, unless you choose another template, you'll work in a style set based on the *default* template. If, while working in the default template, you change existing styles or create additional ones, these are added to the style list for that template. This is also true when you work in templates other than the default. Each template has its own set of styles. So, when assigning styles to menus, you can only work with those contained in the current template.

The procedure for adding styles to menus is similar, the only variation being that you add the items in the Apply Styles folder in the Command list to your menus in the menu list.

You can further customize your menu by adding separators. Separators are those narrow lines on a menu that break the menu into sections, as shown in Figure 1-9. To add a separator, highlight the command or submenu directly above the point where you want the separator to appear, and then click the Separator button.

Figure 1-9: When designing menus, you can use separators to mark off groups of commands and make them easier to read.

Customizing pop-up menus

Seasoned Windows 95 users are no doubt familiar with pop-up menus accessed by clicking the right mouse button. These menus give you quick and easy access to commands and options according to context. In CorelDraw, for instance, when you right-click the text I-beam on selected text you get the menu shown in Figure 1-10. This enables you to perform text formatting and editing tasks quickly, without shunting to the menu bar.

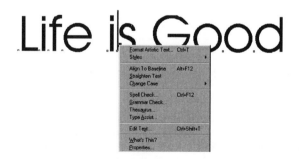

Figure 1-10: Clicking the right mouse button displays a pop-up menu.

Of course, the menu that appears depends on the tool selected and what you click on. CorelDraw ships with several predefined pop-ups. To see a list of them, in the Menus portion of the Customize dialog box, click on the

Menu drop-down list. To edit a right-mouse button menu, scroll through the list and select the option you want to edit. CorelDraw displays the menu layout for that selection. Now, to add, delete, and rearrange the pop-up commands, simply follow the procedure you learned earlier in this section.

Secret

At first glance the capability to customize pop-ups may seem ho-hum. But let's give it some more thought. One of my favorite uses for this option is to assign scripts to the pop-ups. Then, when I right-click on an object, all of my scripts appear. All I have to do is choose the one I want to run on the select object.

Toolbars

Toolbars are palettes of buttons and fields that give you quick and easy access to commands and other features. CorelDraw ships with several predefined toolbars that you can modify to suit your needs, or you can create your own. Over the years, I have found that many CorelDraw users don't even know that CorelDraw has toolbars in addition to the ones that appear automatically. If you're one of those people, you're not alone.

Controlling how toolbars are displayed

To see the available toolbars, choose View ➪ Toolbars. You will see the dialog box shown in Figure 1-11. From here you can choose which toolbars to display, control how the toolbars appear, and create new toolbars.

Figure 1-11: Use the Toolbars dialog box to choose the toolbars you want to display.

By default, CorelDraw displays several toolbars, including the Property Bar, toolbox, and the standard toolbar. To display additional toolbars, select them in the Toolbars dialog box. You can also change the appearance of the toolbars by clicking the Options button in the Toolbars dialog box. You can change the button size and the width of the borders around the buttons. This option is handy if you need to adjust the size of buttons to fit better on your monitor.

When you click OK, the toolbars and the options you select appear on the application desktop. Depending on the toolbars you choose, they will either display at the top of the window (*docked*) or as a separate entity (*floating*) in the application window. You have several options for changing the appearance and location of toolbars. Figure 1-12 shows the Text toolbar displayed three different ways: floating, docked, and resized.

Figure 1-12: You can float, dock, or resize any toolbar.

To float a docked toolbar, move it from its docked position by dragging on a portion of the bar that is unoccupied by a field or button. To dock a floating toolbar, drag it to the position at the top or bottom of the window where you want it to remain docked. To resize a toolbar, drag its sides, as shown in Figure 1-13.

Figure 1-13: To resize a toolbar, drag on the sides or corners.

Adding and removing toolbar buttons

You can add, remove, and rearrange toolbar buttons using the Customize dialog box. You can get there by clicking Customize in the Toolbars dialog box, or by choosing Tools ➪ Customize and then clicking on the Toolbars tab. Both methods bring up the Customize dialog box shown in Figure 1-14. If you want to change a toolbar using the second method, you need to make sure the toolbar is displayed when you open the dialog box.

Figure 1-14: Use the Toolbars sheet of the Customize dialog box to add buttons and fields to toolbars.

The Command Categories field on the left side of the Customize dialog box contains all the available commands and options you can assign to toolbars. The Buttons palette on the right shows the available buttons for the selected category. For example, when you select Text Properties in the Command Categories field, you see all of the buttons and fields designed for changing text attributes. To add a button or field to the Text toolbar, simply drag the button or field from the dialog box onto the toolbar, as shown in Figure 1-15.

To remove buttons or fields, simply drag them off the toolbar. You can change the positions of buttons on a toolbar simply by dragging them while the dialog box is open.

Figure 1-15: To add buttons and fields to a toolbar, simply drag them from the dialog box onto the toolbar. Here, the Font Weight List drop-down list box is being added to the Text toolbar at the bottom.

Easy enough to drag and drop, right? One thing, though: No matter how long you've been using CorelDraw, you probably don't know what *all* of the available buttons mean. To find out, simply rest your mouse pointer over a button for a second. A message appears telling you what the button does. (Macintosh users know this feature as "Bubble Help.")

Secret

Instead of using obscure little icons on your buttons, you can put text on your toolbar buttons. Here's how: In the toolbar, right-click on the button you want to change from icon to text. Select Properties, and then, in the Button Properties dialog box, select Show Text. (You can alter the appearance of the button from here, as well.) When you close Button Properties, the button appears with descriptive text. The problem with this option is that the text takes up a lot more room. When you use text buttons, you cannot fit as many buttons on a toolbar.

Creating new toolbars

In addition to modifying existing toolbars, you can create your own new toolbars in two different easy ways: from the Toolbars dialog box (shown in Figure 1-11) or from the Toolbars sheet of the Customize dialog.

To use the first method, simply click on New and then type the name of the new toolbar. To add buttons and fields, click on the Customize button. Then add and arrange buttons and fields as necessary.

You can perform the second method from within the Toolbars sheet of the Customize dialog box. Drag any button out of the Buttons palette and place it on an *unoccupied* portion of the application window (not on an existing toolbar). CorelDraw automatically creates a new toolbar, naming it Toolbar 1. The next new toolbar would be Toolbar 2, and so on. To rename toolbars, choose View ⇨ Toolbars, right-click on the toolbar you want to rename, and then choose Rename.

Roll-up groups

One of the most useful features of CorelDraw is roll-ups. *Roll-ups* are palettes of commands that make it easy to modify the objects in your drawings. The Blend roll-up, for example, enables you to create blends between two or more objects.

Unlike menus and toolbars, you can't really add and remove options from roll-ups. You can, however, create groups of roll-ups specific to your own personal work habits. You can also specify the default location for each roll-up in the application window.

Roll-up groups are combinations of several roll-ups with related functions. The Effects roll-up group, for instance, contains all of the roll-ups you would use to create special effects, such as adding perspective, blending, creating 3D extrudes, and so on. The Attributes roll-up group contains the Special Fill and Pen roll-ups for modifying an object's lines and fills. You'll find roll-up groups useful because they reduce the clutter caused by the large number of roll-ups CorelDraw has accumulated over the years.

CorelDraw ships with several roll-up groups you can modify, or you can create your own groups. You can modify or create roll-up groups in the application window using the mouse to drag and drop, or you can create new groups in the Roll-Ups sheet of the Customize dialog box.

Creating roll-up groups using drag-and-drop

While CorelDraw's current roll-up configuration is probably fine for most uses, you may find it convenient to create your own task-specific sets. To modify a roll-up group, open the group you want to change by clicking on Tools ⇨ Roll-up Groups. Then you have three choices, as follows:

- **To separate** a roll-up from its current group, simply drag it from the roll-up list in the group, as shown in Figure 1-16.

- **To move** a roll-up from one group to another, simply drag it from one roll-up group list to another, as shown in Figure 1-17.

- **To combine** two roll-ups or add a single roll-up to an existing group, hold Alt as you drag to the title bar of the roll-up or group you want to combine with, as shown in Figure 1-18.

The cursor changes to an arrow with a roll-up icon as you drag the roll-up.

Figure 1-16: To separate a single roll-up from a group, simply drag it from the group to the desktop.

Figure 1-17: To move a roll-up from one group to another, drag it from one group list to another.

Figure 1-18: To combine two single roll-ups, hold Alt and drag one roll-up to the other's title bar.

When you combine two single roll-ups, CorelDraw lets you name the new group whatever you like, as shown in Figure 1-19. Simply click on the selected text *New Group 1* and then retype the name.

Figure 1-19: To rename a new roll-up group, click on the highlighted name and type a new name.

Creating roll-up groups using the Customize dialog box

In addition to creating and modifying roll-up groups in the application window, you can also make changes to group configurations in the Customize dialog box. You can do this by clicking on the Roll-Ups tab. The Roll-Ups sheet of the Customize dialog box appears, as shown in Figure 1-20. The dialog box displays roll-ups and groups according to how they appear in the "arranged" position on the left and right sides of the application window. In other words, they are listed based on the position they line up in when you choose Arrange All from any roll-up flyout menu. Figure 1-21 shows all the roll-ups in the Arrange All position. If you compare Figures 1-20 and 1-21, you can see what I mean.

Figure 1-20: Use the Roll-Ups sheet of the Customize dialog box to customize roll-up groups.

Figure 1-21: All of CorelDraw's roll-ups are organized here in the Arrange All position.

Modifying roll-up groups from this dialog box is a lot like creating new menus and arranging menu options. To add a roll-up to an existing group, open the group by double-clicking on it, and then use the Move buttons or drag and drop a roll-up into the group. You can also use this dialog box to change which side a roll-up lines up on when you invoke Arrange All. To change the stacking order, simply drag the roll-up icon up or down the list. To create a new group, click on the New Group button, name the group, and then move the desired roll-ups into the new group.

You can also direct CorelDraw to display all roll-ups and groups upon opening the program. To do this, choose All Roll-Ups Arranged from the Start-Up setting drop-down list in the lower-left corner of the Roll-Ups sheet in the Customize dialog box. Choosing No Roll-Ups instructs the program to open with no roll-ups displayed. Save on Exit saves the roll-up layout when you close CorelDraw. The next time you open it you'll get the exact same arrangement.

The Color Palette

You have many ways to work with color more efficiently in CorelDraw. In this section, you'll learn how to modify the display of the color palette. Chapter 5 provides a more in-depth discussion of applying and using colors.

You probably already know that you can add and remove colors from the color palette that spans the bottom of the CorelDraw window. (If you don't know how to do this, I'll show you in Chapter 5.) But did you know that you can also change the appearance and position of the color palette? This can make it easier to get to, and you can access all the colors at once rather than having to scroll back and forth. You can adjust the appearance of the color palette by clicking the Color Palette tab in the Customize dialog box, as shown in Figure 1-22.

Figure 1-22: Use the Color Palette sheet of the Customize dialog box to modify the appearance and behavior of the color palette.

Changing the size of the color swatches

If you're working on a relatively small, high-resolution monitor, color swatches in the palette may be difficult to see. You can remedy this problem with the Large Swatches option in the Color Palette sheet of the Customize dialog box. Figure 1-23 shows what large color swatches look like on the color palette.

Figure 1-23: Using the Large Swatches option makes colors easier to see in the color palette along the bottom of the window.

Displaying more colors at once

Secret

Having to scroll back and forth in the color palette can be tedious. In fact, when I'm feeling lazy, I sometimes choose one of the visible colors rather than scrolling through the palette to find the exact hue I need. CorelDraw provides a remedy to temporary bouts of sloth by enabling you to display *all* of the colors on the color palette. You do so by using the Color Palette sheet of the Customize dialog box to adjust the number of rows displayed. You control this setting using the "Display *x* rows while docked" option.

Figure 1-24 shows the color palette with two rows displayed.

Figure 1-24: See more colors at once by adjusting the number of rows displayed in the color palette while it's docked. You can even display all the colors this way.

If you use a small, low-resolution monitor, you may be more interested in saving screen real estate than displaying more colors. An alternative is to place colors you use most at the front of the color palette. You can use the right-mouse pop-up menu to move a color by selecting the Move to Front command. In addition, you can temporarily display all of the colors on the palette by clicking on the upward-pointing scroll arrow in the lower-right portion of the application window, as shown in Figure 1-25. The full palette remains visible until you release the mouse button.

Figure 1-25: Clicking on this scroll button temporarily displays all of the colors on the palette.

Changing the location of the color palette

On large, high-resolution monitors, you sometimes have to drag the mouse a long way from the drawing area to the color palette. CorelDraw provides relief by letting you float the color palette or dock it at the top or left side of the screen. Once you've floated the palette, you can resize it just like a toolbar, as shown in Figure 1-26. To float the palette, simply drag on the gray area around the swatches. To resize a floated palette, drag on a side or corner of the palette, just as you would a toolbar.

To dock the palette at the top or left side of the application window, drag the palette into the position you want, as shown in Figure 1-27. You can tell when the palette is in place when the outline of the palette pops into the new docked position. When you release the mouse button, the palette docks.

As you can see, the customization options for the color palette are extensive. You should experiment to find the right settings for the way you work.

Figure 1-26: To move the color palette to a new position, drag it into place.

Figure 1-27: To dock the color palette, drag it into position and release the mouse button.

The Property Bar

Many professional desktop publishers and designers use graphics programs such as CorelDraw to create graphics for their layouts and then use a desktop publishing program, such as Adobe PageMaker or QuarkXPress, to lay out their pages. People who use desktop publishing programs are familiar with global control palettes that enable you to modify objects according to context. In PageMaker, for example, the Control Palette provides users with readily available controls for modifying selected objects according to which object is selected with what tool.

CorelDraw's new Property Bar is a similar device; however, it goes far beyond the palettes found in popular layout packages. It includes not only the traditional size, placement, rotation, and attributes options, but all sorts of other features. For example, when you select multiple objects, the Property Bar changes automatically. You get controls for grouping, combining, and aligning objects, and more. Figure 1-28 shows what the Property Bar looks like when multiple objects have been selected.

Figure 1-28: When you select multiple objects, the Property Bar provides options for working in that context.

When you apply special effects, such as blends or extrudes, the Property Bar changes to provide special options for modifying the effect, as shown in Figure 1-29.

Figure 1-29: When you select an object containing a special effect, such as a blend, the Property Bar adapts to work with the effect.

Note

In all, about 20 Property Bar contexts exist — more than this chapter has room to discuss. Instead, I'll mention the different Property Bar configurations where they are relevant to the discussion at hand.

Customizing the Property Bar

Technically speaking, the Property Bar is a toolbar, and you modify it pretty much in the same way you do the others. (Toolbar customization is discussed earlier in this chapter.) You customize the Property Bar by clicking on the Toolbars tab in the Customize dialog box.

The primary difference between the Property Bar and other toolbars is that the Property Bar is *context sensitive*. In other words, it adapts itself according to the context in which you're working.

If you're formatting text, for example, the Property Bar displays options pertaining to text attributes, such as point size, typestyle, and so on.

So, when adding, deleting, and rearranging options on the Property Bar, you make changes according to specific contexts. To add buttons for working with text, for example, you first select the Text context from the Property Bars drop-down list. Doing so configures the Property Bar for the desired context, as shown in Figure A.

Property Bar Context List

Figure A: Before modifying the Property Bar, first select the desired context from the context list.

Once you specify the context, then you can make your changes to the Property Bar for working with text. Just follow the same methods described earlier in this section for working with the other toolbars.

Using the Property Bar

Using the Property Bar is pretty straightforward. You modify objects much the same way you modify palettes and roll-ups. To change an object's size, for instance, you can either type new values or use the arrows to change values incrementally. To maintain proportional sizing, be sure to turn on the Maintain Proportional Sizing/Aspect Ratio option. (As with all CorelDraw buttons and fields, you can get a description of the options on the Property Bar by hovering the mouse over the button or field.)

If this brief discussion of the Property Bar has piqued your interest, you can learn more about this new feature of CorelDraw (and discover many techniques for using it) throughout the remainder of this book.

Working More Efficiently

This section explains a few ways to work efficiently. Here you'll learn about a couple of the interface tools that can make your life easier:

- Protecting your work with automatic and last-saved backups
- Saving time with drag and drop

Backing up your work

CorelDraw supports two options for protecting your work — automatic back-ups and last-saved backups. Both backup methods can help you use CorelDraw more efficiently by protecting your work from being lost by mistake.

Automatic backups

The first backup method — automatic backups — happens in the background, while you work. By default, CorelDraw automatically backs up every ten minutes to the directory where the original drawing files reside. The program saves the files with an .ABK extension. If you've ever lost work because of a system crash or power failure, you'll appreciate this feature. In the event of a minor disaster, all you need to do is go to the directory where the .ABK file is saved, change the extension to .CDR and open the file in CorelDraw. All of your work (up to the last automatic save) is restored.

You can change the location where CorelDraw saves its files and adjust how often the program backs up your work by clicking the Advanced tab in the Options dialog box (Tools ⇨ Options ⇨ Advanced). The Advanced sheet of the Options dialog box appears in Figure 1-30. To change the time between backups, simply enter a new value in the Auto-backup field. To change the directory the backup is saved to, select "Always back-up to," and then choose a new directory.

Keep in mind when changing the time between backups that this setting constitutes reconciling a trade-off. If you set too long a time, you may lose a lot of work should disaster strike. If you set too short a time, when working with complicated drawings you could spend too much time having to wait for the program to create backup files.

Figure 1-30: In the Advanced section of the Options dialog box, you can specify backup frequency and set other defaults.

Last-saved backups

Picture this: You spend hours creating a drawing. Then after showing it to your client, you return to the office and spend a few more hours making corrections based on the client's requests. Later, the client says, "I liked it better the other way." How on earth will you get the other copy back?

The obvious remedy to this problem is to save separate versions of the drawing with different names. Unfortunately, CorelDraw does not have a feature for automatically making incremental copies of your work.

Here's another scenario that I have experienced first hand: You work hard on a drawing and get it to look pretty good. Then you start tweaking it — trying this and that. Before you know it, you've completely messed up the drawing you once thought was good. You can easily resolve this problem by retrieving a copy of the last saved version of your work. If you want to be able to do this, you must first adjust a setting in the Options dialog box (Tools ➪ Options ➪ Advanced). After clicking on the Advanced tab of the Options dialog box, mark the "Make backup on save" check box. Now, each time you use Save or Save as, CorelDraw creates a *second* copy of the file with a .BAK extension. To open the backup copy, all you need to do is change the extension to .CDR. Keep in mind, though, that you can't have two files in the same folder with the same name. This procedure will not work, of course, if you have saved the document after making changes.

Saving time with drag and drop

If you've been using Windows for a while, you are probably familiar with drag and drop, the capability of moving or copying an object from one place to another. But did you know that you can drag objects between multiple documents, or even from one application in the CorelDRAW graphics suite to another? This is a quick and easy way to place copies in multiple documents.

Here's how to drag objects from one CorelDraw drawing to another:

STEPS

Dragging Objects Between Drawings

Step 1. Use Tile Vertically or Tile Horizontally (Window menu) to view two or more documents at once.

Step 2. Select the object(s) that you want to drag to another drawing.

Step 3. To drag the object(s) to another drawing, simply drag from one document to another (see Figure 1-31). To drag a copy to more than one drawing, hold Ctrl as you drag and drop a copy in each document.

Figure 1-31: Dragging and dropping objects between drawings is easy.

STEPS

Dragging Objects Between Applications

Step 1. To drag object(s) from one *application* to another, first resize the application windows so both are accessible on your screen.

Step 2. Select the object(s) that you want to move from one document to another.

Step 3. Drag to move the object(s) from the current document to another, and hold Ctrl as you drag.

Note

Drag and drop is actually part of Windows' Object Linking and Embedding (OLE) feature — a big time-saver. Check the Windows 95 Help menu (located under the Start menu) for more information about OLE.

Whatever you use CorelDraw for, the more you use it, the more you'll find yourself needing specific features. With the customize options, it's easy to tailor CorelDraw to fit the way you work.

Summary

▶ You can customize CorelDraw to work the way you do by modifying shortcut keys from the Keyboard sheet of the Customize dialog box.

▶ CorelDraw's menu structure can be modified from the Menu sheet of the Customize dialog box.

▶ To modify or create new toolbars, use the Toolbars sheet of the Customize dialog box.

▶ Roll-up groups can be created or modified in the application window or from the Roll-Ups sheet of the Customize dialog box.

▶ You can change the appearance of the color palette from the Color Palette sheet of the Customize dialog box, and you can float or dock the color palette by dragging on it.

▶ CorelDraw's new Property Bar provides ever-present, context-sensitive controls for quick and easy access.

▶ Using CorelDraw's automatic backup option can save you much aggravation.

Chapter 2

Toolbox Secrets

In This Chapter

You'll learn handy secrets for:

▶ Selecting and manipulating objects with the Pick tool

▶ Reshaping objects with the Shape tools

▶ Creating shapes with CorelDraw's drawing tools

▶ Getting better views with the Zoom tool

Remember when CorelDraw had only about nine or ten tools? Just one or two of the icons in the toolbox had flyout menus for additional tools and features. Today the program has about 25 tools (see Figure 2-1, where many are shown). And they do things you probably never could have imagined back when the program was new.

Figure 2-1: The new CorelDraw 7 Toolbox

In fact, there's so much power behind these new toolbox icons that it would be difficult to explain *everything* you can do with them. This chapter, however, gives you a lot of useful information on how to harness the mostly undocumented power of the toolbox. Each tool in the toolbox has hidden functions, and several new tools — such as the Natural Pen and four Interactive tools — include features never before available in Windows-based graphics applications.

This chapter focuses on how you can configure the tools to behave in different ways. I'll also show you some tricks for using tools. For instance, you can use the Pick tool to manipulate objects in a number of different ways. And the Shape tool has many features that seem almost magical.

Because so many tools exist, they can't all be discussed in one chapter. Many tools — such as the Text, Line, and Fill tools — are related to topics that are the subjects of entire chapters. Chapter 4, for example, is about working with text, so I've saved the discussion of the Text tool for that chapter. Some tools, such as the Interactive tools, are actually extensions of specific features in CorelDraw. In these instances, I discuss the tools in the chapters that cover those features.

The Pick Tool

The *Pick tool* — now there's a funny name. Sounds like you should use it to pitch hay or clean your teeth, not manipulate graphics. Other programs call their version of the same tool the *Selection tool* or *Arrow tool*. Whatever you call it, you can't really work in CorelDraw without it. And you probably already know how to use it — right?

More specifically, you probably know that clicking on objects with the Pick tool selects them. You move and resize objects with it, and if you click twice on an object with the Pick tool, the object goes into rotation & skew mode. Oh yeah. And most people know that you can select multiple objects by Shift-clicking on them consecutively or by dragging a marquee around the objects you want to select. That's about the extent of what most CorelDraw users know about the Pick tool.

But you can use the Pick tool in all kinds of other ways, such as using the Tab key to select objects, performing tasks with the Property Bar, and a host of other useful functions. In addition, you can modify the way the Pick tool behaves. For example, you can change the arrow to cross hairs, enabling more precise moving and resizing. And you can make the Pick tool behave more like tools in other Windows applications.

You can adjust the Pick tool by clicking on the Toolbox tab in the Options dialog box (Tools ➪ Options ➪ Toolbox), as shown in Figure 2-2. As you can see, you have several options for changing the way this tool behaves.

Figure 2-2: Use the Toolbox sheet in the Options dialog box to modify Pick tool behavior.

Using a cross hair cursor

Turn on this option by placing a check mark next to the "Cross hair cursor" option. Figure 2-3 shows what a cross hair cursor looks like. The cross hair cursor works like a T-square on a conventional drafting table. It's like having crossing straightedges that glide effortlessly across your work area. You can use the cross hairs to align objects in relation to other objects or to align them using the rulers.

Figure 2-3: The cross hair cursor makes it easier to align and resize objects properly.

If you're used to the conventional Pick tool, the cross hair cursor might seem a little confusing at first. It's actually very simple to use. The intersection of the cross hairs is used for selection and manipulation. To select an object, simply click the intersection point of the cross hairs on the object. To resize an object, drag the intersection point on the object's handles, the same as you would use the tip of the Pick tool arrow.

Cross hairs are ideal when using CorelDraw for schematics, floor plans, flowcharts, and other drawings where symmetry and precision are crucial. For example, in Figure 2-4 the cross hairs make it very easy to align the drawing objects precisely. Even if you don't use the cross hair cursor all the time, many situations make it far more effective than the traditional Pick tool arrow.

Figure 2-4: Cross hairs enable you to draw and align objects on the fly.

Treating no fill as a solid

Even after many years of using CorelDraw, I still occasionally click in the center of objects with no fill to move or select them. And what happens then? Nothing, of course. Objects with no fill have nothing in them. There's nothing to select. To select or move the object you must click on the object's *outline*.

Secret

The people at Corel are aware that CorelDraw users are sometimes forgetful, and they have included an option that accommodates users' absent-mindedness. You can tell the program to let you select and move no-fill objects like filled objects by placing a check mark next to the "Treat all objects as filled" option in the Toolbox sheet of the Options dialog box. Then, when you click or drag in the center of an object with no fill, you'll get the result you want.

Using Windows mouse actions

If you use other Windows applications, you're probably used to certain things happening when you use your mouse. For example, in many programs when you hold Ctrl and drag on a selected object, you get a duplicate of the original. In CorelDraw, the Ctrl key has a different function. When you resize or draw with the Rectangle tool while holding Ctrl, CorelDraw enables you to draw a perfect square.

You can tell CorelDraw to use the standard Windows mouse actions by selecting Windows Standard in the Toolbox sheet of the Options dialog box (Tools ⇨ Options ⇨ Toolbox), as shown in Figure 2-5.

Select this radio button to make your mouse conform to Windows conventions.

Figure 2-5: Use this option to make your Ctrl and Shift keys conform to standard Windows conventions when using the Pick tool.

Right-clicking

One new feature in CorelDraw you should be sure to take advantage of is the added functionality of the right mouse button. CorelDraw has greatly exploited the power of right-clicking in version 7. Now when you right-click, a bunch of useful options pop up, literally at your fingertips.

Remember

You can add commands to the different right-mouse button pop-up menus for different contexts. If you're already a seasoned right-mouser, you can greatly improve the convenience of this feature by adding the commands *you* use most.

Depending on which object(s) you've selected with the Pick tool, a number of useful options show up by default when you right-click. When a single block of text is selected, for example, right-clicking produces the menu shown in Figure 2-6, enabling you to instantly convert the text to curves (transform it from editable text to a graphic), apply a style, change the stacking order (Send to Back, Bring to Front, and so on), and several other readily available features.

Figure 2-6: Don't reach for a menu when you need to make changes to a selected object. First try right-clicking on the object for a list of pop-up options.

Note

If, while looking over the commands on the right-mouse pop-up in Figure 2-6, you find yourself wondering about some of the commands you see, I discuss most of them in the next chapters. Overprint Fill and Overprint Outline, for example, are prepress options pertaining to successful reproduction on a printing press. They are discussed in Chapter 5, which deals primarily with color.

The Properties option at the bottom of the pop-up menu is particularly handy. Selecting it displays the Object Properties dialog box shown in Figure 2-7. From there you can modify almost every aspect of the object, including typeface, size, style, alignment, fill, outline weight, color, and style — you name it. In addition, you can use the Object Properties dialog box much like a roll-up. By clicking the Apply button as you make changes, you can perform numerous functions without closing the dialog box. Talk about control.

Figure 2-7: When you select Properties from a pop-up menu, you get this extremely useful Object Properties dialog box.

Right-clicking on a graphic or paragraph text object, of course, brings up slightly different menus. As we progress through CorelDraw's enormous wealth of features and shortcuts in the remainder of this book, I'll point out when you can use a right-mouse pop-up command instead of going to a menu. For example, when you right-click on two or more selected objects, you get options for grouping and combining multiple objects. On the other hand, when you right-click on grouped or combined objects, you get commands for ungrouping and uncombining. Group, Combine, and other arrangement and alignment features are discussed in Chapter 3.

Selecting objects with the keyboard

Secret

As your drawings get more and more complicated, with two or more objects stacked on top of one another, it can be difficult, even impossible, to select objects toward the bottom of the stack with the Pick tool. One remedy for this is to use Tab to toggle among objects. To do so, simply select one object and then press Tab repeatedly until the object you want to select is highlighted.

The most efficient way to keep objects separate in complicated drawings is to place them on separate layers. Layers are discussed in the next chapter.

Context-Specific Options on the Property Bar

Because you have so many different options for selecting and modifying objects with the Pick tool, you may have some trouble keeping all the shortcuts straight. I believe the best way to get fast results is by using the new Property Bar.

When working with the Pick tool, the Property Bar changes context according to the type of object you select, as shown in the following eight figures. In the order they are shown, the following objects are selected: Text, rectangle, ellipses (circle), graph paper, polygon, outlines, multiple objects, and dimensions.

In several of these Property Bars, the first six options — Position, Size, Scale Factor, Maintain Proportional Sizing/Aspect Ratio, Angle of Rotation, and Mirror — remain constant, no matter what you've selected. Numerous other options on the Property Bar change according to the context to help you manipulate the object. See Figures A through H.

Figure A: When you work with text, the Property Bar shows the Font List, Size List, Format Text, and Edit Text options. Click on any of these and other options to change text attributes.

(continued)

(continued)

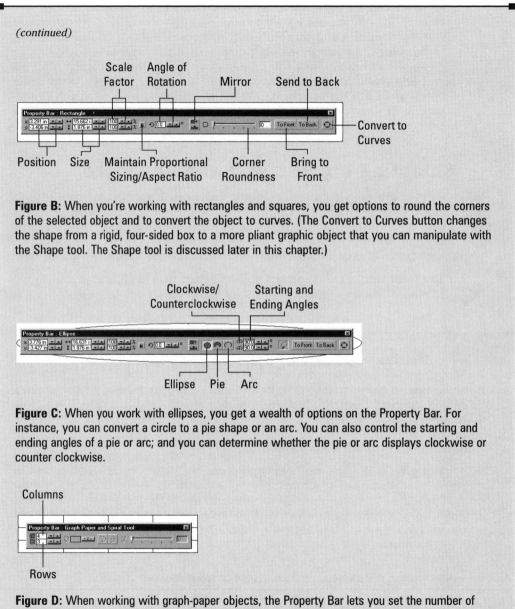

Figure B: When you're working with rectangles and squares, you get options to round the corners of the selected object and to convert the object to curves. (The Convert to Curves button changes the shape from a rigid, four-sided box to a more pliant graphic object that you can manipulate with the Shape tool. The Shape tool is discussed later in this chapter.)

Figure C: When you work with ellipses, you get a wealth of options on the Property Bar. For instance, you can convert a circle to a pie shape or an arc. You can also control the starting and ending angles of a pie or arc; and you can determine whether the pie or arc displays clockwise or counter clockwise.

Figure D: When working with graph-paper objects, the Property Bar lets you set the number of columns and rows. Other options become available when a spiral is selected.

Sharpness

Number of Points   Polygon/Star

Figure E: For polygons, the Property Bar enables you to set the number of points on the polygon, and toggle between a star shape and polygon shape. When in star-shape mode, you can manipulate the sharpness of the points.

Break   Line Style   Auto-Close   Lock to
Apart   Selector   Curve   Connector Node

Line Width
Selector

Start Arrowhead   End Arrowhead
Selector   Selector

Figure F: When you're working with lines and spirals, the Property Bar gives you several options. You can choose line and arrowhead styles, and you can break a line into segments.

Group   Weld   Trim   Intersect

Alig

Combine   Ungroup   Ungroup All

Figure G: When you select multiple objects, the Property Bar provides options for combining, grouping, ungrouping, welding, trimming, intersecting, and aligning objects. (The next chapter discusses these features.)

Style   Units   Prefix   Suffix

Text Position

Dimension Tool   Precision   Show   Dynamic
Modes   Units   Dimensioning

Figure H: For dimension lines, the Property Bar enables you to toggle among the various Dimension tool types, determine the style of text displayed with the dimension line, adjust the level of precision, control the units after the decimal, change the unit of measurement, display unit symbols, use dynamic dimensioning, set suffixes and prefixes, and alter the position of the text on the dimension line. (All of these options are explained later in this chapter.)

(continued)

(continued)

You can set up CorelDraw so the Property Bar displays when you open the program. (By default, if you close the program with the Property Bar displayed, the next time you open CorelDraw the Property Bar will be in the same place you left it.) Try to get in the habit of using this handy new feature.

The Shape Tools

When I first started using CorelDraw, only one tool lurked in the Shape tool position in the toolbox. In those days it was called the node-editing tool. Today three tools exist on the Shape tool flyout: the Shape tool, which is basically a node-editing tool, the Knife tool, which enables you to cut objects into sections, and the Eraser tool, which enables you to remove parts of objects.

Node-editing has always been an intricate part of vector drawing programs such as CorelDraw. The capability of cutting and erasing portions of vector objects, though, is relatively new. These features first appeared in version 6 of CorelDraw. They are truly remarkable feats of programming, and they're extremely useful, too.

Let's look at the three tools in the order they appear on the Shape tool flyout.

The Shape tool

Perhaps one of the most overlooked features in vector-drawing programs is the node-editing tool, such as CorelDraw's Shape tool. The beauty of the Shape tool is that it enables you to manipulate lines in just about every way imaginable. In fact, there's so much that can be said about node-editing that I can only scratch the surface in this chapter.

Nodes are control points on the outline of an object that mark a change in a line's direction or the intersection of two lines. On a square, for instance, nodes exist at all four corners. Depending on the type (or *mode*) of the node, you can manipulate the lines on either side of a node in different ways. You can move the intersection of two lines (as shown in Figure 2-8), or you can curve a line (as shown in Figure 2-9), smooth it, or make it straight and rigid. You do all this by manipulating the nodes.

Figure 2-8: Node-editing enables you to move the control points on a line, reshaping it by extending the node to a new position.

You can create nodes on outlines in two ways. Any time you draw a line with the Freehand tool or another line-drawing tool (discussed in the "Line-Drawing Tools" section later in this chapter) nodes are added automatically where the line changes directions. Nodes are also automatically added when you convert text, shapes (for example, boxes, ellipses, polygons), or symbols into curves (by selecting Arrange ➪ Convert to Curves). Converting an object to curves automatically places nodes at points where lines change direction or intersect. Once you have the nodes, you can begin shaping the object by manipulating its outline.

While you can manipulate nodes in perhaps hundreds of ways, the methods fall under categories, or *modes*. In this section we'll look at some of the more useful modes, including: To Curve, To Line, Smooth, Join, and Elastic.

Figure 2-9: When node-editing curved lines, you twist and stretch the lines, shaping them exactly as you like.

Node Edit roll-up versus the Property Bar

When working with the Shape tool, should you use the Node Edit roll-up, shown in Figure 2-10, or the Property Bar, shown in Figure 2-11?

Figure 2-10: Use the Node Edit roll-up to change the mode of nodes. To display it, simply double-click any node.

Figure 2-11: The Property Bar in node-editing mode.

This is one of those instances when CorelDraw offers too many choices. In this situation the Property Bar is simply a duplication of the Node Edit roll-up. The roll-up takes up less screen real estate and is easily accessible — all you do is double-click on any node. On the other hand, the Property Bar is always available, and, because many of the buttons contain text, rather than those enigmatic little icons, it's somewhat easier to use.

You already know my position — fly the Property Bar and leave it visible for all to see! But then, you might be used to the roll-up.

Note

You may be wondering why only a few of the options in Figures 2-10 and 2-11 are available. When you select a node it is in a certain mode — curve, line, cusp, and so on. When in one mode, only certain other options are available. If you change a node's mode, other options become available.

Using To Line mode and To Curve mode

I discuss these two modes together because they are mutually exclusive. A node cannot be in curve and line mode at the same time. To Line mode makes the line to the left of the selected node rigid. To Curve mode makes the line to the left of the node pliant, enabling you to bend and curve it.

An example should help make these modes clear. In Figure 2-12, I've converted some text to curves. The letters *TELEF* all consist of straight, rigid lines, while the letters *OCUS* contain several curves. The straight lines behave differently from the curved lines when you edit them with the Shape tool.

Figure 2-12: An example of nodes in To Line and To Curve modes.

To move or reshape a line attached to a To Line node, you must drag on the node itself, as shown in Figure 2-13. The line can only be shortened or lengthened. No matter how hard you try, CorelDraw will not let you put a curve in the line.

Figure 2-13: Nodes in To Line mode enable you to reshape lines only in straight, rigid movements.

Lines connected to a To Curve node, however, are flexible. You can arch and bend them as though they were made of rubber or wire, as shown in Figure 2-14.

Figure 2-14: Nodes in To Curve mode are flexible and pliant.

Let's look a little closer at how to manipulate these nodes, in particular the To Curve nodes. No matter how much I tell you about these nodes, you'll still have to practice to learn how to finesse them. But let's see if we can't at least shorten the learning curve. (Or is that learning *curves*?)

Secret

When a node is in To Curve mode, you can manipulate it not only by moving the node itself but also the control points that extend from the node, as shown in Figure 2-15. You can also reshape the line by dragging on the line itself. At first, shaping a line in this manner may seem strange, but once you get used to it you'll find this method to be quite handy.

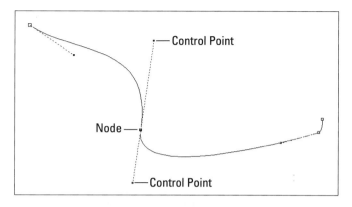

Figure 2-15: Practice shaping a line using a To Curve node and control points.

You have several ways to manipulate a To Curve line:

■ Moving the node itself

■ Manipulating the control points

■ Dragging on the line

When you move the *node* itself, you can drag perpendicular to the line, parallel to the line, or a use a combination of both movements. A perpendicular motion extends the curve, as shown in Figure 2-16. Dragging along the line enables you to move a node's position on the line and straightens the curve, as shown in Figure 2-17.

Figure 2-16: To increase the curve, drag the node perpendicular to the line.

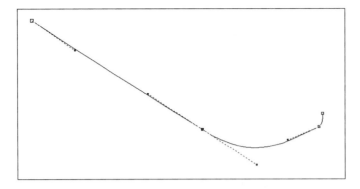

Figure 2-17: To straighten a curve and move the point of control, drag the node with the line.

Manipulating the *control points* enables you to increase or decrease the severity of the curve in two directions, in an *S* pattern, as shown in Figure 2-18. However, there's a bit more to it than that. You can also lengthen and shorten the control points as you drag. Lengthening the control points stretches the curve and reduces the severity of the curving action, as shown in Figure 2-19. Shortening the distance of the control point to the node makes the curving action more radical.

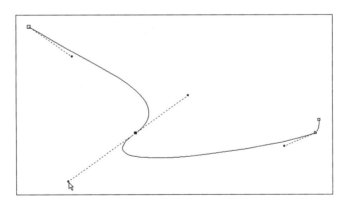

Figure 2-18: Dragging the control points in a swinging motion causes the line to bend in two directions, in an *S* curve.

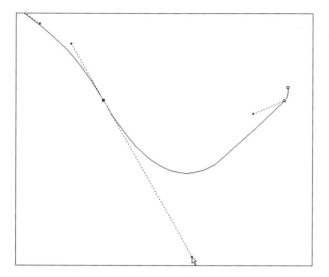

Figure 2-19: Increasing the distance from the control point to the node increases the length of the curve and reduces the curving action.

When you drag on the *line* itself, as shown in Figure 2-20, you get a similar action to dragging on the control points. The line moves in two directions, teetering on the node.

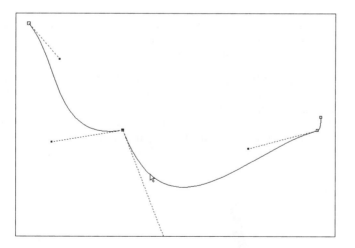

Figure 2-20: Dragging on the line itself works similarly to dragging on the control points. The further from the node you drag, the longer the curve and the less radical the curving action.

After learning so many ways to curve lines, you may be wondering how to *straighten* one. It's simple. Select the node to the right of the line you want straightened and click To Line on the Property Bar. In Figure 2-21, I straightened both of the line segments that do all that curving in the previous figures simply by selecting the nodes and changing them to To Line mode.

Figure 2-21: You can quickly straighten lines with the To Line mode.

And if you want to manipulate only one side of a curve, or a segment on the right side of the node, use the Cusp option on the Property Bar (or Node Edit roll-up).

Drawing smooth lines

If you're like me, you have a hard time drawing with a mouse (I have a hard time drawing with a pencil, too). Your lines wind up bumpy, with two many line segments, or nodes. CorelDraw provides several ways to smooth out bumpy lines. One of these is the *Smooth option*, also on the Node roll-up. Smooth irons the wrinkles out of your lines.

In Figure 2-22, I stretch the rigidity out the line by first converting all the nodes with To Curve and then choosing Smooth. You too can get the kinks out with this simple option. (You don't need to convert one node at a time. You can select multiple nodes just as you would select objects, by Shift-clicking or by dragging a "marquee" around them. A *marquee* is the box you draw around objects with the Selection or Shape tools to select the objects.)

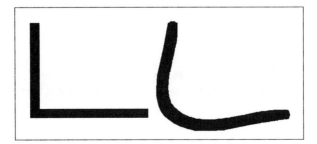

Figure 2-22: Use Smooth to take the kinks out of your lines.

Joining nodes

You can draw two kinds of outlines: open and closed paths. A *path* is the outline itself. An *open path*, though it can take many twists and turns, is a single line. It has a beginning and an end. A *closed path*, on the other hand, is continuous. Perhaps the simplest example of this is a circle, which really has no beginning and end.

The primary difference between open and closed paths is that you can't fill an open path. In other words, you can't make the area surrounded by the outline a color or assign it a gradient fill, and so on. A closed path, then, is a kind of container. Figure 2-23 shows the difference between an open and closed path. While both are circles, the second one is not closed and thus cannot contain a fill.

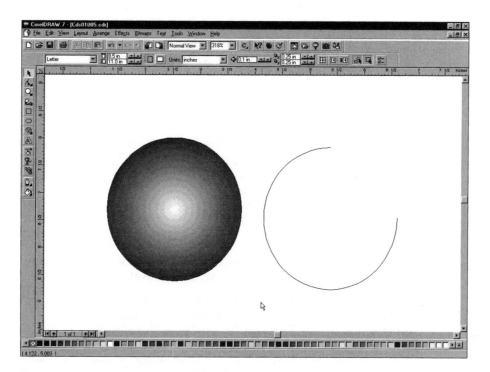

Figure 2-23: An open path cannot hold fills; a closed path can.

The Join option (the third option from the left on the Property Bar) connects two nodes and closes the path. The fourth option on the Property Bar is Break Curve, which you can use to disconnect, or separate, a set of joined nodes. Actually, Break Curve will split any node into two nodes, regardless of whether the path is closed or not. But it's still the option you use to open a closed path.

Another option you can use to close paths is Auto Close Curve, which is the last option on the Property Bar. This option works without your having to select the two end nodes. However, what Auto Close Curve does is draw a line between the two end nodes to close the path, which can severely mis-shape your path. To avoid this predicament, you should place the two end nodes close together or on top of each other before clicking Auto Close Path.

Using Elastic mode

Elastic mode affects the behavior of lines when you move a node connected to two or more selected nodes. If Elastic mode is turned off, all nodes move by the same amount. If Elastic mode is on, nodes move in proportion to their distance from the base node (the node you drag). The end result is that the curve appears to behave like elastic, expanding and contracting in response to mouse movement.

If you're inexperienced at using Elastic mode, it can be difficult to predict how an outline in elastic mode will behave when you manipulate it. However, once you get the hang of it, this is a great way to proportionately stretch and reduce segments of an outline.

The Knife tool

The Knife tool, located on the Shape tool flyout, is pretty straightforward: It enables you to cut a closed path into two closed paths. To do so, you simply click the tool once on the path where you want to start the cut, and then again where you want the cut to end. And voilà! You get two closed path objects. The Knife tool also enables you to cut a closed path in half without closing the two paths. In version 6, this option was turned on from the Tool Properties dialog box. In version 7 you can toggle this option on and off from the first button on the Property Bar (when the Knife tool is selected, natural-ly), as well as from the Toolbox section of the Options dialog box. Having these controls on the Property Bar is a great time-saver.

Another option in the Toolbox section of the Options dialog box is Auto Reduce on Cut, which automatically reduces the number of nodes when you cut a curved line. This function is similar to applying Auto Reduce to a path from the Property Bar when the Shape tool is selected. Auto Reduce removes nodes and smoothes the path, which is faster and more efficient than removing nodes manually.

The Eraser tool

The capability of erasing parts of paths, much the way Eraser tools work in paint-type applications, is relatively new to drawing programs. It's quite use-ful, too. The Eraser tool lets you swipe through a closed path and create two closed paths, or swipe through an open path and create two separate open paths. This feature is straightforward and easy to use. However, in version 7 you can adjust the width of the eraser tip and turn on Auto Reduce nodes on Erase from the Property Bar, rather than having to go into the Tool Properties dialog box.

Line-Drawing Tools

If you've been using CorelDraw for a while, you are probably familiar with most of the tools on the line-drawing tools flyout. However, version 7 includes some significant changes to these tools. First, you may have already noticed that the Dimension tools are now on the same flyout as the Freehand and Bézier tools. Well, actually, a new icon called Dimension Tool is on the flyout — the buttons that used to be on the Dimension flyout now display on the Property Bar when in the Dimension context. Once you get used to this change, it makes working with the Dimension tool much easier.

As you'll see as we move through this discussion of the line-drawing tools, most of the changes to existing tools concern the Property Bar. And while these are useful improvements, the exciting news is the addition of the pressure-sensitive Natural Pen tool, which enables you to draw single-stroke closed paths, allowing for more natural calligraphic effects.

The Natural Pen tool

New to version 7, the *Natural Pen tool* lets you draw closed paths that look like curves. This tool is supposed to emulate a felt-tip or fountain ink pen, and does a reasonable job. The four types of Natural Pen modes are as follows:

- The *Fixed Width* mode draws curves that are the same thickness along their entire length, similar to a thick line or outline. The difference is that the stroke created with the Natural Pen tool is actually a closed path that you can fill with any of CorelDraw's several fill options. The procedure for drawing fixed-width paths with this tool is as follows: Open the Curve flyout and click the Natural Pen tool. Click the Fixed Width Natural Pen Type button on the Property Bar. Type a width in the Natural Pen Width box on the Property Bar. Position the cursor where you want the curve to start. Click and drag along the desired path, like a pencil on paper.

- The *Pressure* mode draws curves that change thickness based on a pressure-sensitive pen or keyboard input. Basically this enables you to mimic the effect you achieve when drawing with a felt-tip or fountain pen by hand. This mode works best when working with a pressure-sensitive tablet, but you can also use your up- and down-arrow keys on the keyboard to adjust the width of the stroke interactively. The following are the steps for using the Natural Pen tool in Pressure mode: Open the Curve flyout and click the Natural Pen tool. Click the Pressure Natural Pen Type button on the Property Bar. Position the cursor where you want the curve to start. Click and drag along the desired path, like a pencil on paper. If you are using the mouse, press the up-arrow and down-arrow keys to vary the pen pressure. If you are using a pressure-sensitive tablet, simply vary the pressure on the tablet, as you would when drawing by hand.

■ The *Calligraphic* mode draws curves that change thickness based on the direction of the curve. This creates an effect similar to using a calligraphic pen. The procedure for creating lines with this mode is as follows: Open the Curve flyout and click the Natural Pen tool. Click the Calligraphic Natural Pen Type button on the Property Bar. Type a width in the Natural Pen Width box on the Property Bar. Type an angle in the Natural Pen Nib Angle box on the Property Bar. Type 0 degrees if you want the pen Nib to be horizontal, and type 90 degrees if you want the nib to be vertical. If you want the pen nib to be slanted, type a value between 0 and 360 degrees. The nib will slant in the direction you set. Then click and drag along the desired path, like a pencil on paper.

■ The *Preset* mode draws curves that change thickness based on preset line types that you choose from a drop-down list on the Property Bar. Here is the procedure for drawing lines in the Preset mode: Open the Curve flyout and click the Natural Pen tool. Click the Preset Natural Pen Type button on the Property Bar. Choose a preset curve shape from the Natural Pen Presets list box. Position the cursor where you want the curve to start. Then click and drag along the desired path, like a pencil on paper.

Figure 2-24 shows the Property Bar in Natural Pen mode and calls out the various options.

Figure 2-24: Here is what the Property Bar looks like in Natural Pen mode.

The Freehand tool and the Bézier tool

When you draw lines in CorelDraw, you usually use either the Freehand or Bézier tool — unless, of course, you need dimensions; then you would use the nifty Dimension tool. The Freehand tool, of course, enables you to draw fluid strokes, from one end to another, as though you were using a pen or pencil. With the Bézier tool you draw lines from point to point, or from Bézier to Bézier. Béziers, sometimes called *Bézier curves*, are the line segments between the nodes on lines drawn with the Freehand or Bézier tool (or text and shapes converted to curves).

Which tool you should use depends on what kind of outline you need. If you're like me, you have difficulty drawing lines, be they curved or straight, with a mouse. When I need a straight line, I use the Bézier tool. The beauty of this method is that all you do is click where you want the line to begin, and then click again where you want it to end. If you need a connecting line segment going in a new direction, simply click again where you want the line to end. CorelDraw automatically connects the new segment to the existing segment. And you can continue to add new segments, ad infinitum. Dot to dot drawing was never so easy! To close the path, simply click on the first node where you started.

Secret

Use the Freehand tool when you need curved or sloping lines. CorelDraw automatically places a node at each place where the line changes directions. If your line has too many ridges and bumps, simply use the Smooth option on the Property Bar to iron them out. You can also smooth lines by deleting nodes at the points where a line makes undesired bends.

You can modify the behavior of these tools from the Toolbox section of the Options dialog box (Tools ➪ Options ➪ Toolbox), shown in Figure 2-25.

Figure 2-25: Use these options to control the behavior of the Freehand and Bézier tools.

- *Freehand tracking* controls how closely a freehand curve matches the movement of the mouse. The lower the number you set, the more accurate the match. Setting this option too low will cause every little bump and ridge to show up, giving you lots of nodes. Setting it higher tends to smooth the line.

- *Autotrace tracking* determines the accuracy of the Bézier tool's bitmap autotrace feature. The lower the value, the more accurate the trace. Autotrace enables you to create outlines based on imported bitmap images. You can then edit the outline as a vector image, enabling you to fill, node edit with the Shape tool, and generally treat the outlines as a CorelDraw drawing. As you know, bitmaps are virtually uneditable in

CorelDraw. (This fact excludes, of course, the effects you can set with version 7's new Bitmap menu, discussed in Chapter 6. In addition, a more advanced autotracing of bitmaps is available in OCR-Trace, covered in Chapter 16.) Figure 2-26 shows an example of an autotraced bitmap. To use Autotrace, import a bitmap (File ➪ Import), and then, with the bitmap selected, click on the object in the bitmap you want to Autotrace.

Figure 2-26: This bitmap was traced with Autotrace.

Manual Tracing

Because of the way they are constructed, many bitmaps cannot be autotraced with the Bézier or Freehand tool. You'll know whether you can autotrace all or a portion of bitmap when you select the Freehand or Bézier tool. If the mouse cursor displays as cross hairs with a thin straight line on the right side of the horizontal cross hair, you can use autotrace on the image. If a small wavy line accompanies the cross hair cursor, you cannot use autotrace.

In these instances you can trace all or portions of the image manually. Here's how: Find a place where you want to begin. Click the mouse at that point. Now move along the edge of the object to a second point, and click again. Continue this procedure until the object is traced. The last click should close the path, as shown in Figure A. To optimize your chances for success with this procedure, you should click at each spot where the object being traced curves or changes direction. Once you've traced the object, you can then use the Shape tool to manipulate the nodes and line segments to customize the trace. This is a great way to turn scanned images into vector objects editable in CorelDraw.

Figure A: To trace bitmaps manually, click repeatedly to add nodes around the edge of the object.

- *Corner threshold* affects when corners, or bends in the outline, are cusped (as opposed to smoothed). Remember that cusped nodes enable you to manipulate Bézier curves on each side of the node independently. A node is more likely to be cusped if the value is lower.

- *Straight line threshold* determines the extent to which a line can vary from a straight path and still be drawn perfectly straight. The higher the value, the less accurate the line needs to be. This is a great option for those of us who can't draw straight lines.

- *Auto-join* sets the distance at which two end nodes join automatically. In other words, when you place an end node close to a node that begins a path, this option sets the distance (in pixels) where CorelDraw forces the two nodes to join and close the path.

The Dimension tool

This tool separates CorelDraw from most other drawing programs. The Dimension tool (which was actually a set of tools in version 6) makes CorelDraw much more adept at creating technical drawings and schematics, even simple blueprints. If you haven't used these tools before, you'll find them remarkably simple — especially with the advent of the Property Bar.

To draw a dimension line, you simply select the direction you want from the Property Bar — horizontal, vertical, or diagonal — and then click where you want the line to begin. Click again where you want the line to end, and then click again where you want the text, or label, for the line displayed. Figure 2-27 shows the three types of lines.

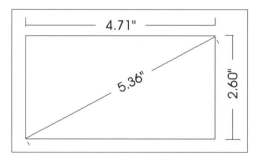

Figure 2-27: CorelDraw has three dimension lines: horizontal, vertical, and diagonal.

The other two line options on the left side of the Property Bar are Callout and Angular Dimension. Callout enables you to quickly direct attention to objects in a drawing, as shown in Figure 2-28. The Callout option works similarly to the other dimension modes. Click once to start the line, then click again where you want the line to end. Click one more time. At that point, you can then type a label.

Figure 2-28: The Callout option enables you to quickly create callouts in your drawings.

The Angular Dimension option lets you call out angles, as shown in Figure 2-29. To use this tool, you click first at the point where your angle begins. In the figure, for example, I clicked at the point of the pie slice. You click again at the point where the angle will be measured from, and then click again where the angle is measured to. Now click to place the label. Voilà! You have angular dimension lines.

Figure 2-29: Use Angular Dimension lines to quickly call out angles.

Changing the Dimension tool options

You're probably already convinced that the Dimension tool is great. But it would be even better if you could make some changes to how it works. For instance, wouldn't it be much handier if you could control where the text label lands in relation to the line itself? Also, by default, the text on the dimensions is much too large for most applications. Oh yeah, and how do you change the scale? Granted, the drawing on the screen is in inches, but floor plans and the like are measured in feet, meters, or yards.

In version 6, to change dimension tool (or any other tool) options you had to go into Tool Properties to change items such as label size, scale, units of measurement, and most other options. This really was a pain, because it entailed opening a dialog box for each change you needed to make.

Once again, the Property Bar comes to the rescue. Now you can change all aspects of how the tool (and the ensuing dimension line) displays and measures. Figure 2-30 shows the Property Bar when in Dimension mode. Let's look at each option in detail.

Figure 2-30: The Property Bar contains a number of useful options in Dimension tool mode.

- The *Vertical*, *Horizontal*, *Diagonal*, *Callout*, and *Angular* buttons determine which type of dimension line you draw.

- The *Style* field enables you to select how the dimension label is displayed. The choices are Decimal, which displays partial units behind decimal points; Fraction, which displays partial units as fractions; U.S. Engineering; and U.S. Architectural.

- The *Precision* field enables you to determine how finite a measurement is displayed in the dimension line label. In other words, how many numbers after the decimal point — tenths, hundredths, thousandths, and so on.

- The *Units* field lets you set the type of measurement, such as inches, millimeters, yards, miles, and so on. Go ahead, click on the drop-down arrow. You have a bunch of options here — one for every type of drawing you can imagine.

- The *Show Units* button determines whether the measurement symbol or abbreviation displays on the dimension line label. When the button is depressed, the unit shows; when not depressed, it does not show.

- The *Prefix* and *Suffix* fields enable you to include additional information with the dimension line label — a brief description, your own symbol, you name it. Prefix, of course, places the text you type into the field before the default label, and Suffix places it after.

- The *Dynamic Dimensioning* button lets you edit the text label on the dimension line. You can change the label to display virtually any thing you want. To edit the label, select the dimension line, click on Dynamic to enable it (enabled is the up position), and then select the text label with the Text tool and type the new text.

- The *Text Position* drop-down list enables you to change the position of the text in relation to the line. You have three position options — above, on, and below the dimension line — and two angle options for diagonal lines: slanted with the line or horizontal. The horizontal option makes the text on a diagonal line slightly easier to read. Figure 2-31 shows the different options available from the Text Position drop-down list.

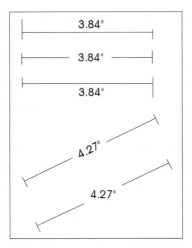

Figure 2-31: The label positions available from the Text Position drop-down list when the Property Bar is in Dimension mode.

Changing the dimension line scale

Secret

Dimension lines are great, but they measure in inches relative to the size of the page you are drawing on. This is of little value if, for example, you are laying out the floor plan for a 600-square-foot office. In this and other design situations, you need to change CorelDraw's units of measurement and scale. Unfortunately, you can't do this from the Property Bar. Instead, you'll have to change the program's defaults from the General section of the Options dialog box (Tools ⇨ Options ⇨ General), or from the Grid & Ruler Setup dialog box (Layout ⇨ Grid & Ruler Setup). Here's how:

■ Open the Options dialog box and make sure that the General section is active, and then click on Change Units. Or choose Grid & Ruler Setup from the Arrange menu. This displays the Grid & Ruler Setup dialog box, as shown in Figure 2-32.

Figure 2-32: Use the Grid & Ruler Setup dialog box to set the units of measurement used in drawings.

■ Use the Horizontal and Vertical drop-down lists in the Units section to change the unit of measurement. The Horizontal option changes the horizontal ruler and the Vertical option changes the vertical ruler. However, when you change the drawing scale in CorelDraw, both rulers will always depict the same units of measurement. The only time you can use different units of measurements on two rulers is when the scale is 1:1.

■ Click the Edit Scale button. This button brings up the Drawing Scale dialog box, as shown in Figure 2-33. From here you can choose a scale from the Typical Scale drop-down list. You have lots of options. Depending on the relative scale of your drawing, you may have to do some math to figure the right scale for your drawing. But most of the more common scales are built in. To show inches as feet, for example, choose 1"=1'. To show inches as yards, choose 1"=3'. You get the idea. If the scale you need is not on the Typical scales list, you can set it by entering the ratio in the Page Distance and World distance fields. Page distance is the measurement for the drawing and World distance represents the real-world scale.

Figure 2-33: Use the Drawing Scale dialog box to set the scale for your drawings.

■ Close all dialog boxes to return to the drawing screen. Your drawing and dimension lines will now reflect the new scale.

Note

Changes to the drawing scale do not affect only dimension lines, but also the rulers, grid, and all aspects of measurement within the drawing. This is the method you should use to change scaling for any type of drawing in CorelDraw, including floor plans, schematics, product designs, packaging, you name it. Note, too, that changing this option while a drawing is open changes the setting for that drawing; setting this option while designing a template enables you to automatically use the new scale settings each time you use the template. You can change the scale for all of your new drawings by first setting the new scale, and then choosing Tools ➪ Settings for New Drawings. Then make sure that Grids and Rulers are set in the Settings for New Drawings dialog box.

Secret

After a while, you may make so many changes with the Settings for New Drawings option that CorelDraw no longer works the way you want. You can return CorelDraw to the default, out-of-the-box settings by deleting the CORELDRW.INI file in the X:\COREL\DRAW folder. When CorelDraw can't find CORELDRW.INI, it automatically returns to its default settings and creates a new .INI file.

Shape-Drawing Tools

On the surface, the shape-drawing tools — Rectangle, Ellipse, Polygon, Spiral, and Grid — seem pretty straightforward. You select one of them and draw your shape. Right? However, there's a big difference in how you control each tool's performance in version 7. All of the options that you once had to go to Tool Properties to change — such as rounded corners for rectangles, or changing the Ellipse tool to draw pies or arcs — are now available from the Property Bar.

Let's look at each tool and see how you can modify its behavior from the Property Bar. Before doing so, however, I want to remind you that you can constrain any of these tools to draw proportionally by holding Ctrl. When constraining the Rectangle tool, for example, it draws perfect squares, the Ellipse tool draws perfect circles, and so on.

The Rectangle tool

The Rectangle tool draws rectangles and squares. The Property Bar options when the Rectangle tool is selected are the same as when a rectangle is selected with the Pick tool, as discussed earlier in this chapter. One nifty feature is that you can round the corners of objects drawn with this tool by using the Corner Roundness slider or field.

The Ellipse tool

The Ellipse tool draws circles, ovals, pies, and arcs. As with the Rectangle tool, the options on the Property Bar when this tool is selected are the same as when you select an ellipse object with the Pick tool. What's hot about the new Property Bar is that you can now switch between ellipse, pie, and arc mode without having to open a dialog box.

The Polygon tool

This tool has a lot of power. It lets you draw polygons (multisided shapes) or multipointed stars with a single mouse stroke. The great news in version 7 is that you can now control what kind of shape, the number of sides or points, and the sharpness of a star's points, all from the Property Bar. The Property Bar options when you select the Polygon tool are the same as when you select a polygon or star with the Pick tool. Again, for those options, see the section on "The Pick Tool" earlier in this chapter.

The Spiral tool

If you've tried to draw a spiral with a mouse or with a pressure-sensitive tablet, you'll appreciate this tool. It draws spirals. You can control several aspects of how the tool does its magic from the Property Bar, such as the number of revolutions or tightness of the spiral. You can also control the same properties from the Toolbox section of the Options dialog box (Tools ➪ Options ➪ Toolbox), which, in the case of the Spiral tool, may sometimes be more efficient, as you'll see in a moment.

First, let's look at controlling how the Spiral tool draws from the Property Bar, shown in spiral context in Figure 2-34.

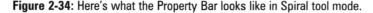

Figure 2-34: Here's what the Property Bar looks like in Spiral tool mode.

- *Spiral Revolutions* controls the number of lines, or loops, from the center of the spiral to the end.

- *Symmetrical Spiral* and *Logarithmic Spiral* are opposites. Symmetrical Spiral makes revolutions that are an equal distance from each other. Logarithmic Spiral creates a spiral where the distance between the loops widens from the center out. Figure 2-35 shows the difference between the two types of spirals.

■ *Spiral Expansion Factor* becomes available when you select the Logarithmic Spiral. It controls the how radically the revolutions expand as they draw outward. A factor of 1 is the same as Symmetrical Spiral, and a factor of 100 is a full expansion.

Figure 2-35: Note the difference between a symmetrical spiral (left) and a logarithmic spiral (right).

Secret

When adjusting the number of revolutions and expansion factor, you may find it more useful to do so from the Toolbox section of the Options dialog box (Tools ⇨ Options ⇨ Toolbox), because you can adjust the factor with the aid of a preview, as shown in Figure 2-36.

Figure 2-36: When adjusting Spiral tool options from the Options dialog box, you get a preview of how your changes will affect the behavior of the tool.

CorelDraw 7 makes it easy to turn a spiral into a closed path. Simply select the spiral with either the Pick tool or Shape tool and then click on the Auto Close Path button. You can now fill the path with a solid fill, a fountain, or however you like. Figure 2-37 shows two closed-path spirals, one with and one without an outline.

Figure 2-37: Examples of filled closed-path spirals, one with an outline (left) and without an outline (right).

Using the Esc Key with the Property Bar

Secret

Many people find it convenient to use the Esc key along with the Property Bar. When you press Esc, the currently selected object is deselected but the Property Bar and the current tool stays selected. This enables you to change tool properties more rapidly and continue drawing (rather than selecting the Pick tool, selecting the object, and then reselecting the drawing tool). For example, you can draw several dimension lines, hit Esc to deselect the last one, change a tool property, and then continue drawing with a new setting.

The Zoom-and-Pan Tool

The Zoom-and-Pan tool (that I'll simply call the *Zoom tool*) controls your view of the current page. It's heartening to see that Corel has performed some maintenance on the Zoom tool. The View Manager and Zoom tool flyout in version 6 had so many choices that it had become mind-boggling. There were so many, in fact, that I had never used some of them. I didn't even know what some of them were. Another tremendous improvement is the Zoom tool context on the Property Bar. This addition is so nifty that you may never find a need to fly the Zoom Manager again. And this says nothing of the new and improved right-mouse button pop-up, which also provides a rich group of zoom options.

Note

If you liked all those options on the Zoom tool flyout, have no fear. You can get them back again. Here's how: Go to the Toolbox section of the Options dialog box (Tools ⇨ Options ⇨ Toolbox), select the Zoom tool icon, and then, in the Zoom & Pan Tool Defaults, select Use Traditional Zoom Flyout. Close the dialog box and check out the flyout — there are all your beloved icons. And one of the things I've missed from CorelDraw versions past is the capability of right-clicking to zoom out, rather than using the right mouse button pop-up. You can get that shortcut back, too, by selecting Zoom Out in the Mouse Button 2 For The Zoom Tool option in the Options dialog box.

I'm not going to go over all the Zoom tool options. To see what they are, hover the mouse cursor over each option on the Property Bar when it's in Zoom tool context to see the pop-up descriptions. (If you don't know what the descriptions mean, click them — you can't hurt your document with these tools.) Instead of covering all the Zoom tool options, it's more productive to cover just panning, marquee zoom, and saving views with the View Manager.

Using the Pan tool and marquee zoom

No matter what type of document you're working on, you often need to zoom in on and center certain objects on your monitor, making them easier to work on. Granted, you can click the Zoom tool directly on an object to enlarge your view of it, but this is hardly precise and is less useful when you want to center several objects at once on your screen.

Two of CorelDraw's features, Pan and marquee zoom, make getting a precise view easy. The first, *Pan* (the little hand on the Zoom tool flyout and Property Bar in Zoom context), enables you to drag your document left, right, up, and down, simply by dragging on the screen. All you do is select the Pan tool and drag in the direction of the portion of the page you want to center, as shown in Figure 2-38.

Figure 2-38: Use the Pan tool to drag your document page into the desired position on your monitor.

Perhaps even more useful is the capability of *marquee zooming* on a specific area on the page. If you're familiar with marquee selecting with the Pick tool, using this feature should be a snap. All you do is select the Zoom tool and then drag a marquee around the area of the page you want to zoom in on, as shown in Figure 2-39. Easy enough, right?

Figure 2-39: To zoom in on a specific area of your page, drag a marquee around the area with the Zoom tool, and then release the mouse button.

Saving views with View Manager

When working on intricate drawings, it's sometimes necessary to intermittently zoom in and out on several specific areas, going to one place, and then another, and then back again. This is especially critical when working on large pages, such as posters and banners, or when working with multipage documents. When you perform these operations manually, you often find yourself zooming in, out, panning, and repeating a lot of time-consuming, tedious steps. You can avoid a lot of this hassle by saving views in CorelDraw's View Manager roll-up, as shown in Figure 2-40.

Figure 2-40: The View Manager roll-up lets you save specific views and reuse them to navigate around your document.

To display the View Manager roll-up, click on the View Manager button on the Property Bar when it's in Zoom tool context, or double-click on the Zoom tool in the Toolbox. Saving views is just as easy. Here's how:

STEPS

Saving Views

Step 1.   Use the standard zoom and pan options to get the view you want.

Step 2.   Click the pop-up menu arrow (shown in Figure 2-41) on the View Manager roll-up to display a list of Options.

Step 3.   Choose New from the pop-up menu. CorelDraw places a new view on the list, naming it *View 1*, *View 2*, or whichever is next, according to the views you've already set for this document.

Step 4.   Click the name of the view and type a meaningful name for the view. (This step is especially critical in documents where you save a lot of views. After a while, View 1, View 2, and so on, are easily forgotten.)

That's it. You can now return to a specific view — just as you saved it — at any time simply by double-clicking it in View Manager. You can also add a view by clicking on the plus (+) button in the View Manager.

Figure 2-41: Use this menu on the View Manager roll-up to add, delete, and rename views.

Secret

One more thing about View Manager. Have you ever wondered what those little icons on the left side of the list of views do? You know, the page and magnifying glass? For a long time I thought they didn't really do anything — though I did wonder why I could turn them on and off.

Actually, they're quite useful. They enable you to modify how your saved views work. When you turn off the page icon (click it and it dims), for instance, you can use the corresponding view to go to the same view *on the current page*, rather than jumping to the page defined in the view. When you turn off the magnifying glass, double-clicking the associated view takes you to the page defined in the view, but at the current zoom level, or the zoom level you were in when you double-clicked the item in View Manager.

In other words, if you want to go to the exact same zoom level on the different page, turn off the zoom icon. To go to a saved zoom level on the current page, turn off the page icon. It just doesn't get any more customizable.

Summary

- You can modify how the Pick tool behaves, such as changing the cursor to cross hairs or treating unfilled objects and filled objects, from the Toolbox section of the Options dialog box.

- The Shape tool enables you to poke and nudge outlines, getting them into exactly the right shape, by manipulating and changing the modes of nodes. You'll also find a lot help for modifying the behavior of the Shape tool and Béziers themselves on the new Property Bar.

- The Knife tool lets you cut open and closed paths into sections, and you can greatly control how the Knife tool works from the Property Bar.

- CorelDraw's new Natural Pen tool enables you to create closed-path pen strokes that emulate artist-like pens. The Natural Pen tool is pressure-sensitive, meaning that you can control the thickness of the stroke from a pressure-sensitive tablet or from your keyboard with a mouse.

- Behavior of the Freehand and Bézier tools is now controlled from the Property Bar, making it easier to draw the desired type of outline.

- Dimension lines provide a wealth of options for drawing floor plans and other types of technical documents, such as schematics and architectural renderings. You can change the scale of a drawing from the General section of the Options dialog box, or from the Grid & Rulers dialog box.

- CorelDraw 7 lets you control various aspects of the shape drawing tools from the Property Bar, including rounding the corners of rectangles and turning ellipses into pies and arcs.

- The View Manager roll-up lets you save various zoom levels on different pages to quickly navigate through complicated documents.

Chapter 3

Aligning and Arranging Objects

In This Chapter

You'll learn great secrets that can help you work more effectively with the following tool, commands, and features:

- Grids
- Rulers
- Guidelines
- Align and Distribute
- Layer Manager
- Grouping and Ungrouping

- Child Objects
- Break Apart and Combine
- The Trim and Weld tools
- The Separate command
- The Intersection tool
- The Nudge and Duplicate commands

CorelDraw comes with a host of grids, guides, rulers, layering tools, and ordering options to help you manage objects and maintain total control over your drawings. In this chapter, I'll explain these features, as well as some artistic tools such as Weld, Trim, Intersect, Combine, and Break Apart. I'll show you how to use these tools to create some interesting effects. For example, you'll see how to use Layer Manager to quickly create a "watermark" graphic that appears beneath the text of a document.

Lining Up Objects

CorelDraw includes a number of tools to help you line up objects in your drawing. The main tools are grids, rulers, guidelines, and Align and Distribute.

Grids

To access the Grid & Ruler Setup, double-click on the ruler and click on the Grid tab. (You can also select the Layout menu and click on Grid & Ruler Setup.) Grids provide a visual reference for the size of objects on your page. When you require exactness, such as with blueprints or scaled street maps, grids are a must. Grids are very flexible, and can be resized with a few mouse-clicks. You can also turn on Snap to Grid (press Ctrl+Y) to make objects you draw conform to the grids you set up on your screen.

Grids are not always visible on your screen. To see them, select View ➪ Grids from the menu bar. (See Figure 3-1.)

Grid & Ruler Setup

Ruler | Grid

○ Frequency
○ Spacing

Frequency

Horizontal: [8.0] per inch

Vertical: [8.0] per inch

☐ Show Grid
☐ Snap To Grid

OK | Cancel | Help

Figure 3-1: Use the Grid sheet of the Grid & Ruler dialog box to control grid options for your drawing.

Secret

When objects have been selected on the page, the Property Bar displays a menu that includes the Snap to Grid option. When you save a document, the current Snap to Grid setting is saved along with that document. Also, the Snap to Grid setting remains active for any new documents you create until you turn off that setting.

Tip

Layer Manager, which is explained later in this chapter, treats grids as a layer. Using Layer Manager, you can print your grid, turn it on or off, and change the color of the grid dots.

Figure 3-2 shows three stars drawn with Snap to Grids enabled. By maintaining the same number of grid dots on either side of the stars, one can be sure of their alignment. Snap to Grids is also extremely helpful when drawing rectangles within other rectangles.

Rulers

CorelDraw's rulers are very flexible. Both the horizontal and vertical ruler can be moved to any part of your page. You can change the measurement units, drag unlimited numbers of guides from your ruler onto the page, or turn the rulers off altogether. You can access the Ruler dialog box by double-clicking on the ruler itself, or by choosing Grid & Ruler Setup from the Layout menu. (See Figure 3-3.)

Figure 3-2: These three stars are evenly spaced because they were drawn with Snap to Grids enabled.

Figure 3-3: Use the Ruler sheet of the Grid & Ruler Setup dialog box to control ruler options for your drawing.

From the Grid & Ruler Setup dialog box you can change the measurement units on your rulers. For example, if a client would like a drawing measured in millimeters rather than inches, CorelDraw's rulers can oblige. In fact, the Ruler menu offers 13 measurement systems, including pixels. Measuring in pixels can be helpful if your final product will be viewed on a computer screen rather than printed onto a page. Oversized work can be measured in meters or yards as well. When working with paragraph text, the rulers mark the height and width of the paragraph. The upper ruler now contains sliding bars that enable control over paragraph indents, margins, and tabs. (See Figure 3-4.) Chapter 4 explains more about formatting paragraph text.

Figure 3-4: This is what rulers look like when you select paragraph text.

Note the changing numbers in the bottom-left corner of the status bar. These are the mouse coordinates. See Figure 3-5. These numbers always display where your mouse cursor is, relative to the bottom-left corner of your page. For example, if your mouse cursor is approximately five inches up and three inches to the right of the bottom-left corner of the page (known as "0, 0"), the mouse coordinates will read something like "3.239, 5.053" (the comma separates the horizontal x axis value from the vertical y axis value). If you've changed your measurement unit to millimeters, for example, these two reference numbers will also display millimeters. In fact, right above these reference numbers is a label telling you what measurement system you are currently using. By double-clicking on the status bar, you can remove the mouse coordinates, or have the status bar display other helpful information. Editing toolbar properties is covered thoroughly in Chapter 9 of this book.

Figure 3-5: Mouse coordinates appear on the status bar.

Secret

If you are creating a blueprint or complex drawing, you might want to make your mouse coordinates "zero out" at the lower-left corner of the design you are making, rather than at the lower-left corner of your page. To set a new location for your starting coordinates (0, 0), drag from the point where your rulers intersect while holding the Shift key. Wherever you release the mouse button, that location will be your new "zero-zero" coordinate spot.

The Drawing Scale dialog box

Figure 3-6 shows the Drawing Scale dialog box. You open this dialog box by clicking Edit Scale in the Ruler dialog box. You can alter the drawing scale to make maps, architectural designs, and other documents that need precise scale measurements. In this example, one inch of Page Distance equals 63,360 inches of World Distance; in other words, the scale is one inch to the mile.

Figure 3-6: Use the Drawing Scale dialog box to create scaled maps with CorelDraw.

Moving the rulers

You can change the position of the rulers by pressing Shift while dragging the rulers in toward your drawing. This makes drawing precision shapes much easier. Figure 3-7a shows a rectangle drawn to exact specifications using moved rulers. CorelDraw comes with a complete set of tools to label measurements on your page. They are Dimension tools, and are covered in Chapter 2 of this book. Figure 3-7b shows the rectangle we just created labeled with Dimension tools.

Figure 3-7a: A rectangle can be more easily drawn to exact specifications with rulers moved close to it.

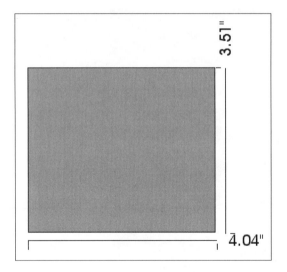

Figure 3-7b: The Dimension tools make it easy to label object dimensions.

Secret

No matter where they are on the screen, rulers can be moved back to their default locations by pressing Shift and double-clicking where the rulers intersect. You can reposition a single ruler by pressing Shift and double-clicking only on it.

Guidelines

To create guidelines, simply begin dragging from any place along your ruler's edge into your drawing. When you stop dragging, a dotted blue line appears.

Using guidelines

Once you have created guidelines, you can use them as visual guides, or you can make objects "snap" to them. For example, you may wish to have a newly created object adhere to the upper border of a rectangle already on your page. You can enable this by selecting Layout ➪ Snap to Guidelines from the menu bar.

Guidelines are also useful for arranging text on a page. Figure 3-8 shows horizontal guidelines used to line up and size artistic text to an exact height.

Figure 3-8: Use horizontal guidelines to make sure text conforms to an exact height.

Creating diagonal guidelines

You'll notice a solid black line at the ends of each dotted guideline. If you
move your mouse to one of these solid black lines, your mouse cursor
becomes a broken double arrow. Drag the line up or down to create a diagonal guideline. Figure 3-9 shows a horizontal, a vertical, and a diagonal guideline. When the mouse pointer passes over a diagonal guideline, the cursor
becomes a split arrow that you can use to drag the guideline and change its
angle.

Figure 3-9: Guidelines on a page can be horizontal, vertical, or diagonal.

Modifying your guidelines

To access CorelDraw's Guidelines Setup dialog box, you have two methods
available, as follows:

■ Select Layout ⇨ Guidelines Setup from the menu bar.

■ Open Layer Manager, right-click on Guides, select Settings, and then
Setup.

The first method is usually more convenient. However, the second method
gives you the option to print your guidelines or change their color.

You can maintain more precise control over your guidelines by using the Guidelines Setup dialog box, pictured in Figure 3-10. You have three tabs to choose from. Use the dialog box to enter exact numerical values for guideline locations, rather than using your mouse and "eyeballing it." Each type of guideline (horizontal, vertical, or slanted) is given its own tab for entering guideline numbers. You may use one of the 13 provided measuring systems for your guides, and set your diagonal guidelines by exact "*x,y*" coordinates or by degree of angle. The Guidelines Setup box enables you to create new guidelines, or move and edit already existing ones.

Figure 3-10: The Guidelines Setup dialog box enables you to position guidelines precisely.

Tip

You can quickly erase all guidelines from your screen by double-clicking on any guideline and selecting Clear All.

Warning

You can also use Layer Manager (explained later in this chapter) to edit guidelines. If you use Layer Manager, make sure to move Layer Manager's black arrow to another layer when you are done. Otherwise, any objects you create will apply only to the Guideline layer. Your screen will be covered with broken blue lines! If you accidentally did this, cut the object and move it to Layer 1, for example, and it will then be a true object, not a guideline.

Using objects as guides

You can also create objects in the Guideline layer and use them as you would other guides. For example, you could create a circle as a guide and make sure everything else you create stays clear of that circle. Or you can create text as a guide, turn on Snap to Guidelines and make sure other layers of text you create snap to that guideline. Figure 3-11 shows text as a guideline.

Figure 3-11: You can even use text as a guideline.

Using text as a guideline can be helpful if you want certain objects to align exactly to text — such as making sure drawn objects fall directly beneath a text heading. Similarly with using objects as guidelines, you can make sure that one object is aligned with another. Later, you can group them and align them both to the page.

The Align and Distribute dialog box

The Align and Distribute dialog box enables you to make sure all your document's objects — including captions — are properly aligned. You can use this dialog box, shown in Figure 3-12, to align objects to each other, to the edge or center of the page, or to grids. You cannot use Align and Distribute to line up objects with guides.

Figure 3-12: The Align and Distribute dialog box lets you align objects in various ways.

You have three ways to access the Align and Distribute dialog box, as follows:

- Select Align and Distribute from the Arrange menu.
- Press Ctrl+A.
- Select the word Align on the far right of the Property Bar. (It becomes visible only if two or more objects are selected.)

Secret

If you align objects to each other, all objects will be aligned to the last object selected.

The Align sheet of the Align and Distribute dialog box enables you to set a horizontal parameter (Top, Center, Bottom) and a vertical parameter (Left, Center, Right), and to choose the Align to Page (edge or center) or Align to Grid options. If you are familiar with CorelDraw 6, you might be wondering what happened to the preview screen. In CorelDraw 7, you may preview your results on the page itself by selecting Preview, and then Reset to try another option. Actually, you need not hit the reset button to try another type of alignment. Just place checks by our new parameters, and select Preview. Use Reset to return your page to the way it was before you began editing. Clicking the "X" in the upper right corner has the same effect as selecting the Cancel button.

Aligning objects

When you are selecting objects to be aligned, think about where you want the objects to end up, and place the last object to be selected on that part of the page. That's because the last object you select will be what the others are aligned to. If you only select one object, you'll need to select one of the Align to Page options, or no action will be taken.

You can combine checkboxes to come up with a great number of alignment options, and so the following are just a few examples of how the Align command works. If you work through these examples yourself, make sure to use the Order command to bring the "PacMan" circle to the front, put the triangle in the middle, and set the rectangle to the back. Figure 3-13 shows three unaligned objects with Center and Center selected. Clicking OK makes the objects look like Figure 3-14.

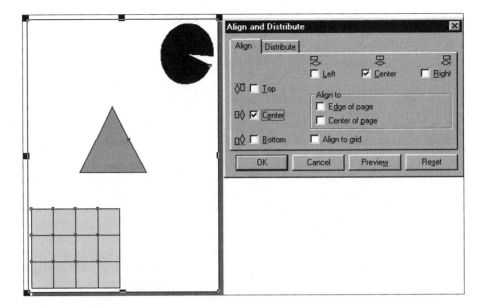

Figure 3-13: These three unaligned objects are about to be centered.

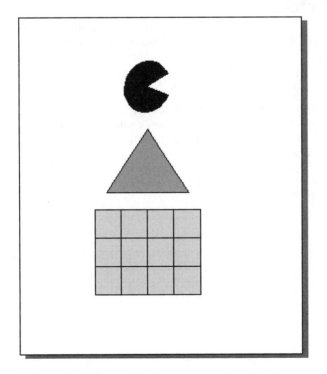

Figure 3-14: The same objects are now center-aligned.

Figure 3-15 shows what happens if you select Top, Left, and Edge of Page. Objects will be aligned to the top left of the last object selected (the triangle), *and also* aligned to the top left of the page. Notice that the rectangle is not aligned in Figure 3-15 because it is not selected.

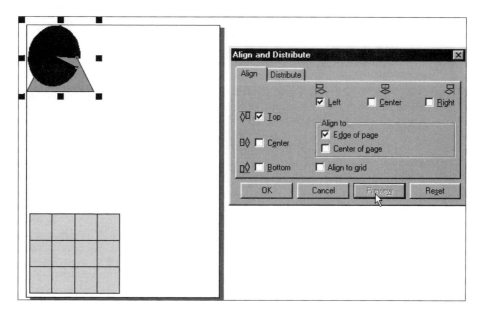

Figure 3-15: The two selected objects are aligned to the top-left corner of the page.

Figure 3-16 shows two objects centered to each other, as well as to the page.

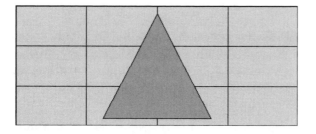

Figure 3-16: These two objects are centered to each other (horizontally and vertically), and to the page.

Figure 3-17 shows how to use Align to center a caption exactly under a rectangle object (the caption is not yet centered).

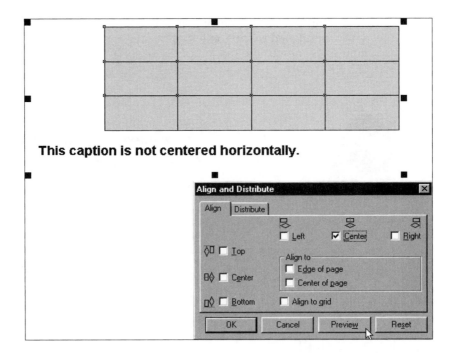

Figure 3-17: To center the caption under the rectangle, you would select the horizontal Center checkbox.

Distributing objects

Click on the Distribute tab of the Align and Distribute dialog box to adjust the distribution of selected objects. (See Figure 3-18.) If you select several objects, you can use Distribute to space them evenly across your page, or across a selected area. As with Align, you can set horizontal or vertical parameters, or both to distribute your objects. For example, if you've just duplicated a CorelDraw object several times, the Distribute command can spread these copies across the top of a page at even intervals.

As with Align, you can click on the Preview button to "test run" your choices before selecting OK. The Distribute option is only available when you have more than one object selected on your page.

Here are some examples of how to use Distribute. Figure 3-19 shows a five-dollar bill that has been duplicated six times using the Duplicate command. Unless you've edited your tool options, this is exactly how duplicated objects look: Each new copy is placed slightly above and to the right of the previous duplicate. The Distribute dialog box is shown with three options checked: horizontal and vertical Spacing and Extent of Page. Selecting OK spreads the dollar bills diagonally across the entire page, as shown in Figure 3-20.

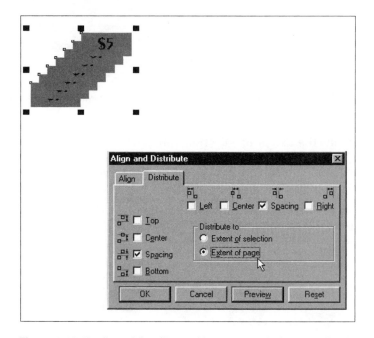

Figure 3-18: The Distribute sheet of the Align and Distribute dialog box lets you evenly distribute selected objects in various ways.

Figure 3-19: Duplicated CorelDraw objects are ready for even distribution.

Figure 3-20: These CorelDraw objects are now evenly spaced with Distribute applied.

The only time the Extent of Selection option does anything is if objects are selected that have room to move within the selected area. If you've just duplicated some objects, as in Figure 3-19, and then you choose Extent of Selection, nothing happens.

Figure 3-21 shows the result of choosing the same objects, selecting the horizontal Spacing command, and choosing Extent of Page. The bills are distributed evenly across the top of the page.

Figure 3-21: This art is now distributed across the top of the page.

Figure 3-22 shows one way you can use the Extent of Selection option. First deselect the five-dollar bills and reselect one. Now Drag it farther up the screen. Doing so marks the path that the remaining bills will travel after you use the Distribute command.

Figure 3-22: Before Extent of Selection is performed, most of this art is bunched together.

Now select all the bills, and choose the vertical Spacing command, and Extent of Selection. The results appear in Figure 3-23.

Figure 3-23: The art is evenly distributed after Extent of Selection is performed.

The remaining CorelDraw object pieces are now evenly spaced across a path led by the first CorelDraw object, bounded within the selected area.

CorelDraw provides many tools for controlling the positioning and order of objects on your page. Still, it's not always easy to keep track of what is supposed to go where. For that task, CorelDraw has provided Layering controls.

Using Layers

Layers are like the transparencies that many people use with overhead projectors. You can place one on top of another to gradually create a completed image. You can draw objects or type text on each layer, and then create a new layer for other objects in the same drawing. Each new layer you create is automatically placed on top of previous layers. While you're working with the new layer, you can choose whether or not you want to view underlying layers. Also, to prevent accidentally changing the work you did on an earlier layer, you can "lock" it in place.

CorelDraw's layers enable you to create one portion of your drawing at a time. For example, for a landscape drawing you might decide to work only on the sky at first and call that portion Layer 1. You could then create a new layer of mountains and call that Layer 2, and then put foliage on the mountains as Layer 3. Why keep them separate? With Layer Manager, you could make the "Mountain Layer" invisible while working on the foliage, and make the "Sky Layer" uneditable, so that you don't have to worry about accidentally moving a chunk of your sky while repositioning a mountain. Layering is great for protecting selected portions of your drawing that you don't want to change.

Layering can also be useful for creating watermark graphics. A *watermark graphic* is a faint background picture that usually appears behind text or another image on a page. (Such graphics are meant to look like real watermarks that are pressed into paper during the paper-making process.) CorelDraw's Layer Manager enables you to create a watermark graphic without your having to specifically duplicate the same picture manually. Also, Layer Manager enables you to specify portions of your work as nonprinting. For example, if you wanted to quickly print out the text portion of a lengthy newsletter, but not the graphics, you could copy all the graphics to their own layer and temporarily render that layer "nonprinting."

Layer Manager

As you can see in Figure 3-24, five icon columns run down the left-hand side of the Layer Manager window. Each icon in the five columns has a different function. For example, the eye icon can make a layer either visible or invisible. When an icon is dimmed, that means the option has been disabled for the corresponding layer. You click on the icons to enable or disable functions for the various layers.

Let's take a closer look at Layer Manager. The first four layers listed on the right-hand side (Grid, Guides, Desktop, and Layer 1) appear by default. You edit the properties of existing layers using the icon commands. You can add new layers by using the flyout menu, which I explain a little later.

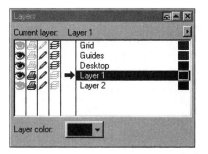

Figure 3-24: In Layer Manager, the visibility of Layer 2 has been disabled. The pointing arrow indicates that any current editing will be done on Layer 1.

The Eye icon

Clicking on the Eye icon that corresponds to a layer renders that layer visible or invisible. For example, if Layer Manager is open, you can turn off grids by clicking the Eye icon on the Grid layer. This saves you from having to hunt for the Turn on Grids menu option.

The Printer icon

Clicking on a Printer icon for a layer renders that layer printable or unprintable. (When the icon is dimmed, you cannot print the layer.) Notice that, by default, the Printer icon is dimmed for the Guides and Grid layers because normally guides and grids are not printed.

The Pencil icon

You can click on the Pencil icon to make a layer editable or to protect it from editing. For example, if you've spent hours on a complex drawing on a particular layer, you might want to click on the Pencil icon for that layer. That way you couldn't accidentally edit the layer. To make changes to it, you would have to return to Layer Manager and click the Pencil icon again.

The Master Layer icon

The Master Layer icon looks like a stack of paper. If you click on the Master Layer icon for a particular layer, every object on that layer appears on every page of a multipage document. That's why the Grid and Guides layers automatically have Master Layer enabled; they usually apply to every page. Figure 3-25 shows a watermark graphic with Master Layer turned on. The shading on the left side of the page will appear on every page of the document. Although CorelDraw has more advanced tools for creating headers and footers, you can also use this technique to place a certain piece of text on every page of a document.

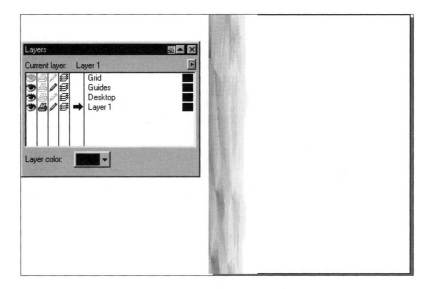

Figure 3-25: You can create a watermark graphic by turning on the Master Layer.

The Arrow column

The arrow in the fifth column indicates which layer is the active layer; in other words, it shows which layer you are working on at the moment. The changes you make only affect the current layer (that is, the layer with the arrow pointing at it). To select a new layer for editing, click in the arrow column next to that layer's name, and the arrow moves there.

Tip If you discover as you're working that suddenly you cannot select or edit anything on your picture, check Layer Manager. You may be attempting to edit an inactive layer or a layer that has been protected.

The Layer Color button

Clicking the Layer Color button enables you to choose a new color for a layer's *wireframe*. (With the Wireframe option, you can move objects around quickly by viewing only their outlines — it's like looking at the object's "skeleton." To view only the outlines, select View ➪ Wireframe.) When you choose a new Layer Color with the Layer Color button, the next time you select View ➪ Wireframe, you will see objects that reside in that layer wireframed with the new color. This view is helpful because seeing all of the shapes in your drawing in the default blue wireframe can be very confusing. Use the Layer Color command to designate a new color for objects on a layer, so you can see those objects better in wireframe mode.

The Layer Manager flyout menu

The Layer Manager flyout menu, shown in Figure 3-26, enables you to move or copy drawings from one layer to another, as well as rename, delete, and add new layers. You can also access the Settings dialog box from the flyout menu, and you can select the Edit Across Layers option.

Switch To Layer

New
Delete
Rename

Settings...

Move To...
Copy To...

✓ Edit Across Layers

What's This?

Figure 3-26: The Layer Manager flyout menu gives you control over your drawing's layers.

When you are working with layers, normally you cannot select an object that is not in the current layer. In fact, if you find yourself clicking repeatedly on an object and you cannot select it, check to see whether the object is on a different layer. If so, you won't be able to select it unless you either move to the other layer or select Edit Across Layers. Edit Across Layers enables you to select any object on any layer that is not locked. A locked layer cannot be edited until it is unlocked.

Adding layers

By default, CorelDraw creates one layer for each new picture (in addition to the Grids, Guides, and Desktop layers). If you want to add more layers, open the Layer flyout menu by clicking on the arrow facing right at the upper right of Layer Manager. Select New Layer, and you'll notice Layer 2 will now be created. For your convenience, the black "active layer" arrow automatically moves to the newly created layer, so you can begin editing it right away.

Using the Settings menu

Within the Layer Manager flyout menu is the Settings menu. (See Figure 3-27.) This dialog box shows you what layer commands are active on the layer you've selected. It also includes two invaluable tools: Override Full Color View and Apply Layer Changes to the Current Page Only.

Figure 3-27: The Layer 1 Settings dialog box lets you control the behavior of an individual layer.

Override Full Color View

If you ever want to view only the wireframe of part of a drawing, but see another part in full color, move the portion to be viewed as a wireframe to its own layer, and select Override Full Color View. From now on, that portion of the drawing will be viewed as if you had selected Wireframe from the View menu, while the remainder of the drawing will be viewed in full color. If a particular portion of your drawing takes very long to refresh, you might want to consider this option.

Apply Layer Changes to the Current Page Only

This command enables you to make exceptions to your layer rules. For example, if you have a drawing that repeats on each page, and you'd like to skip the drawing on page 8, move to page 8 of your document, make that layer invisible, open the Settings dialog box, and then apply this command. For another example, if you would like to print your guidelines only on page 1 of your document, then turn on the Guideline Layer Print icon while on page 1. Open the Settings dialog box and select this command.

As you can see, the various layering options are extremely useful for creating and editing complex drawings. Another important tool that affects the arrangement of objects is the Group command.

Grouping and Ungrouping Objects

Just about every complex picture you create with CorelDraw is actually a group of objects. The Group and Ungroup commands appear under the Arrange menu, and can also be accessed by right-clicking the selected objects and bringing up the Object Properties menu. (You can also group objects by selecting them and pressing Ctrl+G.)

Figure 3-28 shows a CorelDraw picture of a sailboat. This picture is really a group of nine objects. The sail was drawn separately and then grouped with the mast. These objects were later grouped with the hull, and so on.

Figure 3-28: A single CorelDraw object is often really a group of objects.

The boat, when combined with other objects, might later become a harbor scene, which would be a collection of objects grouped together as a "master group." A *master group* is a complete drawing. It can be resized, exported as a different file type, or copied and pasted to another file, all as a group. A master group can also be *ungrouped*. The boat could then be edited individually, recolored and reshaped all on its own, and then grouped again with the rest of the master group. Figure 3-29 shows the layout of the grouping of a typical CorelDraw project.

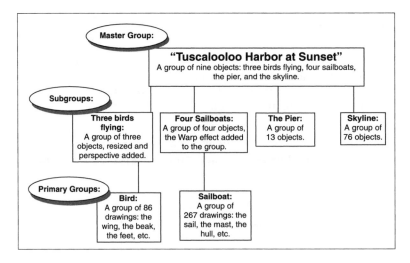

Figure 3-29: A layout of the grouping of a typical CorelDraw project.

Grouping enables you to "section off" portions of your drawing and treat them as if they were a single object. For example, if you created a sky scene with a complicated artistic text pattern on top of it, you could select only the text, group it, and move it to a new page of your drawing, and edit the text without the sky getting in the way.

Even after you've grouped objects, you can still select an object within that group to perform simple editing, such as recoloring. If you wish to perform special effects editing, however, such as Extrude, Rotate, and Contour, you first need to make the object into a *child object*. When you create a child object, you can edit a grouped object without accidentally editing the entire group. For example, while working with a complex drawing of a person, you might decide to rotate only one arm of the person. One approach would be to Ungroup the entire drawing, but you might end up editing more of the drawing than you intended. Then you might have trouble properly grouping the drawing again. To quickly edit a small portion of a group, a better approach is to select only the part of the group you want to edit and press the Ctrl key to create a child object. Here's how it's done:

STEPS

Creating a Child Object

Step 1. Hold down the Ctrl key and select the portion of the object to be edited.

Step 2. Check the status line. It should report that the selection is now a child object.

Step 3. Release the Ctrl key. You can now perform special effects and transform editing on the selected portion and not worry about it effecting the entire group.

Step 4. You have no need to unchild the selected portion when you are finished. Simply move on to the next step in your project.

An example of creating a child object is shown in Figure 3-30, in which the enveloping effect has been applied to *only a portion* of the pencil object on the right. (Enveloping, by the way, is one of CorelDraw's special effects. See Chapter 6 for more information about enveloping.)

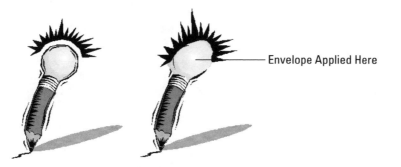

Figure 3-30: Here a portion of the pencil object is selected, made into a child object, and the Envelope effect is applied.

Combining and Breaking Apart Objects

Combining objects is different from grouping objects. The Combine command creates a single object out of two or more selected objects. With grouping, the objects maintain the shape qualities they possessed before they were grouped. The Group command is used to conveniently select objects for moving around the page as a unit. Grouping does not alter the characteristics of the individual objects involved in the group. When you use the Combine command, each object is converted to curves to form one object.

The Combine command

When you apply the Combine command, the areas where the objects overlap become transparent, enabling anything underneath to show through. Figure 3-31 shows how this works. The rectangles and text overlapping each other leave holes where they overlap, enabling a fountain-filled pattern behind the objects to show through.

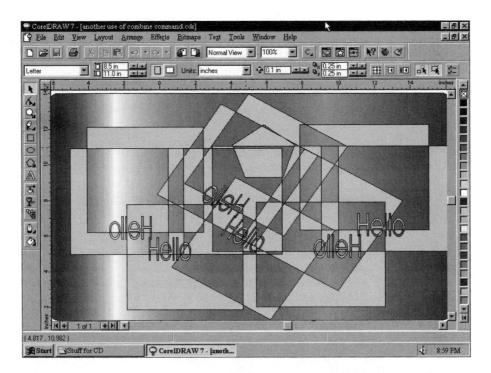

Figure 3-31: The Combine command at work: A series of overlapping rectangles and text shows how the Combine command enables the fill behind to show through.

Here's another use of the Combine command: Suppose you group a number of objects, and one of those objects is a shade of green that you've worked hard at getting just right. It turns out that you would like all the objects, when grouped, to also take on that exact shade. Simply select all the objects, and then select the green object last. Choose Arrange ⇨ Combine. All the objects will be the same color.

The combine command can also be used to quickly make text transparent. In Figure 3-31, the word "Hello" is transparent, just like the rectangles. To try this yourself, create a text object and then make a transparent rectangle. Then select the text first, followed by the rectangle. The text will now be transparent. This procedure is the first step in creating a *text mask*. A text mask works like a cookie cutter that leaves a hole in an object in the shape of the text — as in the word "Hello" in the example. A text mask is handy for enabling a bitmap buried beneath the first object to show through where the text mask is. Figure 3-32 shows another example of a text mask.

Figure 3-32: A bitmap showing through a text mask using the Combine command produces this interesting result.

Here's how you can use the Combine command to create a text mask like the one shown in Figure 3-32:

STEPS

Creating a Creative Text Mask

Step 1. Import a bitmap image into CorelDraw. Make it an interesting, repeating pattern such as honeycomb or brick.

Step 2. Create a rectangle large enough to cover the image you imported. Do not fill the rectangle with any color.

Step 3. Type a word with a bold, clear font. In the example shown in Figure 3-32, I imported an image of crystal as the bitmap and typed the word "Crystal" to form the mask.

Step 4. Drag the word you've typed to the center of the rectangle. The word should be large enough to nearly fill it.

Step 5. Select both the typed word and the rectangle, and click Arrange ⇨ Combine. You now have a transparent rectangle and transparent text.

Step 6. Fill the rectangle around the text with white. (If your background color is something besides white, use it instead.) You now have a mask of text that you can place over any image, and the underlying image will show through the text.

Step 7. Drag the word over the bitmapped image you imported. In the example shown here, the word "Crystal" was placed over a bitmapped picture of crystal. The white surrounding the letters creates the illusion that the rectangle no longer exists, because it is filled with background color.

In order to again work individually with these pieces, you must choose Arrange ➪ Break Apart, not Ungroup.

Text masks are only one example of how you can use the Combine command. Here's another: If you'd like to apply a single fill across several objects, first select them, choose the Combine command, and then apply your fill.

Have you ever tried to apply a blend to *three* objects? You can't. However, if you select two of the objects you want to blend, apply the Combine command to those two objects, and *then* select the third object, you can now apply Blend to the three objects. One more use: If you have created an extremely complex drawing, choose Combine to reduce its complexity. The drawing will not take as long to render onto the page each time you make a change.

The Break Apart command

The Break Apart command, found under the Arrange menu, undoes the work of the Combine command. Let's say you have combined two sails on a drawing of a ship. Then you decide to change the color of one of the sails. Because the two sails are combined, if you were to recolor one, the other would change as well. To recolor only one sail, select both sails and choose the Break Apart command. (You can't use the Ungroup command in this procedure, because the objects are *combined*, not grouped.) Now apply the color to the one sail, and then combine them again, if you wish.

If you use clip art, and are trying to edit only a part of the clip art, you'll find yourself using the Break Apart command quite a bit. That's because clip art is often made up of individual drawn pieces that are combined.

If you break apart combined objects, it might appear as though the smaller objects suddenly disappear. For example, look again at the "Hello" image (Figure 3-31). If I applied Break Apart to that object, each "hello" text would then be an independent object apart from the rectangles. You would only see the rectangles. That's because the text would be underneath. To see the text again, you must select the rectangles, choose Arrange ➪ Order ➪ Send to Back. This, in effect, brings the text to the front, where you can see it.

You can also use Break Apart with the Trim command to fully separate objects that have been trimmed. I explain the Trim procedure next.

Using the Trim Tool

The Trim tool, found under the Arrange menu (or at the far right of the Property Bar) is only available if two or more objects overlap. The Trim tool cuts overlapping areas out of selected objects. Here's how it works: If you select an object that overlaps another and then choose the Trim command, the area where the first object cuts into the second object will be removed from the second object. Or, put more simply, the first object you select *trims* the second object. The Trim tool is often referred to as the "cookie-cutter tool."

The dialog box for the Trim tool is shown in Figure 3-33.

Figure 3-33: You access the Trim dialog box from the Arrange menu.

The preceding explanation shows how the Trim tool works when you click the Trim button on the Property Bar. If you apply the Trim tool by opening the Trim dialog box, you'll have more options to choose from. Here's how to use Trim from the Trim dialog box:

STEPS

Trimming an Object

Step 1. Select a CorelDraw object and place it on top of another.

Step 2. Choose Arrange ⇨ Trim to display the Trim dialog box. Make sure both of the options in the Leave Original area are unchecked.

Step 3. Click the Trim command, and an arrow appears.

Step 4. Click the arrow on the Target Object, the object that is to receive the cookie-cutter cut. The first object disappears, leaving only its shape as a hole in the first object. If you've used a rectangle and a star, the results should look something like Figure 3-34.

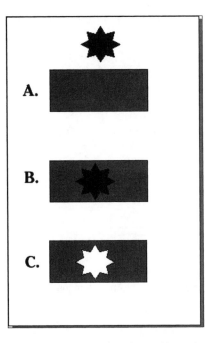

Figure 3-34: Here's the Trim tool in action. A: The star and rectangle are created. B: The star is placed on top of the rectangle. C: The Trim command is applied, leaving a hole where the star used to be.

Figure 3-35 shows an hourglass that was created by trimming the sides away from an oval. This example shows the use of two shapes to create a third shape. The oval object used as a cookie cutter is no longer visible.

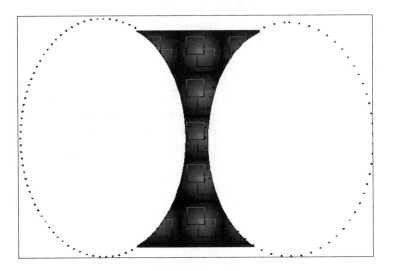

Figure 3-35: An hourglass shape created by using two ovals as trimming tools.

The Trim dialog box provides options to leave both the Target Object and Other Object (the cookie-cutter object) untouched. You can use shapes for editing, and then still have the originals just as they were before you began. Remember, though, that you may have to move the originals out of the way to see your cookie-cutter results.

Secret

You can also use the Trim command to divide a single object into two. Use the Freehand Pencil tool to draw across an object and then select the line. Click the Trim command, point the big black arrow at the object under the line you drew, and click the mouse. Select Arrange ➪ Break Apart, and you can now drag the two pieces away from each other for a "broken" effect, as shown in Figure 3-36.

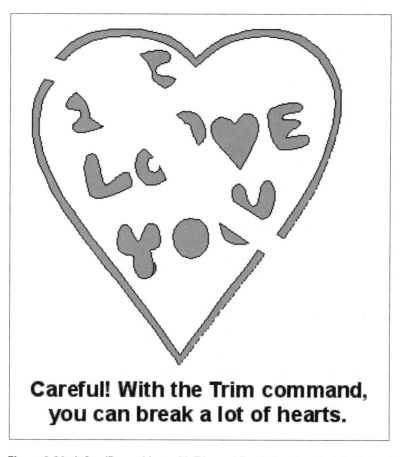

Careful! With the Trim command, you can break a lot of hearts.

Figure 3-36: A CorelDraw object with Trim and Break Apart applied. Don't try this on Valentine's Day.

The Trim command cannot be used with bitmaps; you can only use it with objects created in CorelDraw.

Welding Objects

The Weld tool, which you access from the Arrange menu, erases all internal lines and leaves only the outline when you weld one object to another. Figure 3-37 shows the Weld dialog box.

Figure 3-37: The Weld dialog box lets you attach objects together.

One good application of the Weld tool is for drawing street maps. Figure 3-38 shows a series of intersecting lines. It's not hard to create a street map from this grid-like arrangement. After grouping the lines, select the Node tool (the second tool from the top on the toolbar). Click the grouped objects. When you select an object with the Node tool, you'll find that, instead of seeing bounding boxes, you'll see nodes placed throughout the objects. You can reshape the objects by moving the nodes to a new location, or change the node curve angle with the handles. After arranging the nodes to resemble the streets you want to simulate, apply the Weld tool. The Weld tool eliminates all common boundaries, simulating the appearance of contiguous streets, rather than a bunch of grids on a page. See Figure 3-39.

Figure 3-38: A series of intersecting lines such as these are prime candidates for the Weld operation.

Figure 3-39: The same lines, after using the Node and Weld tools, now resemble a street map.

To use the Weld tool, select the objects you want to weld and then click the Weld command (under the Arrange menu). The selected objects must overlap at some point, or the Weld command will not be available. The cursor becomes a black arrow. With this arrow, click the object group, and every boundary that the objects share will disappear.

When you use the Weld tool on a group of touching shapes, the shapes are reduced to the outline of their combined shape. No lines will exist inside the new shape.

The Weld dialog box has a checkbox labeled Leave Original. By selecting it, you are in essence duplicating the group you wish to weld, and carrying out the Weld command on this exact copy. For example, if you selected Leave Original when creating the map shown in Figure 3-39, the results would be a "before and after." One object group would be transformed, while the original object group would be left unedited by the Weld command.

Here's an example of what you can do with the Weld tool. Figure 3-40 shows a picture of a flower created by using one ellipse and the Weld command (along with the Rotation, Combine, and Extrude commands).

Figure 3-40: This flower was created using the Weld command.

Here are the steps you would follow to create this drawing:

STEPS

Creating an Object with the Weld Command

Step 1.   Create a simple vertically oriented ellipse. Double-click on it and drag the thumb-tack icon to the bottom center of the ellipse.

Step 2.   Select Arrange ➪ Transform ➪ Rotate. The Rotate dialog box appears.

Step 3.   Set the Angle parameter in the Rotate dialog box to –25 degrees, as shown in Figure 3-41. Press the Apply to Duplicate button once, and your ellipse will be duplicated, but at the angle specified.

Figure 3-41: A simple ellipse has had the Rotation dialog box's Apply to Duplicate command applied once.

Step 4.   Press the Apply to Duplicate button repeatedly until you've gone in a full circle duplicating the ellipse.

Step 5.   Place a circle in the center of the ellipse group. Now press the Shift key and select each of the ellipses, making sure none are left out of the selection process. Watch the status bar to make sure the Number of Selected Objects increases each time you try to select one. You should end up with 13 selected ellipses.

Step 6.   Select Arrange ➪ Weld. Make sure none of the Leave Original buttons are checked, and click Weld. You'll see an arrow as shown in Figure 3-42.

Figure 3-42: Apply the Weld command to the ellipses group and the circle by clicking with the large arrow.

Step 7. Click the arrow on the circle. Your ellipses and circle should now be one solid object. If some portions remain unwelded, just click Weld again and select the unwelded portions with the arrow until everything is solid.

Step 8. Color the welded object gray. Place another circle in the center of the object. Select the circle and the object and click on Arrange ⇨ Combine, as shown in Figure 3-43.

Figure 3-43: Apply Combine to a circle and the welded object.

Step 9.   Select Effects ⇨ Extrude and set the Depth parameter to 35, as shown in Figure 3-44. Set the options to Big Back and VP Locked to Object, as shown. Click on Apply.

Figure 3-44: Use the Extrude dialog box to apply the extrude command and create the flower.

Recolor portions of the petals with lighter shades of gray to create a more dramatic effect.

The next time you create objects and want to join them leaving only their common outline, the Weld tool can do the trick.

Remember

Using the Separate Tool

Sometimes, when using the Blend, Contour, or Extrude tool, you may wish to separate the effect portion from the original object. For example, suppose after using the Extrude effect on a star that you want to move the face of the star to a new location. Before you can ungroup the star, use the Separate command to make the star face a separate object from the extruded portion. Then use the Ungroup command, which gives you the freedom to move the star face to a new location. Similarly, after using Contour, you can use the

Separate command to pull the new contoured lines out from the original object. Then use Ungroup to make them movable on their own. Next, move the Contour lines to a new location, if you wish. Figure 3-45 shows an extruded star with its face moved away from the extruded portion. The same figure shows Contour lines pulled away from a star, duplicated and moved around the star at various angles. These effects are made possible by the Separate command.

Figure 3-45: Two objects treated with effects. Applying the Separate command enables you to move the original object away from the effect portion.

You can use Separate with the Blend command. Figure 3-46 shows the two original objects being pulled out of a blend. Now, those two objects, and the blend itself, can all be treated as objects unto themselves.

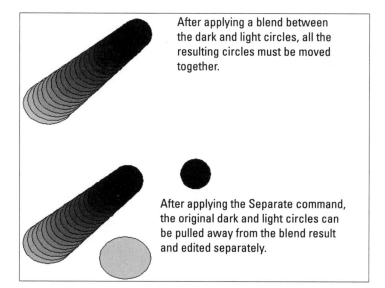

After applying a blend between the dark and light circles, all the resulting circles must be moved together.

After applying the Separate command, the original dark and light circles can be pulled away from the blend result and edited separately.

Figure 3-46: Use Separate to extract the original objects used in a Blend effect.

Using the Intersect Tool

The Intersect command, found under the Arrange menu, creates a new object out of the area where two or more objects overlap. If part of a rectangle overlaps with a triangle, press the Intersect command, and only the portion where the two overlap will be left.

Selecting the Intersect command from the Arrange menu calls up the Intersect dialog box, shown in Figures 3-47 through 3-49. You must click on an object, click the Intersect command, and then click the second object with the arrow. And as with the Trim and Weld commands, you are given the option of leaving the target or "other" (original) object untouched by the process. In essence, this means you perform the command on a duplicate object. And as with the other two commands in this group, Intersect only works with CorelDraw objects. Bitmaps cannot be used.

Figures 3-47, 3-48, and 3-49 show how to use the Intersect tool to create a shape from the area where two circles intersect.

Figure 3-47: One circle overlaps another before the Intersect command is applied.

Figure 3-48: Applying the Intersect command with Other Object checked results in this image.

Figure 3-49: Applying the Intersect command with no option checked results in this image.

Figure 3-50 shows several rectangles and diamonds intersecting with text. When Intersect was applied, the text overlapping the rectangles became a new object. In this example, the objects that were created as a result of Intersect were recolored. This example demonstrates how new objects are created only where the letters actually overlap the rectangles.

Figure 3-50: The Intersect command creates new objects out of text that overlaps other objects.

Let's create a 3D text object horizontally split in half. Because you're actually going to be extruding two split text objects, this technique gives the 3D effect even more substance.

STEPS

Creating a 3D Text Object Split in Half

Step 1. Type a word with a big bold font. The size should be about 86 points.

Step 2. Draw a Rectangle over the top half of the text, and select the rectangle.

Step 3. Select Arrange ⇨ Intersect and put a check by both Target Object and Other Object.

Step 4. Click the Intersect With button and click the arrow on the text.

Step 5. Although you've invoked the Intersect command, nothing looks different because you've elected to leave both original objects alone. Change the color of the text in the rectangle to a dark gray. Only the upper half will be recolored, because you are actually recoloring the copy that was "cut off" by the rectangle.

Step 6. Drag the rectangle down over the lower half of the text and remove both Leave Original option checkmarks in the dialog box.

Step 7. Select the text, and again apply the Intersect command, this time by pointing the big black arrow at the rectangle. If you select the rectangle first, apply the command, and point the big black arrow at the text, you'll get an error message saying that the command cannot be carried out. That's because its very hard to select the text behind the rectangle *after* the rectangle is selected.

Step 8. You now have two text halves. The method you used to carry out the previous command eliminated the originals. Color the bottom half a light gray. So now you have two text objects. Apply a very light gray "hairline" outline to both halves of text.

Step 9. Select Effects ⇨ Extrude and select the lower half of the text. From the Extrude dialog box, the parameters should read Small Back and VP Locked to Object.

Step 10. Apply the Extrude effect.

Step 11. Drag the vanishing point "X" upward and to the right for a more dramatic effect (you'll learn more about perspective and vanishing points in Chapter 6). Click Apply again.

Step 12. Repeat the entire Extrude procedure for the upper half of the text.

Step 13. This procedure causes the top half to be sent to the back. Before you deselect the top half, select Arrange ⇨ Order ⇨ Send to Front. Your top text will now be positioned where it should be.

Step 14. You may now group your text together as you would any finished piece. The results should resemble the text shown in Figure 3-51.

Figure 3-51: You can create a two-tone text object like this using Intersect and Extrude.

The Intersect tool is similar to the Trim tool, except it takes the process one step further. Rather than simply removing the area where two objects overlap, it creates a third object out of the space where the objects overlap. This is a great tool for creating objects that look like they're being sliced, such as the effect of a piece of cheese falling forward after being sliced by a knife. This final example is merely a drop in the bucket of what's possible. The applications are endless.

Duplicating Objects

The Duplicate command is available from the Edit menu (or by pressing Ctrl+D while an object is selected). If you've used CorelDraw for any length of time, you've probably discovered that Duplicate is faster than using Copy and Paste. However, if you are not happy with the way CorelDraw automatically positions an object after duplicating it, you can select Tools ⇨ Options and adjust Duplicate Placement and Nudge. (See Figure 3-52.) You can change these numbers to make CorelDraw deposit the Duplicate item a bit closer or farther from the original.

Figure 3-52: The General tab of the Options Dialog box gives you access to the Duplicate and Nudge controls.

Using the Property Bar with Duplicate

You can also adjust Duplicate Distance from the Property Bar. When no objects are selected, the Property Bar becomes a menu of options for adjusting paper size, "snap to" settings, as well as Duplicate Distance amounts. Hold your mouse momentarily over the set of numbers slightly to the right of the page on the Property Bar. One set of numbers will read Duplicate Distance. Here you can adjust both the vertical and horizontal settings for where duplicates are placed on your page.

Using Duplicate with other effects

The Duplicate command is also built into several of CorelDraw's effects and transform commands. For example, the Position, Rotate, and Mirror commands all contain options that perform their edits on duplicate objects rather than affect the original. The Weld, Intersection, and Trim commands all contain Leave Original options that are, in effect, forms of the Duplicate command.

Use Leave Original and Apply to Duplicate to perform these tasks:

- Perform your effects on a duplicate object so that you can view "before" and "after" objects on your screen simultaneously.

- Apply effects to the duplicate after duplicating to speed up complicated editing chores.

If you're like most people who are used to standard Windows procedures, you probably automatically look for Copy and Paste when you want to reproduce an object on your screen. Not only is using the Duplicate command faster, using the Copy and Paste commands needlessly places the object on the Windows Clipboard. You can avoid this drag on your system's memory by duplicating onscreen objects using the Duplicate command.

Nudging Objects

If you've ever wanted to move a CorelDraw object "just a little bit" in a particular direction, you'll love the Nudge tool. You can nudge selected objects by using the arrow keys on your keyboard. As you may have noticed, though, the problem with the Nudge tool is that the preset nudge amount is usually never quite right.

Secret

You can adjust how far objects are nudged by changing the Nudge Offset amount, which can be set from the Property Bar. Make sure no objects are selected, and the Property bar will display the Nudge Offset amount. Adjust this number to your liking. Both Nudge Offset and Duplicate Distance amounts will be displayed in units matching the measuring system currently being used by the rulers.

Summary

- ▶ Using Grids and Guides is key to making sure all your CorelDraw objects line up on your page. Grids and Guides can be turned on or off and are fully adjustable.

- ▶ Rulers also can be repositioned to suit your needs. The ruler measuring system can be changed. Rulers can be altered to reflect a map scale (for map making).

- ▶ The Align and Distribute command helps you keep control of complicated documents by providing tools to keep everything straight.

- ▶ Layer Manager enables you to separate portions of your page from the others, making it easy to zero in on areas that need editing yet protect the rest.

- ▶ Grouping and Ungrouping draw objects makes it easy to copy, cut, paste, and move complicated composite objects.

- ▶ Break Apart and Combine make it easy to set apart a portion of a complicated object for special effects editing, without having to Ungroup the object.

- ▶ Trim, Intersection, and Weld provide tools for cutting pieces out of CorelDraw objects, slicing them down the middle, and joining them entirely, removing all the boundaries between them.

- ▶ The Duplicate command is far superior to cutting and pasting duplicate objects. By understanding the Duplicate command, you can create special effects on multiple objects quite quickly.

- ▶ The Nudge command makes it easy to move CorelDraw objects even a fraction of an inch with your arrow keys.

Chapter 4

Typesetting Secrets

Computers have put the power of typesetting at nearly everybody's fingertips. Unfortunately, having an arsenal of fonts — CorelDraw 7 comes with over 900 — does not qualify you as a designer or typographer. For the novice, having too many fonts can be a hindrance. Using too many fonts (or using the wrong ones) can make your work look ridiculous, even disastrous.

Numerous books dedicate themselves to the subject of typesetting and design. This chapter covers only the basics of font usage and typesetting. In most cases, font usage in business communications is relatively conservative, so deciding which fonts to use is fairly simple. In graphics and fine art settings, however, almost anything goes — as long as it works.

Many CorelDraw users are unsure about some basic typesetting questions. What exactly is a *font*? What's a *typeface*? When should you use TrueType or Type 1 PostScript fonts? The answers may surprise you. After exploring some of these basic questions, I'll explain some of CorelDraw's special text features, such as fitting text to a path, converting text to curves, and so forth. CorelDraw's text effect features are very powerful, so hang on tight.

Typefaces and Fonts

Before we start talking about type, let's make sure we're speaking the same language. A *typeface* is a style of type, such as Times or Helvetica. Most typefaces can have at least four different attributes: normal (often called "Roman" or "Book," depending on the typeface), **bold**, *italic*, and ***bold-italic***. Some, however, have only one or two styles. Others, such as ITC Goudy Sans, have as many as eight or more. Figure 4-1 shows some different typefaces with their various attributes. Each typeface is a family. The fonts that make up a typeface family look similar, but they each have different attributes.

Baskerville
Baskerville Bold
Baskerville Italic
Baskerville Bold-Italic

Arial
Arial Bold
Arial Italic
Arial Bold-Italic
Arial Narrow
Arial Narrow Bold
Arial Narrow Italic
Arial Narrow Bold-Italic
Arial Black

Brush Script

Giddy Up

Kidnap

Figure 4-1: Typefaces generally come in families made up of text with different attributes.

The term *font* refers to the members of a typeface family that have specific sets of attributes, such as Helvetica Italic.

Another term you should be familiar with is *point size*. The height of text is often measured in units called *points*. Approximately 72 points equal one inch.

Serif and sans serif typefaces

Most typefaces are either serif or sans serif. *Serifs* are the "feet" (or "foundations") at the ends of letter strokes. The most common serif typeface is Times. Others include New Century Schoolbook, Palatino, Garamond, and Goudy Old Style. Most serif typefaces work well for body text because they are easy on the eyes. The serifs help move the reader's eyes from character to character. When used in larger type, serif typefaces appear more decorative.

Sans serif is French for "without serifs." The most common sans serif typeface is Helvetica. Others are Avant Garde, Futura, and Helvetica Black. Traditionally, sans serif typefaces are used for headlines and subheads. Some also work well for contemporary-looking body copy — as long as they are not used for large blocks of text spread across several pages (sans serif text is harder to read at such lengths). Figure 4-2 shows the difference between serif and sans serif typefaces.

Figure 4-2: Serifs are tiny feet at the ends of letter strokes. Sans serif type has no serifs.

Decorative typefaces

Decorative typefaces can be elegant or they can be fun; or they can fall somewhere in between. On the whole, decorative typefaces are hard to read. They work well for short headlines, but rarely for body text. Use them in ads, on flyers, and in newsletter nameplates. Figure 4-3 provides some examples of decorative typefaces.

Bernard Tango

Brush Script

Dom Casual

Binner Gothic

Figure 4-3: Decorative fonts such as these are usually more difficult to read than nondecorative fonts.

The decorative typefaces come in a wide range of varieties. For example, there's elegant, and then there's *really* elegant. Compare Bernard Tango to Brush Script, as shown in Figure 4-3. Bernard Tango is ornate and elegant, whereas Brush Script gets its grace from its simple, hand-lettered look. Both are fun and serve distinct purposes, but they would be difficult to read in large blocks of text.

Again, decorative typefaces work best in short, attention-grabbing headlines, such as in ads and flyers. Some also work well in invitations and announcements, such as the more elegant, hand-tooled typefaces such as Park Avenue and Letraset Hollow.

Typeface tone

Some desktop designers don't realize that typefaces have distinct tones. As you have seen, typefaces can be serious, ornate, or elegant; others can be simple, fun, or cartoonish. Note the differences in the typefaces in Figure 4-4. The words are the same, but the tones vary tremendously. Note that in a couple of the examples, the words *Serial Killer* seem inappropriate.

Serial Killer

Serial Killer

Serial Killer

SERIAL KILLER

Serial Killer

Serial Killer

JERIAL KILLER

Figure 4-4: The tone of a typeface adds greatly to the impact of the words.

Keeping it simple

Using elegant or funny typefaces for headlines and subheads is fine if they fit the tone of your work. If your work is not meant to be particularly elegant, ornate, or funny, play it safe by using a simple sans serif typeface for headlines and serif typefaces for body text. My personal favorite is the combination of Arial Black (Helvetica Black equivalent) for headlines and New Century Schoolbook for body text. Swiss Black is stronger than Helvetica, and Schoolbook is a little less formal than Times.

Remember

Remember that you do not want to use your entire typeface library on each page, or even in each document. A good rule is to use no more than four typefaces per document. Also, you should not use a lot of different point sizes. Avoid confusion by making all headlines the same font. All subheads and body copy should be the same also. Using a variety of typefaces and sizes frequently produces an incoherent hodgepodge that looks more like a ransom note than an effective business document.

Type 1 versus TrueType

Since the advent of Windows 3.1's built-in TrueType font rendering system, many users have become confused about which type of font file is best. Having too many choices can sometimes make computing more difficult.

Actually, whether you use one or the other is not that critical. The speed and quality differences between the two formats are negligible. Many people use both. Depending on my application, I often switch back and forth between them. The type you should use depends on what you're doing with your computer.

Both TrueType and Type 1 fonts are *outline* fonts. Font outlines use a font manager, such as Adobe Type Manager (ATM), and Windows' built-in system for TrueType, to *rasterize,* or *render,* fonts. Both terms simply mean reading information from a font file and then displaying type on a monitor or sending font information to a printer.

Type 1 fonts

Originally, Type 1 fonts were created for use with Adobe's PostScript page description language. To use them in Windows, you must have a third-party type manager, such as ATM, installed. Having to use a third-party utility is a bit of an inconvenience, but once installed it's almost invisible to the user, except when it's time to install or uninstall fonts.

The primary advantage of Type 1 fonts is that they have been around a while longer than TrueType and are therefore the font of choice for desktop publishers and designers. Most desktop publishing service bureaus (establishments where users take their high-resolution printing, slides, and color proofing jobs for printing) use them. This means that if you use Type 1 fonts in your documents, the service bureau is more likely to have your fonts.

Wait a minute! The last statement is not entirely true. Not all service bureaus have all fonts by all vendors. Some, such as my service bureau here in Ventura, California, support only Adobe Type 1 fonts. The fonts on the CorelDraw CD-ROMs are Bitstream fonts (which are fine fonts, by the way). Even though my service bureau and many others have CorelDraw, they don't install the fonts on their system. Getting around this situation is discussed in Chapter 7.

However, this is not as big a restriction as it might seem. An increasing number of service bureaus have TrueType font collections. If yours doesn't, Windows and TrueType provide several solutions. (TrueType font embedding, discussed in the next subsection, is one solution. Embedding TrueType fonts in print files, discussed in Chapter 7, is another.)

TrueType fonts

TrueType, a component of Microsoft's TrueImage, is a PostScript clone. The one area where TrueType prevails over Type 1 is in compatibility, not only among different Windows systems but also across platforms. Apple has incorporated TrueType at the system level in Macintosh System 7, and some software fixes even make it backward compatible.

For a while I hoped that TrueType technology would catch on, making PageMaker, Word for Windows, and other Windows documents (and CorelDraw Mac documents) more readily transportable across platforms easier. Keep in mind that in Windows and on the Mac, we're talking about a built-in type manager, not a third-party overlay. Think of TrueType as system fonts. Another example of system fonts is those that appear when you enter commands at the DOS prompt — you take them for granted. TrueType is not quite that simple, but it's a step or two closer.

TrueType font embedding

Transporting documents from one computer running Windows to another has always been a headache. The only way it works well is if both systems have the same fonts and font manager installed, which, considering all the font products available, is not always the case. TrueType addresses this problem with a feature called *font embedding*. With font embedding, when you create a document that will be read or printed on another computer, you can include the fonts in the file. To do so, when you save a document with Save As, simply select Embed TrueType Fonts Using TrueDoc, as shown in Figure 4-5.

Click here to embed fonts

Figure 4-5: To embed TrueType fonts with your documents, click here.

Working with Text

CorelDraw provides a number of ways to use text in your drawings. Although the options for manipulating type are extensive, you really have only three major categories: artistic, paragraph, and symbols. I cover the following topics:

- Artistic text
- Paragraph text
- Using text styles
- Converting type to curves
- Using the Property Bar for text formatting

Artistic text is entered directly onto the page or drawing area. *Paragraph text* usually consists of larger blocks of text, and the controls you have over it are similar to those in a word processor or desktop publishing package. Use paragraph text to add blocks of text to brochures, flyers, and illustrations.

Artistic text

Artistic text can be manipulated in many ways; for example, it can be colored, filled with patterns or fountain fills, stretched, extruded, or blended. Artistic text is usually decorative and fancy. To enter artistic text, simply click on the Text tool in CorelDraw. The cursor changes to a cross. Click where you want to enter the text and begin typing. You can then edit and manipulate the text in more ways than you can imagine. This section concentrates primarily on manipulating text with the Node Editing (Shape) tool. As you'll see, you can do lots of magical things with this simple tool, which most CorelDraw users don't know. We'll also look briefly at fitting text to paths and converting to curves.

When you select text with the Node Editing tool, each character is given its own node, and the text block is given spacing control handles. Characters can be moved individually with the nodes — up, down, left, right — to create special effects. Text can be spaced interactively with the spacing control handles.

Changing character and word spacing

To increase the space between characters, drag the right spacing control handle to the right. To decrease the space between characters, drag the right spacing control handle to the left. Simple enough, right? Figure 4-6 shows the procedure in action.

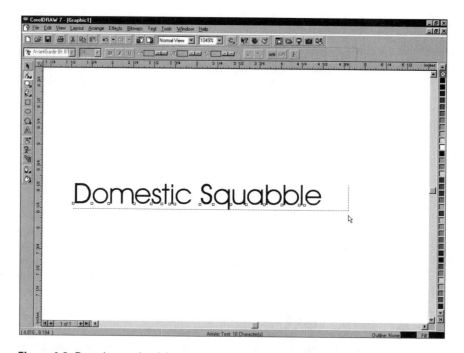

Figure 4-6: Dragging on the right spacing control handle increases the spacing between characters.

To increase the space between words, hold the Ctrl key down and drag the right spacing control handle to the right. To decrease the space between words, hold the Ctrl key down and drag the right spacing control handle to the left. Figure 4-7 shows you how to space words with the Node Editing tool.

Changing line spacing

To increase or decrease the space between lines of text, drag the left spacing control handle up or down. Figure 4-8 shows you how to increase the space between lines with the Node Editing tool.

Figure 4-7: To increase or decrease the space between words interactively, hold the Ctrl key as you drag on the right spacing handle.

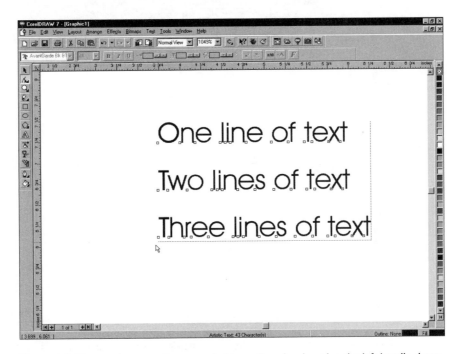

Figure 4-8: You can increase the space between lines by dragging the left handle down.

Horizontal text spacing (*tracking*) and vertical text spacing (*leading*) can also be adjusted with the Spacing option in the Edit Text dialog box. I discuss tracking and leading later in this chapter. Use the Shape tool to edit interactively by appearance; use Spacing when you need precise settings.

Dragging characters off the baseline

You can use the Node Editing tool to move individual characters, or groups of individual characters, off the baseline to create special effects (the *baseline* is the imaginary line on which a line of text sits). To move one character, select the node to its left. To move a group of characters, marquee select the nodes to the left of each character, or hold the Shift key and click on each node. Figure 4-9 shows an example of dragging text from the baseline with the Node editing tool.

As you get more familiar with CorelDraw, you'll find hundreds of uses for manipulating text this way. Some may have already occurred to you.

Manipulating text by dragging individual nodes is a trial-and-error process. Whenever you go too far and want to start over, simply choose Align to Baseline from the Text menu. The text jumps back into its original position. To move a single letter back to the baseline, simply select it before you select the Align to Baseline command. To realign all the text, make sure the text is selected but no individual letters are selected.

![CorelDRAW 7 screenshot showing the text "Domestic squabble" with individual characters dragged off the baseline]

Figure 4-9: To drag a character from the baseline, select the character's node and drag to the desired position.

Figure 4-12: When you change the shape of the path, the text reconforms.

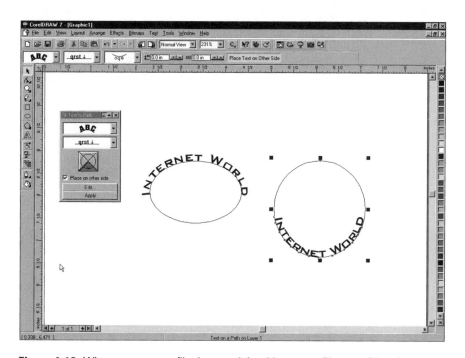

Figure 4-13: When you want to flip the text right-side up, use Place on Other Side in the Fit Text to Path roll-up.

Note

Secret

The preceding options are available from the Property Bar — when you're working with text that has already been fit to a path that is — making it unnecessary to fly the Fit Text to Path roll-up when editing text previously manipulated in this manner.

In Version 7 you can also type text directly on a path. Here's how:

STEPS

Typing Text Directly on a Path

Step 1.   Click the Text tool.

Step 2.   Using the mouse, move the Text cursor near the object.

Step 3.   When the cursor changes to the insertion point cursor, click in your drawing.

Step 4.   Type the text along the object's path, as shown in Figure 4-14.

Figure 4-14: To type text directly on a path, simply click the Text tool on the object's path and begin typing.

If you need to specify values such as the distance between text and object or change the placement of text along the object's path, use the Fit Text to Path roll-up described earlier in this section. You can fit artistic text to the path of objects with open and closed paths.

Converting text to curves

Converting text to curves turns the text into a graphic, complete with nodes and other graphics qualities. This enables you to shape the text with the Node Editing tool in ways you cannot shape regular text. You'll want to be careful, though. This is a one-way street. Text that has been converted to curves cannot be converted back to text.

To convert text to curves, simply select the text string and choose Arrange ⇨ Convert to Curves.

Warning

When you convert text to curves, you can no longer edit it as a text string. Make sure words are spelled properly and that you have assigned all the desired attributes before converting the type to curves.

The following is a typical Convert to Curves procedure, complete with node manipulation:

STEPS

Converting Text to Curves

Step 1. Type the text you want to convert to curves.

Step 2. Make *all* attribute changes, such as font, size, and so on. Remember that you cannot change attributes after you convert.

Step 3. Choose Arrange ⇨ Convert to Curves. The text is now a graphic. Notice that the Status line no longer calls it text. You can use Convert to Curves to manipulate type in almost any way you can think of.

Step 4. Select the Node Editing tool.

Step 5. Select Arrange ⇨ Break Apart. This separates the text into separate editable entities. If you don't understand Break Apart, turn to Chapter 3. You now have several objects with many nodes. You can treat these objects as graphics.

Step 6. Manipulate the nodes as desired.

Step 7. Fill and color the graphic as desired.

Figure 4-15 shows a text graphic I manipulated using the preceding method. In this case, I extended the top horizontal bars of the *T* and *F* letters, and added a gradiated fill.

Figure 4-15: An example of text that has been converted to curves and reshaped.

Paragraph text

Paragraph text usually consists of larger blocks of text than artistic text. To enter paragraph text, click and drag a box with the Text tool. When you release the mouse, a text box appears with the text cursor blinking at the top-left corner of the box. You can type text directly into the frame, or you can import text from a word processor file or paste from the Windows Clipboard. Paragraph text can be moved anywhere on the page, and the frame can be resized and manipulated with the Selection (sometimes called Pick), Node Editing, or Enveloping option, and with many other options.

If you use Microsoft Word, Corel WordPerfect, QuarkXPress, Adobe PageMaker, Microsoft Publisher, or any other text editor or page layout program, you should have no trouble using paragraph text in CorelDraw. In many ways, it's identical. You can justify it right and left, center it, break it into columns, adjust the tracking (the space between characters and words), adjust the leading (the space between lines), and so on. You can even assign styles and "jump" text from one paragraph frame to another. *Jumping* is when you continue blocks of text on new pages, as you've seen in magazines and newspapers.

Because paragraph text in CorelDraw behaves similarly to text blocks in other programs, such as Microsoft Word or QuarkXPress, I'll assume that you already understand how to create, import, and perform basic formatting on paragraph text. So, rather than boring you with old information, this section concentrates on using the new Property Bar to format paragraph text, and applying some of CorelDraw's special effects features on paragraph text.

Formatting Text with Styles

 Picture this scenario: You've laid out a 50-page document in CorelDraw. You take it to your client (or boss) for approval. She says, "Looks great, but I need all the heads switched from Arial to Arial Black, and the body copy needs to be Garamond 12-point, not Times 10-point. And I need it in 30 minutes, please."

So what will you do, rush back to your workstation, select each paragraph one at a time and change them? Wrong! If you formatted your paragraphs with styles, all you need to do is change the style definitions, and CorelDraw does the rest, changing each paragraph tagged with the style to the new format.

CorelDraw supports two text style types: artistic text and paragraph text. Similar to styles in a word processor or desktop publishing package, Draw's styles enable you to use predefined formatting information to instantly format strings of artistic text or blocks of paragraph text. Text Styles are managed from the Styles Roll-up (Layout ⇨ Graphics and Text Styles). You create them by choosing New from the roll-up's pop-up menu. You have three ways to create a new style: First, select the text containing the attributes that you want to incorporate into a new style, and then choose New from the roll-up's pop-up menu. Second, select Copy Properties From from the pop-up menu and then click on the paragraph containing the attributes you want in your new style. And third (this is perhaps the easiest method), use the right mouse button pop-up menu, which is discussed later in the process description.

With either method, CorelDraw creates a new style and adds it to the list in the roll-up. You can then rename the style to anything you like. Once you've created your styles, you can apply them from the Styles roll-up (shown in Figure A), the Property Bar, or from the right-mouse button pop-up menu.

Figure A: You can apply styles you've created by using the Styles roll-up.

You can create styles for the default template — the one that appears when you open a new document — or you can save them in groups as a new template. This capability of creating multiple style sheets, or templates, enables you to prepare predefined shells for creating similar multiple documents, such as a flyer that changes only slightly from month to month. Creating and using templates is covered in Chapter 17.

The following is an overview of creating and using text styles:

- Create the text from which you will create your style.

- Format the text as desired.

- Click and hold the right mouse button on the text from which you want to create a style until the menu flies out. Then choose Save Style Properties as shown in Figure B.

- In the Save Style As dialog box, shown in Figure C, name the style. Notice that you can adjust the properties of the new style by expanding the folders and turning on and off attributes. In Figure C, for instance, you can expand Text and turn off aspects of the new style by unchecking boxes. You can also turn on and off fill and outline formatting.

(continued)

(continued)

■ Click OK.

To rename the style, select it in the Styles roll-up, click the right mouse button, and choose Rename. You can import styles from another template by choosing Template ⇨ Load from the roll-up's pop-up menu and then choose the desired template. To assign a keyboard shortcut to the new style, choose Edit Hotkey from the pop-up. This option displays the Customize dialog box (described in Chapter 1). Click the cursor in the Press New Shortcut key field, and then press the key combination you want as a shortcut.

If you define styles on CorelDraw's default style sheet, they become part of the default new document setup. If you create new styles, you should save them under a new name with the Template ⇨ Save As option in the Styles roll-up pop-up menu.

Figure B: To save a text style, right-click on text for which you want to save the style, and then choose Styles ⇨ Save Style Properties.

Figure C: You can name a new style in the Save Style As dialog box.

Using the Property Bar to format text

When does CorelDraw look like Microsoft Word? When you edit paragraph text from the Property Bar. Look at Figure 4-16. Notice the word processor-like configuration across the top of the screen. From here you can apply styles, change typefaces, change size and other attributes, set alignment, and alter a bunch of other options, including setting tabs and margins from the ruler.

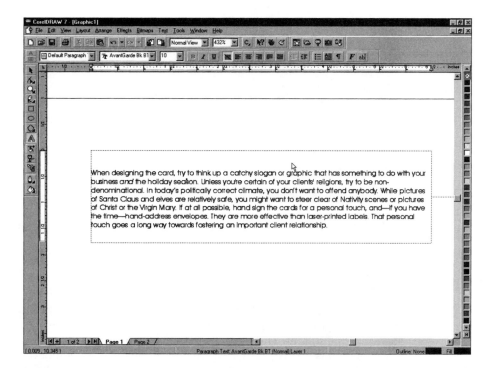

Figure 4-16: The new Property Bar enables you to format paragraph text with word-processor-like ease.

Unfortunately, you cannot set columns from the Property Bar. Instead, to set columns in paragraph text frames, choose Text ➪ Format Text ➪ Frames and Columns, which brings up the dialog box shown in Figure 4-17. From here you set your columns by typing a number in the Number of Columns field. You can choose either to let CorelDraw maintain uniform column sizes by making sure that Equal Column Width is selected, or you can uncheck this option and set individual column and gutter (space between columns) sizes in the Width and Gutter fields.

Number of Columns

Format Text

Font | Spacing | Tabs and Indents | Frames and Columns | Effects

Number of columns: 3

Column width and gutter

Column #: | Width: | Gutter:
1 | 1.062 in | 0.5 in
2 | 1.062 in | 0.5 in
3 | 1.062 in |

☑ Equal column width

Paragraph frame width: 4.186 inches
● Maintain current frame width
○ Automatically adjust frame width

Vertical justification:
Top

OK | Cancel | Help

Gutter
Width
Equal Column Width

Figure 4-17: Use the Format Text dialog box to set columns in CorelDraw paragraph text frames.

Enveloping text

An exciting feature CorelDraw first offered in version 4 was the capability of placing paragraph text in a container and then reshaping the container with the Envelope roll-up. The purpose is to sculpture text in various shapes — stars, octagons, Christmas trees, whatever. This feature is different from PowerClip, which I cover in greater detail in Chapter 6. The PowerClip feature clips, or masks, the text that doesn't fit into the container. Enveloping paragraph text, on the other hand, actually reshapes the text block, adjusting the text flow, to the container. You can create and shape your own envelopes, or you can create an envelope from an existing shape or symbol.

To use an envelope, first create or import a block of paragraph text. Then add a container for the text with the Envelope roll-up. You can then shape the text container according to the type of envelope you choose. As you'll see in Chapter 6, there are four types of envelopes: straight line, single arc, two curves, and unconstrained. You can tell how each works by the icon on its respective button in the roll-up. The icons are labeled in Figure 4-18.

Note

This section looks briefly at using envelopes to reshape paragraph text. For a more complete description of envelopes, see Chapter 6.

The following is an overview of a procedure for reshaping a block of text with an envelope.

Figure 4-18: The Envelope roll-up provides four types of envelopes. You can further modify how an envelope behaves with one of the mapping options directly below the envelope types.

STEPS

Reshaping Text with an Envelope

Step 1. Type or import the text you want to reshape.

Step 2. Use the Format Text (Text ⇨ Format Text) dialog box to make the necessary attribute changes to the text. This is important because making these changes *after* you assign the envelope can change the look of the text inside the envelope container. Keep in mind, too, that you'll get a better-looking text block if you set alignment to Full, so that your text will fill the shape on the right side.

In both drawings and documents, you should not try to justify text over 14 points. You'll get too many unsightly gaps, like broken teeth. In fact, in most cases, enveloping text larger than 14 points probably won't give you the effect you're after.

Step 3. Reshape the box around the text to its best fit, as shown in Figure 4-19. As a reminder, paragraph text boxes are reshaped similarly to graphics and artistic text objects: by resizing the control handles.

(continued)

STEPS *(continued)*

Reshaping Text with an Envelope

Figure 4-19: Once you have created your text and assigned the desired formatting attributes, reshape the box so it fits better around the text.

Step 4. Select Effects ➪ Envelope to display the Envelope roll-up.

Step 5. In the Envelope roll-up, click on Add New.

Step 6. Select the desired envelope type from one on the buttons, or use Add Preset to use one of the predefined envelopes. To assign an envelope from a specific shape (closed path), use the Create From (eyedropper) in the lower-left portion of the roll-up. To do so, make sure the text you want to shape is selected, click the eyedropper, and then click on the shape from which you want to create an envelope.

Step 7. If you chose one of the shaping objects, rather than a preset or custom shape, reshape the envelope as desired. Note that you can also add additional envelopes, as Chapter 6 explains in further detail. Notice that the nodes on envelopes are quite similar to outline nodes editable with the Node Editing tool.

Step 8. When you finish reshaping the envelope, click on Apply.

Add additional envelopes as desired, reshaping and clicking Apply as desired. Remember that you can use Clear Envelope to reverse undesirable effects. Clear Envelope removes envelopes in the order you apply them, from the most recent backwards.

You can make text containers conform to just about any shape imaginable. It's important to remember, however, that too much distortion can make the text difficult to read. Remember that good design is a balance between aesthetics and legibility.

Font Features

Traditionally, the practice of configuring type to print on paper was known as *typesetting*. Nowadays computers enable almost everybody to be "typesetters." However, the difference between professional typesetters and the novice desktop publisher is that the pros use several conventions that non-professionals don't know about. The result is a better-looking page — more polished.

This section discusses some basic typesetting concepts that can help you polish your drawings and other documents. The following topics are discussed:

- Special characters
- Character spacing
- Leading
- White space
- Drop caps

Special characters

Many computer software publishers call uncommon characters *special characters*. There's nothing really special about them. They simply are not on your keyboard — which *does* give them a certain distinction. If you're not familiar with them and how to use them, getting at them may seem like magic.

Most Windows applications let you enter special characters by holding down the Alt key and typing the character's ANSI address on the number pad (DOS programs generally use ASCII, IBM's character set). The software manuals for Windows and many desktop publishing programs have tables showing ANSI address codes. However, this can be cumbersome, requiring too much fumbling around.

Instead, you can use the Windows Character Map, shown in Figure 4-20, to look up character addresses. To find a character's address, simply select a font from the font list, and then select the desired character. If it can be accessed through the keyboard, the keystroke is displayed in the lower-right Keystroke portion of the Character Map window. If a decimal address is required, the address is displayed. You'll find Character Map on the Accessories submenu on the Windows Start menu.

Figure 4-20: Use the Windows Character Map to look up special characters. Choose Start ⇨ Accessories ⇨ Character Map.

You can use Character Map to insert characters into a drawing or document by using the Copy button to copy them to the Clipboard. First highlight the character you want with the arrow keys or by clicking on it with the mouse. Then click the Select button (the character appears in the Characters to Copy field). Next, click the Copy button. Then return to your document, select the same font you selected in Character Map, and select Edit ⇨ Paste. Or you can simply remember the Alt+Number Pad address; however, when using this method, make sure Num Lock is turned on.

Unless your documents contain foreign words or math and science formulas, you will not use most special characters. The following subsections describe some of the more common special characters.

Em dash (—)

The em dash should be used for the dash. It replaces the double hyphen (--) that you probably use on a typewriter or in your word processor. In most font sets, the em dash's decimal address is Alt+0151. I recommend that you use Type Assist to enter this character. (See the sidebar entitled "Using Type Assist.")

Quotation marks

You probably use straight quotation marks (' or "). These are actually foot and inch symbols (typewriters could have only so many keys, so some characters like these had to be used to represent others). Single and double quotation marks should be *opened* (' or ") and *closed* (' or "). By default, CorelDraw automatically opens and closes quotation marks. When you need foot and inch markers, you should find them in Character Map and enter them directly.

Built fractions

Most people make fractions like this: 3/4. This format is not only confusing (compare 22 3/4 and 22$^3/_4$) but it also does not look right. Your character set probably has fraction characters for all quarter-inch and eighth-inch increments. You can make others with your software's superscript and subscript features (for example, $^{16}/_{32}$). You can also create keystroke combination in Type Assist for fractions that you use often.

Using Type Assist

Okay, so Character Map is easier than fumbling through a manual. Still, it requires leaving CorelDraw and invoking another application, and then toggling back and forth. CorelDraw and many other Windows applications provide further relief with a handy feature called Type Assist.

If you use Word or WordPerfect, you might be familiar with features that are similar to Type Assist. What this feature does is automatically insert characters or character strings in response to keyboard input. While writing this book, for example, I used Word's Type Assist to embed special characters, such as an arrow for the following characters: =>. Each time I typed =>, Word substituted ⇨. Each time I entered *cd*, Word entered *CorelDraw*.

In CorelDraw, Type Assist is on the Writing Tools submenu. To access Type Assist, choose Text ⇨ Writing Tools ⇨ Type Assist (here's a case where Type Assist helped automate this writing). This command brings up the dialog box shown in this sidebar. From here you can configure Type Assist. Notice that Corel has configured several special characters for you, including several commonly misspelled words. When you enter the characters on the left side of the list, Type

Assist replaces them with the character or text string on the right.

You have two ways to get Type Assist entries into this dialog box: You can type them directly, filling the Replace and With fields, or you can type the character or string in your document that you want in the With field, select it, and then open the Type Assist dialog box and complete the Replace portion of the pair. To add special characters, use the Alt+Number Pad method described earlier in this section.

Legal characters

The registered name and registered trademark symbols should be set superscript next to the product or company name (for example, Microsoft® Windows™). The copyright symbol usually appears after the word *Copyright* (as in, Copyright © 1997 by IDG Books). Corel has built-in Type Assist replacements for most of these symbols. For the most common, ®, ©, and ™, simply enter the characters (*r*, *c*, or *tm*) surrounded by parentheses.

Bullets

Why use hyphens (-) or asterisks (*) as bullets? These are dull, and you have so many other wonderful characters available. You can even use the hollow box as a check box.

❒ Shoes

❒ Shirts

❒ Socks

CorelDraw comes with several sets of special characters you can use as bullets. But keep your head about you. Too many cute little bullets can look ridiculous. You can create bullets in CorelDraw automatically from the Effects portion of the Format Text dialog box (Test ➪ Format Text ➪ Effects), as shown in Figure 4-21. Simply select the Bullet radio button, choose the symbol font character from the Bullet Category drop-down list, and then select the desired bullet from the scrolling palette. This works on the paragraph where the cursor is blinking, several selected paragraphs, or you can assign the bullet to a paragraph text style. You can also embed the bullet in the paragraph, or you can create a hanging indent bullet by choosing one of the options under Placement.

Choose Your Bullet

Placement Options

Figure 4-21: Use the Effects portion of Format Text to create bullets automatically.

Secret

You can also create your own bullet sets from virtually any CorelDraw graphic, using the program's TrueType font export filter. Simply select the object you want to export as a font, and then choose Export from the File menu. After selecting the TTF filter and selecting OK, CorelDraw asks you to name the font, and enables you to save it as a symbol font. This is a great way to, say, turn you company logo into a font you can enter from the keyboard and resize as you would a type character. (This option is well documented in Help, under Converting Objects to Type Characters.)

Dingbats

Dingbats are a font set of stars, boxes, arrows, and other characters useful for sprucing up a layout. A common dingbat is the pointing hand (☞) used to bring the reader's attention to something, usually a callout, note, tip, or some other special point. Another is the little phone (☎) that advertisers use to indicate a phone number. A standard favorite in a bulleted list is the checkmark:

We offer the following services:

✓ Embalming

✓ Grave site beautification

✓ Lifetime guarantee

Nowadays several dingbat fonts, including Wingdings, come with Windows and several come with CorelDraw. Resist the temptation to use them just because you have them. Although dingbats look nice, they should serve a purpose. A layout sprinkled with cute little dingbats for no apparent reason looks juvenile.

Drop caps/raised caps

Drop caps are enlarged first characters at the beginning of an article, as demonstrated here. Their purpose is to indicate the beginning of a story or the start of a new or important section within a story. But they are also attractive design elements that can break the monotony of large blocks of text. Drop caps can be raised (set high on the line), dropped into the text block, or adjacent (set beside a text block).

Another technique is to use a graphic as a drop cap. Simply create the letter and embellish it in CorelDraw. Then bring it into your layout on the Clipboard.

The possibilities for drop caps are nearly limitless. In a two-color newsletter, you can add color to drop caps. This professional touch adds a little polish to the publication. Another professional technique is to use the color on the logo or nameplate for drop caps.

CorelDraw 7 lets you create drop caps automatically, from the Effects section of the Format Text dialog box (Text ⇨ Format Text ⇨ Effects), as shown in Figure 4-22. You can set either dropped style or hanging indent from the Placement portion of the dialog box, as well as set how many lines the drop cap extends into the text with the Dropped Lines option.

Dropped Lines

Placement Options

Figure 4-22: Use the Effects portion of the Format Text dialog box to create drop caps automatically.

Character and word spacing

Tracking is the spacing between letters and words. *Kerning*, on the other hand refers to the space between specific characters — which is something else altogether. Let's look at them both.

Most software measures spaces between letters and words in *ems*, the space occupied by the capital M, the widest character in a font set. Desktop publishing programs and vector draw programs such as CorelDraw provide extensive control over tracking. The main reason for adjusting tracking is to improve the appearance of type. But you can, at times, adjust it slightly to squeeze more type into an area, or to widen spacing to fill in a blank space. When using it for the latter, though, be careful not to compromise the legibility or overall appearance of your text.

Font sets have default tracking. When you bring text into layout software, it is given the default, except when text is fully justified (each line is then adjusted separately), or if your text style specifies otherwise. Most of the time the default is fine. But at times you'll want to adjust tracking, usually to improve the appearance of headlines and body text.

Adjusting tracking

You adjust the tracking in CorelDraw with the Spacing option from the Format Text command on the Text menu (Text ➪ Format Text ➪ Spacing), as shown in Figure 4-23. You can also adjust tracking with the Node Editing tool, as discussed earlier in this section. CorelDraw provides options for adjusting the tracking between letters and words separately. And you can also adjust tracking for each type of alignment. To do so, simply select the type of alignment for which you want to adjust the tracking, and then make your setting changes.

Figure 4-23: Use the Spacing option in the Format Text dialog box to adjust tracking.

In most cases, the default tracking is fine for headlines. There may, however, be times when you want to adjust it. Use tracking to make headlines more attractive and easier to read. Tracking comes in handy for improving the appearance of body copy, especially for tightening loose type (too widely spaced), and vice versa.

Adjusting kerning

Many people confuse tracking and kerning. Kerning refers to specific pairs of characters, called *kerning pairs*. Kerning pairs are character pairs with combined shapes that can cause unsightly gaps, such as *To*, *AV*, *Ta*, *ff*, and many, many others. Most fonts come with compensation for kerning pairs built in, automatically compensating for the shape inconsistencies. However, sometimes you may find it necessary to make your own kerning changes.

Unlike some desktop publishing software, CorelDraw does not let you make permanent kerning changes to your fonts. Instead, each time you need to change a pair relationship, you must do it by hand. You can make the change manually, by selecting the character you want to kern with the Node Editing tool, and simply moving it left or right, remembering to hold the Ctrl key so that you don't shift the character from the baseline. The second method is to select both characters with the Node Editing tool, and then make adjustments in Spacing (Text ⇨ Format Text ⇨ Spacing).

Leading

Leading refers to the white space between lines of type. Most publishing programs have a default leading of 120 percent of the point size. Ten-point type, then, has a 12-point leading. For smaller point sizes (6–12), 120 percent is just right. Larger sizes tend to look peculiar and take up too much space with 120 percent leading. You will usually want to adjust the leading (set it in your styles) for headlines to about 100 percent.

Another reason to adjust leading is to achieve special effects. This is a matter of taste, and you will want to be careful to avoid making text hard to read.

You adjust the leading in CorelDraw with the Spacing option from the Format Text command on the Text menu, as shown in Figure 4-24. You can also use the Node Editing tool, as discussed earlier in this chapter.

Line Spacing

Figure 4-24: Use the Line option in Spacing to set leading for selected text or for text styles. Setting this option with no text selected changes the program's default.

White Space

Pick up any book or magazine article on document design and layout and you will soon find a discussion of white space. The blank spaces — or what you do not put on a page — are just as important as the ones containing elements. The mentality that I have had to overcome was that blank spaces are wasted ones. Blank spaces are, instead, breaths of fresh air. Each element — headlines, pull quotes, columns, and so forth — should have its own space. Do not crowd elements together so the reader cannot tell where one begins and the other ends.

True, some design elements break up the page, such as graphics and photographs. But a page covered with ink is too full. It is difficult to say exactly how much white space you need. But it is easy to tell when you don't have enough. If it comes down to crowding things together or omitting something, leave something out.

No hard-and-fast formula exists for discerning the right amount of white space. What I do is evaluate my emotional response to the page. If my initial reaction is, "Gee, that sure does look like a lot to read," I find ways to break up the text with visuals and by spreading elements out to give them breathing room.

Summary

▶ A *typeface* is a style of type, such as Times or Helvetica. Most typefaces have four different attributes or styles: normal (often called Book or Roman, depending on the typeface), **bold**, *italic*, and ***bold-italic***. Some, however, have only one or two styles. Others, such as ITC Goudy Sans, have as many as eight or more.

▶ Fonts come in all shapes and sizes, but can be broken into four broad categories: serif, sans serif, display (or decorative), and symbol. Each sort of font has different uses. Serif fonts have little feet at the ends of the character strokes, called serifs. Sans serif fonts have no feet, or serifs. Display fonts can be fancy, frilly, fun, even formidable, and symbol fonts are special figures and icons that usually aren't available in regular fonts.

▶ Some typefaces are serious, some are ornate, and some are elegant; others are simple, fun, or cartoonish. The tone of a typeface can greatly affect the weight of the message.

▶ You have several ways to manipulate type in CorelDraw, including artistic text and paragraph styles. You can also use artistic text with the Node Editing tool. And you can manipulate the paragraph text frames themselves for a wide range of special effects.

▶ When using type in your document, you should be mindful of several industry standard conventions, including the following: Using special characters, adjusting tracking, adjusting leading, using white space effectively, and making effective use of drop caps and dingbats.

Chapter 5

Working with Colors and Fills

In This Chapter

You'll learn useful secrets about:

▶ Color models and color-matching systems

▶ Corel Color Manager

▶ CorelDraw's color palettes

▶ Using CorelDraw's color styles

▶ CorelDraw's fountain fills

▶ CorelDraw's prefabricated textures and patterns

Although it's not as hard as it used to be, getting colors to reproduce properly in electronic publishing environments requires some special knowledge and a lot of patience. The reason for this is, of course, the differences in the ways various devices — desktop printers, monitors, scanners, printing presses, and so on — create color. Some devices, such as computer monitors, for instance, use combinations of red, green, and blue (RGB) to create different hues. Some inkjet printers use RGB, while others use cyan, magenta, yellow, and black (CMYK). These and other differences between devices make for a wide range of variables that affect reproduction of color.

The documentation for many graphics programs lacks clear explanations of how to achieve good color results. Consequently, I've dedicated part of this chapter to explaining the mechanics of getting good results when you use CorelDraw's colors and fills. (In addition, Chapter 7 explains how to use CorelDraw to reproduce colors for a printing press — a process known in the graphic art business as *prepress*.)

The remainder of this chapter covers CorelDraw's immensely useful color and fill tools. One of the great things about CorelDraw is that it provides so many tools for automating tasks. In this chapter you'll learn how to automate many of the tasks related to colors and fills.

Note

Throughout this chapter I'll throw in some tips on how to use color effectively in your documents and presentations. Although my examples focus on CorelDraw, much of this discussion also pertains to the other applications in the CorelDRAW 7 graphics suite.

Color Models

A *color model* is a method for representing color as data. In the electronic publishing and graphics design world, color models provide a way to consistently describe color with number values. CorelDraw applications support several different color models. In this section we look at the ones used most often: the color models RGB, CMYK, and the up-and-coming HiFi (LAB).

RGB

RGB stands for red, green, and blue. By mixing these three colors, you can create just about any color possible — well, any color possible on a computer monitor, anyway. RGB is the model used by your monitor. The screen mixes colors by illuminating red, green, and blue phosphorous lights with an electron gun at the back of the monitor screen. Varying the intensity of each light on the phosphors produces different colors.

RGB, then, is the color model you should use when creating graphics for reproduction or display on a computer monitor. (Or, it's the model you should at least start with. Some other variables also apply, such as the type of application in which you plan to use the image. Images designed for the World Wide Web, for example, often require color reduction through indexing. But I'm getting ahead of myself. You should turn to Chapter 21 for a discussion of using images on the Web, and Chapter 22 discusses using images in multimedia titles and presentations.)

CMYK

CMYK stands for cyan, magenta, yellow, and black (yes, *k* stands for black). CMYK is the process used by most print shops for full color, or four-color print documents. CorelDraw and other applications separate the four colors into plates, one for each color. The printing press then prints percentages of the colors (actually, percentages of each color), one over the other, to mix the desired colors.

Traditionally, CMYK is the model of choice for creating documents bound for a printing press, a color proofing printer, dye-sublimation, full-color poster printer, or print-on-demand applications. In fact, by default the colors you apply in CorelDraw from the color palette are defined with CMYK values.

Note

Printing CMYK separations is discussed in Chapter 7. When printing separations from CorelDraw, the program automatically converts RGB information to CMYK. So you don't need to worry about making sure to use CMYK colors when assigning colors in your drawings. This is also true when you export your drawings to EPS format for placement in a layout. However, if you export to a bitmap format, such as PCX or TIFF, RGB values are maintained. Whenever you export from any CorelDraw application to a DTP layout, you should use either EPS or CMYK TIFF. These points are made much clearer in Chapter 7.

Warning

Wait a minute! Did I say that you don't have to worry about RGB colors getting converted to CMYK? This process works reasonably well for documents printed on desktop inkjet and color printers. But the leap from monitor to printing press is a huge one, with plenty of obstacles along the way — not the least of which is the inherent difference between how colors display on computer screens compared to how they print on printing presses. When working in an environment where the integrity of your color selections is critical, *do not* rely on CorelDraw to make these conversions for you. Instead, read the section in this chapter on the "Corel Color Manager," and then turn to Chapter 7 and read up on printing and prepress.

HiFi (LAB)

Nowadays, the color images you create are more likely to end up in a variety of layouts — print media, multimedia presentations, the Internet, slides, you name it. The problem with most color models is that they are *device-dependent* — meaning that they reproduce exactly the same only on the device for which they were created (device-dependent and device-independent color are discussed in the "Corel Color Manager" section later in this chapter). And even then, they are not exact. Take monitors, for instance. Monitors made by different manufacturers display colors differently. Even different models by the same manufacturer do not always display colors identically.

Hence the need for a color model more flexible than RGB or CMYK. The HiFi, or LAB, color model is not new. It's been around for quite a while — years, in fact. With the advent of color images winding up in so many different media, however, the LAB color model has only recently gained widespread attention. The benefit of LAB colors is that they are not defined according to a specific output medium, but instead more closely to the way the human eyes see color — from CIE color space definitions. (If you don't know what CIE and color spaces are, be sure to read the section on the "Corel Color Manager" later in this chapter.)

Here are some good reasons for using HiFi color when designing images destined for more than one output medium:

- LAB is the color space selected by Adobe for device-independent color. Adobe, the maker of Photoshop and Illustrator, the two leading graphics applications, typically sets the standard for electronic publishing.

- LAB has a significantly larger color gamut than CMYK or RGB. (A color's *gamut* is explained in the "Corel Color Manager" section later in this chapter.)

- LAB has a file size 25 percent smaller than CMYK, meaning less fuss when working with high-resolution, full-color images.

- LAB converts to any format, and you'll always start with the ultimate quality.

Color-Matching Systems

Color-matching systems are different from color models. Color-matching systems provide a consistent way for choosing and talking about colors. Color *models* provide a way to translate colors into numeric values. (A color model is a way of representing colors as data.) As you'll see, color-matching systems are very useful tools for designers and artists.

PANTONE Matching System (PMS)

Often, you use a *color-matching system* to choose a color before you create it with a color model. As you know, color models define colors through values or by mixing percentages of color — usually RGB or CMYK. But this can be confusing. Color-matching systems are composed of predefined colors that you typically select from swatch (or sample) books. When you go into a print shop and choose a color from a chart or swatch book, such as the PANTONE Matching System swatch book shown in Plate 5-1 in the color insert, you are using a color-matching system.

Two types of color-matching systems are available: spot and process. *Spot colors* usually consist of premixed inks. On the printing press, ink is applied to the paper in the premixed color. *Process color* matching system swatches, on the other hand, show colors as they appear when they have been mixed during the print run. A process color swatch book, then, shows the results of mixing the four CMYK values.

Color-matching swatch books take the guesswork out of selecting colors by enabling you to see how they look on both coated and uncoated paper — a much more precise method than trying to choose colors from a monitor.

PMS is the spot color matching system used in most print shops. You should use spot colors when your documents contain one or two colors, because it's cheaper and more precise than process color. When you choose a color from a swatch book at your local printer, it is usually PMS.

CorelDraw has a complete PANTONE color system built in. To use it you must switch to PANTONE Matching System in the Uniform Fill dialog box (click the Fill tool, and then choose the first option on the flyout), as shown in Figure 5-1. (Note that depending on how you left this dialog box the last time you used it, you may have to take a few more steps to get to the PANTONE swatches.) Notice the four icons on the right side of the dialog box. Make sure the second one, Palettes, is active, and then choose PANTONE Matching System from the Type drop-down list.

Figure 5-1: The Uniform Fill dialog box can be set up to use the PANTONE Matching System.

Usually, you match PANTONE colors by names and numbers. To see a list of PANTONE numbers, select Show Color Names from the flyout menu (small arrow-shaped icon in the upper-right portion) in the Uniform Fill dialog box. Figure 5-2 shows the PANTONE swatches with corresponding names. Notice that the names and numbers match those on the PANTONE swatch book shown in Plate 5-1.

Figure 5-2: You can choose Show Color Names to display each PANTONE color with its matching system name and number.

Secret

This list of colors is quite extensive. PANTONE specifies virtually hundreds of colors. If you know the name (or number) of the color you want, you can find it in two ways: First, you can type the name (or partial name) in the Search field. As you type, CorelDraw automatically searches for matches. Second, you can type the exact name in the Name field. CorelDraw displays the appropriate swatch in the list of colors.

Often it's tempting to select a PANTONE color from the list in the Uniform Fill dialog box. Before you do, though, try this experiment. Grab your PMS swatch book (you really should have one if you're working with PMS colors), and then open the Uniform Fill dialog box in CorelDraw, go to the PANTONE Matching System section, and then turn on Show Color Names. Now, in the Search field, type **Reflex Blue**. Open your swatch book to the first strip of colors and find the one labeled PANTONE Reflex Blue. Hold the swatch book up to your monitor and compare the two colors.

Warning

Depending on the quality of your computer's display system and the color calibration and color management options you've set up, the difference between the swatch in the swatch book and the color in the CorelDraw list will be more or less dramatic. In any case, you'll see my point: *Choose your colors from the swatch book. Not your monitor!* The swatch book will always be correct; your monitor may not be.

You can also display the PMS color list and other information from the Colors roll-up, as shown in Figure 5-3. To do so, choose Color Model from the Fill tool flyout, and then, from the Model drop-down list (top right), choose Palettes. Now, from the Matching System drop-down list (second list from top), choose PANTONE Matching System. You can change the color list to show names and numbers by selecting Show Color Names from the roll-up's flyout menu. To select a specific color, type the color name and number in the roll-up's Name field.

Figure 5-3: You can also use the Color roll-up to define and apply colors.

Note

You can choose PMS colors from the Property Bar when using the Interactive Fill tool, as discussed in the "Interactive Fill Tool Magic" sidebar toward the end of this chapter.

Using Spot Colors Effectively

Designers often use spot colors to effectively enhance the message contained in their documents, rather than merely as an aesthetics tool. Using spot colors improperly can detract from the message. Let's look at a few do's and don'ts for using spot color.

Use bright sport colors to attract reader attention or make a point: Colors can signify priorities. People tend to look at the brightest colors on a page or in a graphic first. You can control where their eyes go first by putting the most important material in the brightest colors. This is especially true of charts or other graphics designed to make comparisons, as shown in the color insert, Plate 5-2.

Use spot colors to map information: Use spot color to explain or to enhance the message, not to decorate. Do not use color merely because it's at your disposal. Instead, lead the reader's eye to the significant portions of a page. In a newsletter, for example, use color to draw the reader's attention to the banner or table of contents. In a flyer, highlight important parts of the message with color. Plate 5-3 in the color insert shows an example of effective use of spot color in a newsletter, letterhead, and brochure. When readers look at the page, the colored elements draw them into each piece.

Use spot colors to emphasize: Colors can make new points or different points of view stand out. On a brochure page, for example, use color to introduce a change in topics. On a newsletter page, use color for sidebars or sections containing contrasting arguments. Again, see Plate 5-3 in the color insert.

Use spot colors to symbolize: Certain colors can symbolize the nature of data. The most obvious associations are green for go, red for danger, and amber for caution.

Use spot colors to emphasize distinguishing characteristics: Almost all documents have elements that refer to the document, rather than the subject matter. The most obvious are page numbers, headers and footers, frames, boxed backgrounds, and other recurring objects. You can use spot color to set these objects off from the rest of the document, making it easier for the reader to find them.

Use spot colors as navigation tools: In multi-sectioned documents, many designers use locators to tell the reader where he or she is in a publication. Using color to mark the beginning of each section and subsection helps the reader find material, making using the document more pleasurable. Advertising data in particular is much more effective if information is easily located. You can also use colors to highlight section numbers and locator tabs. You can use different colors to identify separate sections, making each section distinguishable from the others. Plate 5-4 in the color insert shows several examples of using different colors for navigation tools.

Use percentages (tints) of spot colors to make a document appear more colorful: Sometimes called poor-man's color, percentages of spot colors (called *tints* in CorelDraw) make an image or document seem as though you have used many colors. Tints are simply the same colors at lower saturation, which produces lighter shades of the spot color. In CorelDraw, you apply tints from either the Uniform Fill dialog box or Color roll-up (or from the Property Bar when using the Interactive Fill tool), as shown in Figure A. You can set tints at any percentage from 1 to 100. However, you should use at least a 5 to 10 percent variance between tints; otherwise you don't really get the appearance of multiple colors. Plate 5-5 in the color insert shows examples of using tints to create the illusion of multiple colors.

(continued)

(continued)

Figure A

Figure B

Tint Option

Tint Option

Figures A and B: The Tint option in the Uniform Fill dialog box (A) or Color roll-up (B) lets you set the percentage of the color you want to use.

When to Use Spot or Process Color

You should consider several factors before deciding whether to use spot or process colors to print a publication. The three key factors are time, money, and design. Process colors usually require more resources, such as time and cost, than spot colors. Sometimes you can't avoid using process color. Color photographs and full-color drawings, of course, require four-color printing (process colors).

You should use spot colors if you have a limited budget and can accomplish your design using three or fewer colors. If you need to print four or more spot colors, you should use process colors instead, as this color choice then becomes the more cost-saving. The most effective way to get a process spot color is to use PANTONE Process or one of the other color-matching systems. You should also use spot colors when you need to make a precise color match in a corporate logo or some other graphic or when you want to use a special spot-color ink, such as fluorescent or pearlescent.

Other color-matching systems

You may be wondering about all those other names in the list of matching systems. Granted, there's a bunch, including FOCOLTONE, TRUMATCH, PANTONE Process, and others. Mostly these are process color matching systems for which you can find corresponding swatch or match books at art supply stores. Some print shops and service bureaus also sell them.

Basically, these systems are similar to PMS in that you choose colors based on swatches on a printed page. The difference is that these are not premixed inks that you call out at a print shop as spot colors. Instead they are created on process printing presses with mixtures of cyan, magenta, yellow, and black. These color-matching systems are primarily designed to enable you to choose colors based on *how they will print*, instead of how they look on a monitor.

Corel Color Manager

Because you can't depend on colors coming out on a printing press exactly as they appear on your monitor, you need a way to match colors reliably. An excellent way to get all of your output devices in synch is to use a *color management system* (or *CMS*). CorelDraw comes with its own CMS called *Corel Color Manager*. Before going into how to use Corel Color Manager, though, let's first take a look at what it does.

CIE color spaces

Output devices such as printers, monitors, and scanners all define colors differently. The color model used for color definitions is known as the device's *color space*. Most offset presses, many color desktop printers, plotters, and large poster printing devices, for example, specify colors as percentages of cyan, magenta, yellow, and black (CMYK). The color blue in the CMYK model uses the following values: C:97, M:96, Y:18, K:5. The same color on your monitor, which specifies colors with red, green, and blue (RGB) percentages, displays using these values: R:57, G:40, B:107, as shown in Figure 5-4.

Colors defined using CMYK and RGB models are *device-dependent*. In other words, they appear a certain way on a particular device. The color defined in Figure 5-4 would look different on monitors made by different manufacturers — you would see different shades of blue. A color printer would give you yet another color. Depending on paper and some other conditions, the same blue might reproduce in a different shade even when printed on a process-color press.

RGB Values

Figure 5-4: Color models define colors in different ways.

People in the printing and motion picture industries dealt with this problem long before computer graphics came along. In 1930, the Commission Internationale de l'Eclairage (International Commission on Color), or CIE, came up with a system of color standards. Making color models specify color in the same way was an impossible task, so the commission created CIE color spaces that specify color by using the human eye as the rendering method. The CIE specifies colors as people see them. CIE color spaces use mathematical values that aren't dependent on inconsistent variables, such as the design of a particular printer or the composition of a particular ink. It is on these CIE values that color management systems such as Corel Color Manager (and others) base their definitions of colors.

How Corel Color Manager works

To understand how color management systems work, you need to be familiar with two important concepts: gamut and profiles.

Gamut

A device's color *gamut* describes the range of colors that the device can create or, in the case of scanners, sense. Each color device — printing press, monitor, scanner, or printer — has its own color gamut. The CIE color space, based on the human eye, describes the most colors. It has the largest gamut. Color devices cannot reproduce this wide range of colors. In other words, their gamut is smaller than the CIE gamut. In the case of a 300-dpi inkjet printer, for example, the gamut is significantly smaller. Plate 5-6 in the color insert shows the color range for each type of color model and specific devices for reproducing color.

Profiles

Corel Color Manager and other color management systems use *device profiles* to record the color gamut of specific devices. A profile describes the characteristics of each device, as well as other information about its capabilities and limitations. These profiles may be created either by the manufacturer of the color management system or by the manufacturer of the device.

Corel Color Manager uses device profiles to adjust colors between printers, monitors, and scanners. It converts the color data to and from CIE colorspace formats. If the proper device profiles are installed on your system, the Corel Color Manager can turn the colors on your monitor into CIE colors and then convert them to similar colors for your printer, imagesetter, or another output device.

CorelDraw ships with many profiles, including profiles for several different printers and monitors. If your printer or monitor is not included, you can select a similar device, or contact the device maker to try to obtain one, or get information on which included profiles match (or are close to) an included profile. Unlike many color management systems, Corel Color Manager also lets you create your own profiles through a system known as *calibration*, which is explained later in this chapter.

Limitations of color management systems

Corel Color Manager, like other color management systems, does not eliminate the need for traditional color proofing. (If you're not sure what I mean by "color proofing," you should refer to Chapter 7.) Corel Color Manager works best when defining gamuts downward — in other words, when decreasing the number of colors. Computers are much better at reducing information from existing data, rather than increasing it. That makes sense, when you think about it, because increasing data would entail some guesswork. Color management systems reduce one device's gamut to match another — from, say, a monitor to a printer. This is convenient because color monitors have greater gamuts than desktop color printers (just as desktop printers have greater gamuts than printing presses).

The most useful conversion is from what you see on your monitor (RGB) to what rolls out of the color proofing printer and then, finally, the printing press (CMYK). Corel Color Manager transforms RGB color to its internal CIE format and then creates a CMYK equivalent, a process that works reasonably well, but is hardly perfect — as you'll see when we look at actually using color management in your CorelDraw documents.

Preparing to use Corel Color Manager

Getting color right in a graphics environment depends on several factors, including not only the use of a color management system and installing the proper device profiles, but also the proper calibration of your monitor. These steps increase the reliability of colors created and applied in CorelDraw. This section looks at setting up a work area conducive to color management, choosing and setting up a Corel Color Manager, and calibrating your monitor, scanner, and printer.

Tip

Your work environment plays an important role in how you see color on your monitor. The lighting in the room where you work and your monitor's contrast and brightness settings should remain constant for a consistent display of colors. So, if your work area lighting changes throughout the day, when working with color on your computer, you should draw the blinds and work in artificial lighting. If you use fluorescent lights, which can cast a yellow tint, you might consider investing in 5,000-degree Kelvin lighting. But then all this depends on how critical color consistency is to your application.

Once you've gotten the lighting in the room right, adjust the contrast and brightness on your monitor. Contrast adjusts intensity and brightness adjusts the level of black. To make the adjustments, display an image containing a lot of black, then adjust the brightness until you get the best black available, making sure that the black is not surrounded by a gray shadow. Then adjust the contrast until you're pleased with the intensity.

After going to all that trouble of adjusting monitor settings in the correct lighting, it wouldn't be good if somebody came in and readjusted your monitor. (Or if you bumped the controls with a book or software package.) You'd have to go back and do it all over again. To avoid this, tape down the contrast and brightness controls on your monitor.

Once your monitor is adjusted, it's time to fire up the Corel Color Manager wizard, as shown in Figure 5-5. Depending on the devices and drivers you have installed on your system, the first time you launch Corel Color Manager, the wizard configures itself the best it can by checking out your equipment.

Figure 5-5: The Corel Color Manager wizard helps you set up the Corel Color Manager.

In Figure 5-5, for instance, the only device it was able to locate on my computer was the monitor. Which devices Corel Color Manager finds on your computer depends solely on what devices you use and the drivers installed in Windows 95. On my system, for example, I have an HP 855C printer and HP ScanJet 3C. Neither of the drivers supplied by Hewlett-Packard are written in a manner that enables Corel Color Manager to find them. In these situations, you can use Corel Color Manager to manually select the devices attached to your computer.

Corel Color Manager enables you to use device profiles written specifically for your devices, or you can create your own. For most applications, the predefined profiles work fine. However, if you use devices for which Corel has not bundled profiles, or if your application requires highly accurate color correction, you should read the information in the "Calibrating Your Output Devices" section that follows.

Before going into creating your own profiles, though, let's look at the options in Corel Color Manager and what they mean.

- **Scanner:** This option, of course, enables you to tell Corel Color Manager which scanner you use. CorelDraw ships with profiles for most popular scanners. If yours isn't in the list, you can choose Generic Profile, contact the maker of your scanner to obtain a profile, or choose the Generate or Redo Profile option to create your own profile. We'll look at creating a scanner profile in the next section.

- **Monitor:** Use this drop-down list to choose the profile for your monitor. If yours isn't in the list, you can choose a similar monitor, get one from the monitor vendor, or generate one, as described in the next section. What many people don't know about monitors is that although there are plenty of manufacturers, many of them use the same picture tubes. The monitor vendor should be able to help you find a monitor profile among those shipped with CorelDraw.

- **Composite:** Use this drop-down list to choose a profile for your color proofing printer, either your own desktop model or the profile for the device your service bureau uses for composites. (If one is not included with CorelDraw, perhaps you can get one from the service bureau.) If you use your desktop printer for final output, you would still use this setting to choose a profile for your printer. Like the other profiles in this list, you can get one from the printer vendor or generate one.

- **Separations:** Use this drop-down list to choose the separation device on which you proof separated film — usually your service bureau's separation proofing device for creating color keys or match prints. If you don't know what color keys and match prints are, be sure to read Chapter 7. (If a separation device profile is not included with CorelDraw, perhaps you can get one from the service bureau.) Again, these profiles may be available from the device vendor, or you can create your own. However, creating or editing profiles at this level is a highly critical process. You really should rely on the predefined profiles.

- **Monitor Simulates**: The two options here, Composite printer and Separation printer, tell CorelDraw which final output device to simulate on-screen. If you normally take your jobs to the service bureau for separation, you should choose Separation printer. Choosing the Composite printer option tells Corel Color Manager to simulate the output from your desktop, or composite printer — which is fine if this is what you use for final output.

Once you've chosen all your profiles, choose Finish. CorelDraw will use these settings to correct the color among your various devices, and to simulate the final output on your monitor. Keep in mind that if you are creating graphics for display on a monitor, you should not use Corel Color Manager to correct color.

Once you have your profiles set, CorelDraw and the other applications in the suite know what colors your output devices are capable of producing. When working in these applications, Corel Color Manager can now warn you when you define a color beyond the gamut of your printing devices.

Notice the Gamut Color drop-down list in the lower-right corner of the Corel Color Manager dialog box (see Figure 5-5, shown earlier). Use it to tell Corel Color Manager what color to use to show which colors are beyond a device's gamut. You can define colors in the Uniform Fill dialog box, the Color roll-up, or one of the many other CorelDRAW suite application dialog boxes. When you do so, you can turn on the gamut alarm (usually on the dialog box flyout menu), and the program will show you which colors are not available on your printer, as shown in Figure 5-6.

Gamut Alarm area

Figure 5-6: Corel Color Manager profiles enable you to set a gamut alarm to warn you as to which colors are available on your printer. The blotted area (which shows as a bright color on your monitor) shows the colors in current range that your printer cannot produce.

You should not choose colors outside your printer's gamut. The resulting color shift will most likely be one you won't like.

Calibrating your output devices

As I mentioned earlier, for most applications Corel Color Manager's built-in profiles work fine. However, if you don't have a profile for your device — or if you work in an environment where color precision is critical — you can use Corel Color Manager to manually calibrate each of your devices. This section covers the process for each type of device.

Monitor calibration

The profiles in Corel Color Manager assume that the devices adhere to a set of standards. (Printers and scanners are calibrated during manufacturing.) Monitors, however, are subject to so many variables, such as work area lighting, graphics adapters, and so on, that often a predefined profile is simply not accurate enough. Often it's advantageous to calibrate monitors manually. This section shows you how to use Corel Color Manager's monitor calibration utility to get the colors right on your monitor.

Begin by making sure your work area is set up as you normally use it, as explained previously. Before going any further, make sure your monitor has been on about an hour, so that all the phosphors are warm. Now, fire up Corel Color Manager and make sure that the Monitor drop-down list has a check mark beside it (to the right).

Now scroll in the drop-down list and choose Generate or Redo Profile and then click Next. The subsequent dialog box, shown in Figure 5-7, enables you to choose the manufacturer and make of your monitor. Keep in mind here that if you select the exact name and model number from the lists, you'll actually be editing the predefined profile for your monitor. If you're not happy with the results you'll have to reinstall it. What I suggest you do is choose the manufacturer, and then, under Monitor Model, type in something descriptive, such as **My Profile**. Remember, too, that you can create several monitor profiles for the same monitor for different types of graphics work. Use the text box below Monitor Model to make notes about the current profile. If you are creating a profile for an unsupported monitor, of course, you'll have to give it a name, or choose from the two Generic options.

Figure 5-7: Use this section of Corel Color Manager to name your new monitor profile.

On the other hand, if you choose the exact name and model, when you get to the calibration section of Corel Color Manager, the settings are more likely to be close to correct for your device, meaning you shouldn't have to mess around with controls much.

After naming the new profile, click the Next button, which brings up the dialog box shown in Figure 5-8. It is from here that you actually calibrate your monitor. So, rummage through your CorelDraw box and find the scanner target, which you'll need to complete the calibration process. (The scanner target is easy to recognize — it has the same picture of the woman shown in Figure 5-8. I found mine stuffed in the user manual.)

Figure 5-8: Use this dialog box to calibrate your monitor.

Basically, the goal is to get the two pictures — the landscape and woman holding fruit — in the upper-left corner of the dialog box to match the target. You do this by making adjustments to the various settings in this dialog box.

The three settings you adjust are Gamma, Monitor Chromaticity, and Monitor White Point. Let's look at each type of adjustment and what it does:

- **Gamma** controls the monitor's brightness. Adjusting gamma values for your image affects midrange values most. Dark and light values change more slowly. You adjust gamma values using the Gamma box as a reference. The square on the left represents the natural gamma of your monitor, and the square on the right shows current gamma settings. Your monitor's gamma is set correctly when these two boxes match each other. You can adjust gamma one color channel at a time by clicking one of the three radio buttons. When adjusting gamma you should move back from the monitor until the horizontal lines in the left side of the gamma box appear as a solid color. Now, adjust the sliders or enter numerical values until the two sides match. You can adjust all three channels at once by selecting Identical RGB values.

- **Monitor Chromaticity** defines hue and saturation, or chroma levels, for your monitor. Chromaticity is a quality of color corresponding to the monitor's color gamut, or the number of saturated colors that the monitor is capable of reproducing. Because chromaticity values are relatively stable and do not vary greatly between monitors, they usually do not need to be adjusted. In most cases, it's simpler just to select a phosphor, or tube type, from the Phosphors drop-down list, which usually automatically makes the right chromaticity settings for your monitor.

- **Monitor White Point** measures the light produced by the monitor when all electron guns are firing at full intensity. It enables you to define the quality of "pure" white for your monitor. Pure white is expressed as a temperature in degrees Kelvin (K) corresponding to the reflective qualities of different types of light sources, such as the lighting in your office or at your workstation. Different types of lighting affect the cast reflected on your monitor. "Cold" light (Cool White Fluorescent or Fluorescent Three-band), for instance, casts a violet tint, so it reflects from white with a bluish tinge. "Warm" light reflects with more of a red tinge. You can use the slider (that appears when you select the Monitor white point radio button) to compensate for the type of lighting at your workstation, or you can simply choose a lighting type from the Illuminate drop-down list.

While making your adjustments, click the Preview button now and then to see how they affect the targets in the upper-left corner of the dialog box, using your hard copy target as a guide. You can get a larger preview (shown in Figure 5-9) by clicking the button with the magnifying glass icon, making it easier to see how your changes affect the match between the target and your monitor. When you finish making adjustments, click OK to save your changes and return to the Corel Color Manager main dialog box.

Figure 5-9: Click the magnifying glass icon to get a blow-up of the target image.

Scanner calibration

The procedure for calibrating your scanner is much like the one for calibrating a monitor. The primary difference is that for scanners, instead of making adjustments for a preloaded target, you first scan the target and then make adjustments based on the scanned image.

So, if you haven't already done so, find the scanner target in the CorelDraw box. Place it on the scanner bed and fire up Corel Color Manager. In the Scanner list, scroll to Generate or Redo Profile. This brings up the dialog box that lets you choose your scanner make and model, or you can type in your own identifying information. Then click Next.

The ensuing dialog box, shown in Figure 5-10, lets you choose whether to retrieve a prescanned target or scan the target now.

Figure 5-10: To scan the target for the first time, choose Scan Target.

If you've never calibrated the scanner before, you'll need to scan the target before you can proceed. So, select Scan Target and click Next. The following dialog box, shown in Figure 5-11, lets you choose the driver for your scanner, and, if you want, the TWAIN-compliant scanner interface. You can choose one of the drivers Corel has supplied, but they are all 32-bit drivers. If you don't have a 32-bit scanner, you should use the interface software that came with your scanner. In my case, for instance, I use HP's DeskScan.

Figure 5-11: Use the Select Source dialog box to select the driver for your scanner.

After you click Select, Corel Color Manager launches the TWAIN-compliant interface you chose and, depending on which interface software you're using, either prescans the target or waits for you to initiate a prescan.

Here's what I mean. In my case, with DeskScan, the target is automatically prescanned. If you use a Corel driver, the Corel TWAIN dialog box shown in Figure 5-12 appears. Simply click Prescan to tell the scanner to make a pass over the target. The purpose of this pass is to enable you to define the area to be scanned. Once the target has been prescanned, you then use the mouse cursor to position the selection box around the target.

Figure 5-12: The Corel TWAIN scanner interface

In most cases, the scanner interface automatically adjusts itself to the proper color depth for the image being scanned. However, you may need to adjust the resolution. When calibrating a scanner, you should scan the image at the resolution you'll use most often for final output. This depends primarily on how you'll use the image. Images destined for hard copy, high-quality brochures, for instance, are typically scanned at much higher resolutions than images destined for the Internet. (If you don't know which resolution best suits your application, check out the discussion in Chapter 7 about image resolution.) For most full-color images destined for the printing press, you usually scan at resolutions between 200 and 300 dpi.

To set the image resolution in Corel TWAIN, simply choose Custom from the Resolution drop-down list and type in the resolution in the field below the drop-down list. (If you are using your scanner's bundled interface, you should refer to the documentation for setting resolution prior to scanning.) Now click Scan (or whatever initiates your scanner software).

Corel Color Manager now asks you about the target — is it the Corel-supplied target or one supplied by somebody else? Some scanner manufacturers and image-editing programs provide their own target. Choose the target you are using and click Next.

Now you must define the target area so that Corel Color Manager knows which portion of the scanned image to calibrate to. If you placed the target in the scanner straight and defined the scanning area properly, this is an easy task. However, if the target image is crooked, you should first use the rotation buttons (the two buttons with arrows on them) to straighten the target.

To define the target area, you click the mouse cursor on the white crop marks in the lower-right, upper-left, and upper-right corners, as shown in Figure 5-13 (and in case you're wondering why just three of the corners, it's because Corel Color Manager finds the fourth one on its own).

Click in any three of these corners to define the target area

Figure 5-13: You'll use this dialog box to define the target area.

On the first click, the corner you click in magnifies, as shown in Figure 5-14. Then the mouse cursor turns into an L-shape. Line the L up on the white crop marks and click again. You need to repeat this process for all three corners, and then click Next.

Figure 5-14: When you click on the first corner, you'll see a magnified view of the crop mark.

Corel Color Manager provides two options for calibration, as shown in Figure 5-15. You can either let the software perform the calibration for you (Use Defaults), or you can make some minor adjustments yourself (Use Preset Tonal Settings). The method you choose depends on how happy you are with the results of default calibration.

Figure 5-15: The first option accepts the default calibration, and the second option lets you make adjustments based on preset values.

Take the target out of the scanner, and then click the Preview button in Corel Color Manager. Now hold the target up to the screen. If you're happy with the match between the target and the Calibrated Image (right), you're finished calibrating your scanner. If not, click on Close and then select Use Preset Tonal Settings. In the drop-down list, choose Lighten, Darken, or Reduce Contrast, or (if the calibrated image looked like it needed it) click on Darken Shadows. Now click Preview again.

You don't have a lot of choices for adjusting the calibration. So experiment with them, using the drop-down list options in conjunction with turning Darken Shadows on and off, until you get the best match with the target. When you click OK in the Corel Color Manager, you are returned to the main Corel Color Manager screen and the profile for your scanner has been saved. You're done.

Printer calibration

Depending on where you get your proofs and color keys, calibrating a proof and separation printer can be a little more involved than calibrating a scanner and monitor. If you get color proofs and separation proofs at a service bureau, for example, you'll have to work in conjunction with them to print calibration targets. With that in mind, let's go over the process for calibrating a proof printer and creating (or editing) a profile. Remember that if your color proof printer and separation proof printer are separate devices, you'll have to go through the process twice, once for each device.

In the Corel Color Manager main dialog box, scroll through the Composite list and choose Generate or Tune Profile. Then, in the next dialog box, choose your printer make and model, or type in your own identifying text. (Remember, from the discussion about calibrating monitors, that if you choose a Corel Color Manager-supported device, you will alter the default profile for that printer.) Click Next.

As shown in Figure 5-16, Corel Color Manager provides two methods for calibrating a printer. The Scanner Method is the simplest and most common. It involves printing the target file provided by Corel. You then scan the target using a calibrated scanner and Corel Color Manager creates a profile (or edits an existing profile) for your printer. The File Method is more accurate, but it is time-consuming and requires special equipment. You print a target sheet and measure each color square using a spectrophotometer and type the results into a measurements file, and then make some final adjustments. We'll go over the Scanner Method here. The File Method is a bit out of the realm of this book.

Figure 5-16: You can use your scanner to calibrate your printer from a target printed from your printer, or calibrate from a file using a color meter.

Select Scanner Method and click Next. In the ensuing dialog box, select Yes, Print the Test File. You can also select the number of patches to be printed, which can be any number from 40 to 200. The larger the number of patches, the wider the range of samples you give Color Manager to calculate your printer's color characteristics. Corel has set the default number at 200 for maximum accuracy, but 60 or more samples provide adequate results.

Secret

Corel Color Manager launches the Print Setup dialog box for your printer. From here you should make the settings with which you print graphics. For example, on my HP DeskJet 855C, I would click on Properties and set the graphics quality to Best. The settings you make depend, of course, on your printer.

If you use a service bureau to print proofs, rather than printing to a printer on your desktop or network, you need to create a PostScript print file that the service bureau will in turn print for you. At this point you would use Print Setup to set up the print file, which requires, of course, that you have a copy of the printer driver for your service bureau's printer. If your service bureau has CorelDraw 7, it can print the target for you. In either case, you cannot proceed until you have the target in hand, which means that after you create the PostScript file, you will cancel the printer calibration process and then retrace your steps to this point when you have the target. We look at printing PostScript print files in Chapter 7.

Once you've set up your printer, click OK to print the target. Depending on your printer, this may take a few minutes. Once the target has printed, place it on your scanner, making sure that it is straight. (If you're using an inkjet printer, remember to let the ink dry before placing the target on your scanner.)

In the next dialog box, you are given a choice of retrieving a previously scanned target or scanning one. If, of course, this is your first time through this process, you will have to scan the target. So, select Scan Target and then click Next. Now, in the Select Source dialog box, find and select your scanner (preferably, the one you calibrated in the previous section) and then click Select. If necessary, prescan the target, and then make sure that all of it is selected in the scanning area. Scan the target at the resolution you normally print at, making sure that you scan at the highest possible color depth — either Millions of Colors, 24-bit color, or 32-bit color, depending on your scanner.

The Corel Color Manager then displays a screen enabling you to rename the color reference file, or the file that Corel Color Manager uses during the calibration. You can change the name of the file if you want, but I can't think of any reason to do so. Whatever you decide, then click Next. For Corel Color Manager to calculate your printer's characteristics, it has to be able to "place" it to compare the values of the individual patches. So you must align the target, similarly to the method you used to align the target for calibrating your scanner earlier in this chapter. In case you've forgotten, here are the steps.

STEPS

Aligning the Target

Step 1. Use the left and right Rotate Tools to reorient the target in increments of 90 degrees. Rotating the target to landscape position makes it easier to see.

(continued)

STEPS *(continued)*

Aligning the Target

Step 2. Select the Zoom tool.

Step 3. Click on one of the fiduciary marks (the white squares in the corners) to enlarge this area. The cursor becomes a semi cross hair.

Step 4. Position the semi cross hair in the inside corner of the white fiduciary mark on the target file and click.

Step 5. Repeat this for three corners (upper right, lower right, and upper left — Corel Color Manager finds the fourth). The target is now aligned. (See Figure 5-17.)

Step 6. Click OK.

Figure 5-17: Use this screen to align the target by clicking on the small white boxes in the upper right, lower right, and upper left corner.

Corel Color Manager generates the printer profile, and voilà, you're done.

Using Color Manager

Once you have set up all your profiles, you can use Corel Color Manager in any of the graphics-editing programs in the CorelDRAW 7 suite. The procedure is essentially the same in all of the programs — you turn on color correction from the View menu (View ⇨ Color Correction), and you have three choices: None, Fast, and Accurate.

Remember that the purpose of Corel Color Manager is to try to get your monitor to simulate as closely as possible what will finally roll out of your printer, your service bureau's printer, or from a printing press. So when you turn on Color Correction, Corel Color Manager tries to show you on-screen how the document will print. The Fast setting performs an approximation to give you a rough idea of how colors will look, and Accurate tries to give you an accurate portrayal. To avoid heart failure, when working on documents that you know will be printed on paper, I suggest you work in Fast mode while creating your drawing, and then switch to accurate before printing. The color shift will not be nearly as dramatic. And you can easily go back and tweak colors that don't look right.

Corel Color Manager isn't foolproof. In no way does it relieve you from having to take the standard precautions to avoid unpleasant surprises at the print shop. This includes using CorelDraw's gamut alarm (discussed earlier in this chapter under Gamut) to make sure you do not select colors beyond the range of the printing press, and printing color proofs before dropping the job off at the print shop.

Color Palettes

Secret

The use of color palettes involves more than just selecting an object and then clicking on a swatch. For example, as you may already know, to change the color of an outline, you simply select the outline and then open the Outline Color or Pen roll-up from the Pen tool flyout. But you can avoid the extra steps of opening the Outline Color dialog box or Pen roll-up by changing the right mouse button configuration of the color palette options in the Customize dialog box (Tools ⇨ Customize ⇨ Color Palette). By default, when you click the right mouse button on the color palette, you get the pop-up shown in Figure 5-18. You can alter this so that CorelDraw changes the color of a selected outline when you right-click on a color swatch. Simply select the Set Outline Color option in the Mouse Button 2 portion of the Color Palette section in the Customize dialog box.

Set Outline Color
Set Fill Color

Customize...

Move to Start
Move to End

Delete Color

New
Open...
Save
Save As...

What's This?

Figure 5-18: By default, you get this menu when you right-click on the color palette. You can change this so that CorelDraw colors the outline of selected objects when you right-click on a specific swatch.

Using Color Effectively in Charts, Graphs, and Presentations

CorelDraw is perhaps the most versatile of available draw programs. Not only is the draw program itself capable of laying out multiple-page documents, such as newsletters and reports, but it also comes with a wide selection of chart and graph clip art you can recolor and use in your presentations. The purpose of charts, graphs, and diagrams is to make concepts easier to understand. The purpose of presentations is to explain or persuade. Color contributes to the clarity, impact, and memorableness of a presentation. Again, when using color in business documents, the primary goal is to convey your message, not make the piece pretty. Color should be used as a tool. Its aesthetic value is secondary.

It's tempting when using color to use every hue in your arsenal. Remember that you want to make your point. This section lists several rules for using color in charts and presentations. The color insert contains several examples of these points.

Use Color to Make a Point: Use color to emphasize a single point — one pie segment, one trend line, one row of figures, one bullet, one bar or column. Unless you are comparing data, avoid showing two sets of data on the same slide. See Plate 5-7 in the color insert.

Use Color to Make Points Stand Out: Use color to make emphasized elements stand out. Use dark colors — black, blue, purple — for backgrounds. Use bright colors — white, yellow, orange — for the most important words and items. And use neutral colors, such as light blue or green, for unimportant elements.

Use Colors to Bring in New Points: Use color to emphasize new points. Assign the brightest colors to new data and use duller colors to play down information you've already covered. One of the more common uses for this technique is to "build" slides where new bullet points are bright and old points are grayed out, or "dimmed." You can also use dull colors to play down negative or unimportant points. Plate 5-8 in the color insert shows an example of using color to bring in new points.

Use Color to Establish Relationships: Use color to identify recurring or related themes. You can, for example, assign green to all positive aspects of your presentation and orange to all negative data. It doesn't take long for an audience to recognize these trends, especially if you point them out early in the presentation.

Use Color to Build Excitement: You can use color to build your presentation to a climax. Start with a dull neutral color and then gradually build to a bright one. Or start with a dark shade of a color and gradually lighten it until it's a bright hue.

Use Color Coding: Much like using color to establish relationships, you can also color code information. In a series of charts you should use the same colors for related data. If, for example, you want to show trends for a certain department throughout your presentation, use the same color each time you display data for that department. See Plate 5-9 in the color section.

You can also add and remove colors from existing color palettes, or create all-new color palettes. I especially like to use this last option to create palettes for drawings that contain colors not on CorelDraw's built-in palettes, or for creating palettes of spot color tints. Once you've created the palettes, it's much easier to apply tints and custom color to objects, rather than recreating the colors each time you need them.

Adding and removing colors

Different types of drawings and documents require different colors. In fact, seldom do I use the colors on CorelDraw's built-in color palettes. Instead, when working on artwork destined for a printed document, I find it safer (now that I'm used to it) to choose my colors from color swatch books. The problem with this method is that usually the colors I want are not on the color palette. So first I must create them, and then, to use them again in the same drawing (or another one), I add them to the color palette.

Whether you are creating colors for print media or for an electronic document, the procedure is the same (except that the swatch book is irrelevant when publishing for multimedia or the Internet). To add a color to the color palette, you first must create the color. Do this in either the Uniform Color or Outline Color dialog boxes, or from the Color roll-up. The benefit of using the Color roll-up is that you can apply colors to both fills and objects, and you do not have to close the roll-up to apply the color, making it easier to experiment.

So, let's look at adding colors to palettes from the Color roll-up. The first step is to choose the color system from the Model drop-down list for the final output — RGB for the computer screen, CMYK for process-color printing, PMS for spot color printing, and so on. If you are creating artwork for print media, you can also turn on Color Correction (View ➪ Color Correction), in which case the Color roll-up will attempt to show you only colors available on the proof printer you selected in Corel Color Manager (discussed earlier in this chapter under "Corel Color Manager"). Note that if you work in the RGB color model, you can turn on the gamut alarm on the Color roll-up flyout menu. CorelDraw then warns you as to which colors are not available on your proof printer, as shown in Figure 5-19.

— Gamut Alarm

Figure 5-19: When you turn on color correction and the gamut alarm, the Color roll-up shows which colors are not available on your separation proof printer.

As you probably know, you have two ways to create color in the Color roll-up. You can choose them in either of two ways. The first way is by sight in the color selection area by dragging the slider on the right side of roll-up and then selecting your color from the window to the left of the slider. The second way is to enter values in the fields near the top of the roll-up. Again, you should use the first method when designing colors for the screen and the second method for print media.

Once the color is defined, you add it to the color palette by choosing Add Color to Palette. Keep in mind that the color will be added to the current color palette. By default, CorelDraw uses the default Custom Color palette. To add colors to another color palette, you must first open it to make it current, as discussed in the next section.

A quick and easy way to create colors for adding to your color palette is to use the eyedropper in the lower-left corner of the Color roll-up. It enables you to "pick up" colors from objects in you drawing, similar to the Eyedropper tool in Photo-Paint and other bitmap image editing programs. All you do is click the eyedropper button to select it, and then click the mouse cursor (now an arrow) on the object containing the color you want to pick up. The color is displayed in the New Color swatch in the upper-left corner of the roll-up. Now select Add Color to Palette.

You'll also find the eyedropper handy for creating colors based on existing colors in your drawings. Simply use the method described in the previous paragraph to select a color. Make adjustments to the color as you normally would, and then choose Add Color to Palette. While adjusting the new color, you can use the original color as a guide for comparison by clicking the small Swap Colors arrow next to the color swatch in the upper-left corner of the roll up, as shown in Figure 5-20.

Figure 5-20: To use the original color as a guide, click the Swap Colors button.

The color swatch in the upper-left corner of the Color roll-up is actually two swatches: Original Color (top) and New Color (bottom). As you make adjustments to the color in the roll-up, the New Color swatch reflects the changes, while the Original Color swatch remains unchanged — unless you click the Swap Colors button (or choose the corresponding Swap Colors command on the roll-up's flyout).

All of the colors on the default color palette have names, which you can see by selecting Palette from the Color Model drop-down list in the Color roll-up. And you must also make sure that Show Color Names on the roll-up flyout is active. Now, when you click on a swatch in the roll-up's palette, you can see the Name field. To name your new colors, simply type a name in the Name field before you choose Add Color to Palette.

I find naming colors especially helpful when creating palettes of spot color tints. You know, descriptive names, such as PMS 363 90%, PMS 363 80%. This convention makes it a lot easier to choose the right tints in my color scheme. Names are also helpful when designing a series of drawings based on the same color scheme, especially when the drawing contains a lot of similar-looking colors, such as several shades of green for plants and flowers. Using color names is also helpful if you view and edit documents on computers with different display systems and monitors.

Deleting a color from a palette is simple. Simply right-click on the color you want to trash, and then choose Delete from the pop-up menu. You can do this either in the Color Palette (at the bottom of the screen) itself, or in the palette inside the Color roll-up.

Creating new color palettes

The main reason I like to create new palettes in CorelDraw is that the existing one has far too many colors on it already. I don't like scrolling through them. Many of my documents and drawings don't contain a lot of colors. So I like to create palettes containing only the colors I need.

Creating a new palette is easy. Simply choose Palettes from the Model drop-down list in the Color roll-up, choose Custom Colors from the list of palettes, and then choose New Palette from the flyout (or the Uniform Color dialog box flyout). You can also right-click on the Color Palette at the bottom of the screen.

CorelDraw displays the New Palette dialog box. From here you name the new color palette. I suggest you use a descriptive name. (Remember that you can use up to 255 characters in Windows 95.) CorelDraw adds the .CPL extension automatically. When you click Save, the program creates an empty palette and makes it current. Figure 5-21 shows the Color roll-up with an empty color palette.

Figure 5-21: An example of an empty custom palette, ready to receive new colors.

Now, use the method described in the previous section to add colors. To add PMS tints, for example, follow these steps:

STEPS

Adding PMS Tints to a Palette

Step 1. Choose PANTONE Matching System from the Palettes drop-down list.

Step 2. Find the PMS colors for which you want to create a series of tints.

Step 3. Set the first tint percentage in the Tint field.

Step 4. Choose Custom Colors from the Palettes list.

Step 5. Type a descriptive name in the Name field.

Step 6. Choose Add Color to Palette from the roll-up flyout.

Step 7. Repeat the process, adding colors and tints until you have all the desired colors defined in your new palette.

That's it! Figure 5-22 shows the Color roll-up containing several new colors I defined for PANTONE Blue.

Figure 5-22: An example of a new color palette with custom-defined colors.

Secret

You can use this method to create a color palette from existing images, such as, say, clip art. Using the colors contained in tried and proven clip art images (such as those bundled with CorelDraw) is one way to make sure that your colors print properly. To add new color from a piece of clip art, select the object containing the color, and then open the Uniform Fill dialog box from the Fill tool flyout. Then choose Add Color to Palette from the dialog box's pop-up menu.

Color Styles

One of the more exciting new features in CorelDraw 7 is color styles. If you are already familiar with text styles and graphics styles, then using this new feature will be a snap.

Basically, this feature lets you assign style sheets to the colors you create in the Color roll-up or Uniform Color dialog box. You can then reuse each color simply by assigning the style to selected objects. You can also create parent-child styles with other similar colors. If you create a style for the color blue, for example, you can create child colors for other hues of blue, such as light blue, sky blue, and so on. The beauty of the parent-child relationship is that should you decide to change the color scheme, say, for example, from blue to red, all you do is change the parent style and the child styles will follow suit. You can also tell CorelDraw to automatically create styles and parent-child relationships as you work, which I'll show you in a moment.

As with text and graphics styles (both are sometimes called *object* styles), you can create specific color styles for individual templates and copy them between templates. This is a great way to ensure consistent color schemes between documents and to create templates, drawings, and documents with colors you use often.

Creating a color style

It's actually very simple to create a color style. Color styles are created from the Styles roll-up, which is also known as the Styles Manager, shown in Figure 5-23. To open the Styles roll-up, choose Layout ⇨ Color Styles. (You can also choose Text and Graphics Styles from the Layout menu and then click on the Color Styles tab.)

Figure 5-23: Use the Color Styles portion of the Styles roll-up to create and manage color styles.

To create a color style, simply click the New Color Style button. This brings up the New color dialog box shown in Figure 5-24. From here, you create a color as you normally would, type a name for the Style field, and then click OK. (If you forget to name the style, CorelDraw names it Color Style. You can then rename it by right-clicking on the name, and then choosing Rename.)

Figure 5-24: Use the New Color Style dialog box to create color styles.

You can edit a color style by selecting it in the list, and then clicking the Edit Style button (third from the left), which brings up the Edit Color Style dialog box. In addition, you can create color styles from existing objects by clicking the Automatic Create button (last one), which brings up the Automatically Create Color Styles dialog box shown in Figure 5-25.

Figure 5-25: Use this dialog box to create a color style from an existing color in your drawing.

From here you can choose to create a color style based on either a fill or outline color, or both. And you can also create child styles automatically (explained next).

Creating parent-child relationships

Many drawings call for different shades of the same color. In CorelDraw, related colors styles can be linked through a *parent-child relationship*. You can manually create your own child color styles or you can have CorelDraw create them for you automatically (from existing color in your documents).

The manual method

This method enables you to create only one child color style at a time, but gives you far more control over the resulting color associated with the color style than the automatic method. Let's face it, CorelDraw's built-in decisions are not always right for the task at hand — they can't always anticipate your precise needs. To create a child color style, select the color for which you want to create a new child and then click the Create a New Child button (second from the left). This brings up the Create a New Child Color dialog box shown in Figure 5-26. From here you can use the color window to select a hue or the Saturation and Brightness controls to edit the new color. You can also use the Color Name field to assign a color style name other than CorelDraw's default. When you click OK, the child is added to the Styles roll-up.

Figure 5-26: Use this dialog box to create the color and name for a child style.

The automatic method

You can instruct CorelDraw to create child styles automatically from an existing style by clicking on the Create Shades button (second from the right) in the Styles roll-up. This brings up the Create Shades dialog box shown in Figure 5-27. From here you tell CorelDraw how many child colors to create, whether they should be darker or lighter than the current color, and how widely they should vary from the current color.

Figure 5-27: This dialog box lets you create child color styles automatically, enabling you to control the number of child colors, and the variant colors.

The different options are clearly labeled. About the only aspect of this dialog box that is not readily self-explanatory is Shade Similarity. You can adjust the slide to varying degrees of difference and similarity. I've played extensively with this option, and what I've learned is that if you need precision, you should choose your child colors manually. Create Shades is seemingly a bit random. But this option works great if your coloring does not need to be exacting. And it works well for creating shades (or tints) of spot colors, saving you from having to do it manually, though you may find yourself engaged in a bit of trial and error before you get the colors you need. But then a big part of graphics design and layout is trial and error anyway, right?

Fountain Fills

One of the most impressive things about computer draw programs is their capability of automatically creating gradient fills, or what CorelDraw calls *fountain fills*. A *gradient* is two or more colors blending, or graduating, in steps into one another. One exotic type of gradient is a rainbow fountain fill, which consists of several colors graduating into one another.

If you don't already know how to create different types of fills, you should check the online documentation that comes with CorelDraw. Look under "fountain fills." This section focuses on adjusting fills for just the right effect. It also explains two of version 7's great new features, the Interactive Fill tool and the Interactive Transparency tool.

You control fountain fills from either the Fountain Fill dialog box or from the Special Fills roll-up. The benefit of using the dialog box is that it provides more controls than the roll-up, such as the capability of adjusting a fill's edge pad and fountain steps (edge pads and fountain steps are explained later). On the other hand, the roll-up provides a level of interactivity not available in the dialog box. In the dialog box you must make your adjustments, click OK to apply them, and then reopen it to make further changes.

In version 7, however, the Property Bar (in Interactive Fill tool mode) provides most of the controls available in the Fountain Fill dialog box. You can, for example, now control edge pad and fountain steps interactively, almost making the need to open the Fountain Fill dialog box obsolete. About the only thing you need to open the dialog box for nowadays is to create two-color custom fills or to select one of CorelDraw's preset fills. So let's talk about those two options first.

Two-color rainbow fills

Rainbow fills enable you to create multicolored gradients. Rainbow fills are configured from the color wheel Color Blend area in the Fountain Fill dialog box, which you access by choosing the second option on the Fill tool flyout. The Fountain Fill dialog box is shown in Figure 5-28. The three arrow buttons next to the color wheel indicate three options. These options enable you to create a straight blend directly from one color to another, a blend that selects colors clockwise around the color wheel, or counterclockwise around the color wheel.

Figure 5-28: You use the options in the Color Blend section of the Fountain Fill dialog box to configure rainbow blends.

The following procedure creates a blend:

STEPS

Creating a Blend

Step 1. Select the type of blend — Linear, Radial, Conical, or Square — from the Type drop-down list.

Step 2. Use the From and To color palette drop-down lists to select the begin and end colors.

Step 3. Select one of the color wheel options: straight blend, clockwise, or counterclockwise. Color Plate 5-10 shows the difference in how the three options create a blend.

Step 4. Adjust the midpoint and angle (if you don't know what these are, read the "Midpoint, Edge-Point, and Fill Angle" section that follows).

Step 5. Click OK.

Preset fills

Presets are preconfigured fills you can apply to objects, eliminating a lot of experimentation. The reason I like to use presets is that Corel has already optimized them for printing. That way I don't get any surprises at the print shop. You apply presets from the Fountain Fill dialog box. There's a bunch of them. I'll bet you can find one for your needs. Plate 5-11 shows some examples using presets on extruded text.

Fountain steps

Fountain steps refers to the number of increments in the fill, or the number of gradation steps from one color two another. Changing the number of steps affects the fill in two ways: it can increase the overall quality of the fill, and it can actually change the overall look of the blend. Using many steps creates a smooth flow in the blend from one color to another. Using fewer steps creates a banding effect, making the gradation increments more apparent.

You have two ways to change fountain steps: either from the Fountain Fill dialog box, or from the Property Bar when using the Interactive Blend tool. Because the major focus of this book is to show you how to create artwork in CorelDraw more efficiently, lets look at changing fountain steps from the Property Bar.

Depending on whether you select an object that already has a fountain fill, or one that has a solid fill, when you select the Interactive Fill tool from the toolbox, the Property Bar may or may not show the Fountain Step option (last option on the right end). Fountain Step becomes available when you select Fountain Fill from the Property Bar with the Interactive Fill tool selected. To change the number of fountain steps, click the Fountain Step Lock/Unlock button, and then use the controls to set the number of steps. Your changes show on-screen automatically.

Secret

As with all of your work in CorelDraw, when working with fountain fills, you must be mindful of the difference between what's displayed on your monitor and what will finally roll off the printing press. By default, CorelDraw displays only 50 fountain steps. So, if you set your fountain steps higher than 50, you won't see the difference. The reason for the default of 50 is two-fold: One, the higher the number of fountain steps the slower your display system redraws them. Two, depending on the resolution of your display system, most computers cannot really display more than 50 steps. How many steps a device can produce depends on its resolution capabilities. Hence, desktop printers, proof printers, and printing presses are capable of reproducing more steps than you can see on your monitor.

Also keep in mind that at some point too many steps are overkill, and can even cause some older output devices to crash. By default, when you print from CorelDraw or export to a PostScript format, the maximum number of fountain steps is 128, which is plenty for most drawings. Anything higher than that can really bog down a printing device. You also need to consider some other things when printing fountain steps, which we'll look at in Chapter 7.

Midpoint, edge-point, and fill angle

In some of your drawings you may want your fills to flow from certain points in the selected object rather than from end to end. And in radial, conical, and square fills, you may want to change the center of the fill. When you make these kinds of adjustments you are changing the fill's *midpoint.* CorelDraw also lets you change where a blend begins and ends, or adjust the edge-point. And sometimes the effect you're after calls for changing the angle of the blend. In previous versions of CorelDraw, you changed the mid-point and edge-point in the Fountain Fill dialog box. Fill angle could be changed in either Fountain Fill or from the special fill dialog box. Those options are still available in version 7, but the easiest way to adjust them is with the Interactive Fill tool.

Adjusting the midpoint

The midpoint is where the two colors are at their highest point of blending. In a fountain fill between yellow and red, for example, the midpoint would be where the two colors mix at 50 percent each, or orange. In a rainbow blend, the midpoint is the place on the color wheel halfway between the From and To colors. One of the more common uses for changing the midpoint is to adjust color shading.

Still not sure of what the midpoint is? Perhaps an example will help. Figure 5-29 shows the same rectangle with a fountain fill set at different midpoints. To change a fill's midpoint with the Interactive Fill tool, make sure that you have the tool (and the object) selected, and that Fountain Fill is active on the Property Bar. And make sure that the type of fill you want — Linear, Radial, Conical, or Square — is also selected on the Property Bar. Now, simply drag the Fountain Fill Midpoint slider left or right to increase or decrease the midpoint. For a precise setting, simply type the desired midpoint setting in the field next to the slider.

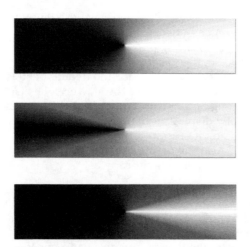

Figure 5-29: Examples of various midpoint settings: 50 percent (top), 10 percent (middle), and 90 percent (bottom).

Changing the edge pad

The term *edge pad* refers to the distance from the edge of the filled object to the point where the fountain fill begins. In other words, you can have a solid color at the edge of the object and a fountain fill nearer the middle, or you can have a solid color on one side of the object and fountain fill at the other.

The Interactive Fill tool enables you to adjust the edge pad in two ways: from the Property Bar or with your mouse. Both methods adjust the edge pad in two directions, or, in the case of radial, conical, and square fills (which blend from the center outward) in four directions.

To change the edge pad with the Property Bar, you change the value in the Edge Pad field, which is the field next to the Midpoint field. When you hover your mouse over it, the label says Fountain Fill Angle and Edge Pad, which actually refers to both fields. Edge Pad is the one on the bottom. To adjust the edge pad interactively with your mouse, drag on the arrow-side of the interactive adjuster (the arrow with a square box on one end and an arrow at the other), as shown in Figure 5-30. As you move the arrow inward, the edge pad increases. As you move it outward, the edge pad decreases.

Figure 5-30: You can adjust the edge pad interactively by dragging on the arrow side of the interactive adjuster.

To adjust only one side of an edge point, you move the square end of the interactive adjuster, as shown in Figure 5-31. As you can see, you can use this method to create blends in virtually any portion of your selected object. And you can move the edge pad to any portion of the object by moving the square end of the interactive adjuster. You can also create a two-sided edge pad by first moving the square end of the adjuster, and then dragging on the arrow end to shorten the adjuster.

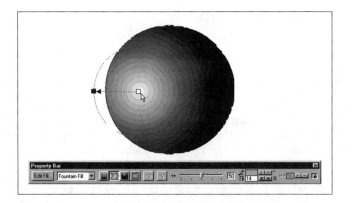

Figure 5-31: To create one-sided edge pads, move the square end of the adjuster, as shown here.

Interactive Fill Tool Magic

Few things in life are slicker than making changes directly on the page with version 7's new Interactive Fill tool. Depending on the type of fill you're working with, the Interactive Fill tool gives you a whole mess of options for manipulating your fills. Let's take a brief look at the various options by type of fill.

When you work with a uniform (or solid) fill, you can adjust your colors by percentages, as shown in Figure A.

Figure A

When you work with PANTONE colors, the Property Bar lets you change colors and tints interactively, as shown in Figure B.

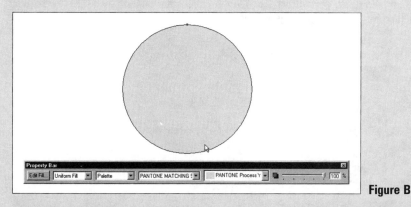

Figure B

When you work with a fountain fill, you can change the edge point and angle interactively with the adjuster, and make numerous other changes, such as type of fill, with the Property Bar, as shown in Figure C.

Figure C

When you work with pattern fills you can interactively switch between two-color and full-color patterns and adjust the size of the pattern, as shown in Figure D.

Figure D

(continued)

(continued)

When working with a texture fill, you can quickly use the Regenerate option and get to the various dialog boxes for editing the textures, as shown in Figure E.

Figure E

When working with PostScript fills, you can quickly switch between the various fill types, as shown in Figure F.

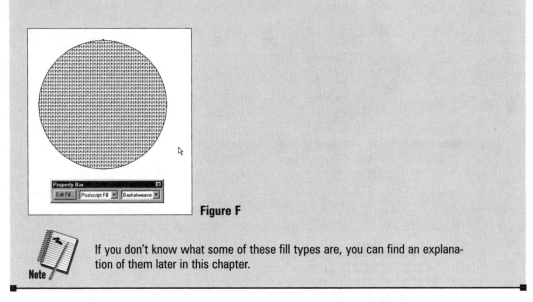

Figure F

If you don't know what some of these fill types are, you can find an explanation of them later in this chapter.

Note

Adjusting fountain fill angles

Depending on the type of fountain fill you are working with, adjusting the angle of the fill can dramatically change the effect of your graphic. In Color Plate 5-12, I adjusted the angle in five different directions to make this point.

You can adjust a fountain fill's angle from the Fountain Fill dialog box, or from the Special Fill roll-up. But by far the easiest method is with the Interactive Fill tool. When you select a fountain-filled object with the Interactive Fill tool, you get the interactive adjuster. To change the direction of the blend, simply drag the arrow in the direction to which you want the fountain fill to flow, as shown in Figure 5-32.

Figure 5-32: To change the angle of a fill interactively, drag the arrow in the direction you want the fill to flow.

You've seen throughout this section how to modify fountain fills in different ways. In many cases you can improve the overall quality of your fountain fills by using a combination of these techniques. While the fountain fill options are quite helpful and enable you to create effects that might otherwise take a long a time to achieve manually, this feature requires trial and error to achieve that just-right effect, and it takes practice to master.

Creating multicolor fountain fills

Earlier in this chapter I showed you how to create rainbow fills from two-color fountain fills. If you need more control over which colors are contained within a fill and where they appear, you can use the Interactive Fill tool to create multicolored (or *custom*) fills. Note that you can also do this from the Fountain Fill dialog box with the Custom option, which is well documented in Help. But you get far more control with the Interactive Fill tool.

You won't believe how easy this is. Say you've got a two-color blend, perhaps red and orange, and you want to add another color. All you do is select the color in the color palette (or from one of CorelDraw's many other color creation options) and then drag it to the filled object. To add the color in the fountain fill, simply place the tip of the mouse cursor on the interactive adjuster dotted line (precisely where you want the color to appear) and release the mouse button. Voilà! You've got a third color in your fill. You can add as many colors as you like with this method.

Figure 5-33 shows a filled object with several colors added. Each square along the adjuster dotted line designates a different color and acts as control point for moving the color in the fill and adjusting its width and midpoint. With the capability of stretching the adjuster with the arrow, moving the square at the opposite end of the adjuster, and dragging on the individual color control points, you have extensive control over the placement, width, and midpoints of your fills.

Figure 5-33: An example of a custom blend. Each square control point represents a new color. You can control the midpoint of each color by dragging on the squares.

To delete a color, simply right-click on the corresponding square.

Predefined Patterns and Textures

As mentioned earlier, one of CorelDraw's strengths is that it not only provides the power the professional artist needs but also many features the nonartist can use. CorelDraw's prefabricated textures and patterns are a case in point. With just a few mouse clicks you can wind up with some rather spectacular effects. But this is not to say that the professional artist cannot also use these impressive fills in their artwork, too. They are robust, completely customizable, and can save hours of tedium in trying to create the same or similar effects by hand.

In this section we take a brief look at CorelDraw's Pattern, Texture, and PostScript fills. Plate 5-13 in the color insert shows several examples of the affects available through using these fills, and these examples don't even scratch the surface of what's available. I'm assuming that you already know that they exist and that you apply them as you would any other fill — by selecting an object and then selecting the fill you want. Consequently, what we'll concentrate on here is modifying the fills to suit your needs and using them in conjunction with the Interactive Fill tool.

Using pattern fills

CorelDraw ships with two types of prefabricated pattern fills — two-color and full-color. Each type provides rather extensive controls over the size and tiling of the pattern and, in the case of two-color fills, the colors used to comprise the pattern. The full-color fills come in two flavors, bitmap and full-color, providing for a wide range of options. Let's look at each type separately.

Two-color pattern fills

Two-color fills are patterns made up of different color foregrounds and backgrounds. CorelDraw ships with several two-color fills, and you can create your own or import them from other graphic files, such as other CorelDraw drawings or Photo-Paint PCX files. You can adjust the size and placement of a two-color pattern with the size and tiling options in the Pattern dialog box, which you get to by clicking on Edit Fill in the Property Bar when the Interactive Fill too is selected. Figure 5-34 shows the Pattern dialog box in two-color mode.

Figure 5-34: The Pattern dialog box in two-color mode enables you to adjust the size of the pattern and the foreground and background colors.

To use this option, select a pattern from the pattern flyout. Choose whether you want the pattern to be small, medium, or large, and then select the desired colors. If you're not happy with the results of the small, medium, or large options, you can adjust the pattern more precisely with the Width and Height options to set precise measurements for the pattern.

You can further adjust the look of the pattern by adjusting the pattern's tiling. To do so, click on the Tiling button, which expands the Pattern dialog box, as shown in Figure 5-34. Similar to edge pads for fountain fills, tiling enables you to set where the pattern begins in relation to the object being filled. You adjust the options in the First Tile Offset option to shift the pattern right or left. Row or Column Offset actually lets you shift the pattern tiles in relationship to one another, distorting the pattern, as shown in Figures 5-35 and 5-36.

Figure 5-35: Use the Tiling option to control offset of the individual tiles that make up the pattern.

Figure 5-36: Offsetting a pattern's tile by column or row enables you to distort the pattern for some interesting effects.

Finally, you can conform the pattern to the size and shape of your object with the Scale Pattern with Object option. This option tries to make the pattern fit the object. Depending on the shape of your object, sometimes this works and sometimes it just makes a mess.

Secret

You have two ways to add new two-color fills to your collection: Create and Load. Create enables you to design fills by filling in a grid, and Load lets you use another graphics file to create a pattern. (My favorite way to create new fills is to scan them. I created a wood grain pattern, for example, by scanning a section of a picture of a bookcase.) Let's look at both procedures.

To create a pattern, follow these steps:

STEPS

Creating a Two-Color Pattern Fill

Step 1. Make sure the object you want to create a fill for is selected. (Note that you can create a pattern without selecting an object by selecting the Pattern Fill button on the Fill tool flyout.)

Step 2. Select the 2-Color fill option.

Step 3. Click on Create. This brings up the Two-Color Pattern Editor shown in Figure 5-37. In this dialog box you create patterns by filling in squares. As you can see, you have three grid size options and several pen sizes available. Pen sizes refer to how many squares are filled when you click in the grid. To erase a filled square, click the right mouse button. Figure 5-38 shows a simple pattern I created.

Figure 5-37: Use the Two-Color Pattern Editor to create patterns.

(continued)

STEPS *(continued)*
Creating a Two-Color Pattern Fill

Figure 5-38: Here is a simple pattern created in the Two-Color Pattern Editor.

Step 4. When you finish creating your pattern, click OK.

If your pattern is not displayed on the pattern button, scroll through the pattern palette and select it. It'll be the last pattern in the palette. To delete the pattern, choose Delete in the Pattern dialog box.

Here's how to import a pattern:

STEPS
Loading a Two-Color Pattern

Step 1. In the two-color section of the Pattern dialog box, click the Load button.

Step 2. In the Import dialog box, find the bitmap image you want to make a pattern from and double-click on it. CorelDraw automatically converts it to black and white. (If you want to use part of a graphic, you should cut the section you want to use out of the graphic and save it in a separate file — before you begin this procedure.)

Once you've imported the image, you can adjust the size with the size or tiling options.

Full-color pattern fills

Full-color fills are similar to two-color fills, except they consist of many colors instead of just two. You can use them to fill objects, or as backgrounds, and you can import your own. You access them by choosing either the Full-Color or Bitmap option in the Pattern dialog box. Full-color fills are created from vector, draw-type images; bitmap fills are created by importing paint-type images (or pieces of images that you snip out).

As with two-color patterns, you can adjust the size and placement of the pattern with the small, medium, and large options; or you can adjust the pattern more precisely with tiling. And you can create your own patterns by importing virtually any graphics file.

Using textures

CorelDraw's texture fills, sometimes called *fractal textures*, are bitmaps that work well as backgrounds and as fancy fills for special effects. CorelDraw ships with several textures that you can use in both CorelDraw and Photo-Paint. You can also modify existing textures or create your own.

Each texture has a different set of options and colors, as in the Texture Fill dialog box shown in Figure 5-39. To change a texture, simply change the values in a text box, or click on the desired color button. If an option is locked, as designated by the lock icon to the right of the option, you must click on the lock to unlock it. To save a texture after modifying it, click on the plus button; to delete a texture, click on the minus button (at the top of the dialog box).

Figure 5-39: Use the Texture Fill dialog box to modify texture fills. The options for each type of fill are extensive and different for each texture. Experimenting is the best way to get the right fill.

You can also change any other aspect of the texture with the options on the left side of the dialog box. These options are quite intricate, however. I could write an entire book on using and modifying these controls, drowning in a bunch of techno mumbo-jumbo about which control does what, but that would be boring. Besides, I don't know all the ins and outs of these fills anyway. I usually use them as is, changing only the colors as needed.

Note two important considerations, though. These are tile size and resolution, both of which are controlled from the Texture Options dialog box, shown in Figure 5-40, which you get to by clicking Options in the Texture Fill dialog box. The default 13 dpi for the textures is really only suitable for viewing in CorelDraw. You'll want to adjust the resolution for the task at hand, be it printing or viewing on a monitor. If you don't know what I mean, refer to Chapter 7. What I suggest you do with the tiling option wherever possible is adjust the pixel size to the size of the object you're filling. Otherwise you must rely on CorelDraw's tiling of the textures — many of these types of textures do not tile without obvious seam lines.

Figure 5-40: Use this dialog box to set texture resolution and width.

PostScript textures

CorelDraw ships with several PostScript textures, such as Bars, Basket Weave, and Bubbles. Some of them are quite useful. Note, however, that CorelDraw does not export PostScript Textures to EPS files well, making placing drawings and containing them in other applications difficult, and, at times, impossible. About all they're really good for is printing from CorelDraw. PostScript textures are accessed by selecting the PostScript Fills option on the Property Bar with the Interactive Fill tool active (or by choosing PS from the Fill Tool flyout).

You can adjust the size and patterns of the fills (as shown in Figure 5-41) by adjusting values in the PostScript Texture dialog box. However, because they are not displayed on the artwork on your monitor, getting them right is a trial-and-error process. You'll have to toggle back and forth between Full-Screen Preview and the default window to see the results. The preview window in this version's PostScript Texture dialog box *does* give you a better idea of how your changes will affect the overall fill.

Figure 5-41: Use the PostScript Texture dialog box to edit and apply CorelDraw's PostScript texture fills.

Summary

▶ CorelDraw and other graphics and layout programs support various color models for defining color. The reason for this is the different ways output devices create color. Printing presses and desktop printers, for instance, use percentages of cyan, magenta, yellow, and black (CMYK) to produce color. Computer monitors, on the other hand use an RGB color model.

▶ The human eye, computer monitors, desktop printers, and printing presses all have different limitations (or gamuts) when it comes to defining color. Hence, programs such as CorelDraw provide color management systems to help compensate. CorelDraw uses Corel Color Manager, which relies on profiles of your hardware to help ensure that what you see on your monitor matches what comes out of the printer.

▶ CorelDraw enables you to create and save your own sets of colors as custom color palettes. You can then use the palettes in any of your CorelDraw drawings or documents.

▶ Version 7's new Color Styles feature enables you to create and apply styles to objects similarly to the same CorelDraw feature for graphics and text styles. As with object styles, color styles can easily be copied between templates, and you can create parent-child relationships between styles for easy updating.

▶ CorelDraw's new Interactive Fill tool makes applying and editing fountain fills — which consist of two or more colors flowing, or graduating, into one another — much easier than wading into multiple dialog boxes.

▶ CorelDraw's prefabricated fills, patterns, and textures provide quick and easy ways to create dramatic special effects. You can edit the patterns to suit your needs, and you can even add and create your own patterns to the fill palettes.

Chapter 6

Automatic Special Effects Features

In This Chapter

▶ Perspective

▶ Envelope

▶ 3D extrudes

▶ Blend

▶ PowerClips

▶ Lens

▶ Rotate and Skew

▶ Stretch and Mirror

▶ Bitmap effects

Have you ever looked at a document — flyer, poster, magazine ad — and wondered, *How did they do that?* Often when I see the work of other designers I am awestruck. Nowadays, though, many of the stunning artistic effects are not necessarily the result of great talent. Instead, a lot of amazing effects can be achieved if you can simply recognize what looks good. Computer graphics programs — once you understand some of their hidden power — have literally given almost everybody the power to create spectacular-looking graphics. And CorelDraw certainly excels in providing tools to help designers whip out some dramatic effects — without a lot of art background.

The term *special effects* is a convenient catchall. This chapter is titled "Automatic Special Effects Features" because it covers CorelDraw's automatic drawing capabilities. (Besides, Corel also calls them special effects.) Not only do these features enable you to create special effects, but they also let you perform standard drawing functions — effects that graphic artists take for granted — easily and automatically. Figure 6-1 provides several examples of effects that CorelDraw enables you to perform automatically, without any particular training. You'll find even more examples of various special effects in Plates 6-1a through 6-1f in the first color insert.

Figure 6-1: Here are examples of three different special effects: Envelope (A), PowerClips (B), and Lens (C).

The possibilities provided by the special effects options are nearly limitless. This chapter discusses many of them, but mostly it shows you how to use these powerful features. Once you've learned how they work, you can experiment further with the automatic draw options to create your own effects.

You'll find all six special effects options on the Effects menu, as follows:

- **Perspective** enables you to create one- and two-point perspective views, such as objects appearing as though they recede away from you. Simply drag the nodes on a bounding box, or the dotted box surrounding the object, to change its view.

- **Envelope** enables you to distort and warp objects in almost any direction by dragging on bounding box nodes.

- **Blend** enables you to blend two objects into one. You can also use this feature to create airbrush effects and shading.

- **Extrude** creates 3D effects by extruding multiple planes and surfaces from a selected object.

- **PowerClips** is an incredibly useful masking feature that lets you clip objects inside other objects.

- **Lens** enables you to apply special effects to designated areas. A prime example is to use the magnify option to blow up part of a map or technical drawing.

Once you master these features, you'll have a new toolbox of effects for sprucing up your documents and presentations. In addition to covering these features, this chapter also looks at the bitmap effects options on version 7's new Bitmap menu.

Perspective

This feature is called Perspective because it changes the view of an object. Basically, Perspective enables you to make objects appear to recede away or loom toward the viewer, giving drawings a 3D aspect. You can get a similar effect by rotating and skewing, but not nearly as easily — without trial and error, that is. This feature makes the 3D creation process almost foolproof.

When you add perspective to an object, an eight-node bounding box surrounds it. You then adjust the nodes to change the object's vanishing point. The vanishing point is the place in the background or foreground where the object disappears at the horizon.

In CorelDraw, perspective drawings can have either one vanishing point, as shown in Figure 6-2, or two vanishing points.

Figure 6-2: When you add perspective, you can adjust an object's vanishing point.

To add perspective to a selected object, follow these steps:

STEPS

Adding Perspective to an Object

Step 1. Select the object to which you want to add perspective with the Pick tool.

Step 2. Select Add Perspective from the Effects menu. The object now has a bounding box.

Step 3. You can manipulate perspective by dragging on one of the nodes, as shown in Figure 6-3. As you drag on a node, a vanishing point "X" appears. Move the X to adjust the vanishing point up or down. Depending on where you drag the bounding box's handles or the vanishing point X, your vanishing horizon will move.

Figure 6-3: To move an object's vanishing point, drag the vanishing point X or the bounding box's handles.

Secret

To create a two-point vanishing horizon, drag directly on one of the square handles on the perspective bounding box or the second vanishing point X, as shown in Figure 6-4. (Each object with a perspective assigned to it has two vanishing points, left and right. If you cannot see one or the other, you can bring either into view in your drawing area by dragging on a corner bounding box handle.) Depending on the size and shape of the object you are applying perspective to, you may have to drag on one of the bounding box handles (on the side for which you want) to bring both vanishing point Xs into view.

Figure 6-4: Use the second vanishing point arrow to create a two-point perspective.

Figure 6-5 shows the result of creating a *two-point* perspective on each of two objects (both objects exhibit two-point perspective).

Figure 6-5: For an interesting effect, you can create a two-point perspective.

Envelopes

Envelopes are bounding boxes you manipulate to reshape objects. Envelopes enable you to bend and warp objects in various ways, as shown in Figure 6-6. The possibilities are limited only by your imagination.

Figure 6-6: You can manipulate objects with the Envelope option in many creative ways.

The Envelope roll-up, shown in Figure 6-7, shows four options as icons: Straight Line, Single Arc, Two Curve, Unconstrained Editing.

Figure 6-7: Use the Envelope roll-up to apply envelopes for manipulation with your mouse.

The first three options primarily affect the sides of objects. The fourth option lets you mold the bounding box similar to the way you manipulate points with the Node Edit tool (discussed in Chapter 2). You'll find the fourth option handy for shaping objects to conform to the shape of other objects, such as sculpturing text to conform and fill an outline, as shown in Figure 6-8.

Figure 6-8: You can use the Create From option in the Envelope roll-up to conform objects to selected objects. In this case, the word "Cheese" has been conformed to the shape of the cheese's side.

You can also use one of several preset shapes by selecting the Add Preset option in the Envelope roll-up. Envelopes can be created from individual shapes with Create From, similar to the way you use Copy Style From. An object can have more than one envelope, meaning that you can bend an object one way, assign a new envelope, and bend the object another way, while still maintaining modifications from previous envelopes.

Creating envelopes

Here is a brief overview of using the Envelope feature:

STEPS

Creating and Applying an Envelope

Step 1.   Select the object you want to warp.

Step 2.   Select Effects ⇨ Envelope.

Step 3. Click on Add New.

Step 4. Drag on a node in the direction that you want to distort the object, as shown in Figure 6-9.

Figure 6-9: To warp an object with Envelope, drag on a node as shown here.

Step 5. After manipulating the envelope bounding box square, in the Envelope roll-up, click on Apply. The object warps according to the shape of the selected envelope size.

Depending on the mode you are in when you click Add New, the envelope will behave in a certain way. Figure 6-10 shows how each mode affects the warping of the object. To select a specific mode, simply click on the button representing it in the roll-up. Single Line Mode enables you to warp the object with straight edges. Single Arc Mode warps an object with curved edges on one side of a control node. Curve Mode warps on both sides of a node. And Unconstrained Editing Mode enables you to reshape and envelope in virtually any direction, as with the Shape tool, discussed in Chapter 2.

Figure 6-10: Choosing different Envelope modes results in a variety of interesting effects.

After you apply an envelope, you can apply more envelopes to shape the object further, or you can continue to adjust the existing envelope. When you apply additional envelopes, the previous envelope disappears, but the warp remains.

Secret

Editing envelope nodes is much like editing nodes on an outline with the Shape tool, as discussed in Chapter 2. The nodes on the envelope bounding box work very similarly to Shape tool nodes. In fact, when you double-click on them, the Node Edit roll-up appears, enabling you to set node properties to curve, to line, and so on.

Click Create From and you can use the shapes in CorelDraw's symbols library to contour text and objects to almost any shape you can think of. To do so, get the desired shape from the symbols palette, and then follow the preceding techniques.

Clearing envelopes

If at any point you don't like the effect of your envelope manipulations, you can retrace your steps with Clear Envelope (Effects ➪ Clear Envelope). This command clears one envelope at a time, starting with the most recent and working backward. You can use this command to undo modifications without losing all of them. Clear Envelope is available only when an object containing one or more envelopes is selected. Another option is Clear Transformations, but it removes all modifications, including any other effects, such as perspectives and extrudes. It also removes font attributes, such as typeface and size. So experiment with Clear Envelope to see how it can help you in ways Clear Transformations can't.

Extrude

Extruding an object gives it the illusion of depth. To create this 3D effect, CorelDraw projects points along the edges of an object and joins them to form surfaces. The results are dramatic, as you can see Figure 6-11. You'll find more examples of extrudes in the color insert (see Plate 6-1f).

Figure 6-11: Use extrudes to give flat objects the illusion of depth.

Extrude works best with text and simple shapes. You control extrudes with the Extrude roll-up and your mouse — or, in version 7, with the Interactive Extrude tool. The success of your extrude depends on several factors, including how you set options such as extrude depth, light source, shading, and rotation.

Granted, creating extrudes with the Extrude roll-up is easier than doing them manually, but it's not always easy to get the effect you're after. CorelDraw ships with several predefined extrudes. To see them, simply click on the Extrude Presets button (first in roll-up), and then scroll through the list.

If you have used previous versions of Extrude, you'll get a kick out of the Interactive Extrude tool. When used in conjunction with the Property Bar, the Interactive Extrude tool contains almost all of the options in the Extrude roll-up, as shown in Figure 6-12. The benefit of the Interactive Extrude tool is that most of your changes happen automatically, without your having to click on the Apply button in the roll-up. Also, the Property Bar contains some controls for setting such options as vanishing point angle, page location, and size of the extruded object, with precise values and coordinates unavailable in the roll-up.

Figure 6-12: The new Property Bar (when in Interactive Extrude mode) includes almost all of the options on the Extrude roll-up.

Controlling extrude depth

Extrude depth refers to the length of the extrude planes behind the extruded object. You can control the depth either from the Extrude roll-up or from the Property Bar when in Interactive Extrude mode. When you control extrude depth in conjunction with the Extrusion Type drop-down list, which contains such predefined options as Small Back, Big Back, Back Parallel, and several others, you can dramatically change the size and shape of your extruded planes. You can also adjust the depth interactively with your mouse by dragging the vanishing point X away from and toward the extruded object.

The options for depth range between 1 and 99, with 1 being the shortest depth and 99 being the longest. Figure 6-13 shows the differences you can achieve by changing the depth. These examples are of the Small Back type. They would look quite different if I used a different type.

Figure 6-13: The object on the left contains a small back extrude set at 10. The object on the right is small-backed with a depth value of 99.

When adjusting your planes with Extrusion Type and Depth, you can also determine the vanishing point angle of your extrude. In other words, you change the direction of the 3D angle, making your extrude appear to go to the right, left, above, or below the extruded object. You can adjust these options from the Vanishing Point Coordinate fields on the Property Bar (in the middle), or you can change them interactively with your mouse, by adjusting the vanishing point X, similarly to working with Perspective, as shown in Figure 6-14.

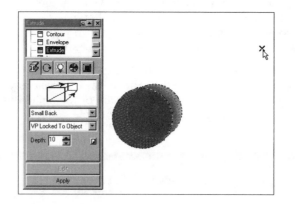

Figure 6-14: You can adjust the vanishing point angle of an extruded object interactively with your mouse.

Rotating extruded objects

Here's a feature that rescues us artistically challenged CorelDraw users — the capability of rotating extruded objects in 3D space. You can pick an object up and move it around — as though you held it in your hands. To do so, click on the Rotation option in either the Extrude roll-up or on the Property Bar. In either case, you'll have to make your rotation adjustments in the roll-up. Figure 6-15 shows the Extrude roll-up in rotation mode.

Figure 6-15: To rotate extruded objects, you can use the Rotation mode of the Extrude roll-up.

You have two options for rotating the object: either by entering rotation values or interactively. To use the first method, click on the icon that looks like a sheet of paper on the right side of the dialog box, and then enter rotation values. I prefer the interactive method, which entails moving the large C-shaped object in the center of the roll-up, as shown in Figure 6-16. It's that simple. As you click and drag on the C, each time you release the mouse button, a dotted replica of the object appears over the original, to show you how your adjustments will affect the object.

Figure 6-16: The left object in this example is a rotated version of the object on the right.

Adjusting shading on extruded objects

When you first start using Extrude, you may not immediately get the effect you expect or want. For example, look at the two extruded objects in Figure 6-17. The top one is an extrude without the shading adjusted, and the bottom is the result of some minor shading adjustments. Shading can be adjusted either from the options on the Property Bar — Use Object Fill, Use Solid Color, and Use Color Shading — or from the same settings in the Fountain Fill dialog box, which you access from the Fill tool flyout. The first two Property Bar options do very little: they simply apply either the fill of the object being extruded to the extrude planes, or some other solid color. These options are more effective when used in conjunction with Lighting, which the next section discusses.

Figure 6-17: Examples of extruded objects with nonshaded (top) and shaded planes (bottom).

The third option is more versatile. Click Use Color Shading in the Property Bar to bring up the Extrude roll-up in Color Shading mode. From here you can assign a From and To color to the extrude fills, further enhancing the 3D effect, similarly to fountain fills discussed in the previous chapter.

Secret

You can set virtually any color you want in the From and To palettes, but you might end up with some rather bizarre shading. My favorite effect is to use the same color in From as the fill in the original object, or the object you've extruded, and then to use white or a light percentage of black in the To palette. This gives the extrude the appearance of 3D shadows.

Secret

Extrudes almost always look better if you add a hairline to them with the Pen tool. The lines delineate the planes. The hairline is the fourth tool on the Pen tool flyout.

Blends

The controls in the Blend roll-up and in the Property Bar (when the Interactive Blend tool is selected) blend one object into another through a series of intermediate shapes. Remember that a blend is a graduation, or gradation, of one object into another. If the blended objects are different colors, the blend steps will also contain intermediate colors. You can specify the number of intermediate steps created and the range of colors blended. You can also fit objects you've blended to a path.

Using blends to create shading

Blending has many applications, but the most common is to create shading, as shown in Figure 6-18 and in the color insert (for example, Plates 6-2a and 6-2b).

Figure 6-18: One of the most useful applications of blending is to create shading. In the flying fish, for example, the shading effect is achieved by blending an object containing the lighter fill into another shape containing the darker fill.

You may be thinking that this feature is a lot like fountain fills (discussed in Chapter 5). In one regard, they are: They enable you to create a fountain fill-like effect with one or more colors graduating into another. However, the difference that makes this feature more appropriate for shading is two-fold: With blends you control the shape of the gradation, and by adjusting the blend steps you have much greater control over how shades are placed.

You create a blend for shading as you would any other, except that the shape and placement of your control objects, or the two objects being blended, is critical to the effect you'll achieve. Notice the cool shading on the lemon in Figure 6-19.

What you can't see in this picture is that blend steps exist between the outer and center control objects. In Figure 6-20, the lemon appears with outlines that show the steps between the outer outline and the final center outline.

Figure 6-19: You can use blending to create cool shading effects.

To achieve a shading blend, you simply draw your outer and inner shapes, and then assign the outer and inner colors. Remember that the two objects do not have to have the same shape. In fact, you'll get a more interesting and lifelike effect if you alter the shapes. You can also control the light source simulation by placing the center, or lighter colored shape, off center, or where you want your light source to emanate from. In the picture of the lemon, for instance, the light source is set at the top center of the lemon.

Figure 6-20: The same lemon in the previous figure with outlines showing the blend steps.

In a blend, the intermediate shapes are dynamically linked, which means you can edit either of the blended (control) objects and the blend conforms automatically. (Note that you cannot blend objects on different layers. Layers are discussed in Chapter 3.) Say, for example, that in the lemon blend you want to change the size or reposition the lighter portion of the blend. All you do is select the control object and manipulate it — CorelDraw conforms the blend to your changes.

Finally, keep in mind that CorelDraw blends objects in the order they were drawn or selected.

Remember

Using the Interactive Blend tool

The Blend roll-up is pretty handy, but not nearly as slick as the Property Bar in Interactive Blend tool mode. You get all the controls of the roll-up plus a whole new range of interactivity, including the capability of creating blends automatically from one object to another, and adjusting the properties of your blends onscreen. The Interactive Blend Property Bar is shown in Figure 6-21.

Figure 6-21: The Property Bar in Interactive Blend tool mode gives you great control over your blends.

The slickest aspect of this new tool is its capability of creating a blend between two closed paths interactively — by simply dragging from one object to another, as shown in Figure 6-22. Simply select the first path with the Interactive Blend tool and then drag to the other path. It just doesn't get much easier.

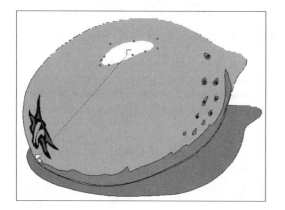

Figure 6-22: To create a blend with the Interactive Blend tool, drag from one object to another.

Now, let's look at the other options available on or through the Interactive Blend tool Property Bar and how they effect your blends.

- **Blend Steps/Blend Spacing:** Use these options to select the number of intermediate shapes you want in the blend. When blending on a path (discussed later), you can specify the spacing between the intermediate shapes. Changing the steps and spacing affects the gradation and the angle of your blends, providing control over light source and other properties

■ **Blend Direction:** Use this option to form an arc or spiral between the start and end objects. Specifying negative values changes the direction of the arc or spiral. Basically, this option rotates the intermediate steps between the two control points, modifying the blend in a circular motion. The problem with using this option when shading is that it actually turns the intermediate objects, which can distort the shape of your image. In most cases you'll want to make very small changes with this setting. You'll have better luck rotating blends used in shading with the Loop option (first button to the right from Blend Direction), which rotates at the halfway point between the two control objects. This can help you change light source without a lot of trial-and-error manipulations.

■ **Direct Blend/Clockwise Path/Counterclockwise Path:** Use these options to specify how colors are blended. If either object has a fill of None, outline colors are displayed. You can blend colors normally with the shortest distance from the start to end colors on the color wheel, or choose a multicolored blend, which blends the colors either clockwise or counterclockwise on the wheel, similar to fountain fills, as discussed in Chapter 5. Rainbow blends can consist of many colors. Use the buttons to blend either clockwise or counterclockwise.

■ **Intermediate Shapes Distribution/Intermediate Color Distribution:** When you blend objects on a path, these options let you adjust the distribution of intermediate shapes and colors. (To blend on a path, select the two objects you want to blend and then click Miscellaneous Options Page, which is the last button on the Property Bar. Select Blend to Full Path. Clicking on this option displays a menu with commands for blending objects along a path. You can edit the path with the Shape tool, and CorelDraw redraws the blend. New Path displays a special mouse pointer for specifying a new path for a blend group. You can also specify a new path for a blend group already blended on a path. Detach from Path separates the blend group from its path.) Now use the Intermediate Shapes and Intermediate Color distribution sliders on the Property Bar. Figure 6-23 shows the results of adjusting these options.

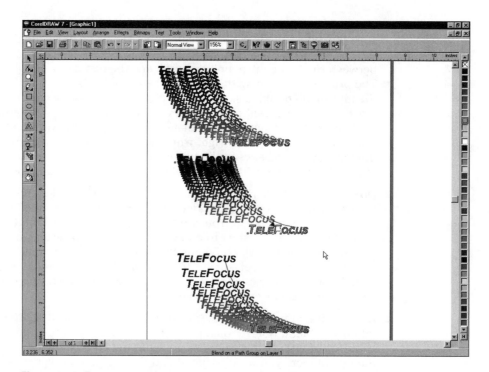

Figure 6-23: Three examples of blending on a path. The first shows default intermediate color and shape distribution. The second shows intermediate shape distribution manipulation, and the third shows intermediate color distribution manipulation.

- **Map Nodes:** An option you should know about on the Miscellaneous Page pop-up is Map Nodes. Use it to make your blends different shapes by mapping them to different Bézier nodes. Selecting this option displays a special mouse pointer for specifying which node on the start and end objects you want CorelDraw to use as the objects' starting node. You can use Map Nodes on an existing blend group or on a new one before blending.

Depending on the fills, some blends may perform differently from what you expect. For a description of how CorelDraw treats different fills, refer to CorelDraw's Help under the Blend roll-up.

PowerClips

Introduced in CorelDraw 5, the PowerClips feature is a great special effects feature that places enormous power at your fingertips. Use PowerClips to paste selected objects into containers, masking out areas of the original object that don't fit into the container, as shown in Figure 6-24.

Figure 6-24: The PowerClips feature enables you to paste objects inside other objects, creating an automatic mask.

In Figure 6-24 I PowerClipped the image of a computer into the letters *PC*. The image shows through only in the areas contained within the letters; the rest of the computer is masked out. The possibilities of PowerClips are limited only by your imagination. Another effect I like to use PowerClips for is clipping text into an object, as shown in Figure 6-25.

Figure 6-25: You can use PowerClip to create all types of effects, such as PowerClipping text into shapes, as shown here.

Lenses

The Lens roll-up contains several lenses that you can apply to objects in your drawings. Applying a lens to an object causes the object to display through the lens. You can only apply a lens to objects with closed paths. Plate 6-3a and 6-3b in the color insert show examples of the Magnify and Tinted Grayscale lenses.

Using the Lens roll-up

Using the Lens roll-up is easy. Simply select one or more objects you want to use as a lens. Scroll through the list of lens effects in the roll-up, and then select the one you want. Depending on the effect you choose, the roll-up provides controls for the effect. Magnify, for instance, supplies a field for setting the magnification level. Tinted Grayscale lets you set the tint color. Transparency lets you set the level of transparency and the lens color, and so on.

In addition to applying basic settings for each lens, you can make several other adjustments from the roll-up, or you can copy a lens, or remove a lens altogether. The roll-up's Frozen, Viewpoint, and Remove Face options help you get the exact effect you want for any type of lens. The first option, Frozen, captures the lens's current contents so that you can move the lens and a copy of the contents beneath it. This is a great feature for creating blowups of portions of maps and technical drawings. The second option, Viewpoint, enables you to use the mouse to change the area covered by the lens. You can move the viewpoint to display a specific part of a drawing through a lens without having to move the lens. The third option, Remove Face, enables you to show a lens only where it covers other objects. In other words, blank areas are not affected by the lens, so that you don't get, say, a tinted lens where you don't need it.

Copying a lens, of course, enables you to make quick duplicates of lens effects for use elsewhere in your drawings.

When working with the Lens feature, remember the following pointers:

- The object (outline or closed path) you use as the lens cannot be a grouped object. You can apply a lens to a group of objects, however.

- When a lens is applied to a group of objects, it is applied to each object individually. You could get some rather bizarre effects.

- Applying a lens to objects on different layers has no effect on the layers.

Choosing a lens

Lenses are powerful features providing for a wide range of special effects. In this section I've provided brief explanations of what each lens does. But to get a good grasp of how each lens actually works, you should create a lens, place it over an object, and then go through the list in the roll-up selecting each type of lens and fiddling with the settings. Let's take a closer look at the following ten lens options:

- **The Color Add Lens:** With this lens, you can mix the colors of overlapping objects. The color you choose in the Color box overrides the color of any object under the lens that is filled with a nonuniform fill. If you place a Color Add lens over an object filled with white, the lens retains its settings; however, the lens color will not display. Basically, this lens lets you tint the objects beneath it with any color (or percentage of a color) you choose.

- **The Color Limit Lens:** Color Limit works similar to a color filter on a camera. It filters out all colors under the lens except the one you specify in the Color box. For example, if you place a green lens over an object, all colors except green would appear filtered out within the lens area. You control the strength of the filter by the value you specify in the Rate box. A rate of 100% lets only green show through. A lower setting lets other colors show through.

- **The Brighten Lens:** Colors under the Brighten lens are brightened by the factor you specify in the Rate box. You can specify a Brighten rate between –100% and 100%. At 100%, the colors approach white. At 0%, the lens has no effect, and at –100%, the colors approach black. You can use this effect for highlighting portions of an image, as shown in Figure 6-26. You can also use this option to correct output brightness. Consider using this lens if one object or area prints too dark or light.

- **The Custom Color Map** lens sets all underlying colors to a color range between any two colors you select in the To and From palettes. You can also choose the progression between the colors. By default, the lens uses a direct route between the two colors. However, you can create interesting effects by selecting the Forward Rainbow or Reverse Rainbow options. These options map colors using a progression that follows a forward or backward route through the spectrum between the two colors you've selected. Areas of the lens that do not cover other objects are filled with the color at the end of the color map.

Figure 6-26: Use the Brighten lens to highlight portions of an image.

- **The Fish Eye Lens** distorts and either magnifies or shrinks the objects behind it, depending on the percentage value you specify in the Rate box. Lenses with positive rates distort and magnify objects by increasing amounts as their rate settings progress from 1 to 1,000. Lenses with negative rates shrink and distort objects by increasing amounts as their rate settings progress from –1 to –1,000. A rate of 0 results in no change to the appearance of objects behind the lens.

- **The Heatmap Lens** changes colors to those in a predefined Heatmap palette, creating a heatmap or "infrared" look. Bright, or hot, colors are mapped to hot colors (yellow, orange), while dark colors are mapped to cooler colors (blue, cyan, red, and purple). The palette rotation value determines where the color mapping begins. For example, a value of 0 or 100% causes mapping to begin at the start of the palette (white), and move to the right (through cyan, blue, and so on). A value of 50% causes mapping to begin halfway through the palette (red) and move to the right and then back to the start of the palette. You'll get some interesting effects from this lens.

- **The Invert Lens:** This lens inverts the colors under the lens to their complimentary colors based on the CMYK color wheel. For example, red becomes cyan, green becomes magenta, and yellow becomes blue.

- **The Magnify Lens:** This lens causes the objects under the lens to be magnified by the factor you specify in the Amount box, creating the illusion that you've placed a magnifying glass over the drawing. The maximum magnify factor is 10. Use this option to blow up portions of drawings and images. See Plate 6-3a in the color insert.

- **The Tinted Grayscale Lens:** Objects under this lens appear as if they've had a tonal scale setting applied to them. Colors under the lens are mapped from the lens color to an equivalent tonal color of that lens. For example, a blue lens over a light colored object creates light blue, while the same lens over a dark colored object creates dark blue. You can use this option to create duotones. See Plate 6-3b in the color insert.

■ **The Transparency Lens:** Colors of objects under this lens are mixed with the lens object's color, creating the illusion that you've placed a piece of transparent film over the object. You enter a transparency rate from 1 to 100% for the lens object in the Transparency Rate box. The greater the value, the more transparent the lens object. At 100%, the lens fill disappears. The color you choose in the Color box overrides the color of any object under the lens that is filled with a nonuniform fill. With the addition of the Interactive Transparency tool, this lens becomes a bit obsolete. The new tool, as you'll see in the next section, is much more adept at creating transparent objects.

Secret

Here's a trick you can use to blow up and call out portions of maps, tables, and diagrams, as the color insert shows in Plate 6-3c. To achieve this effect, you use two lenses, Magnify and Transparency. First, I placed the circle path over the portion of the map I wanted to blow up, and then used the Magnify lens set at x2. I then clicked on the Frozen option in the Lens roll-up, which duplicates the area covered by the lens and pastes it into the mask object, enabling me to move the magnified area anywhere in my drawing. (Note that the Frozen feature works with all the lens effects.)

To create the shaded backdrop, I drew a triangle with the Bézier tool, filled it with a light gray color, and then applied a Transparency lens set at 75 intensity. Voilà! A professional looking blow-up.

The Interactive Transparency Tool

CorelDraw's new Interactive Transparency tool lets you apply uniform, fountain, pattern, or texture transparencies to objects with your mouse for some dramatic effects. You control the direction and position of the transparency using transparency arrows, which you drag across the surface of the selected object. You control the opacity of the beginning and end of the transparency using the Property Bar.

To use this tool, you start by selecting the closed path for which you want to change transparency. The Property Bar takes on the look and feel of the Interactive Fill tool mode (discussed in Chapter 5), except that you are provided with Opacity sliders (Starting Transparency and Ending Transparency) that control the transparency levels of the fill. Starting Transparency controls the more opaque areas in the fill and Ending Transparency controls less opaque areas levels.

Figure 6-27 (Plate 6-4 in the color insert) shows one application for the Interactive Transparency tool. In this example, I simply selected the filled object, assigned it a solid fill, and adjusted the level of transparency with the slider.

When working with fountain fills, discussed in the previous chapter, you can also drag the control arrow across the filled object to control the direction of the fill flow, much like the same feature of the Interactive Fill tool. In addition, you can use the Freeze button (similar to Frozen in the Lens roll-up) to capture the image (or portion thereof) beneath the object containing the transparent fill. This enables you to move the filled object and the captured portion of the underlying object to a new position in your drawing.

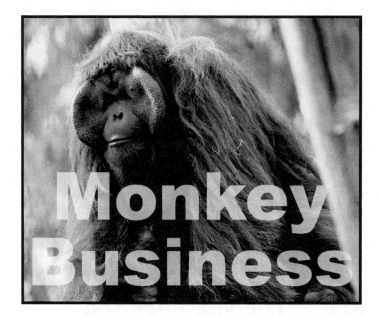

Figure 6-27: Use the Interactive Transparency tool to place transparent fills in objects.

Rotating and Skewing Objects

While it's easiest to rotate and skew objects with the Pick tool (click twice on a selected object to put it in rotate and skew mode), using the Transform roll-up gives you precise control over the amount an object is rotated or skewed by enabling you to enter angles and percentages in text fields. You'll also find that performing the same tasks with version 7's new Property Bar is quite handy.

You can also rotate or skew a copy of an object with the Apply to Duplicate option on the Rotate section of the Transform roll-up, or, when working with the Property Bar, by pressing Ctrl+R (Edit ⇨ Repeat) repeatedly. This procedure works well for creating special effects, such as rotating several copies of an object to create a pinwheel effect, as shown in Figure 6-28. Simply set the amount of angle rotation for the first object, and then click Apply to Duplicate until you have the desired number of copies.

Figure 6-28: Use the Apply to Duplicate option in the Transform roll-up to create a pinwheel effect like this one.

Scaling and Mirroring

The stretching and mirroring options in the Transform roll-up stretch, scale, or mirror (flip horizontally or vertically) selected objects. Use this command instead of using the mouse when you want precise control over the amount of stretching or scaling. Objects are stretched from both sides of their highlighting box. Values greater than 100 shrink them, and values less than 100 enlarge them.

To scale an object, enter equal values in the Scale Horizontally and Scale Vertically boxes. With the Leave Original option, you can stretch or mirror a copy of selected objects, which is helpful for creating shadows and other special effects. While creating a shadow may seem like a simple task, many CorelDraw users don't know how easy it can be with Scale and Mirror. Here's a simple procedure for creating a shadow:

STEPS

Creating a Shadow with Scale and Mirror

Step 1. Create the word or object for which you want to create a shadow, and then enlarge, reduce, or shape it as desired.

Step 2. If it's not already open, open the Transform roll-up.

Step 3. Select Scale and Mirror in the Transform roll-up list.

Step 4. Click on the Vertical Mirror button (bottom of the two buttons on the list).

Step 5. Click Apply to Duplicate. A copy of the original is flipped and placed over the original.

Step 6. Drag the top object down until the bottom of the letters are matched up, as shown in Figure 6-29. To constrain the object so that it moves in a straight line, hold down the Ctrl key while you drag the object down. This ensures that you align objects precisely.

Figure 6-29: Drag the duplicated mirrored object to the bottom of the original, as shown here.

Step 7. Click on the currently selected object to put it in rotate and skew mode.

Step 8. Using the bottom-center arrows, drag to the right or left, depending on the direction you want your shadow to lean, as shown in Figure 6-30.

Figure 6-30: Skew the object by dragging to the left or right.

Step 9. Now you can make whatever changes you want to affect the height and length of your shadow. You can also make it a lighter shade of the same color to give it a more realistic shadow appearance.

Bitmap Effects

Someday, graphics programs may treat vector draw-type and bitmapped paint-type images the same way, eliminating the need for two types of graphics programs. That day is not yet here, however. In the meantime, Corel has added a slew of bitmap editing features to CorelDraw, enabling you to perform all sorts of bitmap-editing wizardry right in CorelDraw documents.

Granted, for the most part, these effects are merely duplications of the same features in Photo-Paint. The benefit of having these features is that you don't have to do your bitmap work in Photo-Paint and then import the images into your CorelDraw drawings and layouts. This really is a time-saver and enables you to make adjustments to your bitmaps based on how they look *in the final document.*

Again, most of the bitmap effects are the same special effects plug-ins you'll find on the Effects menu in Photo-Paint. Plug-ins are covered in Chapter 11. This section here concentrates on the application of bitmap effects in CorelDraw. For a more detailed description of how to use the plug-ins themselves, refer to Chapter 11.

If you understand the difference between vector and bitmapped images (see Chapter 8), you may be wondering why you would want to convert vector images to bitmaps. Yes, vectors are more versatile in terms of scalability, file size, and print times. However, here are some other things to consider. First, if you want to use your images on the Internet or in multimedia presentations, the images must be in a bitmapped format, such as GIF, JPEG, or BMP. Granted, version 7's new Publish to Internet feature (discussed in Chapter 22) will publish an entire CorelDraw page to HTML format, converting the graphics on the page as needed. But if all you need is a graphic, not the entire page, you'll get more utility from Convert to Bitmap (Bitmap ➪ Convert to Bitmap).

Once an image is converted to bitmap format, you can then change its color model (Grayscale, Paletted, RGB, CMYK, and so forth). For World Wide Web graphics, you would use the Paletted option (Bitmap ➪ Convert To ➪ Paletted) to map the colors before saving the image as a GIF file. You would then use Export (File ➪ Export) to save the image to the desired format.

However, electronic publishing is not the only reason you would convert a vector graphic to a bitmap. If you know anything about prepress procedures (discussed in Chapter 7), the following may seem obvious. Sometimes you can get better results on a printing press if you assign different resolutions to certain portions of your documents. In a newsletter layout, for example, photographs can be optimized if you set their resolution separately from the rest of the document. You can do this by converting portions of your document to bitmaps.

When you choose Convert to Bitmap, CorelDraw lets you control resolution (and color depth) during the conversion, from the Convert to Bitmap dialog box, shown in Figure 6-31. You can also use this feature to resample resolution and color depth of existing bitmaps, or images that you import into your CorelDraw documents.

Figure 6-31: Use the Convert to Bitmap dialog box to convert vector objects to bitmaps, or to resample existing bitmaps.

When you convert text and other objects that contain well-delineated edges, such as text, you should also check either the Normal or Super-sampling anti-aliasing option. The difference between the two is that Super-sampling provides optimal edge smoothing.

Summary

▶ Use Perspective to create objects that appear 3D by moving toward a vanishing point. Perspective provides two possible vanishing points, enabling you to create objects that seem to move in two directions.

▶ Use Envelope to warp objects in any way you can imagine. CorelDraw has several types of envelopes that let you create straight-edged warps, curved-edge warps, and even freehand or warps with Bézier control points. You can also apply multiple envelopes, enabling you to apply additional warps to previously warped objects.

▶ Use Extrudes to apply 3D planes to objects, making them appear as though in 3D space. Extrude works well on simple objects, such as one line of text or simple shapes. You can control an extrude's depth, shading, and light source to further enhance the appearance of a three-dimensional object.

▶ Use Blend to blend one object into another. The most common use for this feature is to create shading in drawings and fine art. Controlling various aspects of the blend, such as object shape, blend steps, and acceleration, provides extensive controls over your shading and other blend applications.

▶ Use PowerClips to mask objects inside containers, such as text outlines or simple CorelDraw shapes (for example, boxes, polygons, or stars). This is a great way to create special effects.

▶ Use Lens to place closed paths over objects and then create one of several effects through the container, such as magnify, grayscale, heat lamp, and many others.

Chapter 7

Printing Secrets

In This Chapter

You'll learn the ins and outs of:

- ▶ Resolution and screen frequency
- ▶ Printing on slide recorders
- ▶ Printing on laser printers
- ▶ Printing on color inkjet printers
- ▶ Getting camera-ready
- ▶ Printing color separations
- ▶ Using CorelDraw graphics in your layouts

Each output device — laser printer, monitor, slide recorder, imagesetter — works differently and requires you to prepare graphics in a particular way. Each reproduction device also has its own requirements, as do the media — paper, slides, transparencies, and so on — that it prints on. For example, a grayscale photograph printed on newsprint requires line screens and resolution settings different from those used to print the same photograph on glossy paper.

With this in mind, note that basically graphics reproduction devices can be separated into two types: hard copy and electronic. *Hard copy* is anything you print out — in one way or another. *Electronic publishing* refers to software reproduction, in the form of Web pages, electronic presentations, and multimedia titles. This chapter tells you how to get the best results in reproducing your graphics on hard copy devices, such as laser printers and printing presses. Electronic output is covered in detail in Part IV.

Note

Most of the discussion of graphics output in this chapter pertains not only to CorelDraw but also to all CorelDraw graphics applications, all graphics applications in general, and all DTP applications, such as Adobe PageMaker, Corel Ventura, and QuarkXPress.

The issues involved in going from computer monitor to paper or another hard copy output medium are many, and your knowledge of them determines the success you'll achieve. As we saw in Chapter 5, transferring color from a computer to some other type of medium brings up many issues, such as color shifts, color models, and color management. Being aware of these potential pitfalls is only half the battle. You must also understand several printing and prepress concepts, such as resolution and screen frequency, and several other issues. In this chapter I'll attempt to clear the fog on the road from computer file to printed document, equipping you for a safer trip.

Screen Frequency and Resolution

More than any other variable, screen frequency and resolution play essential roles in how well your graphics reproduce. The purpose of this section is to familiarize you with these terms and to present an overview of their importance. A combination of screen frequency and resolution affects image quality. Resolution is important because it determines the printer's capability of printing higher screen frequencies.

Screen frequency

Screens and *halftones* (these terms are used interchangeably) are percentages of solids. When you tell a program to shade a box at 20 percent, you are creating a screen. Grayscale photographs, where shades of gray are made up of percentages of black, are also screens. So are the percentages of colors that make up a four-color drawing or photograph. Four-color images are created on a printing press by mixing percentages of cyan, magenta, yellow, and black.

Conventionally, halftones are created with a camera. Fine-mesh screens (measured in lines per inch, or lpi) are laid over the object to be *screened*. The mesh separates the image into lines of tiny dots. The size and frequency of the dots determine where the printing press puts ink on paper, thus creating halftones.

Computers and scanners have all but eliminated the need for the fine-mesh screens, but printing presses still work much as they always have. It is important to consider screen frequency when preparing documents for the printing press, for a variety of reasons.

The most important consideration is how ink spreads on different paper types. For example, taking into account the difference in how soft newsprint and coated glossy paper accept ink is crucial. On soft paper, ink soaks in and spreads, running together. Glossy paper is much more forgiving. Ink tends to sit on top of the coating, eliminating much of the spreading.

To compensate, halftones printed on newsprint require a *loose* screen, about 75 to 90 lpi, so that ink dots do not spread together, muddying the image. Coated paper, where ink spread is minimal, works best at 133 lpi or higher so that the coarseness of the screen is not noticeable. The trick is to match the lpi to the paper's absorbency so that as little as possible of the screen's coarseness shows, without degrading the halftone through ink spread.

Another aspect of halftone printing affected by lpi (and resolution) is grayscale. Manipulating screen frequency and grayscale can make a tremendous difference in the quality and clarity of *each* photograph. As we move through this discussion of graphics output, the importance of this relationship between dpi and lpi will become increasingly clear.

Secret

When preparing a document for slide recorders and the print shop, work closely with your service bureau and print shop. Before creating the graphics and laying out the document, decide what medium (or media) the work will be reproduced on (such as paper type, slides, or copier). Then consult your service bureau and print shop regarding the best resolution and lpi settings for that medium. Oh yeah, and don't worry about seeming like a beginner. All professional designers work very closely with their vendors to ensure the best results.

Resolution

Most computer users are familiar with printer resolutions. Hard copy output devices — printers, imagesetters, slide recorders, and plotters — print at various rates of dots per inch (dpi). Most laser printers, for example, print at 300 or 600 dpi. Imagesetters (photo-quality typesetters) print from 900 dpi up to 3,000 dpi and beyond. The benefit of higher resolution is smaller dots. Smaller dots mean more detail and subtleties — sharper lines and curves — and, more important, cleaner halftone screens and photographs.

Calibrating Your Output Devices with Color Management

It certainly makes sense that in desktop publishing, what you see on your monitor should match (as closely as possible) what rolls out of the printer, imagesetter, or printing press. The closer your computer screen matches the completed work, the less guessing you'll need to do. If what you see on your monitor is precise, you save time by avoiding numerous proofs and revisions.

In other words, the computer display should be WYSIWYG, or what-you-see-is-what-you-get. Unfortunately, as any desktop publisher will attest, there really is no such thing as WYSIWYG computing.

However, if all you publish is black-and-white text and monotone graphics, your computer's display does a decent job of representing what pops out of your printer. The problem arises when you work with color. Seldom do the colors on your monitor look the same when printed on a color printer or when you run the print job on a printing press.

The difference arises from the way each device inherently handles colors, making it nearly impossible for them to match. In fact, the same colors look different on each device, and when you move to a printing press, the type of paper the document is printed on also affects how colors appear. These discrepancies have made getting colors right from a desktop system a grueling (and sometimes expensive) proposition, requiring painstaking trial and error and lots of experience. You'll have much better luck if you calibrate your input and output devices, as discussed in Chapter 5.

If you save your CorelDraw drawings in *vector* file formats, which include CorelDraw's native formats and EPS, you don't need to worry much about resolution while creating your documents. These formats are device independent; in other words, they reproduce at the resolution at which they are printed.

However, sometimes it's better to save graphics in *bitmap* format (TIFF, PCX, or BMP) using CorelDraw's export filters. When exporting from CorelDraw, you are given an opportunity during the setup process to select a resolution. After you choose a bitmap format in the Export dialog box (select File ⇨ Export) and click OK, the Bitmap Export dialog box in Figure 7-1 is displayed. From here you can change the dpi in the Resolution drop-down list. You can also set color depth from the Color drop-down list, enabling you to adjust colors for electronic publishing, including such forms as Web pages and multimedia titles (as discussed in Chapter 21). You can also export in a CMYK format, which contains the information necessary for creating four-color separations.

Resolution Controls

Figure 7-1: When exporting bitmaps from CorelDraw, you set the resolution during the export process.

Version 7's Convert to Bitmap option (Bitmap ⇨ Convert to Bitmap) also lets you adjust resolution and color depth without exporting the entire document to a bitmap format, as shown in Figure 7-2. You'll find a number of reasons to convert specific objects inside a CorelDraw document to bitmap format, as discussed in Chapter 6. However, exporting drawings as bitmaps provides much more extensive control over the attributes of the bitmap than does converting objects using Convert to Bitmaps. When exporting bitmaps, for example, you can control not only resolution and color depth but also image size and separate settings for horizontal and vertical resolutions. The importance of setting pixel size for an image is discussed in Chapters 21 and 22.

Figure 7-2: When using Convert to Bitmaps, you can set resolution and color depth.

Printing on Slide Recorders

Slide recorders print documents as 35mm slides. Believe it or not, preparing graphics for slides is easier than preparing them for monitors. For example, you don't have to worry about color depth. Slide recorders can print a wide range of colors.

When using vector, device-independent graphics, don't worry about resolution. The image will print at the highest possible setting. The only type of image you should treat specially is bitmap. The image you see on your monitor is shrunk several times to fit on a slide. Remember that making a bitmap image smaller increases quality.

When scanning or resampling an image for slides, be it a line drawing or a 24-bit photograph, set the resolution to 75 dpi. Higher settings accomplish nothing, except to slow down the slide recorder. If you choose too high a setting, you may overload the slide recorder, causing it to crash. To get the slides to print, you'll have to go back and lower the resolution of the bitmaps.

Line screen and dpi settings for slides are controlled from the Windows printer driver for the slide recorder, which is usually controlled by the service bureau at the time of printing. Actually, when printing slides, resolution or lpi is measured in thousands, or Ks. A 2K slide, then, is 2,000 lines per inch. Slides can be printed at 2K, 4K, 8K, and so on. The higher the K setting, the higher the resolution of the slides. The higher the resolution of the slides, the larger you can magnify the image with a slide recorder without degradation. If, for example, you display 2K slides in a large auditorium with an audience of thousands, your slides will appear rough and jagged. You should set the resolution of your slides according to the size of the auditorium and your audience.

Table 7-1 shows usable slide resolutions for various representative audience sizes.

Table 7-1	Audience Size versus Slide Resolution
Audience Size	**Slide Resolution**
100 to 500 people	2K to 4K slides
500 to 1,500 people	4K to 8K slides
1,500 people or more	8K to 12K slides

Although Table 7-1 provides some guidelines for printing slides, you should also keep in mind the size of the screen and the room where your slides will be presented. If you have no control over placement of the projector and projection size, you'll have to adjust your slide resolution accordingly. Keep in mind, too, that service bureaus charge more as the resolution size increases. An 8K slide can cost more than twice as much as a 2K slide. If you're printing your slides in-house on a desktop slide recorder, chances are it will print at only 2K, or at best 4K (this resolution is set with the printer driver supplied with the device).

Laser Printers

A laser printer is, of course, a common desktop printer that works much like a copy machine. The laser heats spots on the paper, to which toner sticks. A few years ago, they were the desktop printers of choice, until inkjets got so darned good at providing quality output.

Laser printers versus imagesetters

In the early and mid-1980s it was common to use 300-dpi laser sheets for camera-ready art. In 1984, when I first started publishing, I used my laser printer to print text and line art and let the print shop shoot the tricky stuff — screens and halftones. At first, I didn't know I had an alternative. Then I noticed service bureaus springing up all over the place. (A *service bureau* is a vendor where desktop publishers and designers go for output not available at the home office, such as imagesetter film, slides, oversized prints. Today, many service bureaus also create CD-ROMs.) One of them offered to print out a sample document for me, and I was hooked. Service bureaus have machines called *imagesetters,* which are high-resolution output devices for prepress.

A tremendous difference separates 300-dpi laser output from 1,200-dpi (or higher) imagesetter output. Today I use my laser printer primarily for printing proofs. I use a laser sheet for the final output only on occasional small jobs that consist of text and a few rules. As you will see, 300- and 600-dpi printers cannot print screens and halftones very well, especially if you plan to reproduce them. However, the latest generation of PostScript Level 2 600-dpi printers are getting much better at it. Recently, 1,200-dpi laser printers have become more commonplace, and they're coming down in price.

Here is a list of guidelines for determining whether 300- or 600-dpi output is right for your documents:

- Use a 300- or 600-dpi laser printer for black elements only — text, rules, boxes, line art, and so on — not for screens or halftones.

- Use 300- or 600-dpi output for small jobs (less than 1,000 one-page copies). If you are printing 20,000 one-page copies, the added cost (under $10 per plate) of imagesetter output is negligible.

- If the print shop must screen and place very many elements (more than one per page), imagesetter output may turn out to be less expensive than laser output.

- Use 300- or 600-dpi output only if you cannot afford imagesetter output. This is especially true if your newsletter targets the marketing departments of other businesses. Chances are very good that they know and can tell the difference.

High-resolution laser printers

Some laser printers boast 600, 800, 1,000, or even 1,200 dpi. However, these figures can be misleading. Often, the processors in these machines are simply fooled into squeezing more toner into smaller areas. And that's the problem with laser printers in general — they use toner. They spread powder on paper. This process has inherent limitations. The dots are big at any resolution, which restricts their capability of creating halftones.

However, the output from some of them is much crisper and cleaner than that from 300-dpi machines. Edges are smoother, sharper. Screens are tighter. Often this output is quite acceptable. Whether you should use a laser printer for final camera-ready output depends on whether you are pleased with the results. I do not use them for photographs. However, if you have one in-house, and the output is acceptable, that is an entirely different situation.

You should never attempt to use laser printer output for four-color documents. Dot placement is not precise enough.

Setting screen frequency

Whether you use a laser printer or an imagesetter, you'll occasionally need to adjust screen frequency. (Note: The terms *screen frequency* and *line screens* can be used interchangeably.) In CorelDraw, as in many other

Windows applications, you usually set screen frequency through the Windows PostScript printer driver in the Graphics portion of the Print Setup dialog box, shown in Figure 7-3.

Figure 7-3: You can set your line screens from your PostScript Printer driver's Properties dialog box. Most laser printers automatically install the optimal settings.

You can get to this dialog box by selecting File ➪ Print Setup ➪ Properties ➪ Graphics. To change line screens, choose Use Settings Below and type in the lines per inch you want.

What screen frequency is right for your printer? If your printer came with its own Windows driver, the installation program usually installs the driver with optimal screen settings. Notice in Figure 7-3 that my TI Pro 600 is set at 75 lpi. That's because it is a 600-dpi PostScript Level 2 device. Most 300- and 600-dpi Level 1 printers work best when set between 50 and 60 lpi. Imagesetter documents bound for the print shop should be set according to the type of paper planned for the job.

When using spot colors, you can adjust screen frequency for each individual spot-color object. The reason for this is that spot colors are often printed in percentages, or screens (as you learned in Chapter 5). Sometimes it's beneficial to adjust screens separately from the rest of the document. Sometimes, for example, you'll need to adjust screen frequency for paper types.

Printing on different paper types is discussed later in this chapter, under the "Offset Presses" section. Be sure to read this section before printing camera-ready art for the printing press.

In most cases, you shouldn't need to change these settings. If you do, however, get to this dialog box by selecting File ➪ Print Setup ➪ Properties ➪ Graphics.

Laser-printed reproductions

Because of laser printers' resolution and line screen limitations, their effectiveness for reproduction is dubious. Two additional concerns present themselves when you use laser printers for reproduction: expense and cracking.

Expense

Most people think it is less expensive to make copies on a laser printer than at the print shop. Unless your document run is small — say, 100 or 200 copies — this is not so. Toner and laser developer cartridges are expensive, as is wear and tear on your printer. For large runs, the print shop cost (per copy) is small, and it decreases with larger print runs.

Cracking

What would you think if the ink cracked and chipped off your finished documents? Depending on the paper you use, this problem is a distinct possibility. One desktop publisher I know learned the hard way. After paying over $500 for beautiful stone-colored stationery, he discovered that the paper did not hold laser toner. At every fold, the toner fell off, sometimes leaving two or three lines of illegible text. Graphics chipped off as much as a quarter of an inch on either side of the folds. The chipping and cracking were especially embarrassing because the person used the stationery to advertise his desktop publishing business.

One way to avoid this problem is to use paper designed for laser printers. If your local stationer's store does not carry it (most have only white), the store may be able to order some for you.

You should also first test the paper you plan to use for reproduction. Simply print out a page of words and graphics and then fold it several times (or, better yet, wad it up). If the toner cracks, use a different paper. Use laser paper even if you do not plan to fold the document. The reader may fold it, and toner may work itself off in other ways. After all that work your drawings should be durable. They should stand up to time, being passed around, and being thrown into briefcases.

Grayscale images

Just because your scanner, monitor, and graphics package are capable of up to 256 shades of gray does not mean that an equal number of shades will come out of your printer. For example, 300-dpi printers can achieve only about 25 shades of gray, because of their resolution and screen frequency restraints. Their highest screen frequency, before quality degradation, is about 60 lpi. The dots are too big to set screen frequency any higher.

You can calculate what grayscale level an image will print at with this formula:

$$\text{Screen Frequency} = \frac{\text{Printer Resolution}}{\sqrt{\text{Gray Levels}}}$$

In other words, 60 lpi on a 300-dpi printer gives you 25 levels of gray. A number of reasons exist for adjusting shades of gray, the most important being continuous tone quality, or how well graduating shades of gray run together. Other reasons include file size and printing time. The higher the resolution and lpi, the bigger the computer file and the longer it takes to print.

If you set line screens higher than 60 lpi on a 300-dpi printer, the image can become muddied, or blotchy. You can set screen frequency somewhat higher on higher-resolution devices and get improved quality, but for top-quality grayscale images you really should use an imagesetter for final output.

Color Inkjet Printers

Not long ago, you wouldn't see much written about graphics printing on inkjet printers — the output was so poor. However, inkjets have recently come of age. When you use coated paper designed specifically for inkjet printers, the quality is surprisingly good. So good, in fact, that I have used them for promotions for my own graphics design firm.

With that said, these devices still have some serious limitations. You cannot, for example, use the output for reproduction at a print shop — unless, of course, you use a color copier, which can be quite expensive. You can use the printer itself to make multiple copies of your artwork and documents; however, the cost of ink cartridges and the special paper required to get good output makes this solution cost-prohibitive for all but short runs — say, less than 100 copies.

If you use color management (discussed in Chapter 5), however, your colors will print relatively true to what you see on your monitor. And the output is respectable.

Setting resolution for inkjet printers

Most of the newer inkjet printers have two resolution settings, 300 dpi for color output and 600 dpi for black and white. Some claim resolutions of 700 or 800 dpi. When printed from CorelDraw, text and vector graphics print at the highest possible resolution, and bitmaps print at the resolution you set them at. That does not mean, however, that you gain quality by setting your bitmap graphics to 300 or 600 dpi. These devices have the same screen frequency limitations as the laser printers discussed earlier in this chapter. You'll get the best results by scanning and saving your bitmap images at between 150 and 200 dpi for color graphics and at about 300 dpi for black-and-white images. Anything higher simply takes up too much disk space and memory and takes too long to print for little or no gain.

Most of these devices enable you to set print quality with somewhat generic terms, such as "Draft," "Normal," and "Best." You then match the output quality to the type of paper, such as regular copy or printer paper, premium inkjet paper, transparencies, or glossy paper. My Hewlett-Packard 855C, for example, provides some simple but useful controls for controlling output, as shown in Figure 7-4. You'll get the best results by tweaking these settings and matching them to paper you use. What I usually do is use a normal setting and copy paper for printing drafts and then bump up the quality settings and paper type for printing the final outwork. You can get to these settings by clicking the Properties button in the Print dialog box.

Figure 7-4: You can dramatically affect print quality on most inkjets by adjusting settings in the device's Properties dialog box.

The convenience of these types of printers is that they enable you to easily revise and print materials on demand, as needed, a few pieces at a time. I find this a useful and cost-effective way to print occasional proposals, stationery, and other quick and dirty documents as needed, rather than getting multiple copies at the print shop and then throwing a bunch of them away when they're outdated.

Adjusting screen frequency for inkjet printers

Unless your inkjet printer is a PostScript device, you can't really make adjustments to line screen settings, apart from adjusting the print quality as described in the previous section. If your inkjet is a PostScript device, however, you change line screen settings as you do for PostScript laser printers, as discussed earlier in this chapter.

Oversized-Poster Printers

Occasionally, you may benefit from a relatively new class of print devices, the oversized-poster printers, such as LaserMaster's DisplayMaker. Basically, these devices print on continuous sheets 36 inches wide or more, enabling you to create huge posters and murals directly from your CorelDraw files. In effect, these are really big inkjet printers, at least in terms of the resolution and line screens settings you make in your documents.

When you need just a few posters or other oversized artwork, these devices are much more cost-effective than offset printing, and the output is superb. When designing for these devices, you should use the same settings that you would for your desktop inkjet. You should also get color profiles for Corel Color Manager from the printer manufacturer or your service bureau to ensure good color correction.

Getting Camera-Ready

After you complete a drawing, a newsletter, or some other document, you need to make it "camera-ready." Making a layout camera-ready requires attention to detail — fine tuning. This section explains how to successfully transfer documents from your computer to the print shop.

Offset presses

In conventional printing, *camera-ready* means exactly what it implies — creating a layout ready for the printer to take pictures of. The printer then uses the negatives to create metal plates for the printing press. For most print shops, "camera-ready" means no other preparation work is necessary before photographing. If the printer must paste up, shoot halftones, mask, or white-out areas — in short, do anything — you'll incur an additional charge. And you lose control of that part of your layout.

Camera-ready also means having a separate board, or plate, for each color. For example, say your four-page newsletter is black and blue. Your camera-ready art will have eight pages — one for each color on each page. Color separations are discussed in detail later in this chapter. For now, just be aware that they are part of the process of making work camera-ready.

Today, most camera-ready art is created from computer files on imagesetters. Nevertheless, you can still use the conventional paste-up method, and you can adequately reproduce some documents and graphics from laser printer output, especially output from high-resolution laser printers.

Imagesetters versus Printers

Imagesetters are never used as mass reproduction devices. Instead, they are used for printing camera-ready art for an offset printer or for silk-screening processes. Throughout this book the terms *printer* and *imagesetter* are used more or less interchangeably. However, a big difference distinguishes them. Imagesetters are the output devices of choice for desktop publishers and graphics designers. Unlike laser printers, they do not use toner. Instead they use a process similar to photography. The page, a plastic-coated paper (or film), is actually developed in chemicals. The result is higher resolution (because the dots are much smaller). This means cleaner output — crisp and clear lines and type, as well as fine screens and halftones. Also, most laser printers are not capable of hairlines and crisp small (under 10 point) text. Imagesetter output contains finer lines and more detail. Although high-resolution lasers improve subtleties somewhat, they still print dark and are not really capable of hairlines.

Today, several manufacturers make imagesetters, but their output quality levels are comparable. They print at several resolutions from about 900 dpi to over 3,000 dpi. The higher resolution is more expensive and takes longer to print.

Windows 95 supports most imagesetters. The few that are not supported usually supply their own printer driver. Be sure to check with your service bureau to see which imagesetter they use. If a third-party printer driver is required, the service bureau can provide it for you.

When you're making a document camera-ready for an offset printer, you need to adjust the screen frequency appropriately. You should take two factors into consideration: the paper to be used and the camera that the print shop will use to create the negatives.

Compensating for the paper

The most critical issue here is the paper's absorbency. The most significant absorbency factor is whether the paper, or *stock,* is coated — one or both sides treated with a sealant. Many kinds of coatings are in use. For our purpose, the most common are gloss and dull gloss.

Coated stock is less absorbent than uncoated because ink does not seep into the paper's fibers. Instead, it sits on top of the coating. On uncoated stock, the paper absorbs the ink, spreading out the dots. To allow for the spreading, a coarser screen is needed. Use higher screen frequencies for coated stock and lower frequencies for uncoated stock.

Another factor in paper absorbency is softness. Thousands of paper types continue to flood the market. A good rule of thumb is to use lines per inch frequencies from 70 to 90 for newsprint; 90 to 100 for bond, such as stationery; and about 133 or higher for coated or glossy stock. If you need more precision, your print shop should be able to tell you what screen frequency works best for the paper you choose.

Taking the camera into account

If you will be having negatives and metal plates made from your camera-ready output (a necessity for documents containing photographs and screens), consider the limitations of the print shop's camera. If your screens are tight (say, over 120 lpi), some cameras cannot discern the dots, making the image blotchy and ugly. Other cameras, however, can handle such frequencies adequately. Consult the print shop for the best lpi setting for the shop's equipment.

If your final layout will be from a 300-dpi laser printer, have the print shop prepare all images except monotone line art (and, perhaps, some black-and-white drawings, if you are pleased with how they print). The coarse screens and halftones that 300-dpi devices produce may have been acceptable a few years ago, but not today, not with so many high-resolution imagesetters available at service bureaus.

Printing to film

One very powerful alternative to conventional offset printing is *printing to film*. This is exactly what it sounds like — the document comes out of the imagesetter as a negative. The procedure (which is explained in more detail later in this chapter) is not much different from printing positive paper sheets on a high-resolution imagesetter, and the benefits are many. In this section we examine the advantages of printing your documents on negatives.

No matter how good your print shop's camera (and the person operating it) may be, some clarity and detail are lost during shooting. Printing to film ensures the best possible reproduction of your layout (except for, perhaps, full-color photographs, which are still a bit tricky to reproduce on a computer). When high quality and a professional appearance are important, print your layout to film.

Screens and halftones are screened exactly as you set them. When you print to film, you eliminate the possibility of underexposure or overexposure, camera alignment problems, and a number of factors that can be influenced by human error. Once you learn the intricacies of printing to film, you'll find no substitute for transferring print data directly from your computer to a negative.

Printing to film is most advantageous when you need tight, high-resolution screens and halftones for reproduction on coated paper. Imagesetters are capable of much higher line screen frequencies than the cameras used in conventional prepress printing.

Printing camera-ready art

To print in CorelDraw (and other CorelDraw applications), select File ⇨ Print, which opens the Print dialog box shown in Figure 7-5.

Figure 7-5: The Print dialog box is the gateway to a wealth of print options.

Monotone, spot color, and process color printing

Camera-ready art can be prepared as any of three types: monotone, spot color, and process color. Each type requires slightly different treatment.

To print a black-and-white component on a laser printer, simply click OK. You can also choose to print to a range of pages or to print to a file. Notice also the For Mac option. When you select Print To File, For Mac becomes available. This option prepares the print file for processing on a Mac-based system.

To print color separations and control other prepress factors, click the Options button. As you can see in Figure 7-6, this is a very useful dialog box. In fact, it is so powerful that all of its uses are not immediately apparent. Although often you only need to click OK to print a drawing, the process can be a little more complex when you're printing camera-ready art.

Figure 7-6: The power behind CorelDraw's printing options becomes apparent when you look at the Print Options dialog box.

Preparing camera-ready art for the print shop can entail a number of steps, depending primarily on the drawing and the type of reproduction.

If you are proofing on a PostScript laser printer and printing final output on an imagesetter, the first step is to select the correct printer, the paper size, the resolution, and the line screen, for example. If you are printing to a file or making separations, you have several other options to set.

Secret

When proofing a drawing larger than your laser printer supports, you can use the Fit to Page option in the Print dialog box to force the page to fit the current page size, or you can use the Scaling option in the Windows PostScript printer driver Options dialog box.

Printing options

The Prepress toolbar in Print Preview sports several handy options. The *I* icon stands for "file information." When you turn this option on, it prints a message outside the margins naming the file, the print date, and several other bits of useful information, such as whether color management is turned on or off, as shown in Figure 7-7. The icon that looks like a piece of film sets whether to print positive or negative. Remember that negative film is the best way to print in full color. However, my service bureau likes to control the negative switch on the imagesetter, so I don't make my separations negative. Note also that if you are creating art for silk screening (T-shirts, sweatshirts, and so on), your separations should be positive.

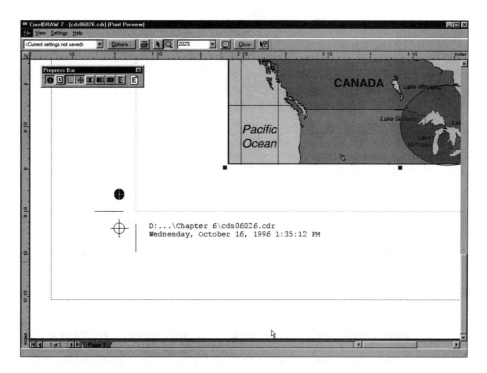

Figure 7-7: Use the *I* icon (at the left end of the Prepress toolbar) to print file, date, and other information on your plates.

The *E* icon lets you set emulsion up or down. Emulsion up is the standard setting for most print jobs.

You may also want to include *calibration bars* for the print shop to use to make sure inks are mixed properly. For color documents, click the color icon below the preview. For grayscale, select the grayscale button. These bars are also helpful when printing to a proofing printer, such as a dye-sublimation printer, discussed later, or when printing color keys, also discussed later. Figure 7-8 shows a page with the calibration bars turned on.

Figure 7-8: Your printer and the service bureau can use these bars to determine whether your colors are printing properly.

Registration marks and crop marks

To ensure that pages are the right size and that they are straight, and to ensure that color separations overlay properly, the print shop will need some guidance: registration marks and crop marks. *Registration marks* are small target-like figures that print on each separation. To ensure proper overlay, the print shop aligns the plates on the registration marks. *Crop marks* are lines in the corners of pages that tell the print shop where to crop (or cut) the pages.

Crop marks are required for almost all offset press runs, including black and white. On letter-sized pages, however, some print shops can use the edges of the laser printout as crop marks. Registration marks are required for color separations. You can access both by clicking either the Preview button or the Options button in the Print dialog box. I prefer using the Preview method, which enables you to see how the registration marks and crop marks will print, as shown in Figure 7-9. To apply crop marks in Preview mode, simply click the third option on the Prepress bar.

Crop Marks   Registration Mark

Figure 7-9: Crop marks indicate the edges of the page. Turn them on from Preview or with Print Options.

For letter-size drawings printed on letter-size sheets, the print shop can use the edges of the paper as crop marks. If the document contains spot color, however, the printer may still require registration marks on separations. If so, you can place them directly on the page. You can draw registration marks and place them in white space at the top, bottom, and sides of the page, as shown in the left margin in Figure 7-10. The printer can mask them out after creating plates.

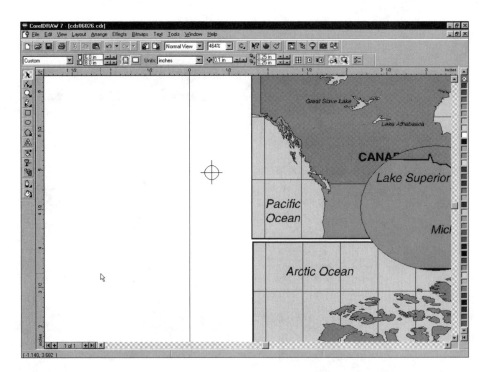

Figure 7-10: When printing spot color pages that are the maximum size your printer allows, you can draw registration marks in blank spaces on your document.

Remember

Remember to place your marks inside a quarter-inch margin. Most lasers cannot print to the edge of the paper.

When your pages are smaller than the printer's paper size, you can use CorelDraw's crop mark and registration mark settings, as long as your drawing is at least one-half inch or so smaller than the actual paper size.

Printing Oversize Pages and Bleeds

When printing pages, especially color separations, to the edge of the paper supported by your desktop printer, to get crop marks you really should take your job to a service bureau for output on oversized paper. For example, if your page is 8½ by 11 inches and you need crop and registration marks, your service bureau can print your plates on oversized, or "extra-sized," sheets. Your letter-sized document would actually be printed on 9½" by 12" paper, making space for crop and registration marks. This is also true of legal (8½" by 14") and tabloid (11" by 17") pages, which should be printed on extra-sized paper to accommodate the crop marks.

Another design element that requires special treatment is bleeds, which is an unfortunate term for documents on which the artwork (ink) runs to the very edge of the paper, such as the cover of this book. To achieve a bleed, you design your artwork so that it runs slightly over the edge of the page, as shown in Figure A. The actual bleed is achieved during trimming. When the print shop cuts the paper, it slices off the portion of the artwork that extends past the edge of the page. This method ensures that you don't get any white slivers on the edge of the paper, a possibility were you to design the page with artwork abutting the edge of the paper.

Your bleed doesn't need to extend far over the edge of the paper; about an eighth of an inch will do.

Figure A: When designing pages on which the artwork extends to the edge of the paper, place the art so that it slightly overlaps the edge.

Working with a service bureau

Not so long ago, desktop publishing service bureau operators hated to work with non-Macintosh users. "Oh," they would say dourly, "you use *Windows*," as if it were some kind of disease. For a while I was the only desktop publisher in my area who used IBM-compatible equipment. Everybody else used Macintoshes. Today, many people use IBM-compatible electronic publishing stations. But most service bureaus still lean toward Macintoshes.

This section explains how to prepare your documents to be printed on a high-resolution imagesetter. Different service bureaus have different requirements as to how documents should be prepared. Some service bureaus can print directly from CorelDraw or your layout program. Others require you to print to a PostScript file. Similarly, some service bureaus have a large inventory of fonts available, whereas others require you to include the fonts with your documents.

You will need to find out what your service bureau's particular requirements are. Often, all you need to do is call up the service bureau and say "I want to bring in a CorelDraw file for output." The service bureau personnel will tell you what format they prefer.

Before taking any of the following steps, call your service bureau. Ask them what type of imagesetter they use, and find out whether the fonts you use (all of them) are available. If Windows does not ship with a Windows printer driver for the imagesetter, ask the service bureau to supply you with the proper printer driver. If you are using fonts other than Adobe Type 1 PostScript fonts (those included with the CorelDraw package are Adobe

Type 1), you should also find out if the service bureau has the same brand (such as Bitstream, Z-Soft, and TrueType).

Configuring your printer setup

When working with a service bureau, keep in mind that you are actually creating your document on one computer and printing from another. In this situation, you may need to compensate for the configurations of the different devices.

Adding printers in Windows

In order to use a printer, you must first install it from Printer Setup or from the Printers dialog box. You can get to Printers from the Windows task bar (Start ➪ Settings ➪ Printers). To further modify or adjust a printer's settings, you can get to Printer Setup from the Print or Print Setup commands in almost any Windows application. Use the Printers dialog box's Add A Printer icon to create separate printer definitions for each printer. Use Printer Setup to switch printers from within an application or during a printing session.

Adding a printer is not as complicated as you may think. Figure 7-11 shows the Printers window, which you access from the Settings submenu on the Windows Start menu. You begin all printer installations from here by clicking the Add Printer icon, which invokes the Add Printer Wizard. Now simply follow the step-by-step directions. In most cases you'll set the printer port to LPT1; however, if the service bureau does not support CorelDraw (or your version of CorelDraw), you'll want to direct the printer's output to a file, as explained later. (You can also change the printer's port from Print Setup after it's installed.)

Figure 7-11: Use the Printers window to install a printer.

Printer drivers

A *printer driver* is software that intermediates between an application and a printer. Basically, it translates the document into code the printer uses. Hundreds of printers divvy up the market, and Windows 95 and Windows NT ship with many different printer drivers.

Windows defines all of its PostScript drivers in one file, PSCRIPT.DRV. This makes it easy to switch between the different PostScript printers.

Printing to a file

After adding a printer, you'll need to tell Windows where to send the data. If the document will be printed on a printer located at the service bureau, you should send the data to a file. You can do this using the Add Printer Wizard by selecting File as the port. (See Figure 7-12.) Then you can give the service bureau a self-contained PostScript print file.

Figure 7-12: If your service bureau does not support CorelDraw (or your version of CorelDraw), you can set the printer's output to a file.

If you did not set the output to File during installation, you can do so during printing from the Print dialog box from within CorelDraw. Simply select Print to File in the Print dialog box, as shown in Figure 7-13. If you are taking the file to a service bureau that uses only Macs, be sure also to click the For Mac option. Now when you click Print, you will be prompted to name the print file.

Figure 7-13: You can print to a PostScript print file by choosing the Print to File option in the Print dialog box.

If your document contains fonts not supported by the service bureau, you should also go to the Options portion of the Print Options dialog box (File ⇨ Print ⇨ Options ⇨ PostScript Preferences) and make sure that the Download Type 1 Fonts and Convert True Type to Type 1 checkboxes are selected. (See Figure 7-14. If you don't know the difference between these two types of fonts, refer to Chapter 4.) This will ensure that the proper fonts are printed when the service bureau runs the file.

Figure 7-14: Use the PostScript Preferences dialog box to download fonts if the service bureau does not have them.

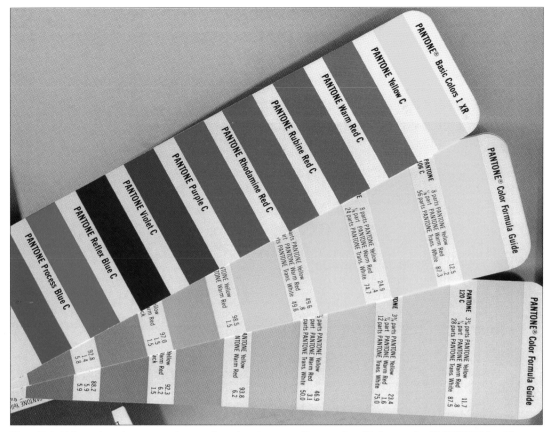

Plate 5-1: When choosing spot colors at the print shop, you'll more than likely use the PANTONE Matching System swatch book. This is a precise way of choosing premixed spot colors. You should use this method rather than relying on your monitor.

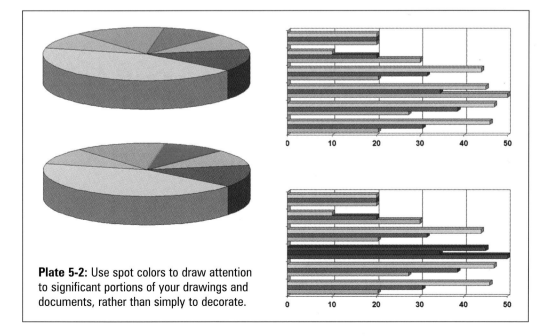

Plate 5-2: Use spot colors to draw attention to significant portions of your drawings and documents, rather than simply to decorate.

WestNet News

Resource Management News for Our Clients and Friends

Human Resource Management Consultants

1155 Port Avenue, Culver City, CA 92800   July, 1997 - Vol. III   Tel: 805-240-1188, Fax: 805-240-1189, AOL: sjenson

Team Conflict: Taming the Savage Beast

What to do when your crews become unruly.

The federal education loans and grants Sue received while in college should have been enough to help her live and study in reasonable comfort--but she spent far too much on alcohol.

Sue started drinking when she was 16. She drank moderately at first, only on weekends, usually. This pattern followed her into college, where she continued to drink only on those nights when she didn't have school the next day. Sometime in her senior year, she started drinking during the week.

One year after she got out of col-

lege, Sue got married. Marriage, her two children and a career as a medical technician in a major California hospital was nothing like what she had expected--by the second year she was drinking every night and having a couple of drinks during her lunch breaks.

By age 25, Sue was spending hundreds of dollars a month on alcohol. But she didn't even suspect she had a problem. She began coming

When your work team gets out of hand, it seems like an impossible beast to tame.

in late to work, making a lot of mistakes, and sometimes not showing up at all. Her dulled senses and negative

If They Would Just Grow Up

How to handle immature employees

Ask Mike Lusk, Regional Sales Development Manager for Allstate Insurance, what he attributes his company's success to, and his answer is simple--traditional values. Allstate, both locally and worldwide, practices the concepts of service, value and community involvement, and it has paid off. From the writing of their first policy in 1931, the company has done nothing but prosper. According to Lusk, customer satisfaction are responsible for Allstate's tremendous growth.

Part of the reason for Allstate's enormous success can be found in its roots. Allstate Insurance is the brain child of General Robert E. Wood, who was the president of Sears & Robuck Co. in 1931. Allstate is a member of the Sears Financial Network. However, big companies do not always do well just because they are big. Allstate's growth is due primarily to the company's attitude toward its customers and a sense of civic duty.

The Allstate mission statement is:

Few things are less frustrating than an immature team member.

a

WestNet

Human Resource Management Consultants

b

Our Global Team

Australia
Decision Dynamics
61-2-442-232 (Telephone)
61-2-442-235 (Fax)
randsag@ibm.net

Canada
PMB. Consultants
416-425-6624 (Telephone)
416-425-2832 (Fax)

Mexico and Latin America
Quest
1-714-581-9478 (Telephone)
1-714-581-9456 (Fax)

US
West Net
Tel: 805-240-1188
Fax: 805-240-1189
AOL: sjenson

Helping People With People

WestNet
1155 Port Avenue
Culver City, CA 92800

Bulk Rate
U.S. Postage
Paid
Permit #2043
Culver City, CA

Helping

People

With

People

WestNet

Human Resource Management Consultants

c

Plate 5-3: Rather than cluttering up your documents with random color, instead use color to direct the reader's eyes to specific portions of the page. In newsletters (a) and letterhead (b) you can use color to call out the newsletter name and company logo. In brochures (c), use color to label information, making topics easier to find.

Plate 5-4: Use color in longer documents to mark the beginning of each section to help readers find material and stay oriented. Use color to highlight section numbers, to distinguish individual sections, and so on.

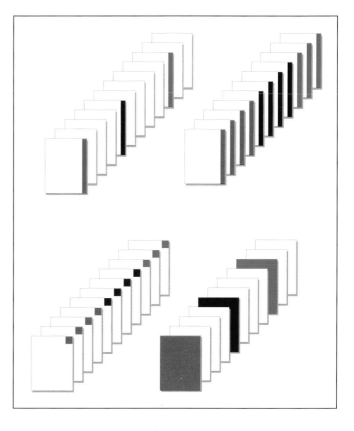

Plate 5-5: Sometimes called "poor-man's color," different percentages or *tints* of spot colors create the illusion of multiple colors. In the pie chart, for example (a), the various tints make it seem as though several different colors are in use, rather than just one. When using black and a spot color, as in this annual report cover (b), you can use percentages of both colors, widening your range of color options.

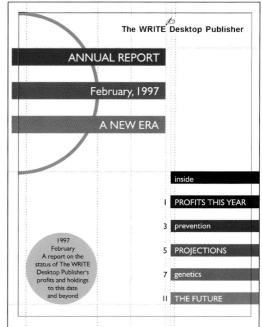

a

b

Plate 5-6: This graph shows the vast differences between what colors the human eye can see and what color devices are capable of reproducing. Notice that process printing presses have the most severe limitations.

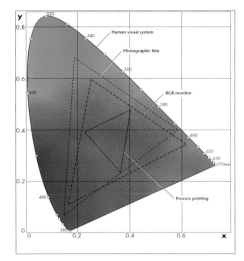

Plate 5-7: Use color in your charts to draw the viewer's eyes to the most important element on the chart.

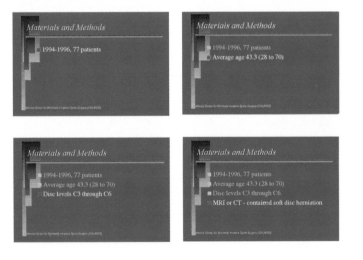

Plate 5-8: Use bright colors to bring in new points and dull (dim) colors to play down points you've already introduced (a). You can also use the build effect with charts, enabling you to talk about one group of data at a time (b).

a

b

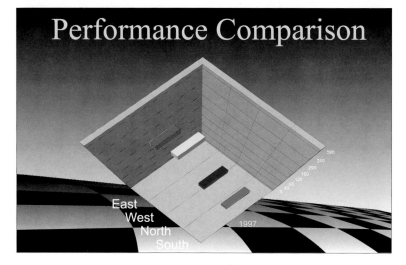

c

Plate 5-9: Use the same colors for related data. If, for example, you want to show trends for a certain department throughout your presentation, use the same color each time you display data for that department (compare a, b, and c).

Plate 5-10: Examples of how the straight (top), clockwise (middle), and counterclockwise (bottom) options affect fountain fills.

Plate 5-11: Here are a few example of effects you can achieve with fountain fills and extrude.

Plate 5-12: These examples show how changing a fill angle can affect the look of your drawing. The angles shown here are 90º, 180º, 270º, 360º, and a radial fill at 90º.

Plate 5-13: With CorelDraw's textures and patterns, you can create custom art with just a few mouse clicks. From two-color to full-color patterns to fractal textures, literally thousands of options are available from which to choose.

Plate 6-1: Here are some examples of what you can achieve with special effects: Envelope (a), PowerClips (b), Lens (c), Perspective (d), and Blend (e).

a

b

c

d

e

Plate 6-2: Examples of shading achieved with the Blend feature. Notice the highlights in the fish's back, the dog's legs, and at the top of the circle in the New Year's design — each achieved by blending two different-colored objects.

Plate 6-3: You can use lenses to highlight and call out portions of your drawings. In this example, the Magnify lens (a) zooms in on a portion of the map. The Tinted Grayscale lens (b) highlights a specific area on the map. In addition, you can use two lenses, Magnify and Transparency, to call out portions of a map (c). This third example shows the power of Lens. The circle path over the portion of the map uses a Magnify lens set at x2. The Frozen option in the Lens roll-up is selected, which duplicates the area covered by the lens and pastes it into the masking object. You can move the magnified area anywhere in the drawing.

a

b

c

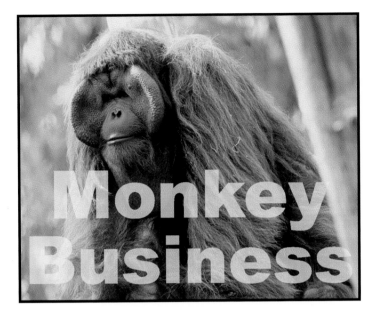

Plate 6-4: Use the Interactive Transparancy tool to place transparent fills in objects. Transparencies created with the Interactive Transparency tool give the appearance of placing tinted film over an object, making the transparent object seem opaque.

Plate 7-1: Unless you knock out the dark color under the light color, the dark color will show through.

Plate 7-2: When printing light colors over dark colors or two overlapping light colors, you can avoid unsightly gaps from press misregistration by trapping. In this example, I have changed the trap to red so that you can see it.

Plate 8-1: You can create a variety of images with Photo-Paint. Here, a plug-in helped create the planing effect on the Statue of Liberty (a). Elements from two different pictures were combined to create the image of the hands and globe (b). The screen capture depicting Advanced Teamware's Web page contains several different effects you can achieve with Photo-Paint (c).

Plate 8-1a

Plate 8-1b

Plate 8-1c

Plate 8-2: This embossed photograph shows an example of an artistic image created with Photo-Paint.

Plate 11-1: An example of the kind of effect you can achieve with the third-party plug-in from MetaTools, Kai's Power Tools. The tiling effect was achieved with KPT Planar Tiling. The multiple curling was done with KPT Page Curl.

Plate 13-1: "Chess Wars"

Plate 13-2: "Alien Visitors"

Before printing to a file, be sure to also check the proper separation and printer mark settings, as discussed in the section named "Color Separations" later in this chapter.

Secret

If you have a desktop PostScript printer, you can ensure that the file prints properly by copying the file to your printer — which is essentially the same thing your service bureau does with your print files. To copy a PostScript print file to your printer, follow these steps:

STEPS

Copying a PostScript Print File to Your Printer

Step 1. In Windows Explorer, find the print file you created from CorelDraw.

Step 2. Right-click on the file.

Step 3. From the pop-up menu, select Copy.

Step 4. Scroll in left window of Explorer until My Computer is visible, then double-click the icon to open My Computer.

Step 5. In the right window of Explorer, double-click Printers to open the folder.

Step 6. Right-click on the PostScript printer to which you want to copy the file.

Step 7. Choose Paste from the pop-up menu.

Windows copies the file to your printer and the document prints, enabling you to check your separations, and to make sure fonts and printer marks print properly. (Printer marks are discussed in the "Color Separations" section that follows.)

Note

You have a number of different ways to set up a print file. This is the method I use because I find it to be the most convenient.

Getting your files to the service bureau

If the service bureau has a PC with your program installed, and the fonts you use, it can print your documents directly to an imagesetter from the original document file. If the service bureau does not have your program or fonts, you should print your document to a PostScript print file, as explained earlier.

I prefer this latter method, because I maintain control — and my service bureau gives me a 20 percent discount. The one drawback is that if for some reason your file doesn't print, the service bureau can't do much to help. In most cases either a PostScript print file prints or it does not. With document files, the service bureau can open a document and try to figure out why it does not print.

However, print files tend to be huge, often much larger than will fit on a conventional 1.44MB floppy disk. In these situations you will need some kind of removable medium, such as a SyQuest or Iomega Zip drive, to transport your files to the service bureau. You should check with your service bureau to see which devices they support before investing in a removable drive. (Removable media are discussed in Chapter 23.)

As an alternative to removable media, most service bureaus have electronic bulletin board services or Web sites to which you can transmit your files via modem. If that is the case, you'll probably want to compress the file using some kind of compression utility. The most common are PKZIP and WinZip.

Quick press reproduction

Many cities have small "quick" or instant press print shops. What usually makes them quick is they don't use the negative and metal plate method on their printing presses. Instead, they use *paper* plates, eliminating a few steps. In some cases, this can be a little less expensive. The paper plates reproduce halftones and screens much better than a photocopier, but not as well as metal plates.

This process is good for short press runs that do not require the highest quality. For longer runs, the cost of the negatives and plates used in the more conventional method becomes negligible, because the per-copy price drops substantially as the quantity rises. A major cost factor in printing is the number of *passes* (times paper runs over the press) required. Quick presses tend to run small sheets, increasing the number of passes. Large presses use large sheets that hold several pages, decreasing the number of passes. Many of them can also print more than one color at a time, further eliminating additional passes.

If you want the final document to reproduce your camera-ready art as closely as possible , use the metal plate process, which requires film, from either your computer or your print shop's camera. As you know, in the conventional process, the print shop shoots negatives and uses them to "burn" plates for the press. These extra steps cost a little more (from $10 to $20 per plate), but you gain substantially in quality. Screens and halftones reproduce clearly. Small type and fine lines print crisper and cleaner. You will be more pleased with the results.

If your document requires a large press run (say, more than 1,000 copies), look for a volume print shop with a large press. You will save money on the number of passes. Once, on a 9,000-copy press run, I found a $3,000 price difference between a quick press shop and a volume printer.

Color separations

As you saw in Chapter 5, you have two basic ways to print color on a commercial printing press: using spot-color inks or process-color inks. When you use color in your documents, print shops often require a separation for each color used. This process is not always as straightforward as it seems. This section looks a little closer at preparing your documents for the printing press.

Both processes — spot and four-color — have slightly different requirements. We will look at spot color first.

If your final layout will be printed on an imagesetter, print the separations on a laser printer first. Make sure that each of the colored elements is on the right plate.

Preparing spot color documents

Spot color differs from process color in that instead of mixing inks to get colors, the printing press uses premixed ink in the desired color. This approach poses some special problems, especially in printing one spot color over another, such as in logos, or, say, newsletters with sidebars and announcements in colored boxes.

Knockouts

Printing spot separations in graphics and layout software works fine, except when colors overlap. Depending on the colors involved, a solution can be tricky. When printing a light color, such as yellow, over a dark one, such as black, the black will show through — unless you create a *knockout*. Because the black shows through the yellow, discoloring it, you do not want black ink directly under the yellow ink. A knockout is white space, or paper (rather than ink), in the area where the top color will print. Color Plate 7-1 illustrates a knockout. Notice that no black ink prints where the yellow overlaps.

A problem occurs only when you have a lighter color over a darker one. You can, for example, print black over almost any color without the color showing through. And overprinting, or printing one spot color over another, works just fine for several other color combinations. No hard-and-fast rule exists here. The best approach is to check with your printer before trying to overprint colors.

Knockouts are very important when you are working with screens and halftones. You cannot put any color behind a grayscale halftone without a knockout.

By default, CorelDraw automatically knocks out overlapping spot colors, which is good, but this feature poses another problem — the possibility of press misregistration, which you eliminate by trapping, as discussed a little later in this chapter.

Overprinting in CorelDraw

Although CorelDraw automatically knocks out overlapping colors, sometimes you'll get better results from overprinting.

You can tell CorelDraw to overprint using the right mouse button Overprint Fill menu option, shown in Figure 7-15. Simply select the object you want to overprint, click and hold the right mouse button, and then select Overprint Fill. If the object has an outline, you should also select Overprint Outline.

Figure 7-15: Overprinting is controlled from the right mouse menu pop-up.

Secret

You can tell CorelDraw applications to overprint all black objects by choosing Always Overprint Black in the Separations area of the Print Preview dialog box. This saves time by eliminating the need to set all black items in a drawing to overprint. Follow these steps to set Always Overprint Black:

STEPS

Setting the Always Overprint Black Option

Step 1. Click File ➪ Print Preview.

Step 2. Click Settings.

Step 3. Click the Separations tab.

Step 4. Enable the Print Separations checkbox.

Step 5. Enable the Always Overprint Black checkbox.

Always overprinting black creates a color trap (see the section on "Trapping" that follows) by causing any object that contains 95 percent black (or more) to overprint any underlying objects. It is a useful option for artwork containing a lot of black text, but it should be used with caution on artwork with a high graphics content. If your service bureau recommends a black threshold value other than 95 percent, click the Options tab, choose Overprint Black Threshold from the Special Settings Option list box, and change the setting as required.

Trapping

The problem with knockouts in graphics software is that they are too precise. They knock out exactly the overlapping areas. Printing presses, on the other hand, do not register precisely; that is, they do not print in exactly the same place on each piece of paper. As paper passes through the press, it stretches and moves slightly. Most presses register to within .005 of an inch. This may not seem like much, but it is enough to leave undesirable white gaps between two colors. So if, for example, you are printing yellow text inside a black box, some of the copies will have noticeable white lines between the colors.

To ensure that knockouts print without registration gaps, you should trap them. A *trap* is a small outline around the darker element that prints over the lighter one. It compensates for the press's lack of accuracy. Color Plate 7-1 in the color insert shows an example of a trap. In CorelDraw you can create traps in several ways. Creating a trap is easy: simply use the Outline Pen tool to create .005-inch outline around the object being trapped, and then change the color of the outline to the color of the object being trapped. Next, from the right mouse button pop-up, choose Overprint Outline.

Secret

Until you've done it a few times, you may find trapping to be a little tricky. But you don't have to do it yourself. You have four options: you can take your drawing file to a service bureau that supports CorelDraw and let the technician there do the trapping. Or if your service bureau uses Macs, export the drawing to Adobe Illustrator 3.0 format (select File ➪ Export) and provide it to the service bureau for a technician to trap. (If your service bureau uses CorelDraw Macintosh, save the file as a CorelDraw 6.0 file.) Your third option is to print the drawing to a file and let the service bureau use its automatic trapping software to do the trapping.

Warning

One word of caution, though — if you export to Adobe Illustrator format, be sure to convert your text to curves (as described in Chapter 7). The service bureau's Macintosh system probably will not have your CorelDraw fonts installed.

Additionally, you can tell CorelDraw to automatically trap objects. Here's how:

STEPS

Automatically Trapping Objects

Step 1. Click File ⇨ Print Preview.

Step 2. Click Settings.

Step 3. Click the Separations tab.

Step 4. Select the Print Separations checkbox.

Step 5. Select the Always Overprint Black checkbox.

Step 6. Select the Auto-Spreading checkbox.

Choose either to type a maximum trap value or always to use a fixed trap amount. When you use the Maximum Trap Value option, the size of the trap assigned to an object depends on the maximum trap value and the object's color. The lighter the color, the larger the trap. The darker the color, the smaller the trap. If you want the spread width to be fixed, then enable the Fixed Width checkbox. The Maximum Value box changes to the Width box when you select the Fixed Width checkbox. Use this box to set the width of your traps.

I prefer using fixed traps rather than letting the software determine the size of the trap. If you choose fixed traps, call your print shop to see what size traps they recommend. Keep in mind, though, if you set this value too low, small text may be illegible when auto-spreading is applied. And some small objects may be distorted. In fact, that CorelDraw tries to trap everything in the document is a good reason to exercise extreme caution when using fixed traps.

Note

You can also set Always Overprint Black and Auto-Spreading when exporting to EPS format. Simply select them in the Auto-Trapping section of the EPS Export dialog box.

Process (four-color) color separations

CorelDraw has the power to do terrific process color separations, especially when you use the color management system, Corel Color Management, discussed in Chapter 5. In process-color printing, the printer uses four translucent inks — cyan (C), magenta (M), yellow (Y), and black (K) — to reproduce colors. By printing different sizes and combinations of CMYK ink dots close together on a page, the printing press simulates hundreds of different colors.

If the dots are positioned properly, the result is a rosette pattern that helps to create the color illusion. If the dots are off even slightly, an unsightly moiré pattern prints instead, breaking the color illusion. Halftone dots also vary in size — small dots are used to print lighter areas, and larger dots, to print darker areas. In the final printed piece, your eye uses the dots to perceive dozens of different colors.

Don't take my word for it. You can see what we're describing by picking up any magazine and flipping to a color photograph. If you look very closely at the color photograph (you may even want to grab a magnifying glass to help), you will notice small dots of color that make up the image. Up close, those dots look like cyan, magenta, yellow, and black dots. From a distance, though, your eye merges those colored dots to perceive a simulation of the range of colors from the original photograph.

Prepress tools

Corel Color Management, discussed in Chapter 5, is not so efficient that it eliminates the need for conventional prepress tools, such as color proofs, color keys, and press checks. These traditional devices are often still required to make the transition from screen to paper. They can help you, your service bureau, and print shop professionals to get the desired results. You should know, however, that CorelDraw provides most of the tools you'll need to correct these and other problems.

Color proofs

Color proofs assure you that the colors you see on your monitor match the data sent to the printer or imagesetter. The best color proofing device is a dye-sublimation printer. Your service bureau probably has one. If the colors in your dye-sublimation printout look right, you're well on your way to good reproduction.

Color keys

Color keys are created from the final separated film you give to the print shop. For an additional fee (usually about $60 per full-color page), your service bureau or print shop can create a key consisting of acetone sheets, one sheet for each separation plate. When the four clear plates are overlaid, you get a very good representation of how the final page will look.

Press checks

A press check is the only foolproof method for getting the results you desire. This is exactly what it sounds like. The print shop sets up the press, runs off a couple of copies, and invites you to check the colors. Some print shops charge for press checks. Some shops do the checks themselves, comparing the copies to the color key.

Whether you use one or all of these methods, once you get the output in hand, your service bureau or print shop professional should be able to tell you what adjustments you need to make. As any graphics designer will tell you, the only way to get good four-color processing is through communication with all the parties involved.

Printing CorelDraw Graphics Using Other Applications

The concepts covered in this chapter are also important when you import CorelDraw graphics into other applications, such as PageMaker or WordPerfect. Resolution and screen frequency settings are just as important in a PageMaker layout as they are when printing from CorelDraw. The overprinting and trapping concerns also remain. To get spot and process color separations, you must print from an application that supports these features. The application must also be capable of separating imported graphics, which few layout applications can do. (As of this writing, no word processors support color separations.)

Note

Many of the settings you choose in CorelDraw are maintained when you import them into other applications. Screen frequency settings, traps, and overprints that you set in CorelDraw, for example, are maintained when you export to an EPS file and then import the graphic into a Ventura Publisher layout. You should note, however, that it is necessary to use EPS format — no other.

Size, color, and resolution settings made in CorelDraw, CorelDream 3D, and Photo-Paint are maintained when exporting to bitmap formats, such as PCX, TIFF, and BMP. However, layout programs do not separate all bitmap formats. In most cases you'll need to export as a CMYK TIFF, although some layout programs do have the capability of converting other formats. PageMaker, for example, can convert RGB TIFFs to CMYK, and it can also separate Photoshop files.

Check out compatibility issues before you attempt to print with a layout or word processing program.

Summary

▶ In offset press printing you should note two important settings: resolution and screen frequency. Resolution refers to the dots per inch of an image, and screen frequency refers to the lines of dots per inch. Getting the optimal reproduction results requires a balance between these two settings.

▶ When printing to slide recorders, remember to keep the resolution of your graphics low, about 75 dpi. Slide resolution and line screens call for settings such as 2K, 4K, and so on.

▶ When printing on laser printers, keep in mind that they have limitations in respect to screen frequency, thereby limiting the number of shades of gray they can print. Remember too that laser printer output does not always reproduce well on a printing press and you can never use it for four-color separations.

▶ When printing on color inkjets, match graphics quality to paper quality through the Properties dialog box, and keep in mind that printing multiple copies on an inkjet can be expensive.

▶ Camera-ready art is artwork ready for the print shop or service bureau to create negatives from with their camera. Nowadays, many designers go beyond camera-ready by printing to film.

▶ When printing color separations, you will often find it necessary to knock out and trap your colored objects to avoid discoloration and press misregistration snafus. When printing process separations, be sure to use Corel Color Manager, and take advantage of the other proofing tools at your disposal, such as dye-sublimation proofs, color keys, and press checks.

▶ When you are using CorelDraw graphics in your layouts in other software programs, many of the trapping, knockout, and other separation issues remain relevant.

Part II

Supporting Applications

Chapter 8

Corel Photo-Paint

In This Chapter

I'll go over some of the basics about Corel Photo-Paint and introduce you to some little-known facts and features of the program. You'll learn:

▶ What you can do with Photo-Paint

▶ Managing raster format versus vector images

▶ Navigating the Photo-Paint interface

▶ Basic image-editing techniques

What Is Corel Photo-Paint?

Corel Photo-Paint is a powerful image-editing tool that functions along the same lines as Adobe Photoshop. It helps you complete several different graphics editing tasks, including:

- Working with nontechnical illustrations

- Enhancing images and photographs

- Using a scanning interface

- Using special plug-in filters to edit, enhance, and apply special effects to images

- Resampling raster graphics for various types of output, including offset press, multimedia titles, slides, and World Wide Web graphics

- Converting images between several color models, including CMYK, RGB, grayscale, and the Internet-ready GIF format

Before reading this chapter, you should have a basic understanding of CorelDraw, the vector image editor included in the CorelDRAW package.

You can create many different types of graphics with Photo-Paint. Plate 8-1 in the color insert shows a few examples of the many different types of images you can create in Photo-Paint.

Nontechnical illustration

Photo-Paint and programs like it are the applications of choice for creating aesthetically pleasing images, such as those you see all over the World Wide Web and on magazine covers. The program gives you access to a host of tools that let you paint much as an artist paints on canvas. In addition to its simulations of artists' tools, such as pens, pencils, and brushes, Photo-Paint provides you with several tools and techniques that were certainly not available to the old masters — tools such as air brushes and special effects plug-ins (discussed in Chapter 11). Color Plate 8-2 shows an example of an aesthetically satisfying image created with a computer.

Photographic image editing

If you've ever wondered how ad designers and Hollywood types place a person's head on someone else's body, or how they recolor the sky, sea, or eyes in photographs, now you know: they do it with programs such as Photo-Paint. This program gives you the power to control the inferences your audience draws from photographs.

The capability of enhancing and editing photographs and other raster images includes correcting the exposure in underlit or overexposed images and removing imperfections such as dust, scratches, and stains. You can also patch tears, delete or add objects — you name it. In the course of this chapter and the three that follow it, I'll show you how.

Scanning

Photo-Paint is fully TWAIN (Technology Without An Interesting Name) compliant, meaning that it works with most desktop scanners. Photo-Paint interfaces readily with the software that comes with many scanners, with any TWAIN-compliant third-party software, and with CorelScan (another application that comes with CorelDRAW 7), permitting you to scan images directly into Photo-Paint from any of these sources.

During the scanning process, you can resize, adjust brightness and contrast, adjust shadows, and make any number of enhancement settings to improve the quality of the image, so that it prints or displays on a Web page optimally.

Plug-In Filters

Here's an aspect of Photo-Paint that conventional artists and painters could surely have used: plug-ins are small applets that you can install in Photo-Paint that enable you to provide a wealth of enhancements to your images, such as embossing, beveling, textures, and more — much more. Photo-Paint comes with a number of plug-ins, and you can purchase several others, such as Alien Skin's Black Box and MetaTools' KPT Power Tools.

Plug-in filters are so handy that we've included an entire chapter (Chapter 11) about them. In the meantime, Figure 8-1 shows an example of a Web banner created with the Black Box's Bevel plug-in, just to get you interested.

Figure 8-1: In this Web banner, an Alien Skin plug-in was used to bevel the edges of the banner and the text.

Resampling raster graphics

As you've seen repeatedly throughout this book, different types of media require different graphics resolutions and line screens. Images headed for the printing press should be set to much higher resolutions than images designed to display on a computer screen. You can use Photo-Paint to prepare images for the various media types you'll be using. To do so, choose Image ➪ Resample. This brings up the Resample dialog box, shown in Figure 8-2. From here you can adjust image size and resolution.

Figure 8-2: Use the Resample dialog box to change the resolution and size of your raster images.

Color model conversion

Different media types require different color models just as they require different resolutions. Printing presses, for example, require CMYK separated images. Multimedia titles and the Internet require RGB or indexed-color images. In addition to editing, enhancing, and resampling images, you can use Photo-Paint to convert your raster graphics between various color models. Part IV of this book covers preparing images for electronic media. In the meantime, you should know that you change color models in Photo-Paint from the Convert To command on the Image menu. The various models Photo-Paint supports are on the Convert To submenu.

Raster Graphics Versus Vector Graphics

The tasks introduced in the previous sections have one major aspect in common: they all directly relate to *raster* images. Before using the Photo-Paint interface, you should understand what raster images are and how they differ from the vector images you create in CorelDraw.

The major difference between vector images and raster images is that vector graphics represent shapes mathematically, whereas raster graphics represent shapes as patterns of dots or pixels. This difference explains why both formats are necessary — each type has its own particular uses.

Vector graphics

Drawing programs — such as CorelDraw, Micrografx Designer, or Adobe Illustrator — are used to create vector graphics. Vector graphics are drawn mathematically, using lines and curves rather than the fixed dots used in bitmaps. The immediate advantage of this format is that the files are generally much smaller than bitmaps and usually don't take as long to print.

More important than file sizes and print times is the fact that vector graphics are scalable and support many aesthetic qualities better than bitmaps. (When an image is scalable, you can resize it without degrading quality. This concept is discussed in further detail later in this section.) Vector graphics are much better adapted than bitmapped graphics at handling drawings consisting of lines and arcs, or images in which elements are well-defined, such as the one shown in Figure 8-3.

Notice the detail of the drawings in Figure 8-3. Fine lines are truly fine, text is sharp, and flat surfaces are well-defined. The vector format's capability of supporting high resolutions enables more control over detail, also making it ideal for technical drawings and diagrams.

Vector graphics also provide more control over the final output resolution. Because they are device independent, they do not have a fixed resolution. In other words, you can print a graphic at whatever resolution, measured in dots per inch (dpi), your final output device supports. Bitmapped graphics, on the other hand, retain the resolution at which they were created.

Figure 8-3: The vector graphics format used by CorelDraw is more efficient at creating graphics with intricate details, such as text and smooth lines.

Often, the quality of a graphic depends largely on the resolution. This happens for many reasons. The most significant is that as resolution increases, dots get smaller, allowing for more flexible dot placement within an image. This translates into smoother lines and more evenly spread fills.

Vector graphics are also better at high-resolution fountain fills, such as CorelDraw's linear and radial fills and blends shown in Figure 8-4, and at all sorts of other special effects you can't achieve with the same level of success in bitmapped graphics.

Figure 8-4: Vector graphics are capable of smooth fountain fills, blends, and other special effects that require high resolution.

Another advantage of vector graphics is that many of the variations on this format, such as CorelDraw's CDR files, Encapsulated PostScript (EPS), Designer's DRW files, and some others, provide direct support for Type 1 and TrueType fonts. What this means is that, as with a word processor or desktop publishing file, you can open and close a file as often as you like, even import it into other programs, and the text remains editable.

When you use type in a bitmap editor, it becomes part of the graphic, a bitmap itself, and is no longer editable as a text string.

Because they are drawn mathematically and retain their resolution, vector graphics, unlike bitmapped graphics, can be resized without losing quality. (To a certain extent, bitmapped images can be reduced without loss of quality. However, reducing them too much can cause loss of clarity. You will have little or no luck, on the other hand, enlarging them in your layouts.)

When you enlarge a bitmapped graphic, you'll notice that jagged edges appear. This effect increases as the image gets larger. The vector graphic, by contrast, retains its quality no matter how big you make it.

Encapsulated PostScript graphics

Although Encapsulated PostScript graphics don't directly pertain to Photo-Paint, we can't really talk about vector graphics without mentioning them. Adobe's Encapsulated PostScript (EPS) graphics format is the most widely used and most versatile form of vector graphics. It is the graphics format of choice for desktop publishers and designers for a number of reasons. EPS graphics are mentioned in this discussion of the vector format (as well as several times throughout this book) because it is important to keep in mind that they are the standard CorelDraw-type graphics format.

PostScript is the format used by most of today's high-resolution typesetting equipment and slide recorders. As you saw in the discussion of graphics output in Chapter 7, it is a must for reproducing quality four-color documents on an offset printing press.

A drawback to EPS graphics is that you need a PostScript printer or other PostScript interpreter, such as a PostScript cartridge, to print them.

Other vector formats

Other vector formats include CGM, DRW, and the default formats of several other CorelDraw programs, including CorelDraw's CDR. Many of these formats do not require PostScript printers; however, they are not as versatile as PostScript in handling type and providing numerous resolutions and fills. You cannot take full advantage of many of CorelDraw's fills and special effects without a PostScript printer. An exception is CorelDraw's native CDR format. Not many applications support the CDR format. For example, such leading desktop publishing packages as QuarkXPress and PageMaker haven't supported it.

Note

The times they may be a changin'. Version 6.5 of Aldus PageMaker now supports CorelDraw files directly, eliminating the need to convert them to EPS before placing them in layouts.

If you have a non-PostScript laser or inkjet printer, such as an HP-compatible (a printer that uses Hewlett-Packard's Printer Command Language, or PCL), you can still print almost anything you create in CorelDraw, with a few limitations.

Raster (bitmapped) graphics

Raster graphics (also called *bitmapped graphics*) are created in bitmap editors, or paint programs, such as Photo-Paint. Nowadays, however, most paint programs are referred to as image-editing, photograph touch-up, or digital darkroom software. Granted, most of them have become much more adept at photograph enhancement, but no matter what you call them, they're still bitmap editors.

Vector graphics have several advantages over bitmapped graphics. Bitmapped graphics consist of grids of dots in fixed patterns and print in blobs, much like a rubber stamp. Each dot is programmed into a computer file. If a graphic contains a lot of grayscale or color information, the file can be gigantic and take a long time to print. Depending on the image, bitmapped graphics can also lack some of the aesthetically valuable features offered by vector formats. They do not, for example, reproduce curved and fine lines or text nearly as well. Nor are they as flexible in creating intricate shadings and certain special effects.

Bitmapped graphics are *device dependent*, which means that they retain the same resolution, no matter the capabilities of the device you print them on. This is not to say that bitmapped formats are all bad. In fact, they are essential to desktop design and publication of electronic documents, such as multimedia titles, presentations, and documents to be posted to the Internet. The same characteristics that make them unsuitable for some images make them perfect for others. The way they use dots makes them ideal for lifelike images, such as photographs and some sketches and painting-like graphics.

Grayscale and color photograph scanning requires bitmapped formats. In fact, print shops have used a similar procedure to prepare photographs for printing for years. Using special cameras (today, many shops use scanners), they turn a photograph into a halftone (or into color separations for color pictures). A halftone is a translation of the picture in dots, which makes it possible for the printing press to reproduce it. A closer look is taken at halftoning in Chapter 7, where we discuss preparing images for printing and layout.

Raster graphics differ radically from vector graphics. A bitmap editor modifies each individual pixel on the screen, changing the hue, saturation, and color for each pixel that needs to be modified. (This process is also called "mapping"; hence the name *bitmap* graphics.)

Full-color bitmaps at high resolutions create huge files. Here's why: as the number of colors (and the resolution) goes up, the information in the file increases dramatically. The address of a simple black or white pixel contains the location of the pixel and whether the pixel is black or white. The address for an 8-bit image must contain the location of the pixel and which of 256 possible colors or shades of gray the pixel is, and the address for a 24-bit image must contain the information about which of 16.7 million possible colors the pixel should be. As color depth increases, so do the address information and the file size.

Bitmapped Graphics and CorelDraw

As mentioned, Photo-Paint is the program you should use to create and edit bitmaps. However, you can also import and export some bitmap file formats to and from CorelDraw.

Although you can't edit bitmaps in CorelDraw, you can import them into your drawings. An example is including a photograph on a flyer. Another reason to import them is for tracing, either with CorelDraw's autotrace feature or manually with your mouse or a pen stylus. Once a bitmap is traced, you can delete it and edit the outline in CorelDraw as you would any other vector element.

You can export anything you create in CorelDraw to any of several bitmap file formats, including PCX, TIFF, and BMP. You may want, for instance, to edit bitmap images in Photo-Paint or another bitmap editor or to use them in computer presentations on a monitor. As you've seen (or will see) in Chapters 7 and 23 in the discussions of graphics output, bitmaps work better on computer monitors than do some vector formats.

Another important aspect of raster images is resolution, or the number and size of the pixels that are used to construct the image. Bitmaps often define resolution in numbers like the following: 640 × 480, 800 × 600, and 1024 × 768, which are basic monitor resolutions in pixels. However, when you create high-resolution (200 to 300 dpi) image bitmaps for printing, the number of pixels increases dramatically. The larger the numbers, the smaller the pixels, and smaller pixels mean higher resolution and finer detail — as well as larger files. If you combine high resolution and high color, you can easily wind up with files that exceed 100MB.

This concept is dramatically demonstrated by a simple exercise:

STEPS

Seeing the Effect of Resolution on File Size

Step 1. Open a high-resolution file in Photo-Paint, and then choose Image ⇨ Info. You will see an information box similar to the one shown in Figure 8-5.

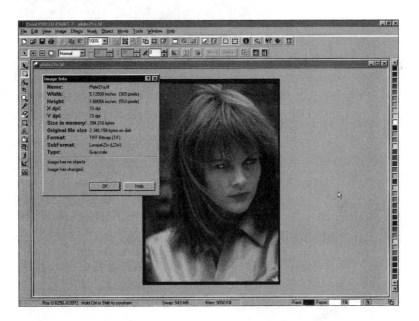

Figure 8-5: Image information for a high-resolution graphic appears in the Image Info dialog box.

Step 2. Notice that this graphic consumes just about 6MB of memory. (File sizes vary greatly. Your graphic's size will differ.)

(continued)

STEPS *(continued)*

Seeing the Effect of Resolution on File Size

Step 3.   Now convert the image to an 8-bit (256 color) image by choosing one of the 8-bit options from Image ⇨ Convert To. Reopen the Image ⇨ Info dialog box, shown in Figure 8-6.

Figure 8-6: Image information is revised after the image has been converted to 256 colors.

Notice that the file size has been cut to almost one sixth of the original.

Step 4.   Now, change the resolution to 72 dpi by choosing Resample from the Image menu. (Be sure the Maintain aspect ratio checkbox is checked.) Reopen the Image Info dialog box, shown in Figure 8-7.

Figure 8-7: Image information is further revised after the resolution has been decreased to 72 dpi.

Notice that our original 4MB file is now only 394K.

Unfortunately, there is no such thing as a free lunch, and each step in the preceding exercise diminishes the quality of the image as well as its size, especially if you're printing the image on a printing press.

Because raster graphics are constructed of pixels, they do not magnify with great success. Zooming in, increasing the size of the photo, or decreasing resolution also increases the size of each pixel. This can result in an unacceptable condition called pixelization.

Secret

Images almost always scale down without any significant loss of quality. Unfortunately, they seldom scale up without suffering quite a bit. Here, then, is one valuable rule of thumb to keep in mind when working with raster graphics: Always attempt to scan or acquire your images in a size that is as big as, or bigger than, what you will be using.

Converting raster images to vector images

Converting a raster graphic into a vector graphic isn't as easy as the opposite process, and usually the conversion is not very successful. To make the conversion, the computer has to interpret the patterns of pixels in the raster image as shapes and then figure out how to write the directions to draw them.

Some tracing programs, such as OCR-Trace (discussed in Chapter 15), can convert raster graphics to vector graphics, but the results are often less than perfect, especially with full-color photographs. You can give it a try with OCR-Trace, but don't say that I didn't warn you.

In Chapter 5 you learned about manipulating color in CorelDraw. Most of the information in that chapter applies to Photo-Paint as well, but note one significant addition: always remember when you are drawing in a four-color mode, CMYK for example, or using process or spot colors, that the monitor is displaying the images in the RGB model. What you see on the screen is seldom what you get when you take your work to a printing press.

Always have a sample book of colors near you, and frequently check your image against it; post-press surprises are seldom pleasant ones.

Introduction to the Photo-Paint Tools

At first blush, the CorelDraw and Photo-Paint interfaces look a lot alike. But if you look a bit closer, they suddenly start to appear distressingly dissimilar. The toolbars have different items on them, the Property Bar looks as if it had one too many, and extra tools are even stuck here and there about the interface.

Well, once you realize that the two programs are designed to do two quite different things, you can start to appreciate the differences. I'm assuming that you bought this book because you own and use CorelDraw, and that you don't know a lot about Photo-Paint. Pouring over the manual is of doubtful value, so we will approach Photo-Paint on a slightly more introductory level. Realize, however, that Photo-Paint is a highly complex program, one that takes a lot of effort on your part to learn. We can't cover all the information you need to become proficient at image manipulation in just four chapters. Our purpose is to introduce you to some basic concepts and techniques.

Fortunately, you already know many of the elements of Photo-Paint, because quite a few elements in the interface are the same as in CorelDraw. Fortunately, too, Photo-Paint is a first-class gas, a whale of a lot of fun, and well worth any time that you can spend with it.

Familiar CorelDraw tools

If you have learned CorelDraw, you already know three sets of Photo-Paint tools pretty thoroughly: the zoom tools, the shape tools, and the fill tools.

All of these operate much like their CorelDraw counterparts. You also know quite a bit about the object, node, and text tools, even though they work in some substantially different ways. So let's start by looking, quite briefly, at some of these differences.

The Object Picker tool

You already know about the selection, or Pick, tool, which is called the Object Picker tool in Photo-Paint, the first tool on the Toolbox shown in Figure 8-8. The second (Object Transparency) and third (Object Transparency Brush) tools on the flyout are new to you. The second, or middle, tool is used to make a transparency blend, or to make the colors of an object fade into the image background color. The third tool is similar, except that the transparency effect is limited to a brush stroke.

Figure 8-8: The second and third Object tools differ from those of CorelDraw.

Remember

The entire concept of transparency may be new to you if you haven't played with paint programs before. Remember, Photo-Paint mimics the work of a paint-on-canvas artist. This means that the paint can be more or less transparent as it is laid on.

The Zoom tool

The Zoom tool is the fourth button down and performs the same duties for Photo-Paint as it does for CorelDraw. However, you'll notice one major difference that you're sure to love. Once you activate it by clicking the Zoom Tool button, you can then operate it entirely by left-clicking your mouse to zoom in and right-clicking to zoom out.

The Node tool

Here again, the first tool (the Path Node Edit tool, similar to CorelDraw's Node Editing or Shape tool) is familiar to you. The second (Repeat Stroke) tool is used to load the characteristics of any brush you have saved (see the section on the Paint tool later in this chapter) so that you can tweak its settings and reapply it to an image or a path. The Node tool buttons are shown in Figure 8-9.

Figure 8-9: The familiar Node tool has a partner to help you with your painting.

The Text tool

The text tool operates much as it does in CorelDraw. However, note one significant difference: the Photo-Paint text tool creates rasterized images of the fonts. This means that words you create in Photo-Paint greatly increase the overall file size.

Secret

Photo-Paint is not intended for typesetting. If you need to include text in a document, it is highly recommended that you perform all image editing in Photo-Paint and then move the finished image into CorelDraw, where you can add vector-based text. Your letters will be cleaner and sharper, and the file will not be bloated with a lot of excess information.

At times, however, it's easier to add text directly to an image, so that the text will become an integral part of the design. In these cases, go ahead and do it, but don't count on the same level of quality that you could get by using vector-based tools.

The Fill tool

The Photo-Paint Fill tool is very similar to the Fill tool in CorelDraw. You can fill an irregular object with any color selected. You can also make a solid fill or a gradient fill across a mask or a masked area. These techniques are discussed in Chapters 9 and 10. You'll need to learn to use them both to make good use of the Fill tool.

The Property Bar

You may already be familiar with context-specific Property Bars in CorelDraw. The Property Bars in Photo-Paint work essentially the same way, but you will want to become familiar with all the new options, which change with each tool you select. The same information in the Property Bar is also available in the various roll-ups for each particular tool. (See Figure 8-10.) This is how the folks at Corel built even more flexibility into your paint area — mix and match your use of the Property Bar or the roll-ups — it's your choice! Chapter 9 explains the Photo-Paint Property Bar in detail.

Figure 8-10: The Photo-Paint Property Bar is shown for the Mask tool. As with CorelDraw, the Property Bar in Photo-Paint changes with each tool selected.

Secret

Many times when you are working with tools in Photo-Paint, you will want to use a combination of settings from the Property Bar and a tool's settings dialog box. Double-click the tool you want to use, and the appropriate Settings roll-up menu opens. You can then display or hide the Property Bar with the Show/Hide Property Bar icon on the toolbar (it is the button right next to that red apple doodad), giving you access to all of the variations of any tool settings.

Unique Photo-Paint tools

Although artistic masterpieces are not traditionally crafted from scratch in paint programs, Photo-Paint does give you some powerful tools that enable you to create works from scratch.

To get a feel for these new gadgets, go to File and select New to open a new image. You'll see the dialog box shown in Figure 8-11. Notice that the Create a New Image dialog box enables you to set the color depth, resolution, and size of the image you want to work with. The last two lines in the dialog box let you know how much memory the image will consume, and how much you have available.

Figure 8-11: The Create a New Image dialog box controls basic image properties.

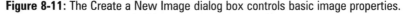

Quite a few tools that you haven't seen before appear here: masking tools, the Crop tool, the Eyedropper tool, Eraser tools, the Image Sprayer tool, the Paint tool, the Effect tool, and the Clone tool. Many of these are quite simple to use, and many aren't. In this section, you'll learn about some of the really cool capabilities of this program.

The Paint tool

Have you ever asked yourself why artists always seem to have a zillion brushes sticking up from old coffee cups? As any artist knows, each brush does a special thing because it has a special shape or texture. Every artist knows that each brush has a function, and you just can't do anything without the proper tools.

Well, you can now go those artists one better. Double-click the Paint tool — it's the third one up from the bottom of the Toolbox, and it looks like a paint brush. This opens the Tool Settings roll-up, shown in Figure 8-12, revealing the paint tools available to you. Now click the Type drop-down list to see the many brushes.

Figure 8-12: You can choose from among several possible expressions for different paint tools.

You can set the characteristics of the brush shape, including the texture of the paint that is laid down by the brush, and you can control other properties of brushes; for instance, you can turn a brush stroke into a series of dabs. Along the Property Bar you can select brush type, paint mode, nib shape and size, transparency, softness of the brush edge, and antialiasing. Click the last two icons on the right to pull down roll-ups.

It is tough to describe the flexibility and types of paint tools available in Photo-Paint. Open the brush Tool Settings dialog box by double-clicking the brush tool. With your blank new file open, select any medium type you want and experiment — moving from spray can to watercolor to air brush. Many predefined types are already available. If you are an experienced artist and you do not find a tool to your liking, customize one as your own and save it to use again by clicking the Save Brush button and giving your new tool a name. You can now use this tool anytime in the future.

You'll need to experiment a lot with all of the various tool settings. Bear in mind as you go along how different this is from CorelDraw. For instance, you have settings for brush transparency and soft edge. When you are painting, one color bleeds into another, and paint seldom completely covers what is underneath. If you are artistically inclined, you will be tempted to lock yourself up with your computer, appearing only now and then to feed yourself. This can be great fun.

If you haven't discovered the fact already, note that Photo-Paint is much more demanding of your computer than is CorelDraw. Creating works of art on a memory-challenged 80486 can become an exercise in frustration, and even the fastest CPU can and will bog down when it attempts to perform some of the more intense Photo-Paint tasks, such as painting with complex brushes and doing masks. We'll talk about masks in a bit and in full in Chapter 10.

As a rule, you need a pretty quick CPU (80586 or Pentium), as much uncompressed hard drive space as you can afford, and as much memory as your borrowed bucks can buy. If you have 32MB of RAM, you should do all right when you start getting into intensive Photo-Paint operations.

The Crop tool

Everybody knows what cropping is. It's simply cutting away unwanted portions of an image, leaving a desired portion. Using the Crop tool (fourth from the top) is a piece of cake. Do this:

STEPS

Using the Crop Tool

Step 1.   Select the Crop tool.

Step 2.   Drag a marquee box around the part of the image you want to keep.

Step 3.   Adjust the size of the marquee box by dragging its sizing handles.

Step 4.   Double-click in the image area to accomplish the crop.

Figure 8-13 shows an example of what cropping can do for a picture.

Figure 8-13: Good cropping can turn a ho-hum photo (right) into a zinger (left)!

The Eyedropper tool

Many times you will want to load your brush with a particular color that appears in an image or the mixing area, and you will have absolutely no idea what the name of that color may be.

Use the Eyedropper tool to select the color you want following this procedure:

STEPS

Using the Eyedropper Tool

Step 1.   Select the Eyedropper tool.

Step 2.   Place the cursor on the color in the currently displayed image, or color in the mixing area that you want to use.

Step 3.   Left-click to set the paint color, or right-click to set the fill.

Note

When a large color sample is taken with the Eyedropper tool, the color result is an average of the colors included in the area sampled. So be aware — the end result may not actually exist within the sample. You can get a more precise color by narrowing the size of the Eyedropper brush tip from the Tool Settings roll-up (with the Eyedropper selected).

The Eraser tools

The Eraser tools flyout, shown in Figure 8-14, has three tools. The first tool (the Local Undo tool) is used to undo the last action you did to an area with one of the paint tools. The second tool (the Eraser) works like a traditional eraser, except that it paints with any color you choose for the paper color, and the third tool (the Color Replacer) replaces only the current paint color in the image with the paper color. Slick!

Use the Eyedropper tool to select a new current color to replace with the Color Replacer tool. You can adjust the size and shape of the eraser brush from the Tool Settings roll-up or from the Property Bar (with the Eraser selected).

Figure 8-14: A suite of three tools in Photo-Paint averts many disasters. Try the Local Undo and the Eraser. The Color Replacer tool works in conjunction with the Eyedropper.

The Image Sprayer tool

Most of the time when you paint, you lay down a path of color using one of the paint tools. However, it is possible to paint with images. Instead of laying down a swath of yellow, for example, you can lay down a swath of images of your favorite cat's face. Click the Open File folder on the left side of the Property Bar to load any paint graphic. Then spray with the Image Sprayer tool (fourth from the bottom in the Toolbox). You can also edit the size, frequency, and transparency of the image you want to spray from the Tool Settings roll-up or the Property Bar (with the Image Sprayer tool selected). Figure 8-15 shows an example of the Image Sprayer's handiwork. Watch out taggers, Corel's on your turf!

Using the tool takes a little practice, though. See Chapter 9, "Advanced Photo-Paint Techniques."

Figure 8-15: The butterflies were sprayed (superimposed) on the brick wall. The more quickly you move the cursor, the more transparent the sprayed images become.

The Effect tool

The Effect tool (second from the bottom) is used to smear, smudge, alter brightness and contrast, and change the hue, as well as to sponge, tint, blend, sharpen, and undither images. Use the Effect tool much as you would use a brush or the Image Sprayer. (See Figures 8-16 and 8-17.)

Figure 8-16: The original image of a butterfly is blurred against the background.

Figure 8-17: The new image has been sharpened and brightened to bring out the butterfly against the background.

Chapter 11 describes effects further. For now, it is enough to know that you can build and use a zillion different way-out special effects to spice up your images.

The Clone tool

The Clone tool (at the bottom in the toolbox) is one of the most awesome and powerful tools in your Photo-Paint repertoire. You will use this tool to perform all manner of touch-up tasks on images, correcting flaws in negatives, removing scratches from film, or even removing unwanted elements from the background of an otherwise great photo.

The Clone tool copies things from one location in an image to another, so it has two cursors — one to show the origin and one to locate where the cloned information will be placed. Probably the best way to understand what the Clone tool does is to view an example of the tool in action. See Figure 8-18.

Figure 8-18: Here is an example of cloning with the Clone tool.

Secret

Perhaps the greatest secret to using the Clone tool is to work with the image displayed as large as possible. If, as in this example, you are taking pieces of the background from the close neighborhood of the element you want to paint over, get as close to the element as you can.

Three lesser secrets to using the Clone tool include selecting the proper origin, establishing a checkpoint, and patience. Selecting the proper origin comes with practice. Establishing a checkpoint is something that needs to be in your everyday bag of tricks.

Setting a checkpoint is a valuable practice — try it. When you start to get into some intense image manipulation, establish a place that you can return to if everything suddenly goes wrong. You do this by choosing Checkpoint from the Edit menu. Now if something you do turns out wrong or you don't like its looks, you can always get back to where the image was right by choosing Restore to Checkpoint from the Edit menu. Cool.

To use the Clone tool, follow these steps:

STEPS

Using the Clone Tool

Step 1.   Zoom in on the area you want to change.

Step 2.   Select the Clone tool from the drawing toolbar.

Step 3.   Click a location from which to copy an element.

Step 4.   Paint with the new cursor.

It sounds easy, but it takes some practice.

Watch that tool size. The Clone tool, like all the other tools in Photo-Paint, has a settings dialog box, as well as special settings available on the Property Bar. Keep the nib size reasonably small. It is a lot easier to keep resetting the origin (right-click and choose Reset Origin from the shortcut menu) than to try to go back and clean up. Figure 8-19 shows the Tool Settings dialog box for the Clone tool.

Masking tools

The purpose behind Photo-Paint is to let you mess around with raster images. Up until now, everything we have shown you could be directly applied to, or done on, the entire image that was displayed on the monitor. However, you will seldom want to work in such broad strokes.

Rather, you will want to modify one part of an image, say by making a brown eye blue. To do this, you need some method or tool that enables you to choose one small part of an image, while at the same time protecting the rest of the image from unwanted change.

Figure 8-19: Use the Tool Settings dialog box for the Clone tool to adjust significant settings.

This process is called *masking*, and you can use a whole series of tools in Photo-Paint to open small areas in an image for change. This beats the masking tape you use to protect your cabinets when you paint your kitchen!

The Masking mechanisms available to you are the Rectangular, Circle, and Freehand masking tools (see Figure 8-20). You can also select similar colors over an area with the Magic Wand. Scissors creates an irregular mask by following edges, whereas the Mask Brush tool creates a mask from Brush Strokes. Last but not least, you can also Transform a Mask. For a detailed description of masking, turn to Chapter 10.

Figure 8-20: The Masking tools flyout offers a variety of means for masking.

Drawing Tools

Unlike CorelDraw, Photo-Paint is pixel-oriented and has only a very limited selection of actual object drawing tools. You can create a Rectangle, an Ellipse (or circle), a Polygon (any irregular shape), and straight Lines. When creating objects in Photo-Paint, you can choose to fill the object with a color or to leave it hollow. You can also control the line weight (thickness) of the object border, just as you would in CorelDraw. (See Figure 8-21.)

Figure 8-21: The Photo-Paint Tools flyout offers access to the program's somewhat limited selection of drawing tools.

Summary

▶ Corel Photo-Paint is a bitmap editor rivaling Adobe Photoshop in power to create paint-type images. You can also use it to edit and scan photographs, apply special effects plug-in filters, and carry out a wealth of other bitmap image-editing procedures.

▶ Photo-Paint's raster format differs from CorelDraw's vector image format in that images are created as grids of dots, rather than as mathematically drawn arcs and lines. Raster is the ideal format for photographs and painting-like images.

▶ The Photo-Paint interface differs from CorelDraw's in having many different tools for creating paint-type effects, such as smudging tools, painting brushes, and even an image sprayer, sometimes called an image hose.

Chapter 9

Advanced Photo-Paint Techniques

In This Chapter

You'll learn some advanced tips and techniques for working with:

▶ The Property Bar in Photo-Paint

▶ Photo-Paint's Toolbars

▶ Colors

▶ Objects in Photo-Paint

▶ Other Photo-Paint features

Using the Property Bar in Photo-Paint

The Property Bar is an extremely powerful toolbar. It changes according to the context with any tool you select. By default, it is attached to the top of the screen, right beneath the standard toolbar. The Property Bar enables you to quickly and easily make major adjustments or do some fine-tuning with any tool you use. If you select the Object Picker tool, for example, the Property Bar reveals options to adjust the alignment and opacity of the object, repositioning, and duplication. In this context, the Property Bar also provides a drop-down menu that changes the mode of the Object Picker, enabling you to distort and resize any object on your screen without digging through a menu to find the right tool. I've mentioned only a few options here. In all the Property bar provides from 8 to 15 options for each of the Object Picker's seven modes. The Property Bar changes with each of the 14 tool groups found on the Photo-Paint toolbar (on the left side of the screen), and it changes again when you select an individual tool within each group.

Secret

You can float your mouse pointer over the Property Bar to reveal two different kinds of tool-tips:

■ Tool-tips near the tools themselves

■ Detailed descriptions that appear on the status bar

These tips can be extremely helpful because the Property Bar can contain as many as 24 tool options per tool. (No floating tool-tips are available as you use the Tool Settings roll-up.)

The Photo-Paint Property Bar in different contexts

Let's take a look at how the Property Bar's features change depending on the tools that you're using in Photo-Paint.

The Object Picker tool

In Photo-Paint, the Property Bar has a drop-down menu for the Object Picker tool (sometimes called the "Object tool" for short), as shown in Figure 9-1.

Figure 9-1: Here is what the Property Bar looks like while the Object tool is selected. The corresponding drop-down menu is open.

You'll find a few more options on this drop-down menu than on the toolbox flyout for the Object tool. The additional icons on this drop-down menu rotate, scale, resize, skew, distort, and add perspective to the selected object. Keep your eye on the status bar to be sure which tool you have selected.

Secret

You need not go through the trouble of selecting a tool from the drop-down menu whenever you want to choose a different tool. Each time you click an object with the Object tool, you can activate a different tool depending on the number of times you click. Click once to move the object, twice to rotate or skew the object, three times to distort the object, and four times to drag the object with the perspective tool. Notice that the type of bounding marker changes each time you click.

Selecting a tool within the Object Picker submenu causes the other options on the Property Bar to change. Look at the Property Bar each time you select a new Object Picker option. The Property Bar's adjustable parameters change according to your selection. Figure 9-2 shows the Property Bar with the Rotate mode selected. Some of the Rotate options are things you could do just as easily by double-clicking on the object itself and rotating by hand.

But using the numerical values on the Property Bar gives you more accuracy. For example, using the Property Bar, you can move the "center point" that an object rotates around and alter the transparency of an object.

Figure 9-2: The Property Bar (split to show detail) shows these options with the Rotate mode selected for the Object Picker.

The Mask tool

When you select a tool from the Mask tool drop-down menu, the Property Bar changes depending on the tool you have selected. With the Property Bar, you can make your mask *subtract* from the selected area, rather than add to it. You can also change your mask to an XOR mask tool, which enables you to make several unique masked areas on one picture. Feathering, Anti-Aliasing, and Float controls are available on the Property Bar. Masking options are explained in more detail in Chapter 10. You can also open the Channel and Objects roll-up with a single mouse-click. These roll-ups are dis-

cussed later in this chapter. Figure 9-3 shows the Property Bar with the
Scissors mask selected.

Figure 9-3: The Property Bar appears this way with the Scissors Mask selected.

The Path Node Edit tool

Figure 9-4 shows how the Property Bar looks when the Path Node Edit tool
(or "Node tool," for short) is selected.

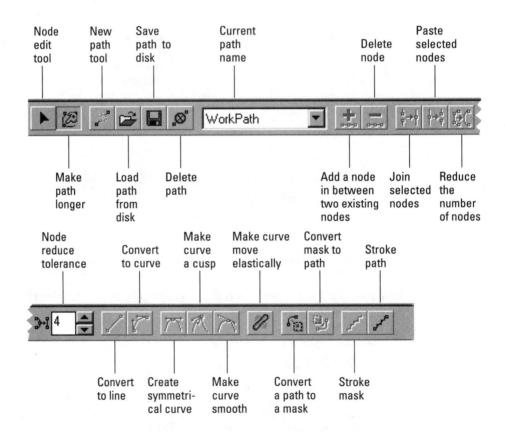

Figure 9-4: The Property Bar takes this form when the Node tool is selected.

The first button on the left of the Property Bar is the Node Edit tool. Use the Node Edit tool to reposition nodes you've already created and to turn line nodes into curved nodes. When it is selected, you cannot add new nodes (that is, new steps along the path) in your drawing, except by using the "+" button on the Property Bar.

The next button activates your tool for placing new nodes on your picture. The next four buttons Create New, Save, Open, and Delete existing paths. You may have several paths open on one document simultaneously. You can save any path with the extension .PTH and name it anything you like.

Note

The New Node tool is not the same as the Add Node button (the plus sign). The Add Node button inserts a new node between two selected nodes. The New Node tool lets you lay down new nodes on your picture by hand to extend your path.

The next menu item opens a drop-down menu, the Current Path Name menu. This menu shows the name of the path you are currently working on. Because you can have more than one path open in a document at once, that drop-down menu can contain several entries. "Work Path" is the default name for the first path created in any document.

The Add tool (the "+" button) places a new node between the selected node and the one right before it. The Delete tool (the "–" button) removes any node you have just clicked on. You can also use the plus and minus signs on your numeric key pad to add or delete nodes. The next three tools can be used to join, break apart, or reduce the number of nodes on a path. The Reduce button eliminates any nodes on a path that are not adjusting that path's direction in some way. Reduce Tolerance is the numeral next to the Reduce command. Set from 1 to 10, it affects how aggressively the Reduce command works to find nodes it can get rid of and still maintain your path's shape. Setting this number higher than 6 causes some real alteration in the way your path looks.

The next six buttons change the selected node into various kinds of curves or lines, such as sharp curves (cusps), symmetrical curves, or smooth curves. The "rubber band" button turns on Elastic mode, which makes the line near the selected node behave like a rubber band when manipulated.

The next two tools turn the selected path into a mask, or a mask into a path, and the final two tools stroke the selected path or mask. Stroking causes the currently selected paint tool to trace the path once. Your path or mask will then have a brush stroke around its perimeter. Repeating this command thickens and accents the brush stroke.

The Crop tool

Figure 9-5 shows the appearance of the Property Bar when the Crop tool is selected. When eyeballing an image with the Crop tool is not precise enough, the Property Bar provides a numeric entries dialog box for more precise cropping. The Tool Settings roll-up gives you an option to change the measuring system you use to crop your picture. That way, if you are using the Crop tool, you can switch to the metric system on the fly.

Figure 9-5: The Property Bar looks like this when the Crop tool is selected.

The Crop tool Property Bar also contains Crop to Mask and Crop to Border commands. Crop to Mask reduces the size of your picture to the area just surrounding the currently selected mask. Crop to Border opens a dialog box that enables you to crop your image according to paper color, the current paint color, or a color picked from your picture with the eyedropper. (See Figure 9-6.)

Figure 9-6: The Crop Border Color dialog box offers choices for cropping according to color.

The Zoom tool

Figure 9-7 shows the Property Bar while the Zoom tool is selected. It contains a numeric zoom option drop-down menu and magnifying buttons that enlarge or shrink your view of an object when you point and click. Also included are the Normal, Actual Size, and Zoom to Fit tools.

Figure 9-7: The Property Bar has this form while the Zoom tool is selected.

The Eyedropper tool

Figure 9-8 shows the Property Bar while the Eyedropper tool is selected. Normally, the Eyedropper tool samples one pixel of paint from the image. The active paintbrush color changes to the exact color that the Eyedropper tool lands on. The Property Bar enables you to select a range of pixels from your image. The *average value* of those pixels becomes your paintbrush's active color. Click the Eyedropper tool while "3X3" is selected, and Photo-Paint averages the surrounding nine pixels. Select "5X5," and the surrounding 25 pixels are averaged. The average becomes your paintbrush tool's color. Select Custom, and you can click and drag an area as large as you like as your sample. Select Point, and Eyedropper returns to selecting single pixels.

Figure 9-8: The Property Bar takes this form while the Eyedropper tool is selected.

Secret

To change the fill color rather than the paintbrush color, press Shift while using the Eyedropper tool. Pressing Ctrl changes the paper color.

The Eraser tool

Figure 9-9 shows the Property Bar while the Eraser tool is selected.

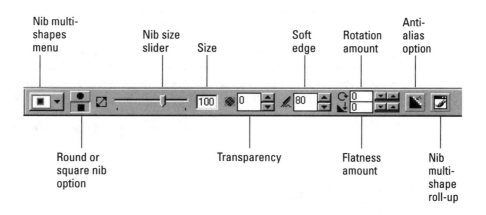

Figure 9-9: The Property Bar appears like this while the Eraser tool is selected.

Many of the Erase features of the Property Bar have to do with nibs. A *nib* is a tool attribute that hasn't been discussed yet. For now, think of nibs as like strands of hair on the tip of your paintbrush. The tip of your brush can be square and thick, skinny and round, and so on. Your brush tip can render "brushy" strokes that show off individual brush hairs, or it can apply paint in thick gobs. Or your brush tip can have a soft edge that gets rid of any jagged, pixelated edges to your brush strokes. Or it can lay down hard lines like a No. 3 pencil. Figure 9-10 shows the different Eraser effects that can be achieved by changing the nib attribute.

Figure 9-10: A portion of this image on the left has been erased with a soft-edge eraser. The image on the right has no soft edge.

As you view the Eraser tool Property Bar from left to right, the first tool allows selection of the nib shape. Scroll all the way down to see all of the different shapes. (See Figure 9-11.) The number next to each shape is the nib size. Besides selecting interesting angles and orientations for your eraser tool, you can insert pictures and symbols. The size and edge quality of these pictures take on the properties you select with the other Eraser tool parameters.

Figure 9-11: You can use either the Eraser tool Property Bar or the Nibs roll-up to select some interesting shapes for your nib. The number near each shape is the nib size.

The next two buttons assign a round or square shape to your eraser, and the slider bar determines eraser size. The Transparency number, set to zero by default, determines how much underlying image remains after you use the Eraser tool. If Transparency is set to zero, none of the underlying image shows through.

The next number, the Soft Edge setting, determines if the image next to the erased area fades out or stops abruptly. The next two buttons determine the angle and flatness of your eraser tool. You don't need to adjust any of these settings unless you aren't satisfied with the built-in eraser shapes.

The second to last button turns on the antialiasing feature. (Antialiasing smooths out the edges of edited bitmaps. It is explained in more detail a little later.)

Secret

The final button is a link to the Nibs roll-up menu. At first glance, this menu looks just like the first item, Nib Shapes. But look closely at the arrow pointing right on the right side of the Nibs roll-up. (See Figure 9-12.) Click the arrow, and you'll see that you can save your edited brush tips (nibs) for later use. You do this by clicking Add Currently Used.

Figure 9-12: The Nibs roll-up menu is available from the last button of the Eraser tool Property Bar. Here you can save eraser shapes for later use.

Tip

In Photo-Paint, an eraser is simply a style of brush that applies the paper color. So when you save a Create From Mask item as a brush, it can be used as an eraser as well. Conversely, any mask saved as an eraser can be used as a brush as well.

Drawing tools

The Property Bar changes depending on which shape is selected. It provides a unique selection of options for each shape, as well as a few options that are common to all shapes (such as opacity controls and scaling).

Figure 9-13 shows how the Property Bar looks when the Rectangle tool is selected. You can set the Fill and Outline types, do away with the Fill altogether, or change the transparency of the drawing itself. The Line Width value defaults to 20, which can be a little wide for most uses. The word "Normal" is part of the Paint Merge dialog box. Photo-Paint provides extensive control over special-effect color merging modes that can create some rather striking effects. The Anti-Alias tool also appears on the Property Bar.

Figure 9-13: The Property Bar takes this form when the Rectangle tool is selected.

If you want to create a shape that is not immediately embedded into the background, click Render to Object on the Drawing tool Property Bar. With Render to Object checked, your drawing will have a marquee and can be resized and edited like any other object.

Secret

The way to make rounded rectangles in Photo-Paint is to increase the Roundness value. It's the third number from the left on the Property Bar. You cannot change the roundness of a rectangle that has already been created, however.

The Fill tool

Photo-Paint's Fill tool enables you to fill a mask, an object, or an entire page with color, a fountain fill, bitmaps, or textures. The tools for editing and selecting Photo-Paint fills have greatly improved over the years. The Fill tool Property Bar provides Transparency and Paint modes, as well as Anti-Aliasing options. You'll also find Color Toleration controls, for determining how sensitively your fill will interact with colors surrounding the area to be filled. But to really edit your fill, you'll need to click the Fill button on the far left of the toolbar. Do so, and you'll see the Tool Settings dialog box, as pictured in Figure 9-14.

Figure 9-14: The Tool Settings dialog box
offers access to various fill types.

Choose Uniform Fill (the color wheel button, the first button on the left) and
click Edit, and you'll see the Edit Uniform Fill dialog box. (See Figure 9-15.)

Figure 9-15: The Edit Uniform Fill dialog box controls colors and other
attributes of uniform fills.

Uniform Fill has four ways to select colors for your fill. Pictured is the Color Blender, which enables you to combine four colors into a custom blend. Also included is a color Mixing Area that resembles an artist's palette.

Fountain Fill enables you to adjust the fill's source colors, fill shape, spectrum direction, and number of steps. Pictured in Figure 9-16 is the Edit Fountain Fill dialog box with the Cylinder 19 preset being edited. Moving any of the seven fill points (pictured where the mouse cursor is) adds new color variations to the selected fill.

Figure 9-16: The Edit Fountain Fill dialog box affords access to further fill options.

Clicking on the "checkerboard square" icon on the Tool Settings Roll-Up enables you to choose a bitmap fill. You can import an image in any common picture file format to be used as a Photo-Paint fill. Options are included to stretch the bitmap so that it fits the selected area, or to tile it according to your specifications.

Click the Texture icon (farthest from the left) on the Tool Settings Roll-Up and choose Edit. You'll see the Edit Texture Fill dialog box shown in Figure 9-17. Photo-Paint comes with hundreds of preset textures available from the four libraries included on the CD. As you can see from the number of options pictured in Figure 9-17, each texture can be edited within an inch of its life. This dialog box is one of Photo-Paint's most distinctive creativity tools.

Figure 9-17: The Edit Texture Fill dialog box affords access to bitmapped textures.

The Gradient Fill tool Property Bar

Pressing and holding the Fill tool reveals the Gradient Fill tool. The Gradient Fill tool has its own Property Bar. It contains an option to use two colors as starting and ending points on the spectrum for your fill. Thus, rather than simply fade from blue to red, your fill can consist of the entire color wheel from blue to red, either clockwise or counterclockwise. You can also fade from the paper color (usually white) to any other color.

The Paint tool

When the Paint tool is selected, the Property Bar reveals options for brush type; nib size and shape; transparency and Soft Edge amount; and links to the Nibs roll-up, Brush reset options, and Tool Settings roll-up. Of particular interest are the Brush reset options. Having this tool handy enables you to edit existing brushes with total abandon, knowing that you can restore them at a moment's notice, if you wish.

Figure 9-18 shows the Property Bar for the Paint tool with the Paint Mode drop-down list open.

Figure 9-18: The Paint tool Property Bar is shown with the Paint Mode drop-down list open.

Paint modes, sometimes called merge modes or apply modes, are the rules you can choose when painting on a background, combining objects, or applying a mask to an image. Most often, the word "Normal" appears in the Paint Mode field because paint is usually applied (and objects are usually layered) according to the normal rules. For example, normally you want the color red to appear red. But when you apply an alternative paint mode, you can change the rules. Each mode in the drop-down list (Subtract, Texturize, XOR, and so on) represents a different algorithm that can be applied to the relationship between the selected object (or paint tool) and the background. Figure 9-19 shows a couple of examples of different paint modes.

Difference Mode

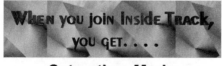

Saturation Mode

Figure 9-19: Here are two examples of special effects created by special paint modes.

The Text tool

Figure 9-20 shows the Property Bar as it appears with the Text tool selected. Beyond the basic font and paragraph formatting options, notice that the Character and Line Spacing tools are immediately accessible, which is a real plus for creating aesthetically pleasing bitmapped text. When you start adding shadows and layering font masks, extra space between characters is needed. One feature worth pointing out is the Render to Mask option, which is available from the Property Bar as well as from the Tool Settings roll-up. The text tool enables you to change font and font sizes even after the text appears on your picture. The text remains fully editable in a bounding box until you select a different tool.

Figure 9-20: The Property Bar assumes this appearance with the Text tool selected.

One feature worth pointing out is the Render to Mask option, which is available from the Property Bar as well as from the Tool Settings roll-up. The text tool enables you to change fonts and font sizes even after the text appears on your picture. The text remains fully editable in a bounding box until you select a different tool.

You must select Render Text to Mask before you create your fancy text, not after. Otherwise your text will be completely embedded in the background as soon as you select a new tool.

A Specimen of Text Effects

This ominous tribute to premillennial anxiety (Figure A) is brought to you by Photo-Paint's totally revamped Text tool, which now converts text to objects or masks, performs lighting effects, and creates instant drop shadows.

This image was created using the Fill texture called "Mineral Speckled, Two Colors." Text was created and the Render Text to Mask command was used. The Spray Can Paint brush was applied to the text. (See Figure B.) The text was turned into an object, copied to the clipboard, and pasted back into the image several times using various paint modes. (See Figure C.) Lighting effects and drop shadows were also applied. The image is included on the CD for you to edit and experiment with.

Figure A: This is our basic image, "1999."

Figure B: Spray-painting the text after it has been changed to a mask has this effect.

A Specimen of Text Effects *(continued)*

Figure C: The text, as an object, has been pasted back in, with the paint mode changed.

The Image Sprayer tool

Figure 9-21 shows the Property Bar while the Image Sprayer tool is selected.

Figure 9-21: The Property Bar takes this form with the Image Sprayer tool selected.

Figures 9-22 and 9-23 give you some idea of what you can do with the different settings.

Figure 9-22: An image has been filled with the Moondrops texture, followed by three brush strokes. The brush was loaded with a Photo-Paint preset "Flags." Note the options selected on the Property Bar.

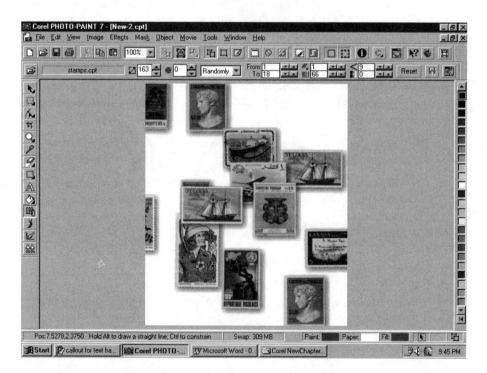

Figure 9-23: Before painting, these images of stamps were set to be sprayed smaller and spread farther apart than the previous image. Notice that without the background, the stamps appear more vivid.

The Image Sprayer Property Bar enables you to adjust the size of each image as it appears on your picture. Because the Image Sprayer tool works with several pictures applied as one paintbrush stroke, the Property Bar provides controls for the sequencing of those images. For example, you can have Photo-Paint apply "blue butterfly, red butterfly, yellow butterfly" in a sequence, or you can have the images applied in a random order. The Property Bar offers you the choice of whether to spray on your images "thin-ly," meaning with lots of space between each object, or "thickly." Spraying on your images more densely creates, for example, an effect of thick foliage, or of rocks piled on top of each other.

The Brush tool

With the Brush tool Property Bar (Figure 9-24), you can adjust brush shape, size, softness amount, and antialiasing. The Property Bar provides a complete list of brushes. Although both the Brush tool Tool Settings roll-up and the Property Bar provide icons of the brush types, only the Property Bar enables you to pass your mouse over the brush icon to see a tool-tip that tells you the name of the brush.

Figure 9-24: The Brush tool Property Bar has this appearance.

Figure 9-25 shows some of the effects you can achieve with the different kinds of brushes.

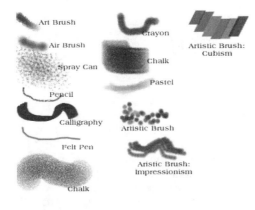

Figure 9-25: The standard Photo-Paint brushes produce these stroke examples.

With Photo-Paint 7, you modify each brush by selecting its *brush type*, perhaps more properly called a brush *method*. For example, within the Pencil category, you must choose between 2B, HB, Sharp & Hard, and Sharp & Soft pencil types. Similarly, the Chalk brush can be further defined by choosing Soft Rub, Medium Rub, and Hard, Square Rub.

Some of these brushes might appear impractical coming right out of the box, but tweaking them with the provided tools (see the Brush tool Property Bar, Figure 9-24) pays great dividends. From the Property Bar, you can adjust brush shape, size, softness amount, and antialiasing. Also, the Property Bar provides your only complete labeled list of brushes.

Special brush nibs

As mentioned earlier under the Eraser tool, the Nibs roll-up (which can be accessed from the Brush tools Property Bar) presents some unusual brush stroke possibilities. Figure 9-26 shows a handful of strokes applied using some of these nibs (brush tips).

Figure 9-26: Sample strokes use nibs from the Nibs roll-up.

Customizing a brush

From the Property Bar, click the Tool Settings roll-up button and select tab two or three. These tabs provide tools for painting with a bitmap or texture, adding watercolor properties to your brush, making color and hue variations to your brush stroke, and choosing options for saving your brush with the other preset brushes. Pictured in Figures 9-27 and 9-28 are the second and third tabs of the Brush tool Tool Settings roll-up.

Figure 9-27: The second tab of the Brush tool Tool Settings roll-up is selected.

Figure 9-28: The third tab of the Brush Tool Settings roll-up is selected.

From these menus, you may add a texture to your brush or import a bitmap to use as a brush texture. Adding a brush texture does not add color to your brush but simulates raised areas and depressions on your painting according to the colors of your texture bitmap. Light colors are interpreted as raised areas, dark colors, as depressions. Figure 9-29 shows a painting employing the "Coins" texture, which is a preset texture included with Photo-Paint.

Figure 9-29: Some brush strokes are shown employing the "Coins" texture.

Secret

To make the texture show through more, increase the "Soft Edge" of your brush.

Watercolors

The second tab of the Brush tool Tool Settings roll-up shows options for adjusting Watercolor settings of your brushes. These controls only apply if you are currently using a watercolor brush. The options control the Bleed and Sustain Color amounts. How "wet" do you want the painting to look? Should the colors bleed together aggressively or keep to their own? Figure 9-30 shows a few strokes using Photo-Paint's Watercolor brush. The canvas is sparse because I wanted to show the gradual fade that the Watercolor brush produces.

Figure 9-30: The Watercolor brush is shown at work. Note the tapering of the brush stroke.

Dab, spacing, and color variation control

The third tab of the Brush tool Tool Settings roll-up controls how many "dabs" of paint should be applied when you apply a single stroke. When applied with color variation, this tool can be useful for creatively "filling in" an empty area. Spacing refers to the amount of space in between the brush hairs of your brush. This creates the appearance of one of your brush strokes creating two or three parallel strokes.

The Color Variation controls can provide many a "happy accident" on your canvas. (See preceding Figure 9-28.) Use these HSL sliders to control the introduction of random color into your brush strokes. A high number means, for instance, that your brush stroke is more likely to introduce a little blue or green if you are currently using red. Lower numbers keep to your chosen hue but still interject a bit of random color play into your painting.

Saving a custom brush

At the bottom of each tab of the Brush tool Tool Settings roll-up dialog box is a Save Brush option. You'll be prompted to provide a new brush name. Your brush will be saved as a new *brush type* under the brush category itself. Think of your new brush as a new style or iteration of the main brush group. For example, if you are working with the Pointillism brush, edit it, and decide to save the edited brush as your own, remember that the Pointillism brush is a brush type of the Artistic Brush group. The next time you open Photo-Paint, look for your new brush: click the Artistic Brush icon and open the brush type menu (see Figure 9-24, the Brush tool Property Bar). Your brush will be there.

Using a Bitmap as Background for Gradient-Filled Text

This image (Figure A) was created using multiple layers of text converted to objects and applied to a bitmap background. Character spacing has been increased to make room for the drop shadow effect. Wide letter spacing also creates room for the letter contouring that occurs when you apply several layers of text with various paint modes, as was done here. This picture is also included on the CD, with all layers intact, for your experimentation.

Figure A: Here is another fancy-text example.

The Effects tool

The Effects tool Property Bar looks a lot like the Brush tool Property Bar, but the drop-down menus provide effects that are completely different. Figure 9-31 shows the Property Bar with the Brush Type menu open.

Figure 9-31: The Effects tool Property Bar is shown with the Brush Type menu open. The Effects tool roll-up shows the tools to choose from. The Property Bar shows the Brush Type menu for the Swirl tool.

With Photo-Paint, brushes are not limited to applying color but can be used to apply effects such as Smudge, Hue, and Blend. Similarly, the Paintbrush tool doesn't have to be shaped like a traditional brush but can apply effects to your picture in the shape of a Swirl, a Motion Blur, or a Rake, for example. So with the Photo-Paint Effects tool, you need to select two main parameters before painting on an effect:

- The Effects tool itself, such as Smudge, Tint, Undither, as well as the usual Brightness and Contrast tools. These are accessed by clicking the icon farthest to the left on the Effects tool Property Bar.

- The shape of the Effects tool, referred to as *brush type*. This is the first drop-down menu on the Effects tool Property Bar. Not only can you choose unusual shapes for your effect, but you can alter the effect mode by, for example, changing Sponge Add to Sponge Remove.

Figure 9-32 shows an image altered using Swirl, on the background, and Blend so that the color surrounding the horse itself appears to fade into the swirl background. This image is found on the accompanying CD, with all the layers intact, for your editing fun.

Figure 9-32: The horse is resting on a background that has been blended and swirled using the Effects tool.

The Clone tool

The Clone tool Property Bar provides options to change the clone type and method. Clone type refers to cloning your image using "painterly" styles employed by famous artists such as Van Gogh and Seurat. The all-important Clone from Saved tool is found here, which enables you to open the previously saved version of your current file and clone a portion of that image back into your current image. Use the Clone Method tool to make your cloning appear more like a brush stroke. The Cloning Method menu contains dozens of brush stroke choices for you to experiment with. The Clone tool Property Bar includes the usual Nib Shape and Size, Transparency, Anti-Aliasing, and Soft Edge tools, as well as links to the Brush Reset dialog box and the Clone Tool Settings roll-up.

Placement of the Property Bar

Because the Property Bar is rather long, often containing more than a dozen options, you may find it too cumbersome to work with as an attached bar. You can make it into a floating toolbar simply by pressing and holding your mouse down on any portion of it and dragging it into your image. Next, dragging inward from either side of the Bar causes the tools to double up in rows and become a wider, taller rectangle, rather than a short, skinny one.

Working with Photo-Paint's Toolbars

Photo-Paint has more than a dozen toolbars. Right-clicking on any open toolbar reveals a toolbar list. A check appears by each of the toolbars currently open. Whereas the Property Bar contains options to edit and refine the selected tool, each toolbar contains single-click access to the tools themselves. For example, the Paint Tools toolbar contains 16 brush types. The Movie toolbar contains buttons to stop, start, and record your movie. Often, each toolbar contains the same tools found on the toolbox on the far left of the screen, but expanded to provide easier access. Photo-Paint's toolbars are:

- Property Bar
- Version 6
- Standard
- Mask/Object
- Movie
- Roll-ups
- Toolbox
- Paint Tools

- Effects Tools
- Clone Tools
- Mask Tools
- Objects Tools
- Node Tools
- Zoom Tools
- Undo Tools
- More Tools

Note

The More Tools toolbar contains a menu for any personalized toolbars you create, as well as the Shape and Fill Tools toolbars.

When a toolbar appears on the screen, it appears as a floating toolbar. Pushing a floating toolbar rapidly up toward any side of the screen causes it to anchor there. Anchoring can sometimes cause toolbars to "double-up" two-to-a-row. This causes some of the tools to be hidden below the screen viewing area. Be careful not to anchor more than three or four toolbars at a time.

Arranging your toolbars

You can arrange your toolbars any way you like. If you wanted, you could reduce your work area to about an eighth of your screen space by filling it up with toolbars. (See Figure 9-33.) Photo-Paint forces you to spend a little time choosing the tools you really want to have handy. You'll need to keep the rest hidden under their menus.

Figure 9-33: All Photo-Paint's toolbars have been placed on the screen.

Resist the temptation to make your screen look like Figure 9-33. Remember that any tool you need can be accessed by selecting View ⇨ Roll-Ups or right-clicking on any blank toolbar space.

Here are a few helpful tips for placing toolbars on your screen:

Tip

■ Some toolbars, such as the Roll-Ups toolbar, take up less than half a horizontal screen. Others, such as the Node and Repeat Stroke toolbars, take up only two spaces. If you drag these minitoolbars next to each other, they stay put and create one long toolbar. This is better than taking up lots of vertical space with tiny toolbars.

■ Toolbars will snap to the position you drag them toward. They can be anchored up, down, right, or left. Any toolbar can be a floating toolbar.

■ Whatever you do, don't put away the Property Bar.

■ Get to know the Command Recorder. With it, you can automate routine tasks, making some toolbars unnecessary.

■ Instead of having lots of toolbars up, learn some keyboard shortcuts for oft-repeated tasks. Use the Customize Toolbars dialog box to create new shortcut key commands.

Customizing your toolbars

Figure 9-34 shows the Customize dialog box with the Toolbars tab selected. Open it by Selecting View ➪ Toolbars ➪ Customize. In this example, the Tools folder is open, and the mouse is hovering over the Pen Settings tool button. By dragging that tool button to any toolbar on the screen, you can cause it to remain there and be operative whenever the toolbar is opened. (By the way, if you own a stylus, this feature enables you to customize Photo-Paint to support your stylus's pressure settings and special features.) That's how easy it is to customize a toolbar.

Figure 9-34: The Customize dialog box Toolbars tab can be attached to any toolbar.

The Toolbars tab is on top. From here, you can take any menu function and place it on a toolbar. The folder icons to the left represent the menus. Click any folder icon, and you'll see a ready-made icon for each command under that menu. If you want instant access to a command, just drag it to any toolbar on your screen. It's as easy as that.

Note

Clicking on the Menu tab enables you to move commands from one menu to another. The Keyboard tab enables you to assign shortcut keys to almost any Photo-Paint function. The Roll-Ups and Color Palette tabs can be used to set new options for those features.

Customizing the status bar

Secret

Just as you can customize Photo-Paints toolbars, you can modify the status bar to suit your own work habits. Right-click the status bar. Click Customize. The Toolbar Customize dialog box appears. At this time, you may open any folder of commands, such as those found in the File or Edit menu. Notice icons appear on the right, one icon for each command found in the opened menu folder. Drag any icon you like to the status bar and it'll stay there. You are not removing it from its "home" menu but merely making a copy of it and moving it. Figure 9-35 shows my own modified status bar, to which I have added the "What's This?" icon, which is usually located in the Help menu. Any time I forget what a tool button or menu item does, I can simply drag this icon to that item and click.

Figure 9-35: A customized Photo-Paint status bar has the "What's This?" icon added.

Getting Your Colors Right

Just as important as editing your document with clever tools and special effects is the job of making sure your final color values are something to be proud of. Photo-Paint enables you to adjust color ranges in your document, select a palette from among many choices, change the overall hue of your document, and alter the color composition of your work in many ways.

Screen dithering

When you must work in 256-color mode, use screen dithering. Found under the View menu, screen dithering combines pixels to simulate colors available only in the 65,000 or 16 million color ranges. Two types of screen dithering are available: ordered, which is fast, and error diffusion, which is more accurate but takes longer to render.

Color correction

Choose View ➪ Color Correction to open the Color Correction menu. Color Correction helps keep your colors accurate in two ways:

- It ensures that the colors you select and use in a particular picture are allowable under the parameters you've set in Corel Color Manager.

- It enables your screen to display colors as they will appear in your printed work.

Within the Color Correction menu are four options:

- **Accurate:** This choice lets you trade speed for accuracy depending on the size of your image and your need for the most accurate color viewing.

- **Fast:** This choice lets you trade accuracy for speed depending on the size of your image and your need for the most accurate color viewing.

- **Gamut Alarm:** If you pick a color that is out of range according to your Color Manager system profile, your monitor will display that color as an ugly neon green. Gamut alarm permits you to choose a color besides neon green as your "alarm color."

- **Simulate Printer:** When you pick a color to use in your picture, Photo-Paint replaces it with the nearest color that your printer can print.

Color hue control

Select Image ➪ Adjust ➪ Color Hue to open the Color Hue Control dialog box. (See Figure 9-36.) It always opens with the current picture on display.

Figure 9-36: The Color Hue Control dialog box opens with the current picture.

Photo-Paint's Hue Control option enables you to increase the presence of a chosen hue in your picture. The effects are more subtle than simply tinting.

Each of the panels at the bottom half of the dialog box shows the results of accenting a particular hue in your picture; hence the panel names: More Green, More Red, and so on. Happily, you aren't simply adjusting the hue for the entire color range of the picture. Look at the checkboxes under the Adjust menu. You may increase magenta for the shadows of your picture and increase yellow for the midtones of your picture, for example. The flexibility of adding several subtle effects gives this tool a much wider application than tinting.

Click one of the six frames below, and the large frame on the upper right, Result, will show your picture with the adjusted hue value. The upper frame on the left, Original, enables you to compare "before" and "after" close up. The frame on the upper right will continue to show your updated hue choices if you've chosen more than one adjustment. You are not limited to adjusting only one parameter. The slider labeled Step controls how *much* More Green or More Yellow, for example, you apply by clicking.

The "hand" and "magnifying glass" icons enable you to pan across your picture, should it be larger than the screen can display, or zoom in on a particular portion. Click the small icon under the Results frame if you'd like to view the Results twice as large.

Secret

The Color Balance option, accessed by selecting Image ⇨ Adjust ⇨ Color Balance, is just like Hue Control, except that it employs sliders rather than panels of pictures to click.

Color tone control

Select Image ⇨ Adjust ⇨ Color Tone to open the Color Tone Control dialog box. (See Figure 9-37.) It operates the same way as the Color Hue dialog box. Use this feature to make your image lighter or darker, to increase or decrease color saturation, or to raise or lower overall image contrast.

Figure 9-37: The Color Tone Control dialog box enables control of saturation and contrast.

Color transform commands

These commands, found under the Image menu, are useful for correcting lines in scanned images, inverting all the colors in your picture, and simplifying the shades of color in a complex picture.

Deinterlace

The Deinterlace command (Image ➪ Transform ➪ Deinterlace) removes lines created by scanning or capturing video images. To replace the discarded lines with color, choose one of the four methods provided. Experiment to see which brings the best results.

Invert

Invert reverses all the colors in your image, creating a "photo negative" effect.

Posterize

Posterize reduces the number of colors in your image, creating a "'60s pop art" effect. This option is useful when a printer is not capable of reproducing all the colors used in a particular complex image.

Level equalization

Choose Image ➪ Adjust ➪ Level Equalization to bring up the dialog box displayed in Figure 9-38.

Figure 9-38: The Level Equalization dialog box offers choices to improve the color value of images.

Level Equalization improves the color value of images that appear too dark, too light, or too lacking in contrast. To let Photo-Paint make the adjustments for you, bypass this dialog box altogether and select Image ➪ Adjust ➪ Auto Levels instead. Level Equalization spreads the color pixels more evenly between the darkest and lightest portions of your picture. Three problems occur that Level Equalization can fix. Here are the techniques:

■ If your picture is too light, your mission is to get Level Equalization to redistribute pixels along a darker scale.

■ If your picture is too dark, you want to set up a lighter range, hopefully replacing some of the darkest pixels with lighter hues.

■ If your picture is too muddy and lacks contrast, you'll want to increase the spread, making Level Equalization spread pixels across a larger range of color values.

Why not just use Brightness/Contrast or Darken/Lighten? Because you'll lose shadows and depth. If you overdo those controls, your picture will look flat. Level Equalization lets you redistribute *the range* of pixels, rather than just add some at the top or the bottom.

Here's how to use Level Equalization:

You have an Eyedropper tool for selecting what you would like to be the lightest and darkest colors in your picture. You will be using one eyedropper to select the lightest pixels in your picture and another eyedropper to select the darkest.

Now if you simply go ahead and select the lightest and darkest regions as they are right now, nothing will change. But your job is to use these eyedroppers to skew the scale in the right direction:

■ If your picture is too dark, then you should use the "dark extreme" eyedropper to select a region of your picture that is not as dark as the darkest black.

■ If your picture is too light, then you should use the "lightest color" eyedropper to pick out a color that is not quite as white as the whitest part.

■ If your picture lacks contrast, then go ahead and select the true "darkest" and "lightest" regions with your eyedropper, but then set the Input Value Clipping arrows and the Output Range Compression arrows for wider ranges than you find them. Doing so spreads the colors in your pixels across a wider range.

You may have to experiment with eyedropper selection ranges to achieve optimal results.

Figure 9-39 shows a muddy picture before and after a trip to the Level Equalizer.

Before

After

Figure 9-39: Level Equalization has improved a picture's contrast.

Warning

Don't select Color Correction unless you've already created a system profile with Corel Color Manager. When you create a system profile, Corel Color Manager creates a record of the colors your computer hardware and software are truly capable of producing. Until you've created a Color Manager system profile, Color Correction won't have anything to adjust to.

Color channels

A channel holds color information about your picture. If you're working with an RGB picture, your picture contains three channels: one describes how much red is in your picture, one, how much blue, and one, how much green. If you select Image ⇨ Split Channels To, your picture will display a new image for each of these three channels. These images "were there all along," so to speak. That's because whenever you create a new image with Photo-Paint, channel information is automatically created for the image. In Figure 9-40 the Channels roll-up shows a picture that was split into its RGB channels. Images can be split according to any of several color models: CMYK, HSB, HLS, YIQ, and LAB.

Figure 9-40: The Channels roll-up shows a picture split into RGB channels.

Having divided your image into separate channels, you can now perform edits on each individual channel image and recombine them (select Image ⇨ Combine Channels) to create some interesting color qualities. For some interesting special effects, try spitting and combining channels according to different color modes. Experiments such as these can fall into the category of the "happy accident." You'll never know unless you try it.

Secret

You'll notice that when you split your image into channels, each channel appears in grayscale. To have the channels appear in their respective colors, select Tools ⇨ Options ⇨ Display and click the Tint Channels checkbox. Doing this has no effect on the how channels are combined or operate.

Note

There's another type of channel called an Alpha channel. Alpha channels are used for masks, which are the subject of the next chapter, Chapter 10.

Working with Objects in Photo-Paint

Before getting into the secrets of working with objects in Photo-Paint, let's review the difference between three of the most important elements you use in Photo-Paint: masks, paths, and objects.

A *mask* is a selection of pixels on the surface of an image. You make that selection by choosing color ranges or by area. A masked area is then edited. Masks are not necessarily a sharply bordered, carved out selection; they are simply temporary aids for setting aside a portion of an image for editing. They can be gradual or feathered. The edited effect you perform on the masked area need not end abruptly. Masks are covered thoroughly in Chapter 10.

A *path* is a shape or a line created by the Node tool. The Node tool is capable of great precision, and paths are usually highly detailed outlines of a portion of a bitmapped image. Paths can be lines. They need not be closed shapes. A path can be copied and reapplied to the same image, and it can be treated with special effects. A path can also be stroked with paint and then removed, leaving the paint behind on the canvas. Unlike a bitmap, a path never loses the integrity of its shape — no matter how much you enlarge it. Paths can be saved as .EPS files and opened in other applications, even vector-based programs such as CorelDraw.

Objects are bitmapped images that occupy their own layer in front of a background image (or on top of it, if you like). They need never be merged or combined with the background image. They can be reshaped and edited, and they can be merged with other layers to create special effects. For example, in Photo-Paint, you can create a drop shadow on an object with only a single mouse-click.

Note

Not all selecting tools have the same capabilities. The Object and Mask Transform tools are both used to select things, but if you click a mask with the Object tool, nothing happens.

The Objects roll-up

Figure 9-41 shows the Objects roll-up, accessible by choosing View ⇨ Roll-Ups ⇨ Objects. The Objects roll-up shows two objects and one background. One object, the balloon group, is selected and available for editing. As an object, it is floating above the background image on its own layer. Consequently, it can be recolored and reshaped without affecting the underlying image. The man is also an object. To see a marquee around the objects on your page, select Object ⇨ Marquee Visible. The Objects roll-up contains options to make chosen objects invisible, uneditable, and merged with the background image. You can also experiment with paint modes and transparency levels using the Objects roll-up. The object you are editing will have a bounding box around it in the roll-up.

Figure 9-41: The Objects roll-up is shown with a corresponding picture.

In Figure 9-41, the photo composition of a man in very warm clothing chasing balloons around the Easter Island statue was assembled using objects in Photo-Paint. Here's how you can recreate this image:

STEPS

Creating a Composite Image Using Objects

Step 1. Open the image CLRCAST.CPT (found on your Corel CD) and use the Magic Wand tool to select the man and his clothing. The Magic Wand tool is one of the Mask Selection tools, the second tool from the left on the toolbox. Press and hold your mouse button to see the drop-down menu of Mask selection tools. You'll have to play with the Tolerance settings to make sure you get only the pixels you want, with no white or blue. Remember that higher tolerance settings increase the likelihood of selecting unwanted pixels. Tolerance values can be adjusted from the Tool Settings dialog box for the Magic Wand tool. See Figure 9-42.

Figure 9-42: Extract the climber from the snow and turn him into an object.

Step 2. Select Create From Mask from the Object menu. This converts your mask into an object. Copy it to the Windows Clipboard.

Step 3. Open HEAVYRIP.CPT, also found on your Corel CD. Open the Objects roll-up as well.

Step 4. Select Paste from the Edit menu and choose Paste as Object. Position the man as he appears in Figure 9-41. You'll need to use the Object Rotate tools to obtain the angle shown. This is done by clicking twice on the man with the Object Picker tool and rotating him to your liking.

Step 5. Open the Balloon image. If you are not a fan of balloons, you may open a similarly sized object. We are going to be converting the balloon group to a mask and painting a shadow of the balloons on the Easter Island statue, so if you use a different image, keep that in mind.

Step 6. Using the Magic Wand tool again, select the balloons, convert them into an object, and copy them to the Windows Clipboard.

Step 7. Paste the balloon group as an object into the Easter Island image. Position them as shown in the picture. Notice your Objects roll-up shows two objects now. Instructions I now give for moving and copying the balloon group will not work unless the balloon group is selected in the Objects roll-up.

Step 8. While the balloons are selected, click Mask ⇨ Create from Object. Make sure there's a checkmark by Marquee Visible in the Mask menu. You'll see "marching ants" around the balloons. Actually, the balloons haven't been touched. They're not selected at all. It's the mask you've just created from the balloon group object that is selected.

Step 9. Using the Object Picker tool, select the balloons and click Edit ➪ Cut.

Step 10. Switch to the Mask Transform tool. Make sure you're using the 4-way arrow, which moves masks. Move the "marching ants" mask over to the lower middle of the Easter Island Statue, where you see the balloon shadow positioned in the final version of this picture (Figure 9-41).

Step 11. Use the Distort tool to stretch the balloon shadow downward slightly. Select Mask ➪ Feather and choose 1 for Width, and Middle for Direction.

Step 12. Making sure the mask is still selected, choose the Fill tool and make the fill color black. Fill the mask with the shadow color. If the shadow edges appear too sharp and not natural enough, chose Mask ➪ Feather again, use the same settings as in step 11, and again fill the widened mask with black paint.

Step 13. Select Edit ➪ Paste ➪ Paste as Object. The balloons will reappear. Reposition the balloon group with reference to the light source in the picture, making the shadow as realistic as possible. Position the man so that it looks as if he is truly after those balloons. By now I'm sure he wishes he'd brought something cooler to wear.

The Object menu

The Object menu contains three interesting commands that deserve special attention: Tag WWW URL, Clip Object to Mask, and Defringe.

Tag WWW URL

If you have an object selected with the Object tool, clicking this command creates a clickable HTML map from it. (The command does not destroy or alter the object itself.) After clicking, you'll see a screen showing the object you clicked. You'll be asked to type in a Universal Resource Locator (URL) and make any comments that will help you remember where clicking on this image will lead you. When you save your image, you'll be asked to save the image as an .HTM file as well. The object's coordinates and image data are saved as a clickable region within the .HTM file itself. Simply put, the Tag WWW URL command creates an HTML image map from your object.

Clip Object to Mask

Let's quickly review the difference between an object and a mask. An object is a bitmap that floats above the background image in its own layer. A mask is a way of setting aside a portion of the surface of an image for editing. So, yes, you can apply a mask to an object just as easily as you can to a background image.

Here's how the Clip Object to Mask command works:

STEPS

Using the Clip Object to Mask Command

Step 1. Use a masking tool on an object to set aside some pixels for editing. When you are done, use the Object Picker tool to make sure the object is selected.

Step 2. Select Object ⇨ Clip Object to Mask. Any part of the object that covers an area outside the mask will be clipped off.

Figure 9-43 shows an object on a background with a mask applied to it. The background is the crosshatch pattern. Above that is the archaeological site with the two tourists walking. The mask is the area surrounded by "marching ants." It was selected using the Magic Wand masking tool. The purpose was to select all of the archaeological site but leave out the blue sky.

Figure 9-43: The object is the archaeological site. The mask covers all of it except for the blue sky. "Marching ants" show the mask's boundaries.

Figure 9-44 shows the results of clicking Clip Object to Mask. The sky is gone from the archaeological site. You see no more sky in the object because it has shrunk down to the size of the mask.

Figure 9-44: The object has shrunk down to the size of the mask.

Figure 9-45 shows the composite picture, after the special effect, "The Boss," was applied. Special effects are explained in detail in Chapter 6.

Figure 9-45: The composite picture is complete.

The Defringe command

The Defringe command, found under the Object menu, is used when a selection you imported as an object was not trimmed very well. Sometimes a fringe of white pixels (not necessarily white, actually) gets imported along with your image. The Defringe command removes the fringe of pixels. You specify the width of the fringe to be removed. Figure 9-46 shows imported text as a bitmap sorely in need of defringing. Figure 9-47 shows the results of the operation.

Figure 9-46: The text bitmap was cut out of another picture and placed against the new backdrop. A white fringe got imported with the bitmap.

Figure 9-47: Here's how the same composition looks after the Defringe command was used.

Other Photo-Paint Features

Photo-Paint 7 includes so many new features that it's not surprising that a handful of tools defy easy categorization. For instance, there's the Repeat Stroke tool, the Command Recorder, and the Navigator pop-up.

The Repeat Stroke tool

The Repeat Stroke tool appears on the same toolbar as the Node tool. You can view this toolbar by selecting View ⇨ Toolbars ⇨ Node Tools. (See Figure 9-48.)

Figure 9-48: The Node and Repeat Stroke tools appear together.

Click the Repeat Stroke tool, and your mouse becomes a point-and-click paintbrush. Click your canvas and a paint stroke appears. The Repeat Stroke tool roll-up (see Figure 9-49) enables you to edit your strokes. Increase the stroke number so that clicking once creates several strokes. You can also assign randomness to your brush stroke, which brings kind of a crosshatch "driving rain" feel to your picture. You can assign a certain degree of random size and direction to your brush stroke, which could create an "impression-ist" feel if applied with discretion. Figure 9-50 shows some interesting brush strokes generated with the Repeat Stroke tool.

Figure 9-49: The Repeat Brush Stroke tool roll-up permits you to repeat brush strokes to achieve special effects.

Figure 9-50: These strokes have been created with the Repeat Brush Stroke tool. The Simple stroke is selected.

Notice the drop-down menu on the Tool Settings dialog box. It says the word Simple. No other entries appear in the menu. That's because the only way to load an entirely new brush stroke is to load it from a path you have created with the Node tool. (That's why the Node tool and Repeat Brush Stroke tool are in the same toolbox.) Here's how to make a new brush stroke that can be used as a Repeat brush stroke in your painting:

STEPS

Making a New Brush Stroke Available as a Repeat Brush Stroke

Step 1.   Use the Node tool to create a path on your canvas.

Step 2.   Select Stroke Current Path from the Tool roll-up dialog box.

Alternatively, you can load a saved path from an earlier session: Using the Node tool, make a path that looks like the brush stroke shape you'd like to make.

Step 3.   Save the path as a .PTH file, as you would any path.

Step 4.   Select the Repeat Brush Stroke tool and click the right-facing arrow next to the drop-down menu that says "Simple" on the Tool Settings drop-down menu roll-up. A Save/Load/New menu appears. Select Load Path as Stroke. The path is loaded onto your canvas.

Step 5.   The next time you click the canvas, the path will be stroked with the brush type and style you have selected.

If the brush stroke style you have selected is too "out there," you're likely to get undesirable results when you apply it to a path.

The Command Recorder

Command Recorder records your actions, keyboard sequences, toolbar clicks, and paint strokes. It saves them as macros, or *scripts*. Command Recorder displays your actions as single lines of text, and you can use the Command Recorder roll-up to relocate, edit, and delete any action. Figure 9-51 shows the Command Recorder roll-up in the process of recording a command sequence. The record button (red) is pushed, and Insert New Commands is enabled. Then click the right-facing arrow to access the Save/Load/New menu. After completing your command sequence, press Stop (Command Recorder's buttons function like those of a tape recorder), and save your script. It will be saved as a .CSC file and can be opened and executed by clicking on it.

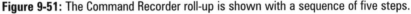

Figure 9-51: The Command Recorder roll-up is shown with a sequence of five steps.

The Command Recorder is similar to Corel Script Editor, which is examined later in this book. (See Chapter 18 for a more complete discussion of scripts.) Script Editor is a complete scripting tool that can be used to create large macros in Corel that include buttons, radio buttons, multiple choice checkboxes, and other Windows tools.

Secret

As with any graphic-based macro recorder, it is best to avoid mouse-oriented commands that involve clicking on a toolbar. A particular toolbar might not be in the same location the next time you use Photo-Paint. Use keyboard commands and menus, rather than toolbars, to design scripts.

The Navigator pop-up

If you open an image that is significantly larger than the screen, you'll notice a small white square at the bottom right of your picture. When you click and hold this square, a miniature version of your picture appears. Notice the gray bounded box inside the Navigator screen. You'll find that you can maneuver this box in and around your picture to determine which portion you want to view. See Figure 9-52 for an example of the Navigator pop-up in action.

Figure 9-52: The Navigator pop-up is shown in action.

The Undo list

The Undo list, accessible by selecting Edit ➪ Undo List, holds each edit you've performed on your picture, keeping them available for you to undo any procedure as far back as the most recent save. (See Figure 9-53.) Saving your work clears the Undo list. You may undo as many procedures at one time as you like. Selecting all procedures on the list for Undo has the same effect as reverting back to your last saved version of the image.

Figure 9-53: The Undo list lets you work back to your last save.

The Movie menu

Photo-Paint's Movie tool creates a simple .AVI file from a series of pictures you create. Figure 9-54 shows the Movie menu when you first open it.

Figure 9-54: The Movie menu appears like this when you begin your project.

The only active control is Create from Document. Here's how it works:

STEPS

Creating a New Movie

Step 1.   After creating a picture, select Movie ⇨ Create from Document.

Your picture now has plus and minus signs in its bottom-left corner. These are your Add Frame and Rewind to Beginning tools.

Step 2.   Click the plus sign at the bottom-left of your picture. The dialog box shown in Figure 9-55 appears.

Figure 9-55: The Insert Frames dialog box lets you add frames to your movie.

Step 3.   Add as many frames to your movie as you like. The new frames will be blank .AVI frames, not .CPT files. You can now go back and use any paint or editing tool to create a movie from your individual .AVI frames.

Step 4. After creating a few frames, choose Movie ➪ Movie Control. (See Figure 9-56.) These are the controls for playing back, fast forwarding, and rewinding your movie.

Figure 9-56: The Movie Control menu controls the movie's play.

Step 5. Your .AVI file's control menu (Minimize ➪ Maximize ➪ Move) in the upper-left corner now has a Close option. Select this, and you'll be prompted to save your .AVI file on your hard drive.

Step 6. Your project can be played back on Windows Media Player or any device that plays .AVI files.

Summary

▶ The Property Bar changes with every tool you select. Knowing what's available on the Property Bar saves you from having to hunt for tool options from a list of menus.

▶ A myriad of paint brushes come with Photo-Paint, and you can even create your own brushes.

▶ Photo-Paint's color correction and color editing tools can make your image work successfully when you move it from the computer screen out into the world of printed material.

▶ The Repeat Brush Stroke tool, the Navigator pop-up, and the Movie menu are among the tools that you'll find extremely useful.

Chapter 10

Photo-Paint Masks

In This Chapter

You'll look more closely at masks. You'll learn:

▶ What masks are used for

▶ How to create masks

▶ How to float masks

▶ How you can brush masks onto an image

▶ How to create a mask from text

▶ How to use color range masks

▶ How to feather masks

Masking Fundamentals

You use masks to select an area of your image you wish to modify in some way. After you apply a mask, your image is divided into two areas: the selected area and the protected area. The area where the mask is applied is the *selected area*. Any editing you do to the selected area affects *only that area*. The rest of the image is protected. No pixels outside the selected area will be altered. You can also select an area with a mask tool and then invert the mask. When you do that, the area that used to be protected becomes the selected area for editing, and vice versa.

Only one mask can appear on your image at a time. That is because masks are temporary selections. Clicking outside the selection terminates the mask.

Creating masks

You have two methods for creating masks:

■ Area selection

■ Color range

For *area selection,* you use a tool to select a group of pixels conforming to the shape of your chosen tool (for example, a rectangle, an ellipse, or a polygon shape, and so on). By definition, all pixels selected using this kind of mask are contiguous. In other words, all of the pixels are in some way connected to other pixels in the selected area.

For *color range* masks, you select an area or areas based on the color of the pixels. For example, you might use the Color Mask tool or the Magic Wand tool to select areas of your picture that have a certain shade of red. A mask created by a color range tool does *not* have to be all the same color. You can use a tool to select a range of color — say, from orange to yellow — depending on the particular tool's capabilities. The Color Mask tool, for instance, lets you use the Eyedropper to pick a large range of colors from your image for masking. Masks created by color range tools are not necessarily composed of contiguous pixels. You can select pixels for this type of mask that are not connected to each other at all.

Adjusting mask transparency

Every mask has a transparency value. As mentioned earlier, you use masking to select one area of your image and protect another. But you can set your mask so that a certain amount of the editing process will be blocked. For example, if you create a mask and color it red, you can adjust the mask so that the red "fades out" around the edges of the mask. This helps create much more realistic effects than sharp mask borders. A simple mask, one that allows the full effect of an effect to show through, has a transparency value of zero.

Although you couldn't tell by looking at it, a mask is actually a gray-scale cover applied on top of your image. (Think of it as being like a wire-mesh screen with loosely or tightly woven mesh.) A simple mask with *no* transparency would then be entirely black; its pixel value would be zero. Entirely transparent areas of the mask would be white, or have a pixel value of 255. Portions of your mask that allow half of an effect to show through would have a 127 pixel value. For example, if you applied a "cloud" effect to an area where the mask began with no transparency and gradually became 50 percent transparent, you would see clouds begin to appear over the partially transparent portion of the mask. If you applied the same "cloud" effect to a masked area that moved dramatically from zero transparency to full transparency, you would see a sharp border where clouds would suddenly appear. To apply these graduated effects, use the Interactive Transparency tool found on the toolbox. While your mask is selected, press and hold the mouse button over the Fill tool, and you'll see this tool "fly out" from the toolbox.

Moving masks

You can move a mask in any of three different ways:

- You can use the Mask Transform tool to move the boundary of the mask without affecting the underlying image.

- You can move both the mask and the portion of the image that is covered by the mask.

- You can move both the mask and a *copy* of the portion of the image covered by the mask. (This is called "floating" the mask.)

Using the Mask Transform tool

It's important to understand the difference between the mask itself and the portion of the image under the mask. Figure 10-1 shows the Mask Transform tool. You use this tool to move the "marching ants" boundary, which shows the outline of the mask itself. When you use the Mask Transform tool, you move the mask from one portion of the image and use the mask to protect pixels in another part of the image. The area of the image that was originally protected by the mask remains unchanged.

Figure 10-1: With the Mask Transform tool, this oval mask can be moved without affecting the underlying image. Any new editing performed will now affect the area where the mask is moved.

Remember

Remember that the Mask Transform tool has its own drop-down menu of shape-changing effects, such as Distort, Perspective, and Scale. (Figure 10-2 shows this drop-down menu, which is available from the Property Bar — not the toolbox.) When you repeatedly click your image with the Mask Transform tool, you can scroll through these effects with each click. You will see the bounding boxes around your mask change depending on the particular effect selected. The status bar tells you which one is operative at a given moment. Move the bounding boxes to preview the effect. You'll find that the bounding boxes move differently depending on which effect you are applying. For example, the Perspective tool's bounding boxes move forward, then inward or outward, depending on if you want a "narrowing" or "broadening" Perspective effect. The Distort tool allows you to move any bounding box irrespective of the others. To apply the effect, click inside the boxes. (The status bar also prompts you through this procedure.) Hold your mouse over any of the Mask Transform tool buttons for a tool-tip about what it does.

Figure 10-2: The Mask Transform tool's drop-down menu is reached from the Property Bar.

Moving the mask boundary and the underlying image

When you want to move the selection itself (the image under the mask), select any mask tool, such as the Magic Wand or Lasso tool, click *inside* the marquee, and drag. You'll be cutting a portion of the image out, leaving a hole where it used to be. Unless you've changed the paper color, that hole will be white.

Floating a mask

You can also "float" a mask. When you *float* a mask, you copy the selected portion of the image to the Windows Clipboard without leaving a hole in the image. To do this, click Mask on the menu bar and choose Float before moving the selection. You could use this feature to build an object from several identical smaller objects, such as creating a flower from petals, or a checkerboard effect from a series of identical squares.

Saving masks

If you want to preserve your mask for later use, you need to save the mask to disk or save it as a channel.

To save a mask to disk, choose Save from the Mask menu. A mask can be saved as a .PSD, .CPT, 24-bit .TGA, or .TIF file. Adobe Photoshop 3 or 4 recognizes masks saved as .PSD files. (The masks open as active selections.) A .TIF or .TGA file that contains an alpha channel opens in Fractal Design Painter 4 or Photoshop 3 or 4 with the mask as an active selection.

You can also save the mask as an *alpha channel*, referred to in Photo-Paint as a *mask channel*. Alpha channels are sections of your image set aside for storing mask information. These channels can be reopened later for editing the masked area. Saving complex masks as alpha channels means that you don't have to create the same mask later. You can save several alpha channels in a single painting. This practice is one way to work around the limitation of the software not being capable of having more than one mask open at once in your document. By saving and reloading masks as alpha channels, you at least don't have to create them again. Also, saving a mask as an *alpha channel* allows the mask to be edited in other programs that use them.

The Mask Overlay option

When you are creating a complicated mask on your image, it's often helpful to see only your mask selection. Select Mask ⇨ Mask Overlay, and your entire image except the masked portion will be covered with a red tint. You can turn this overlay on or off without affecting the image itself.

The Invert Mask command

Secret

If the portion of your image that you wish to mask is very complicated, in terms of shape and color, and the other part of the image is simple, you can select the portion that's easily masked and then invert the mask (click Mask ⇨ Invert). Now the difficult portion of your image will be masked. This technique is much easier than spending hours trying to outline the exact shape of complex, irregular pictures. Figures 10-3 and 10-4 show the Invert Mask command at work.

Figure 10-3: The background is masked on this image using the Magic Wand tool, which is explained a little later.

Figure 10-4: After using the Invert Mask command, the flower itself is masked.

Area Selection Masks

Press and hold your mouse pointer over the main masking tool (near the top of the toolbox), and you'll see the seven area-selection masking tools on a flyout from the toolbox. They are:

- The Rectangular Mask tool
- The Elliptical Mask tool
- The Irregular Polygon Mask tool
- The Brush Mask tool
- The Scissors tool
- The Lasso tool
- The Magic Wand tool

Only the Rectangular, Elliptical, Irregular Polygon, and Brush Mask tools select a simple bounded area without reference to the color of the pixels involved. The other three area-selection masking tools — Scissors, Lasso, and Magic Wand — have both area-selection *and* color range capabilities. (Those tools are discussed later in this chapter.)

Figure 10-5 shows the selection of tools when you click and hold the masking tool button.

Freehand Mask tool
Rectangle Mask tool
Scissors Mask tool
Mask Brush tool

Circle Mask tool
Lasso Mask tool
Magic Wand Mask tool
Mask Transform tool

Figure 10-5: The flyout menu showing the area-selection masking tools.

The Property Bar and Tool Settings roll-up change depending on the tool you select. Figure 10-6 shows the Property Bar's four tool options when you choose one of the area-selection tools.

Create a
new mask
Subtract from an
existing mask

Add to an
existing mask
The XOR
Mask button

Figure 10-6: These are the first four options on the Property Bar when an area-selection masking tool is activated.

If you are starting a new mask on your image, the arrow should be depressed. If you are adding to a mask, you should click the plus (+) sign. Use the minus (–) sign to remove a portion of an existing mask. You use the double-squared tool for XOR masking.

The Area Mask Operations menu

The drop-down menu next to the first four tools (see Figure 10-5) is the Area Mask Operations menu. While using the Rectangle and Ellipse tools, you will find the following four settings available:

■ **Normal.** The tool has no angular or scale constraints.

■ **Fixed Size.** Clicking your picture "drops" a mask of a specific height and width. Next to the drop-down menu are two numerical data boxes. You may input any number (measured in pixels) for the mask's width and height.

- **Rows.** This option selects a small but wide strip of an area, similar in appearance to a row of spreadsheet data.

- **Columns.** The option selects a tall but thin strip of an area, similar in appearance to a column of spreadsheet data.

When you are using the other area-selection mask tools, this drop-down menu allows you to switch between two types of Color Tolerance modes: Normal and HSB. The HSB mode is helpful for intelligently narrowing the scope of pixels you want to select with your tool. You can, for example, make your tool ignore an area that is particularly dark or highly saturated with color, while selecting pixels that are otherwise quite similar.

The Brush Mask tool

The Brush Mask tool paints a mask onto your picture. Using the paintbrush Property Bar and the Tool Settings roll-up, you can create any type of brush, brush size, number of bristles, transparency amount, or stroke quality; in fact, any brush parameter besides color can also be used to modify the Brush Mask tool. Using the Zoom tool with the Brush Mask tool, you can build a very precise mask that still has some personality to it.

Figure 10-7 shows some rather "painterly" strokes rendered with the Brush Mask tool.

Figure 10-7: The Brush Mask tool is shown at work.

Other area-selection masking tools

Now let's look at a handful of other tools that employ methods for selecting shapes and areas (rather than color ranges).

The XOR Mask tool

Figure 10-8 shows the XOR (pronounced *X-O-R*) Mask tool in action. When you create a mask and then add it to a prior mask, you unmask the area where your new selection overlaps with the preexisting mask. In Figure 10-8, the black area and the light gray area are selected. The dark gray between them is no longer selected because it is the overlapping area. The XOR effect can be used for creating masks that overlap. The XOR effect allows an underlying image to show through where the masks converge.

Figure 10-8: The XOR Mask tool is shown in action.

The Anti-Alias option

Anti-Alias is an option that can be used with almost all of Photo-Paint's mask tools. It is especially useful for area-selection masks. (The Anti-Alias button is found on almost every tool's Property Bar, usually toward the right end. By default, antialiasing is enabled.) With Anti-Alias enabled, the tiny jagged edges that are inevitably included with your mask selection are smoothed out. The need for antialiasing is simply part of the process of working with bitmaps rather than more precise vector images. Unless you have an affinity for jagged edges, leave the Anti-Alias option selected.

Expand/Reduce

Expand/Reduce expands or reduces the size of your mask according to the number of pixels you choose. This is a simple area command that takes no consideration of the colors of the surrounding pixels. Select Mask ⇨ Shape from the menu bar and then choose Expand or Reduce.

Text masks

Text is always created as an object. However, you can convert text to a mask to create a stencil effect with the text. Figure 10-9 shows four smaller pictures converted to objects and pasted onto a textured background. The text "Be Here Now" was created and then converted into a mask. The mask was cut, leaving only the hole for the underlying image behind the four pictures to show through. The phrase "Be Here Now" then became visible as a stencil "cutout." You can create raised or embossed effects by pasting the previously cut text over the cut out area as an object and then applying paint modes. The text in Figure 10-9 was created using this technique along with the Luminosity paint mode.

Figure 10-9: An image has been created by converting text to a mask.

Here are the steps for creating Figure 10-9:

STEPS
Converting Text to a Mask

Step 1. Create a background with a fill or a bitmap.

Step 2. Paste in four square images as objects, and place them evenly over the background. You must select images that contrast highly against the background. (That's because after you remove the text stencil, the background image shows through as text.) High contrast with the top images will make the results more legible.

Step 3. Use the Text tool to create a brief text phrase. You may have to try selecting a font size several times until you've covered just the right amount of image with your text.

Step 4. For maximum effect, position your text evenly over all four square image objects.

Step 5. Because the text is an object, you must click Mask ➪ Create from Object, and then cut the text, which is now a mask.

Step 6. This leaves a hole the underlying image can show through.

Step 7. Try applying the text again, positioning it over the hole, and experimenting with Paint Modes.

Secret

You can also use objects as stencils, turning them into masks and removing the mask, leaving a hole in the image that matches the outline of your object.

Color Range Masks

Unlike area-selection masking tools, color range masking tools are based on the color of pixels rather than shape or contiguity. For example, if an image has lavender colorings and you want to shift the lavender to more of a red, you can use a Color Range mask to select the lavender, and change it to red. Also, if you were working with a picture of a man with gray hair and wanted to change the gray hair to black, it would be much easier to use a Color Range mask tool to select the hair than it would be to attempt following the hairline's uneven edges with an Area Mask tool.

Color Tolerance

The color range masking tools in Photo-Paint include an option for you to assign a level of "color tolerance" to the tools. When using a color range masking tool, such as the Magic Wand, you can assign rules that tell the tool to select one shade of a color for masking and leave another shade untouched. Will your tool select, for example, only pixels *very similar* to the red spot where you clicked the tool, or will it cast a wide net and pick up anything in your picture that is even *remotely* red? This is called setting the *color tolerance level*. The higher you set the color tolerance level, the more pixels will be selected by the mask. When you set a low color tolerance level, the tool selects only hues very similar to the spot where you actually clicked the tool.

The Color Mask tool

Let's first take a look at the Color Mask tool. This is a remarkable tool. When you load a picture in Photo-Paint and select Mask ⇨ Color Mask, a dialog box appears that frames the picture you loaded. (See Figure 10-10.) You can create a color mask by clicking any area in the picture you wish with the Eyedropper tool. The rectangular boxes on the right side of the dialog box fill up with your color selections. You'll also notice that your mask grows larger with each color you pick from your picture. Figure 10-10 shows the Eyedropper tool (which automatically comes up with the dialog box) poised and ready to select an area of dark color. Notice that the top rectangle is filled with the same color that the Eyedropper is selecting. You may select as many (or as few) colors from your picture as you wish. Although the Color Mask screen shows only ten sample boxes, you can scroll down further if you want to make more than ten selections.

Figure 10-10: The Color Mask dialog box shows the Eyedropper at work.

You can use the Pan tool (the hand) to move other portions of your image into the viewing screen. The Smoothing slider bar changes how tolerant of color variances your Eyedropper tool should be. One very helpful tool is the Overlay button (the eye). It places a red tint over all masked areas of your image. Any part of your image that is not tinted is not masked. This helps for spotting "holes" in masks that are supposed to cover a uniform area.

Notice that the Create From field in Figure 10-10 shows a drop-down menu that says Sampled Colors. This indicates that you're creating your mask with colors sampled from your picture. The drop-down menu has other options, enabling you to create a mask from colors in any available color pallet.

Using the Color Mask Tool to Change a Background

Go into Photo-Paint and open the file named BRUSHES.CPT, an image that comes with Photo-Paint in the Samples folder. Use this file to practice changing the background by using the Color Mask tool.

STEPS
Changing the Background Using the Color Mask Tool

Step 1. Select the entire blue background using the Color Mask dialog box and Eyedropper, leaving the dog entirely untouched by the masking. Click the Overlay button (the eye) to make sure "all the blue" is gone. See Figure A.

Figure A: The tinted overlay makes it easier to select unmasked areas.

Step 2. After closing the Color Mask, you might see areas of blue that are not entirely masked. Use the Brush Mask tool to add to the mask, making sure that Additive mode is enabled. See Figure B.

Figure B: Touch up the mask with the Brush Mask tool.

Step 3. Invert the mask so that the dog is selected by selecting Mask ⇨ Invert, and then cut the mask to the Clipboard. This leaves an area of white where the dog was. See Figure C.

(continued)

(continued)

Figure C: Use the Invert Mask command.

Step 4. Choose Effects ⇨ Fancy ⇨ Alchemy. This kind of effect makes changes to your whole image if an area is not selected. Using the default settings (Threads, Random), click OK, and close the Alchemy dialog box.

Step 5. Select Edit ⇨ Paste ⇨ As New Object, and reposition the dog so that all the white is covered. (See Figure D.)

Figure D: Paste the dog back in as a new object.

The finished image is shown in Figure E.

Figure E: Here is what the file named BRUSHES.CPT looks like after changing the background.

Other color range masking tools

Several other color range masking tools exist besides the Color Mask tool. Some of them work alone; others need to be used in combination with area-selection masking. Here's an overview of the other color range masking tools.

The Grow command

After using one of the area mask tools (such as the Rectangular Mask tool), select Mask ⇨ Grow. The mask expands to include all the pixels that are similar in color to the ones along the edge of the current marquee. The Grow command uses the color tolerance level of the current paintbrush or painting tool. Look at Figure 10-11. Clicking the Grow command would expand the existing mask to include most of the lower rocks below the lighthouse, but not the lighthouse itself. In this case, to include the upper rocks near the lighthouse, color tolerance level would have to be increased to about 25.

Figure 10-11: The Grow Command expands this mask to include most of the lower rocks.

The Similar command

Select Mask ⇨ Similar, and your current mask grows to include pixels anywhere in your picture that are within the current color tolerance level. The difference between the Similar command and the Grow command is that Similar includes pixels *anywhere* in your picture, whereas Grow expands your mask only to contiguous pixels.

The best way to set a color tolerance level for working with commands such as Grow and Similar is to double-click the Magic Wand tool in the toolbox. The Tool Settings roll-up appears. You can then easily set the color tolerance level in that dialog box for use with these commands.

The Smooth command

Select Mask ⇨ Shape ⇨ Smooth to find this command. If you've created a color range mask, the smooth command blends the colors in the pixels around the edges of the marquee. The result looks a lot like feathering, which is explained a little later. Rather than creating areas where the background shows through (which is what feathering does), you are blending the colors around the parameter of your mask. With the Smooth command, you need to enter a value in the Radius data box. The larger the number, the more the colors will blend together.

The Paint on Mask command

This command is easily confused with the Brush Mask tool. With Paint on Mask, you are not painting a new mask onto your image. *You are painting degrees of transparency onto an existing mask.* After you've selected Mask ⇨ Paint on Mask, your image turns black, except for the masked area, which is white. Your color choices are degrees of gray because the level of transparency of your mask is measured by the degree of gray present on the mask. Figure 10-12 shows a picture that was altered using the Paint on Mask command. The masked area, which is white, originally had no gray pixels because it was entirely masked. (In other words, there was no transparency to the mask at all.) The area surrounding the mask is black, because no mask is present there. The figure shows a stroke of a paintbrush on the mask area, in a shade of gray. After the Paint on Mask command is turned off, that mask will have a somewhat translucent area where it was painted with a brushstroke. If a lighter shade of gray had been used, it would be less transparent. Darker shades of gray would create almost total transparency.

Figure 10-12: A masked area is shown with Paint on Mask turned on. One brushstroke is over the mask.

Figure 10-13 shows a powerful special effects tool associated with the Paint on Mask command. While Paint on Mask is turned on, if you paste any image onto the mask, it will be interpreted according to its relative shades of gray and thus modify the mask — just as if you had painted it on with brush strokes. You do not need to convert your image to grayscale to use this feature. For Figure 10-13, an oval mask was applied to the psychedelic background image and then filled with butterflies. While Paint on Mask was turned on, the apple object was pasted onto the mask. The apple had so many dark shades of gray that it behaved almost as a "cutout," revealing almost all of the butterfly image provided by the mask. If there had been lighter shades of gray, you'd see more of the background image and less of the butterflies, which are found only on the mask.

Figure 10-13: An apple is pasted onto a mask, modifying only the mask's grayscale qualities. The mask shows through.

The Stroke Mask command

After creating a mask, select Mask ⇨ Stroke Mask, and the Paint Tool dialog box appears. You can then select a brush style of your choice to stroke your mask's border. You can stroke with any color, and you can even instruct Stroke Mask to go around the mask more than once, to introduce an element of randomness to strokes after the first. Stroke Mask can place its stroke(s) inside, on top of, or outside the mask's border. Figure 10-14 shows some hearts that were masked and then stroked inside the mask border with the Stroke Mask tool.

Figure 10-14: The Stroke Mask Tool is shown at work.

Tools for Both Area and Color Range Selection

The Magic Wand, Lasso, and Scissors tools have color tolerance controls that allow them to select a broader or narrow range of pixels beyond what they would normally select as Area Mask tools. (Figure 10-15 shows all masking tools on the toolbox.) Remember that the Mask Transform tool is also part of this drop-down menu.

Figure 10-15: These masking tools appear on the toolbox.

Figure 10-16 shows a mask created with the Freehand Mask tool (the third tool from the left). The mask was stroked with a single brush stroke. (Click Mask ➪ Stroke.) Remember that this tool requires you to double-click when finished selecting.

Figure 10-16: A mask is created with the Freehand Mask tool, with one brush stroke applied.

The Lasso Mask tool

The Lasso Mask tool deserves special attention because after you carve a mask around a particular area, the Lasso Mask tool "shrinks down" to select any obvious boundary or object inside the scissors marquee. How well it picks out the object inside the scissors marquee depends on your fine-tuning of the color tolerance settings.

Secret

You can apply constraints to several Shape Masks using the Ctrl and Shift keys. Pressing Ctrl while using the Rectangular and Ellipse Mask tool constrains the shape to a square or a circle, respectively. The Shift key applied with the same tools expands your selection from the center rather than starting at the left or right. (Give it a try. This is a very helpful option.) Using the Ctrl key with the Mask Brush constrains the brush to vertical or horizontal movement.

The Scissors Mask tool

The Scissors Mask tool finds the obvious edges in your picture (areas where the pixel colors change very abruptly), and, if you "cut" with the scissors tool near the edge, the mask marquee will be placed right at the edge. The Scissors Mask tool is also helpful in adding freehand selected areas to an already existing color-range created mask.

The Magic Wand

Click a pixel with the Magic Wand tool, and all nearby pixels will be included in the selection according to Color Tolerance levels that you define on the tools Property Bar. With this tool, you simply click the color you want as it appears in your picture. Click in an area that has direct, contiguous communication with the other pixels you want included in your mask.

Feathering

Feathering is probably the most important tool in working with masks. Feathering gives your area selection fuzzy edges. If you are working with a Rectangular mask, for example, you might not want that rectangular shape to remain as harsh and sharp when blended with other portions of your picture. Feathering creates interesting collage effects where one image blends nicely into the next. Feathering helps blend the pixels from one image into the next with a nice tapered graduation.

Select Mask ➪ Feather to open the Feather dialog box. (Note that both Objects and Masks have their own feathering tool.) As shown in Figure 10-17, the Feather dialog box allows you to select how wide the feathered area should be. The feathering command creates feathered pixels on *all sides* of your mask. This effects how deeply into the image you want the feathering process to cut. Larger numbers cut deeper into the edges of your picture to produce a highly feathered image. The drop-down menu (default to "Average") controls how gradually you would like the pixels to blend into the background image, or how pronouncedly they should seem to rest on top of the background. Choosing Average creates more blending into the background, and Middle makes the mask appear to rest on top of the background.

Feather		
Width: 8	Direction: Average	OK
	Edges: Linear	Cancel
		Help

Figure 10-17: The Feather dialog box controls blending options.

Figure 10-18 shows a portion of a complex image showing several blending techniques. The trumpet, in the foreground, stands out, with several images feathered behind it.

Figure 10-18: This composition features feathering.

Feathering one side of a mask

Here's a technique for combining two very different pictures into one image. Let's combine a picture of a lighthouse with a photo of downtown San Francisco to create a surrealistic landscape.

Open the lighthouse image, cut it to the Windows Clipboard, and paste it as an object onto a New Image, leaving lots of blank paper around it. (We'll be squeezing two blended photos onto this canvas. Figure 10-19 shows a mask drawn widely around an image of a lighthouse. The mask cuts through the lighthouse image on the right side. That's because when you invoke the feather command, you'll want the feather to cut into only the right side of the image. Notice the huge feathering amount in the dialog box (144 pixels). If you put the mask any further toward the center of the photo, you'd get some degree of feathering on all four sides.

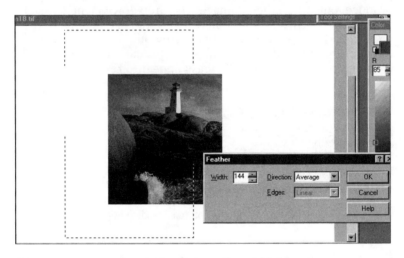

Figure 10-19: A technique for feathering only one side of an image.

You can also perform this effect by applying the Object transparency tool to one image and then the other. The Object transparency tool is the second tool that "flies out" from Object Picker when you press and hold the mouse over it. When you drag the Object Transparency tool across an object, the tool becomes an arrow facing the direction you drag. The transparency increases in the direction you drag the tool. Dragging a short distance results in abrupt, steep transparency curves. Dragging a long distance results in a more gradual tapering of transparency.

If you create the mask as it is in Figure 10-19, the deep feathering effect appears only on the right side of the image. After you click OK, your image should show only the mask. Click Object ⇨ Clip Object to Mask, as shown in Figure 10-20. The next figure, Figure 10-21, shows the results of this action. Only one side of the object is feathered.

Figure 10-20: After feathering a large mask, select Clip Object to Mask.

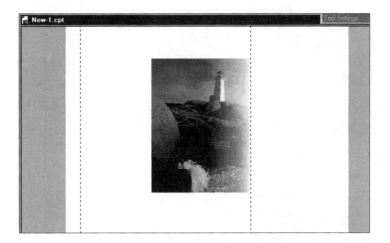

Figure 10-21: The results of Clip Object to Mask, a feather on one side.

If you repeat this procedure on another photo, creating the feather on the left side, and then blend the two feathered images together, the final image should look something like Figure 10-22. This figure shows the mask boundary still visible, so you can see how the city photo was treated with the same effect, but on the opposite side. (Don't forget to experiment with the Interactive Transparency tool as well.)

Figure 10-22: The finished composition combines two feathered images.

Blending images with feathering

Figure 10-23 shows a blend of two photographs for an ethereal composition. First the photo of the river was altered to accommodate the size of the door. Then the feathered door was added.

Figure 10-23: A composition shows a feathered object inserted into a river scene.

I'll retrace the steps to show how it was created.

STEPS

Adding a Feathered Image

Step 1. The original image (see Figure 10-24) was not tall enough to accommodate the "sailing-into-the-door" effect. To create a blank space on the canvas, I adjusted the paper size. (Select Image ⇨ Paper Size). Figure 10-25 shows the Paper Size dialog box. Making the Paper Size larger gives an image room to expand. In this case, let's make it about twice as tall as it is now and place the existing image at Center Bottom

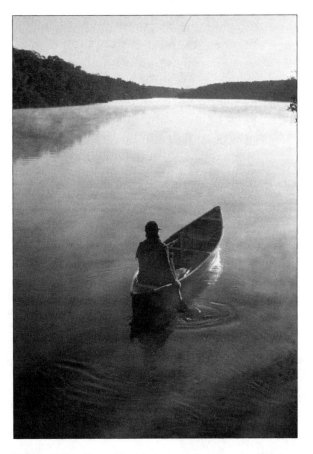

Figure 10-24: The original boat image is shown before it was altered to accommodate the door.

(continued)

STEPS *(continued)*

Adding a Feathered Image

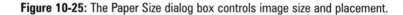

Figure 10-25: The Paper Size dialog box controls image size and placement.

Step 2.   I then converted the river image into an object. I selected the entire image with the Rectangle Mask tool and then clicked Object ⇨ Create from Mask.

Step 3.   The Perspective tool was used on the river scene to create the illusion of the river's horizon being farther away. I selected the Object Picker tool and clicked the river scene. I clicked on object several times until the status bar showed "Perspective on the Image." I then dragged the image's upper boundary toward the top of the paper. Making the image narrower while dragging created a deeper perspective effect. This procedure was followed once on the right side of the image and then again on the left.

Step 4.   I then used the Distort tool to make the image into a true rectangle again.

Step 5.   I copied the object to the Clipboard and pasted it as a new image. This got rid of the first image, which had been converted into a mask.

Step 6. I opened a photo from Corel's Doors of San Francisco collection and pasted it at the top of the river photo. The door itself was selected and feathered at about 100 pixels. Figure 10-26 shows the feathered door before it was placed in the river image.

Figure 10-26: The feathered door is shown before being placed into the river image.

Step 7. I then copied the feathered image to the Clipboard and pasted it as an object onto the river image.

Step 8. Finally, I added a second boater behind the first one. Because the boater was a narrow figure, this contributed a "long, deep journey" feeling to the composition. To do this, I selected the boater with the Magic Wand tool, clicked Object ⇨ Create from Mask, and pasted it a bit upriver and to the right of the original.

So whenever you want to blend images more naturally, diminishing any harsh lines between the images, think of the Feathering tool. Remember that higher feathering values cause images to fade together more gradually. Lower feathering values cause more abrupt combinations.

Using Masks to Create a Framed Picture

Here's a masking technique that enables you to create an interesting photo composition using a photograph of a piece of wood as a background.

STEPS

Further Practice with Masking and Feathering

Step 1. Starting with a background photograph of a piece of wood with daylight shining across it, a mask was made by double-clicking the Rectangle Mask tool. This selects the entire wood background.

Step 2. Select Mask ⇨ Shape and set the Reduce value to 80 pixels. If the wood background image you begin with is sized differently than this one, you may need to select a different pixel range to get the frame effect, as shown in Figure A.

Figure A: An image of wood has a mask around it to create a frame.

Step 3. Double-click the Fill tool to bring up the Tool Settings roll-up and click the Texture option (the first button on the right). Select Textured Blends Vertical from the list.

Step 4. Fill the outside border of the image with the Fill tool. It will be filled with the texture.

Step 5. To create the "thickening" effect of the frame, Select Object ⇨ Create from Mask. (Make sure the mask is still selected when you do this.) Select Edit ⇨ Paste ⇨ As New Object. Experiment with various Paint Mode tools as you blend the new frame you just pasted from the Clipboard with the existing one. I found that "Texturize" created a nice effect.

Step 6.   Open an image of a flower with a dark background. The dark background makes it easy to use the Magic Wand tool to select the background. Click Mask ⇨ Invert so that the flower itself is selected. When selecting the background with the Magic Wand tool, make sure the Additive Mode (the plus sign) is active.

Step 7.   While the flower is selected, again choose Object ⇨ Create from Mask, and copy the flower to the Clipboard. Paste it as a new object into the framed wood image. Select Object ⇨ Create Drop Shadow, if you like. Your results should look similar to Figure B.

Figure B: The finished product shows the flower on the wood.

Removing holes

Sometimes when you are selecting a large contiguous area of your image, small "islands" of nonselected portions remain. That's because the color tolerance settings of your tool have not been set broadly enough to pick up these stray pixels. Sometimes these holes in your mask are too small to be conveniently snapped up with the tool you are using. While the mask is selected, choose Mask ⇨ Shape ⇨ Remove Holes, and all unselected areas enclosed in the mask will become part of it.

Setting the threshold

While a mask is selected, click Mask ⇨ Border ⇨ Threshold to remove feathering from a mask. You'll be prompted to select pixel values between 1 and 255. That's because feathering, as a component of your mask, is actually a shade of gray. By selecting a pixel value, you are actually choosing a cut-off value for your feathering effect. The result is sharper edges around your mask.

Summary

▶ Adjusting a mask's transparency can give you greater control over how images blend with special effects.

▶ The various mask tools such as Invert and the Mask Overlay option are useful for working with both area-selection and color range masks.

▶ With the Paint on Mask tool, you can paint degrees of transparency onto an existing mask.

▶ The Brush Mask tool is an area-selection masking tool you can use to paint masks onto an image.

▶ With feathering, you can get rid of harsh mask edges, and you can even blend two different images together.

Chapter 11

Plug-Ins for Photo-Paint and CorelDraw

In This Chapter

▶ Using plug-ins for enhancing and touching up images

▶ Using plug-ins for creating special effects

▶ Third-party plug-ins

Programs such as Photo-Paint are often referred to as having an "open architecture." *Open architecture* means that other small applets (for example, plug-ins) can hook into the application, providing additional features and enhancements to the host application. In the case of Photo-Paint, the program supports standard Adobe Photoshop plug-ins. Many plug-ins ship with Photo-Paint, and you can purchase others from third-party vendors such as Alien Skin, Adobe, MetaTools, and many others.

Located on the Effects menu, plug-ins are arranged in groups (on submenus) by category. Some provide additional image enhancement, while others can apply complex special effects. Photo-Paint plug-ins include categories for blurring, sharpening, distorting, lighting, adding noise and texture, and applying stylistic effects, such as embossing, page curling, beveling, and many, many other effects.

Plug-ins can add tremendous new dimensions to your images and to your design process. Although a thorough discussion of every available plug-in lies beyond this book's scope, in this chapter you'll get enough information to get fired up and ready to use plug-ins with Photo-Paint and CorelDraw.

Using the CorelDRAW 7 Plug-Ins

As you may already know, *filters* are important pieces of software that you use to import and export graphics and text files. In CorelDraw, for example, you can import several different file formats, such as EPS, TIFF, Microsoft Word documents, and so on. CorelDraw also lets you export to several non-native formats. In paint programs, such as Photo-Paint, you can also open and save different formats through filters. In addition to using import and export filters, you can use special pieces of software called *plug-in filters* (also called *plug-ins*). Essentially, these plug-ins work the same way as other filters. They hook into a host application and enhance its capabilities.

Note

With CorelDRAW 7 you have the capability of applying plug-in filters in both CorelDraw and Photo-Paint. Even though you cannot edit bitmaps directly in CorelDraw, you can apply plug-ins to bitmaps imported into your drawings. Consequently, this discussion of plug-ins pertains in large part to both Photo-Paint and CorelDraw. In CorelDraw, you'll find the plug-ins on the Bitmap menu.

In Photo-Paint, plug-ins are applied from the Effects menu, as shown in Figure 11-1. While the arrangement of plug-ins on the menu seems to have no rhyme nor reason, they can be broken into two basic categories:

■ Touch-up and enhancement plug-ins

■ Effects plug-ins

Most of the plug-ins apply effects of one sort or another. The touch-up and enhancement plug-ins can be found primarily on the Adjust, Blur, Noise, and Sharpen submenus.

Figure 11-1: Use the commands on these submenus to apply plug-ins to your images.

Many more plug-ins are available than this chapter can cover. In fact, plug-ins provide so *many* options that the only way to get a good handle on them is to experiment with them first-hand. Nevertheless, here is a brief overview of some of my favorites.

Touch-up and enhancement plug-ins

A "touch-up and enhancement" plug-in is basically one that improves the quality of an image (rather than applying a special effect). These types of plug-ins enable you to adjust brightness, color, sharpness, and remove noise and flaws. You get the picture. And yes, believe it or not, blurring or softening an image can sometimes improve its overall appearance.

Whether you are applying a touch-up plug-in or an effects plug-in, the procedure is primarily the same. You simply select the plug-in you want from the Effects menu, which brings up a dialog box similar to the one shown in Figure 11-2. From here you can make adjustments to the plug-in's action, and get previews, before you apply the filter, of how your changes will affect the image. The preview feature is a big help, as it can take a long time to apply some filters to large, full-color images.

Figure 11-2: This typical plug-in dialog box for adjusting, applying, and previewing plug-ins introduces you to the sorts of options available.

When applying a plug-in, Photo-Paint provides a wide range of options. For example, you can move the image in the Original window with the grabber hand to see how your settings affect a specific portion of the image, as shown in Figure 11-3. Or you can zoom out of the image (right-click with the Zoom tool) to see how your changes affect the overall image, as shown in Figure 11-4. You can also fill the viewing area with a preview image, giving you a larger, better view to judge the results, as shown in Figure 11-5. To use this option, click the button to the left of the Preview button. Aside from these basic instructions, each plug-in is different and performs varying tricks on the image, so my best advice is to monkey around with the controls.

Figure 11-3: Use the grabber hand to move the image around in the Original window.

Figure 11-4: Use the Zoom tool to zoom in on specific areas of the image to preview how plug-in settings will affect your image. (Here the image is zoomed out.)

Figure 11-5: Click on the button next to the Preview button to fill the viewing area with the preview window.

The Sharpen plug-ins

You'll find one of the most useful groups of plug-ins on the Effects menu on the Sharpen flyout. While several good plug-ins lurk here, the two that I find the most helpful are Find Edges and Sharpen. Find Edges does exactly what the name implies. It finds hard surfaces within an image and sharpens them. This plug-in is a great way to make objects within an image appear more clearly.

Sharpen attempts to eliminate blur, or to make an image more clear. While it doesn't succeed on all images, it does a good job on many. Check out the images in Figure 11-6. I applied the Sharpen plug-in resulting in the "after" image. Pretty cool, huh? How much a picture needs sharpening depends totally on the image, of course. Too much sharpening can distort the image. My experience is that you should apply Sharpen incrementally, a little bit at a time. At the point you've gone a little too far, use Undo to go back a step.

Before   After

Figure 11-6: Use the Sharpen plug-in to clear up blurry scans.

Dust and Scratches plug-In

Sometimes that just-right photograph for your project isn't in the best of shape. It might be scratched, or maybe you spilled coffee or ketchup on it.

Who knows? Technology to the rescue. You can clean up many image flaws with the Dust and Scratches plug-in available on the Noise submenu. In Figure 11-7, for instance, the image was edited with this plug-in to remove scratches and stains.

Before   After

Figure 11-7: Touch-ups made with the Dust and Scratches plug-in can help prepare this image for newspaper publication.

In most cases, with this filter you'll want to work on the area with the flaw you want to remove, so select the area with one of the selection tools, as shown in Figure 11-8. Then open the Dust and Scratches plug-in and adjust the settings until you get the effect you want. You'll need to do this for each area of the image you want to touch up, which may seem tedious. But it's much better than using an image with glaring flaws, or not being able to use it at all.

You can get a similar effect by using the Sharpness plug-in on the Adjust submenu. In fact, this method provides several preview windows, allowing for a more interactive approach to cleaning up your images.

Secret

As the previous example demonstrates, you can apply plug-ins to selected portions of an image. Many of the plug-ins work within a selected area, on a mask, or on a separate object layer, enabling you to apply enhancements and effects with discrimination, making for some pretty unique results. For more information about using masks, refer to Chapter 10.

Special effects plug-ins

If you're not familiar with Photo-Paint and plug-ins, you'll be pleasantly surprised at all the things you can do with Photo-Paint's special effects plug-ins. The CorelDRAW package comes with hoards of them, and if they don't do everything you need, you can buy additional plug-ins from third-party vendors that produce just about every kind of effect imaginable. And then some. Again, each plug-in does different things to images, so they all work differently. In this section, I'll go over a few particularly cool plug-ins. But don't stop at just these favorites. Try out some other plug-ins on your own.

Figure 11-8: When using the Dust and Scratches plug-in, first select the area you want to touch up before invoking the plug-in.

Emboss

This plug-in can make you seem like a real artist without you really trying. When you use Emboss an image, you raise its edges, giving it a 3D effect. The Emboss dialog box, shown in Figure 11-9, lets you adjust the depth and level of the 3D effect and the direction of the light source, and provides four different color effects to choose from.

Figure 11-9: Set emboss depth, light source, and other options with the Emboss plug-in dialog box.

Figure 11-10 shows an image embossed with several different settings. You'll have a lot of fun using this effect.

Figure 11-10: The first image is the original. The second image was embossed with an Emboss Color of Gray, a Depth of 3, a Level of 100, and a Direction of 90 degrees. The third image was embossed with an Emboss color of Paper, Depth 2, Level 100, Direction 0 degrees.

Page Curl

If you surf around the Web at all, you've probably noticed this effect used a lot. It also shows up on many software packages and in magazine adds. You'll find Page Curl on the 3D Effects submenu on the Effects menu, which displays the dialog box shown in Figure 11-11. The effect recreates the look of paper being curled, or peeled back, as shown in Figure 11-12.

To use the Page Curl dialog box, you first specify which corner you want to curl with one of the four Adjust buttons. Then specify whether you want the curl to be horizontal or vertical. Now adjust height and depth of the curl. If necessary, move the image in the Original window so you can see the corner you're curling. You can get a preview at any time by clicking on the preview button, as shown in Figure 11-13.

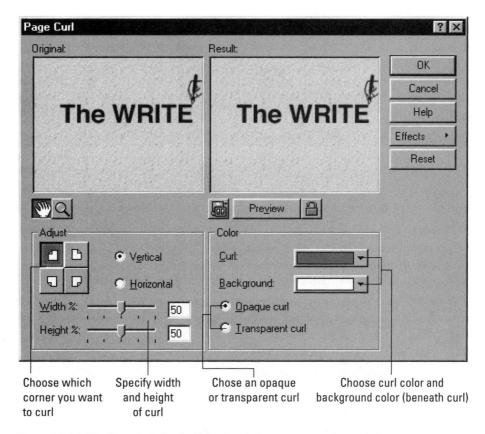

Choose which corner you want to curl

Specify width and height of curl

Chose an opaque or transparent curl

Choose curl color and background color (beneath curl)

Figure 11-11: The Page Curl plug-in dialog box helps you create that curled page corner effect you see in magazines and on the Web.

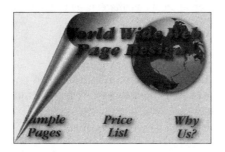

Figure 11-12: Example of effect achieved with the Page Curl plug-in.

Figure 11-13: Use the Preview option to gauge your progress as you adjust the curl.

To change the color of the curl itself, or the background beneath the curl, simply choose new colors from the drop-down palettes. You can also set the curl to transparent, which is a neat effect, as shown in Figure 11-14.

Figure 11-14: Use the Transparent option to create an interesting curling effect.

Perspective

Here's an attractive effect. This plug-in lets you manipulate an entire image in 3D space. And it's remarkably easy to use, as you can see from the dialog box shown in Figure 11-15. All you do is adjust the corners on the little box in the lower-right corner of the dialog box.

Figure 11-15: The Perspective plug-in dialog box makes it easy to adjust an image's perspective.

You have two ways to manipulate your image: Perspective and Shear. Perspective works similarly to the Perspective roll-up in CorelDraw (discussed in Chapter 6). Use it to narrow and widen the sides of the image to make it appear to be moving toward a vanishing point, as shown in Figure 11-16.

Figure 11-16: Use Perspective to tilt your images toward a vanishing point.

The Shear option enables you to manipulate the image as though you are rotating it in your hand, turning it to its side, on its back, and so on, as shown in Figure 11-17.

Figure 11-17: Use Shear to rotate the image in 3D space.

Using Third-Party Plug-ins

In addition to the many plug-ins that come with Photo-Paint, several collections are also available from various third-party vendors, such as Alien Skin, MetaTools, Adobe, Pegasus, and a host of others. As a rule, Photo-Paint supports industry-standard, or Adobe Photoshop plug-ins. However, this technology changes all the time. Be sure to check for compatibility with Photo-Paint 7 before you buy.

Secret

As a rule, when you install a plug-in package, the installation program looks for Adobe Photoshop's *plug-ins* subdirectory. For your plug-ins to work with Photo-Paint (and CorelDraw), they must be installed in the plug-ins folder inside the Corel folder, or the folder where you've installed your CorelDRAW files. If you use Photoshop or another image-editor, you can also access the plug-ins by creating shortcuts of your plug-ins photoshop directory and placing them in the Corel plug-ins folder. Or you can add any folder on your system to the list Photo-Paint uses to search for and access plug-ins in the Options dialog box (Tools ⇨ Options ⇨ Plug-In Filters ⇨ Add), as shown in Figure 11-18.

Figure 11-18: Use this dialog box to tell Photo-Paint where to find additional plug-ins.

While I can't begin to cover all of the plug-ins available, this section lists and describes a few of my favorite collections. You can find several others by searching for "Photoshop plug-ins" on the World Wide Web.

Alien Skin's Black Box

This nifty set of ten or so plug-ins is great for creating buttons and other graphics for the Web. It enables you to do several neat effects, such as cutouts, carves, and several others. The three plug-ins I find most useful, though, are Inner Bevel, Outer Bevel, and Drop Shadow. Figure 11-19 shows examples of all of these effects.

Figure 11-19: Example of bevels, drop shadows, and buttons created with Alien Skin's Black Box.

You can get a hold of Alien Skin at http://www.alienskin.com.

Kai's Power Tools

Perhaps the best of all plug-ins, Kai's Power Tools from MetaTools is a collection of texture and gradient designers with more options than you can imagine. You'll find KPT "lite" (a special version) in the CorelDRAW box that installs when you install Photo-Paint. The full version provides a wider range of plug-ins and design options.

You can use the Texture Designer to create virtually any texture of any color. One of my favorite tools in the collection is KPT Planar Tiling, which actually creates an abstract tiling of the entire image, as shown in Figure 11-20 and in Plate 11-1 in the color insert.

Figure 11-20: An example of a KPT Planar Tiling effect from Kai's Power Tools.

You'll find a demo version of Kai's Power Tools on the CD-ROM included with this book. You can contact MetaTools at: http://www.metatools.com.

Adobe Gallery Effects

Adobe makes its own collection of paint-program plug-ins called Gallery Effects. Actually, Adobe has three different collections available: Classic Art, Volumes 1, 2, and 3. Basically these are texture generators covering a wide range of possibilities, such as Chalk & Charcoal, Angled Strokes, Note Paper, Patchwork, Fresco, Graphic Pen, Stamp, Spatter, Texturizer, and many others. Each set contains 16 plug-ins that promise hours of fun and rewarding experimentation.

You can reach Adobe at: http://www.adobe.com.

Summary

▶ The terms *plug-ins* and *filters* are often used interchangeably. They both do the same thing — add functionality to an application, whether it's to enable a program to import and export foreign file formats, enhance and touch up images, or apply special effects.

▶ You can apply plug-ins to images in Photo-Paint from the Effects menu and in CorelDraw from the Bitmap menu. The filters work similarly in each program, except that they work only on imported bitmaps or portions of your drawing that you convert to bitmaps in CorelDraw.

▶ Plug-ins come in two basic flavors: enhancement/touch-up and special effects. The former are for improving image quality and the latter are for special effects or stylizing images or portions of images.

▶ In addition to using the many plug-ins that come with CorelDRAW, you can purchase collections from various third-party vendors, including Alien Skin, MetaTools, Adobe, and Pegasus.

Chapter 12

Dream 3D

In This Chapter

You'll learn how to use the following CorelDRAW 7 features:

▶ Scene Wizard templates

▶ Perspective windows

▶ Low, medium, and high res rendering

▶ Virtual Trackball

For CorelDRAW users, CorelDream 3D holds the least rewarding "out of box experience." Many factors — such as the little castles you have to line up perfectly, the paths you have to build along splines, and the difficulty of knowing what you're looking at — have kept many users from exploring Dream 3D. However, CorelDRAW 7's version of Dream 3D includes a Scene Wizard that gives you more than just while-you-wait instant 3D pictures. The Scene Wizard provides starting points for you to include models that you choose, position objects the way you like, and even import graphics from CorelDraw and Photo-Paint. In fact, you can create some unique works of art with Dream 3D just by knowing how to manipulate and edit existing objects, without having to learn practical 3D modeling (the subject of the next chapter). So don't just skip over this somewhat intimidating program. Stop in and have a little fun.

Note

You should be aware, though, that of all Corel applications, Dream 3D requires the most horsepower. Even with 16MB of RAM, with this program I tend to make a lot of trips to the coffee maker in between steps. If you're patient, however, the results are rewarding. Three-dimensional modeling is the wave of the future, and nothing else looks quite like it.

Before You Get Started

Several of the projects I've created with Dream 3D can be found on the CD-ROM that accompanies this book. The projects are saved on the CD-ROM as complete Dream 3D projects, so you may load them, deconstruct each piece, and work along with the project if you wish. If you "lose your place," you can always reload the finished work again from the CD-ROM.

However, to make Dream 3D projects on your computer look like the projects shown in this book, please read the following:

The way I've used Dream 3D in this book is by showing four perspectives on the screen simultaneously. That way, when you move an object "up," for example, you can see the results of your movement from various angles. When working with 3D, this instantaneous feedback is all-important. Many times, you'll think you are moving an object "up" toward the top of your screen, and later, when you look at the scene from another angle, it turns out you were moving it forward, not up.

However, when you open CorelDream 3D, you'll only seen one perspective window, not four. The problem with working with only one perspective window is that, in order to switch to different viewing angles, you have to right-click on any white, blank area in the window, select View, and then choose a view type. Each time you change views, you'll have to do this.

On the CD-ROM that accompanies this book, I've included templates that will enable all of your 3D projects to open with four perspective windows up and running. To work alongside the lessons in the book, you pretty much need to load and work with these templates. This makes what you see on your screen match the screen layout shown in the book. You may load the *CorelDRAW 7 Secrets* Dream 3D template or load the project itself from the accompanying CD-ROM.

Loading the recommended templates

Note

The following directions require that you insert the *CorelDRAW 7 Secrets* CD-ROM in your CD-ROM drive. If you've installed CorelDRAW 7 to run from your CD-ROM, then these instructions will not work for you. You must first exit from all CorelDRAW programs, insert the *CorelDRAW 7 Secrets* CD-ROM, open the folder titled "Chapter 12," and copy the file called "Corel Secrets Workspace Template.d3d" to your hard drive. You may then remove the *CorelDRAW 7 Secrets* CD-ROM and replace the CorelDRAW program CD-ROM as you would normally. Finally, to load the required Corel Secrets Templates and follow along with this book, start with the third step that follows.

STEPS

Loading Templates

Step 1. Put the *CorelDRAW 7 Secrets* CD-ROM in your CD-ROM drive.

Step 2. Open the folder titled "Chapter 12."

Step 3. Double-click on the icon titled "Corel Secrets Workspace Template." If Dream 3D is installed on your computer, that file opens automatically in Dream 3D. Take a minute to look at all four windows.

The larger window to the left that fills most of the screen is the Reference window, also known as "Perspective Window of Doc1:1." This window displays the projections of your 3D objects on three different walls. Looking at this window gives you an idea of how your objects are positioned in three dimensions.

The window to the upper right shows the view of your objects from above. This window, called "Top View," or "Perspective of Doc1:2," is good for checking objects that have been moved forward or backward.

The window below shows the view from the right. Look at this window to see if objects moved from top to bottom are really where you want them. This window is called "Right View," or "Perspective of Doc1:3."

The fourth view, or window, shows the view from the front. Doesn't it look just like the first view? Not really. Moving objects in the fourth window will only move them "up" or "down." This limitation is desirable, because objects moved in the first view can be moved along all three axes, which can get confusing. This fourth window is called "Front View," or "Perspective of Doc1:4."

If objects appear too close or too far away in any of these views, use the Zoom tool to move closer or farther away from the objects. The Zoom tools work similarly as in other CorelDraw programs.

Now that you are a little acquainted with the four perspective windows, select window ➪ Workspace ➪ Save. You'll be asked to name your workspace. Do so.

From now on, any project you begin or file you open in Dream 3D will open with these four windows showing. You'll also notice that the title of the workspace you saved appears as one of the choices under the Workspace menu. (Select Window ➪ Workspace to see these choices.)

As mentioned previously, make your screen open with CorelDraw 7's default Workspace by selecting one of the default settings from the same Workspace menu.

To restore the default screen, simply select Window ➪ Workspace, and then choose the default setting for whichever screen resolution you work at. After choosing the default screen, your workspace will again consist of one perspective window and the hierarchy window (which I explain in the next chapter).

If you have trouble working with the template, check out the sidebar titled "What If the Template Doesn't Look Right to Me?"

Working without the template

Without the template, you can still follow along with the tutorials from the conventional CorelDream 3D view by changing views every time you move an object. In the following projects, the accompanying pictures show three, or sometimes even four, views at a time. To follow along without multiple views, right-click on any blank, white space inside the image window and select View ⇨ Type (See Figure 12-1). Choose one direction from the menu. The change on your screen is instantaneous. You'll see all of the screen objects from whichever view you select. The *main* view, the view that shows all of the 3D projections, is called the Reference view. Right-click again on any blank area to switch to a different view. You may do this as often as you wish, switching views back and forth to move an object into just the right position

Figure 12-1: Right-clicking on any blank, white space in a window brings up a shortcut to change views on the fly.

Scene Wizard Templates

The Scene Wizard is more than just a collection of ready-made templates. Although you can use a Scene Wizard as a complete template, adding, perhaps, a company logo or personal art object, Scene Wizard also functions as a starting point to create more individualized scenes and projects. See Figure 12-2.

Figure 12-2: The Scene Wizard screen asks you to select from four different scene templates.

Each of the four main Scene Wizard categories, Logo Template, Photo Studio, Indoor Scenes, and Outdoor Scenes, moves through several phases of creation, asking you for input as your scene is built. For example, the Photo Studio template might look rather unremarkable at first glance, but click Next, and you'll see that you can choose from 24 lighting effects and angles for your project. So in actually, the Photo Studio template is your key to beginning a project with excellent lighting effects already in place. This gives you more time to be creative, rather than having to fuss with light faders.

Additionally, when using the Outdoor Scenes template, you'll notice that twelve scenes have been created for you, but you need not stick with their chosen backdrops. The real work in creating those templates went into getting effective lighting, fog, and camera angles. You could change the background of one of those scenes and be well on your way to creating an outdoor scene all your own.

Experimenting with the Indoor Scenes template is informative because you can have some say in how the room structure is built. If you choose Step by Step after clicking Next, you'll see the Configure Your Room screen, as shown in Figure 12-3. You are given eight Room styles from which to choose, including various wall-and-floor combinations, and subsequently, eight

Indoor Mood Lighting choices, including TV studio, Shadow effects, and multiple spotlights.

Figure 12-3: The Configure Your Room screen is available from the Indoor Scenes template.

For company logos, don't be deceived by the simple bulb image on the opening screen of the Scene Wizard. Inside are ten customizable company logo templates, each producing an unusual effect. So, the Scene Wizard is a collection of templates that give you room to bring a personal touch to even a simple project, without your having yet learned a stitch about 3D modeling.

Secret

Scene Wizard employs only basic serif and sans-serif fonts in its scenes. That's because each user has different fonts on his or her system. But you can easily replace the default Scene Wizard fonts with another font.

One important note: You can apply these Scene Wizard templates to already existing scenes. If you've created a 3D environment with some objects, but have not yet found the right lighting, try applying one these templates to your project. If you decided that a cloudy sky would be the perfect backdrop for some 3D objects you've created, you need not make one from scratch. Just apply the one included in Outdoor Scenes.

After you selected a scene and are finished choosing options for it, click Finish, and your computer screen will fill with four perspectives of your scene, as shown in Figure 12-4. Perspective One is front and center. The other three perspectives fill the right side of your screen.

Figure 12-4: The four perspective windows appear after Scene Wizard creates an indoor scene.

Everybody who uses a 3D program like Dream 3D for the first time always has the same response after clicking the Finish button at the end of the Scene Wizard process. Namely, "Where is it? Where is my work of art?"

What you see are simple models of the objects that are involved in creating your scene. These objects can be moved around, built upon, cast with different lights, shaded with different textures, and rendered against different backgrounds. After you have finished manipulating the objects in this wire-mesh mode, you can chose to *render*, or ray-trace, your scene into a real picture, something you can actually send to your publisher or to Mom.

Ray-tracing refers to the amazing mathematical process that brought us this new world of 3D modeling. Ray-tracing, miraculous as it is, also takes a really long time on most computers. That's why you are encouraged to spend a lot of time working in the wire-mesh mode building your scene and making sure the cameras are really pointing to the objects you *think* they are pointing to. Then, when you render your object (Select Scene ⇨ Render, and chose from various quality settings. We'll get into that later.), you'll have a better chance of seeing what you hoped to see.

What If the Template Doesn't Look Right to Me?

If the views shown in the four windows do not look similar to the four-at-a-time views shown in this book, you may need to adjust each screen one by one until the objects are centered. Click inside one window, and do the following:

Use the Zoom tool to zoom in or out until you've located the objects inside the wire-mesh screen. You should see some gears and the word "Industrial."

Use the scroll buttons on the bottom and right side of the window to reposition the objects so that they are in the center of the screen. The numbers at the bottom left of the window (1:2, 1:8, and so on) represent the zoom values. If the template originally places the objects so that they are *too close* for viewing, the zoom value will read something like "2:1" or "8:1." If the template placed the objects *too far away* for accurate viewing, the zoom value will perhaps read "1:4" or "1:8."

To view the three smaller windows to the right, use zoom values of 1:2. To view the main, larger window on the left, use a 1:1 zoom. But first, the objects must be located and centered. If the objects and the wire-mesh screen are quite far away, you might initially only see a small, blue screen in your window. Once it's centered, use the Zoom tool to bring the object closer so that it fills most of the screen. If the objects in the window are too close, you might only see a huge section of the wire-mesh screen filling the entire window. Zoom out to 1:2, and reposition and center the objects.

After centering and resizing your view of the objects, you can change the viewing angle of each window by right-clicking in any white, blank space in the window. Choose View ⇨ Type, and then click the type of view you want for that particular window.

The Dream 3D projects in this book are arranged as follows:

- The largest view (the view on the left side of your screen) uses the Reference view, meaning it shows projections of its objects on several walls to simulate 3D space.

- The second view (the view at the top right) uses the Top view. This view is good for moving objects from forward to backward, because you can view everything from the top.

- The third view (the screen in the middle right) provides a view from the right. This view is useful for moving objects up or down, meaning *higher* or *lower*.

- The fourth view (the view from the front) is good for moving objects from right to left or from left to right.

Choose Window ⇨ Save Workspace, and name your workspace anything you wish. After naming it, the workspace will be included in the list of available workspaces shown on that same menu. Now, anytime you open a new project, you can load this workspace, and your new project will offer the same four views of your saved workspace.

If you are using a smaller monitor, you may not see all of the windows that Dream 3D opens by default. The Objects Browser and Hierarchy of Doc.1 (or current document) are actually open and available, but you may only see the blue bounding window at the bottom of your screen. To view the Objects Browser, if it's not already visible, select Window on the Dream 3D menu, scroll down, and click. Then, locate the corner of the window and drag it into view.

Dream 3D scenes include a background, either a bitmap, a color, or color gradient. However, you will not see your background until you render the scene, as it is not visible in the Perspective or Modeling mode.

Perspective Windows

Each perspective window represents the point of view of an existing camera. You know you are viewing Perspective One, because the window is labeled, "Perspective of Doc1:1." The other perspective windows are labeled "Perspective of Doc1:2," "Perspective of Doc1:3," and so on. Looking at Figure 12-4, the blue box-like object near the front of the screen is really a camera facing away from you, toward the objects visible in that perspective window. You also notice a rectangle with a small circle in it projected onto the opposite surface from you. That rectangle represents what a camera is pointed at, in this case, Camera One, Perspective One. (See Figure 1-5.) If you double-click on the camera, you'll see the Object Properties dialog box. (In Dream 3D, cameras and lights are thought of as objects.) The current tab says Camera, confirming the type of object with which you are working.

Figure 12-5: The camera as it appears in the Perspective window.

To see that you can switch to more than one camera even now, move to the Window menu and remove the checks by all of the Perspective options except Perspective of Doc1:1. Now, maximize Perspective of Doc1:1. Drag the scroll bars up, and you'll see a camera facing down on the objects. Drag the scroll bars to the left, and you'll see another camera. You can now return the other perspective views to their former positions on your screen by selecting them from the Window menu. Click the Windowed or Restore button to make Perspective of Doc1.1 return to its former size.

The red object that appears to be floating in air is a light, as shown in Figure 12-6. Double-click on it, and you'll see more information about the type of light it is, its positioning, and its brightness features. You'll see that the Object Properties dialog box for this light offers more tabs than a camera. These special lighting features, such as linking lights to geographical planes and viewing lights through gels, will be covered later in this book. You'll also notice a red-orange rectangle projected on the floor and opposite walls of the light. The projection onto the floor represents where the light is facing. The projection on the opposite wall represents where the light fixture exists on that particular 3D plane.

Figure 12-6: A light as it appears in the Perspective window.

Using the other perspective windows

The other perspective windows off to the side of the screen represent the views of other cameras. For example, if you maximize the window called Perspective on Doc1:2, you'll see the objects created by Scene Wizard from the top down. You will not be able to see a camera or light present in all views.

Tip

Why is the "top-to-bottom" camera helpful? After all, you're probably not going to render scenes from this unflattering perspective. But once you get to know Dream 3D, you'll be *joining* objects together. In order to do this well, you'll need to see objects as they join in *all three* dimensions.

Finding the floor

Doesn't sound too hard, does it? (Depends what you did last night.) Guess again. The picture in Figure 12-7 shows a bicycle that appears to be seated directly on a surface. But the way 3D space works, we're not sure yet if it is or not. Figure 12-8 shows the same object viewed from another perspective window. But to be 100 percent sure, you'd have to see it from all three angles.

Figure 12-7: This bicycle may or may not be sitting directly on the surface.

Figure 12-8: We can see the same object from an additional plane to help us position the bike.

Figure 12-9 shows the bicycle as I first dropped it down onto the surface. There's the bicycle, embedded inside the floor. 3D programs are like that. They'll let you cross and mesh objects as you wish. The trick is to get them to mesh together in a way that makes geometric sense. Looking again at the main perspective window (the largest) in Figure 12-9, you'll notice that it provides projections on three sides so that you can tell where exactly the camera is hitting the opposite wall and where the light beam is falling. Notice that the other two perspective windows, "Perspective of Doc2:3" and "Perspective of Doc2:2," only provide a view of one axis. But that help is enough.

Figure 12-9: These three views of a bicycle show that it is positioned incorrectly on a platform.

If I were to use the Selection Arrow (the pointer in the upper left-hand corner) to click on the bike in Perspective One and attempt to pull the bicycle up on top of the platform, I would really be pulling it towards me, along its x axis. From Perspective One, known as Perspective of Doc2:1, I cannot pull an object up, along its y axis. But look at "Perspective of Doc2:3." You are given a direct cross-table view. Consequently, your pointer can reposition the bicycle up and down by dragging the bicycle in that window only. Notice that the smaller view is from a camera positioned to aid you in moving the bicycle towards the middle of the platform. If you tried to reposition the bicycle in and out by dragging in Perspective Three, you couldn't do it. It is by using the Selection Arrow tool in each of these three views that I was able to position the bicycle truly on top and in the center of the platform. Figure 12-10 shows the properly positioned bicycle.

Figure 12-10: The properly positioned bicycle is shown in all three perspective windows.

Understanding the window names

While you may have many scenes open in Dream 3D at once, take note that the "Doc" referred to in "Perspective of Doc2:3" means that there was another scene opened before this one was. (Hence, the title "Doc2:X.") The "3" in "Perspective of Doc2:3" means that this window represents the third camera created to view this scene. It is possible to have many camera views (perspectives) associated with a scene. Therefore, you could potentially have a window titled "Perspective of Doc4:5." A perspective window titled as such would represent the fifth camera view created for the forth document, or scene, that was open at this time.

Secret

When you position an object in one perspective window, be sure to keep an eye on how it moves in the other windows. Check the object's position *in each window* before moving your object too far along one plane. You might end up with only a piece of your object in the actual rendered viewing area.

Photo Studio Scene Wizard

The bicycle pictured in Figure 12-11 is the rendered (ray-traced) version of the scene modeled previously. Each model is a combination of groups of objects connected together at specific joints. These objects are treated with colors, and shaders and textures are available that can modify those colors. Lights are objects also, shined onto surfaces that cause shadows to be cast onto backgrounds. And the cameras that show the view from a specific angle are also objects, in that they can be made to possess various lens qualities and moved around the scene at will.

Figure 12-11: The rendered bicycle picture.

Figure 12-12 shows you how it all began, with one of the Scene Wizard templates, specifically, the Photo Studio template. The light setting "Left 30%/ Right 100%" was chosen, as you can see from the figure. Each light combination brings out different surface qualities of the object(s) in the scene and casts unique types of shadows. After selecting a type of lighting, the Scene Wizard prompts you to select from one of six backgrounds, ranging from sky to wallpaper to no background at all. Following this choice you can select a prop for your scene, perhaps a stool on which to place an object, or, as in the case of the bicycle, a marble checkerboard floor on which to set the object. These choices are built into your scene. Of course, when you select Finish, all you immediately see is the wire-mesh "cut-out" box that represents the 3D universe used in building your scene. This three-sided projection area is the perspective window of Doc1:1.

Figure 12-12: The Photo Studio Scene Wizard prompts you to choose from a variety of lighting effects.

Rendering

If you've jumped ahead a bit and placed an object of your choice on one of the props provided by Scene Wizard, you might want to go ahead and render this object to some format or picture file, and see what it *really* looks like.

When you choose Scene ⇨ Render, you'll see a drop-down menu of rendering choices. (See Figure 12-13.) Some specialized rendering choices are available in this menu, but what concerns us now is knowing the following:

■ How to render a picture quickly, just to make sure all the objects that concern you are really in your view (See "Secrets of the Production Frame," which follows.)

■ How to render at a higher quality a picture of a scene you really like

Figure 12-13: The Scene menu with the Render drop-down menu exposed.

I explain rendering choices thoroughly later in this chapter, but for now, know that the Render Settings menu item contains choices regarding type of file output, size and resolution, as well as which camera should be used for the rendering. Below that is the Render menu. At first, render with Low Res Review to check your scene. This is similar to a photographer taking a picture with a Polaroid camera first, just to be sure that the lens sees what he or she does. Use Medium Resolution when you are fairly happy with the results and want to preview the subtle blends and textures that Low Res Review is not going to pick up. Finally, render with High Resolution when you're entirely happy with your work. Rendering at High Resolution can take several hours and appears to require more than 100MB of contiguous hard drive space on your computer to use as swap space. The rendering choice labeled "CPT Pre-Production Medium" creates a file 800 × 600 pixels at 150 dpi. The choice labeled "CPT Pre-Production High" creates a 1024 × 768 pixel file at 300 dpi. The trouble with using the last two modes for rendering is that, once you feel conformable adjusting the Production frame (we'll discuss that next), those settings might not match your picture's proportion.

At the end of the rendering process, you'll be given the choice to save your picture in one of several file formats.

Note

After ray-tracing a scene, Dream 3D returns you to a maximized version of Perspectives Two or Three. This can be disconcerting to a new user. To return to the default perspective window setting, first click the Restore (windowed) button of the maximized window's control menu. Now select Window from the menu and click Perspective of Doc1:1. It will appear maximized as well. Again, click the Restore button from that document's control menu. You'll now have all four perspective views available as they were before.

Rendering and your camera

When you finally render a picture, you're going to have to choose one view to render to. It will be a view seen by one of the three or four perspective windows with which you've been working while developing your scene. So as you're working along, moving and editing objects, start thinking about which one of those views really looks like a picture. When you are happy with how things look, select Scene ⇨ Render Settings and click on the Camera tab. Generally speaking, the title of each perspective window relates to the camera number. For example, the view "Perspective of Doc3:4" would be a view of what the fourth camera sees. From the Camera tab of the Render Settings dialog box, open the drop-down menu and select the camera that corresponds to the view you'd like to render. After you select a camera, do a Low-Res Review render to be sure you've picked the right one. If you haven't, simply select a different camera. If you don't like any of the views, readjust the Production frame, and rotate objects and lights until one of the cameras suits you. In the next chapter, I talk about manipulating camera angles, lens qualities, and views.

The Production frame

Select View ⇨ Production Frame, and you'll see a black, thin box frame squared around your objects. This is the Production frame. It represents what you will actually see when you render a scene. It's important to keep this frame in view because none of your editing outside the production frame (except for adjusting lights, of course) will show up in your rendered output.

You can resize and move the Production frame by selecting it and using the bounding boxes to resize and drag it from inside the boundary. Figure 12-14 shows the results of the Production frame being sized around a large area. Figure 12-15 shows the results of the Production frame "shrunk in" closer around the rendered objects.

Object placement

Let's review the concept of looking at several perspective windows one more time. Figure 12-16 shows the Objects Browser and three perspective windows, one large and two small windows. The kayak clip art object was dragged to the main Perspective window; however, look closely, and you can see it from two other camera views in the two other perspective windows. Perspective of Doc1:2 presents an overhead view, and Perspective of Doc1:3 presents a view from the left. To be sure that your object is positioned correctly, you must check each perspective to see if the object is truly lined up in the way it appears from Perspective One. Sometimes, for example, a boat can appear to be "in the water" in Perspective of Doc1.1, but when viewed in another perspective window, it's clear that the boat is slightly above the waves. Check your object's location in several perspective windows before ray-tracing your picture.

Figure 12-14: Because the Production frame is sized around a large area, the rendered picture shows the wider area.

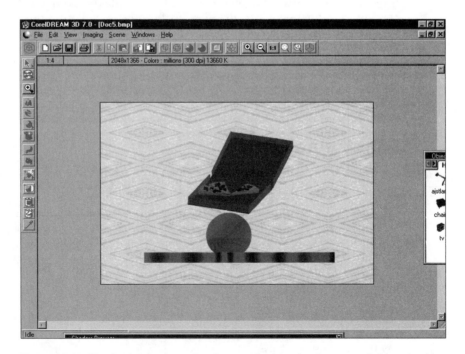

Figure 12-15: The Production frame has been resized to closely surround the main objects, and the rendered picture reflects this.

Figure 12-16: The kayak was dragged and dropped onto the scene. The three views help determine where the object is really located.

Logo Templates

It would be a shame to think that the only thing the Scene Wizard "Arabica Coffee" is good for is making a coffee commercial. (See Figure 12-17.) We're going to take advantage of the dramatic lighting and background scheme provided by this Scene Wizard and add new text, get rid of the cup of joe, and learn about three important Dream 3D features while we're at it. When we're finished with this, you'll understand a bit about grouping and ungrouping objects to recolor them, using and editing shaders that affect the texture of your object, and using the Virtual Trackball to rotate objects in any direction.

Figure 12-17: The Logo Templates Scene Wizard offers several selections from which to choose. Here the "Arabica Coffee" logo is selected.

If you'd like to follow along, click the Logo Templates Scene Wizard, click Next, select the cup of coffee logo, and again click Next. You'll be prompted to write in some text. Type, Caldwell Bowling, one word for each space.

Next, we'll deconstruct and remove the cup of coffee from the scene, as shown in Figure 12-18. You'll see that the cup of coffee is made up of groups of objects. The coffee steam plumes are three individual objects that remain ungrouped. The saucer is a single object as well. The cup of coffee, however, is a construction of several objects. Using the Selection Arrow, click directly on a steam plume. A bounding box appears around one. While one steam plume is selected, click on the Arrange menu. You'll see that Ungroup is not an option because each steam plume is a single object. Press the Delete key, and that plume of steam is gone. Do so with the other two plumes. Now select the saucer. Clicking delete rids us of that in one easy operation. But click on the coffee cup and look inside the Arrange menu. You'll see that Ungroup is an available option. The coffee cup is really two joined objects. Still, pressing Delete once removes the entire cup from the screen. That's because the objects are grouped and will respond together to such commands. We now have the words "Caldwell Bowling" alone on the screen. Actually, lights, cameras, and backdrop are still alive and well, so "Caldwell Bowling" is not really alone at all. The lighting and backdrop manipulation that was created with this Scene Wizard template will still apply to whatever we create next, as long as we don't change those entities ourselves.

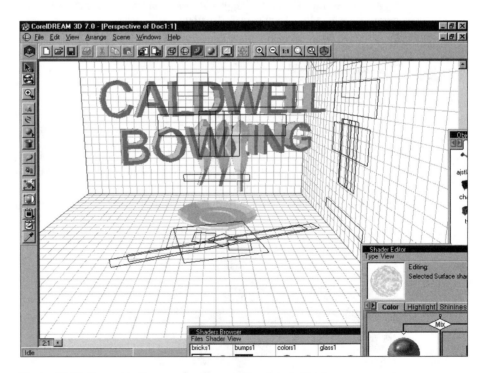

Figure 12-18: Removing the cup of coffee and its related objects.

Open Object Browser and click the Sports tab. Drag the bowling ball and pins icon, and drop it in the picture. Figure 12-19 shows my first attempt. Notice the bowling pins are placed clumsily in front of the letters. And yes, once again, no amount of repositioning the bowling pin in Perspective One is going to move the pin *behind* the letters. As you can see in Figure 12-19, the window labeled "Perspective of Doc5:2" shows a camera angle best suited for dragging the bowling pin "in and out." So drag the bowling pin backward, behind the letters with the Selection Arrow. Your view should be a view from above, as shown in that same figure, in order to move the pin correctly. Finally, the correct placement is shown in Figure 12-20.

Figure 12-19: The first placement of the bowling ball and pins.

After moving the pin in front of the letters, get ready to color the bowling ball. Because the scene's background is black, it won't do to have the bowling ball be the same color. However, most objects need to be ungrouped to be recolored. Select Arrange ➪ Ungroup, as shown in Figure 12-21, to ungroup the bowling pin and ball. It will then be possible to select the bowling ball individually.

Figure 12-20: The bowling ball and pins are correctly placed.

Figure 12-21: After selecting Arrange ➪ Ungroup, the bowling ball and the pin can be selected individually.

When recoloring objects in Dream 3D, you don't drag the color shader onto the object, as you do in some 3D programs. You simply select the shader that represents the color you want to switch to, and click the Apply button, which is found in the lower-left corner of the Shaders Browser. Figure 12-22 shows the Shaders Browser.

Figure 12-22: The Shaders Browser

The reason it's called Shaders Browser and not "Color Changer" or something else is that many components are involved in creating a modified surface for your objects, and color is just one of them. Because 3D rendering is so accurate and can create such finely detailed appearances on surfaces, you can make precise changes in an object's reflective qualities, such as how metallic it looks, the degree of wood grain that should show through the color, and so on. When you double-click on any Shader ball in the Browser menu, you'll see the dialog box shown in Figure 12-23.

I cover the Shader Editor dialog box in detail later in this chapter, but you should know that inside it are sliding faders to modify how shiny or bumpy your object's surface is. For example, if your surface has a plaster-like texture, how deep should the pits and bumps be? If your scene includes a light shining on your surface, should the surface reflect mostly the light's color, or should it maintain a deep color quality of its own? All of these surface qualities and more — many more — are editable in the Shader Editor dialog box.

Getting back to modifying your bowling ball, select Marble from the Shader Browser, and double-click on it. This brings up the Shader Editor dialog box. You'll find that the dialog box opens to the Color tab. Double-click on the color square itself and a three-fader Color dialog box opens in the upper-right corner of the screen. The three faders are RGB controls. To make your bowling ball blue like mine, drag the R fader to the left and the B fader to the right. The color rectangle on the Shader Editor itself will reflect the color change. As shown if Figure 12-24, the Color dialog box doesn't limit you to RGB color editing. Other modes are available from the drop-down menu.

Figure 12-23: The Shader Editor dialog box lets you modify the surface of the bowling ball.

Figure 12-24: The Color dialog box allows you to edit your object in RGB color mode, among others.

Figure 12-23, the Shader Editor dialog box, shows the edited marble settings I used to make the marble surface more apparent in the scene itself. The changes will be reflected in the small square (with the sphere inside). Click the Apply button to change the bowling ball surface to match what you've created in the Shader Editor.

Figure 12-25 shows the ball and pin while still ungrouped, with the Shader Browser open. The bowling ball has a new color and texture.

Figure 12-25: The ball and pin are still ungrouped, and the Shader Browser is still open.

With your Selection Arrow (the arrow on the upper right of the Dream 3D toolbar), move into any perspective window in which it's easy to make a clear selection of both the ball and the bowling pin. While pressing Shift, select both objects and click Arrange ⇨ Group from the menu. You'll notice the second object you select is surrounded with red bounding boxes, rather than black. That's because you can make the second object respond in certain ways to any editing you perform on the first object. This is called *linking*, and I deal with this form of editing later in this book. For now, you need both objects selected because you're going to tilt the bowling pin and ball to simulate a collision between the two.

Secret

With Dream 3D, you cannot use the Selection Arrow to "drag" a square around multiple objects you'd like to select. You'll have to select one, and then the other. That's because as you learn more about Dream 3D, you'll see that the *order* in which you select objects affects how they relate to each other.

The Virtual Trackball

The Virtual Trackball, shown in Figure 12-26, rotates the angle of objects in three-dimensional space. It is the second tool from the top of the Dream 3D toolbar. Usable in any view, you can rotate objects a little bit to the right, and then up, for example. (It combines X-Y-Z rotation with Pitch, Roll, and Yaw. More on that later in this book.) It is perfect for creating the random kinetic appearance of a bowling ball hitting the pins.

Figure 12-26: The Virtual Trackball rotates the angle of objects in three dimensions.

Secret

If you don't see the Virtual Trackball, but instead see a single curved arrow at that toolspace, press and hold your mouse button down a little longer over the toolspace. The Virtual Trackball will appear. The single curved arrow is the One Axis Rotation tool.

Figure 12-27 shows what happens when you move the Virtual Trackball tool into one of the perspective windows, click on an object, and begin dragging in a certain direction. Along with the usual bounding boxes, you'll see a circle around the entire perimeter of the object(s) you are manipulating. Look closely at that figure and you'll see a little arrow in the perspective window, Doc2:2. That arrow means you've placed the Virtual Trackball over an area that can be rotated or twisted in some way. Notice that the same circle is present in the other perspective windows as well. In this example, I've used the Virtual Trackball to raise the pin farther up off the ground, while the ball is tilted downward, simulating impact.

Figure 12-27: The Virtual Trackball moves both the ball and pin together.

Figure 12-28 shows the bowling pin and ball now tilted. I also moved the pin closer toward the letters. That's because the white coloring of the pins will produce an excellent shadow surface for the letters. Besides, ray-traced objects look so good close up that you don't have to worry about hiding imperfections, as with bitmaps.

Figure 12-28: The bowling pin and ball, now repositioned, are ready for rendering.

While working on a project such as this, you should be doing Low-Res Review renderings every time you make a change. By doing these frequently (Choose Scene ⇨ Rendering ⇨ Low Res Review), you'll see what changes to make to your Production frame, when objects have moved out of camera view, and so on. After you've checked everything, try a Medium Resolution rendering to be sure you've placed the objects in the most flattering light, showing off the their textures and shadows. Then, it's time for the High Resolution render. Figure 12-29 shows the bowling ball scene rendered in High Resolution mode and saved as a .TIF file. (I talk more about saving to different file types later in this chapter.)

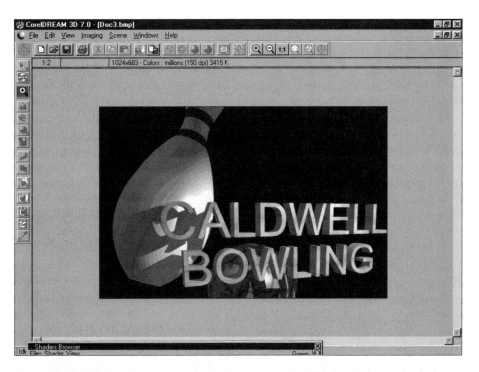

Figure 12-29: The bowling scene is shown here rendered in High Resolution mode. And to think this all started with a cup of coffee!

Creating a Unique Scene

Now, create an entirely unique scene. Start with a Scene Wizard called Foggy Morning.

STEPS

Making a Scene

Step 1. First save and delete anything that's already open on your Dream 3D screen. When you save a project as the default file type (.d3d), you are not erasing or replacing any Scene Wizard files, even if you started your project with a Scene Wizard.

Step 2. You do not have to delete every single perspective window to get rid of the current project. Just select "Perspective of DocX:1," where X is the number of the document you are working on, and delete it by clicking the "X" in the perspective window's Control menu. The other perspective window associated with that project will close, also.

Step 3.   Now you are free to begin a new project without having eight perspective windows to wade through. Select File ⇨ New ⇨ Scene
Wizard ⇨ Next ⇨ Outdoor Scene ⇨ Foggy Morning.

Step 4.   Your scene will open to be modeled, and what you'll see is a
whole lot of nothing. That's because the Foggy Morning scene
includes only cameras, lights, and a background. You will not see
your background until you render it.

Step 5.   Drag the Object Browser out to where you can see it. Open the
Transportation tab, and place the airplane called *wrigfly2* onto
Perspective One. (See Figure 12-30.)

Figure 12-30: The wrigfly2 airplane object is placed into the Scene Wizard,
"Foggy Morning."

Note that the plane is too close to the ground to stir much interest. Look
closely at the perspective window labeled "Perspective of Doc7:3." It is this
window that enables you to move an object up and down, for example, closer or farther from the ground. Once again, trying to adjust an object along
this geometric plane in Perspective One will do no good. Use Perspective
Three, which is a view from the left. Place the Selection Arrow tool inside
that window and drag the airplane up. Use "Perspective of Doc7:2" (the view
from the top) to drag the airplane closer toward the front of the viewing
area. Figure 12-31 shows the plane in the air.

Figure 12-31: The plane is now airborne.

After checking and repositioning the Production frame, render the plane now. But before doing so, tilt the right wing toward you so you can see some of that nice wood grain in the rendering. Figure 12-32 shows the airplane in Perspective Three, which shows us the best angle for tilting. Right next to it is the Low-Res Review rendering I did immediately after, just to check my work. Figure 12-33 shows the fully rendered plane against the preset "Foggy Morning" backdrop.

Figure 12-32: It's easy to tilt the airplane the way I want by using Perspective Three. Next to it is the Low-Res Review to check my work.

Figure 12-33: The fully rendered "Foggy Morning with Airplane" picture.

While the bitmap of the foggy morning is attractive, the concept of *fog* in 3D programs means creating a simulated fog with lighting and special camera effects so that the other objects in your scene seem to be moving in and out of the fog, rather than the object being plastered onto a picture with fog in it. Figure 12-34 shows another scene rendered with the same airplane, but with the fog features calculated from the Scene ➪ Atmospheres dialog box (more on this topic later in this book).

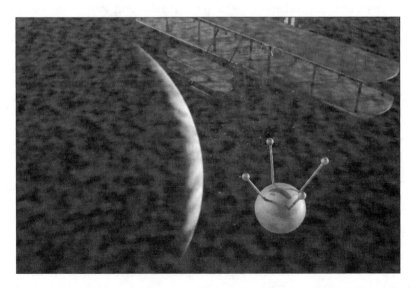

Figure 12-34: The same airplane is rendered in a scene that includes fog provided by the Dream 3D fog algorithm.

Figure 12-35 shows the Render Effects dialog box with the Backdrop tab showing. This is accessed by selecting Scene ⇨ Backdrop. A drop-down menu is available. Scroll through the options and select Map. The dialog box will now include a floppy disk icon. Clicking it enables you to search your hard drive for a bitmap to use as the backdrop for your objects. Many file types are allowable, including .CPT, .TIF, and .BMP. You'll see a tiny picture of the bitmap you've selected. Looking closely at the figure, you'll see that you are given options for how the bitmap may be placed, tiled, or rotated. You can make a "quality versus speed" choice regarding the rendering of your bitmap. For this project, I did not change any of the default settings.

Figure 12-35: The Render Effects dialog box is opened to change the backdrop bitmap for the airplane scene.

Figure 12-36 shows the airplane rendered with the new bitmap. I called it "Chess Wars." Still, it needs embellishment. The plane is positioned at a boring angle, and besides, I want to tell you about how to position two objects so that it looks like they are touching one another.

Figure 12-36: The airplane is rendered with a new backdrop called "Chess Wars."

I decided that in order to negotiate a path through all of these attacking chess pieces, the airplane needed some glasses. Figure 12-37 shows my first humble attempt at positioning sunglasses from the Objects Browser onto nose of the airplane. First, you must shrink the glasses somewhat. To do this, position your Selection Arrow over squares at the corners of the bounding box and drag inwards. You can do this in a precise, numeric way also, and I deal with that method in the next chapter. Figures 12-38 and 12-39 show two angles necessary to work with in order to really get the glasses up against the airplane's nose. Both of these perspective windows are provided by default by Dream 3D, so you don't have to create your own camera angles — yet, anyway. Please note that the bounding box containing the glasses is *tilted*, meaning that it will be necessary to do some positioning with the Virtual Trackball.

Figure 12-37: Positioning the sunglasses from the Object Browser

Figure 12-38: A sideways view of getting the sunglasses on the airplane's nose

Figure 12-39: A top view of getting the glasses on the airplane's nose

Figure 12-40 shows the glasses positioned correctly on the nose of the airplane. Once the airplane and glasses are grouped together, the airplane can easily be positioned at a much more interesting angle. The glasses add a comic "face" focus. Now, move to the Edit menu and select Numerical Properties. (Make sure you don't accidentally select Properties.) As shown in Figure 12-40, the Numerical Properties dialog box displays data boxes for the size and positions of both the glasses and the airplane. Dream 3D provides highly precise control over the exact positioning and sizing of objects that are joined. The method I'm showing you here in this chapter, positioning by hand through various perspective windows, is not appropriate for creating the complex objects of which Dream 3D is capable. But such a method serves well for now.

Figure 12-40: The glasses are positioned correctly and the airplane is reoriented in space.

Now that the plane looks good, let's move a camera around to the front and slightly below eye level to take advantage of the comical, off-angle appearance. The steps to do this are as follows:

STEPS

Positioning the Camera to the Front

Step 1. In the Reference window (Perspective One, the largest window), zoom out so that you can see several cameras.

Step 2. With the Selection tool, choose one of the cameras, and move it toward the front of the airplane, facing it.

Step 3. Select both the Camera and the Airplane/Glasses group. Then choose Arrange ➪ Point At (or press Ctrl+M). The camera will now face the center of the object or group.

Step 4. Using various views to check your positioning, move the camera slightly below eye level and to the front. Choose Scene ➪ Render ➪ Low Resolution Preview to make sure the camera is positioned where you want it.

Step 5. Don't forget that you can load the file "Chess Wars" from the accompanying CD-ROM (found in the Chapter 12 folder). Use that file to experiment with various camera angles, moving them around and rendering at low resolution until you come up with something you like.

Step 6. Figure 12-41 shows the newly created camera pointing at the airplane's bespectacled face.

Figure 12-41: The new camera is pointing directly at the airplane's front.

Advanced users of 3D programs will howl that I have not discussed the "Hot Point," which is the adjustable focus point on which any camera or light will focus. Yes, it can be moved and edited. This topic is covered in the next chapter.

Figure 12-42 shows the rendered version of the airplane in "Chess Wars." A light was added, directed primarily at the glasses. This was done by selecting the Create Light tool from the toolbar and placing it in Perspective One. In the next chapter, you'll explore light positioning. You'll also learn about hierarchy, how to create objects from the tools in the toolbar, and how to join objects with the Numerical Properties dialog box. You'll also work further with this picture, adding text and changing the backdrop.

Figure 12-42: The rendered version of the airplane.

Summary

▶ Scene Wizard templates give you more than just while-you-wait instant 3D pictures. You can work on them to come up with exciting, original scenes.

▶ Perspective windows show different points of view of existing cameras.

▶ When you position an object in one perspective window, be sure to keep an eye on how it moves in the other windows.

▶ The Virtual Trackball rotates the angle of objects in three-dimensional space.

▶ By following the steps explained in this chapter, you can create an interesting and unique scene using Dream 3D.

Chapter 13

Advanced Dream 3D Techniques

In This Chapter

You'll learn about:

▶ Using the hierarchy window

▶ Adding text to scenes

▶ Editing shaders and shader channels

▶ Using the Alignment and Numerical properties dialog boxes

▶ Adding backdrops

▶ Using the Render Area, hot point, and the 3D Paint tool

▶ Creating objects from scratch in the Modeling window

▶ Duplicating with Symmetry

The Hierarchy Window

First, let's look at a very important window that is created along with the Reference window every time you begin a Dream 3D project. This is the Hierarchy window. The *hierarchy* is a diagrammatic arrangement of all the objects in your scene. You can view it as one of your windows, from the same menu you'd use to view a perspective window. (Choose Window ⇨ Hierarchy of Doc X:X.)

Now, let's complete the "Chess Wars" picture begun in the preceding chapter by adding text, and let's bring text into the picture by using the hierarchy. By dropping the Text icon onto the hierarchy list, you can easily control where your new text object should go in relation to other objects. Remember that in Dream 3D, objects include lights, cameras, and models. Figure 13-1 shows the Text tool being dragged below Camera 4.

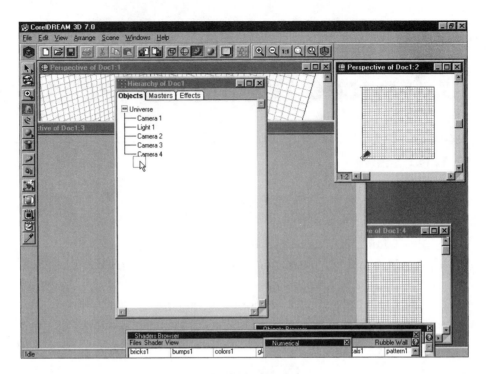

Figure 13-1: First drag the Text tool to the Hierarchy window.

After dragging the Text tool onto the main perspective window or the hierarchy, you'll see the Text dialog box. (See Figure 13-2.) It gives you control over letter bevel size, the depth of your text object, and the usual font control tools such as letter and word spacing. Remember, though, that your text object's "depth" can be controlled in the Perspective windows with the same tools you use to resize all objects.

Secret

When you are choosing a font size, here's a quick rule of thumb. Cut the font size in half, and you'll know your text object's approximate height in inches. The default text font size when you open the Text dialog box is 72. This setting creates a text object approximately 36 inches high.

After you've chosen your text and closed the dialog box (by clicking the Done button), the hierarchy names your text object appropriately. (See Figure 13-3.)

Figure 13-2: Use the Text dialog box to set various text attributes.

Figure 13-3: The hierarchy list now shows the text you've added.

As you can see from Figure 13-4, objects you've just created will initially appear partially out of sight, or sometimes completely out of site from the main Perspective window (Perspective of Doc1:1). I had to hunt through two additional views to see where the text I created would be initially visible.

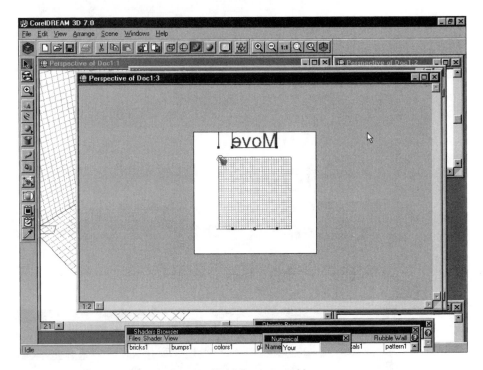

Figure 13-4: The text object just created initially appeared here on my screen.

Look at the window label in Figure 13-4. It says "Perspective of Doc1:3." Now look back at the window label of the Text dialog box. It also says "Perspective of Doc1:3." It should come as no surprise that this window is the only place you can initially locate the text object you have just created.

This text was actually created in its own scene, as we are creating it here, and then it was cut and pasted into the "Chess Wars" picture. I then decided to separate the words "Your Move" into two groups of letters and place the words at different distances from the camera. Figure 13-5 shows how initially the two words appeared one behind the other, unreadable when viewed from above. I had to change to another perspective window so that I could select each group of letters and move them to a new position. (See Figure 13-6.) Note that Figure 13-6 also shows a camera added "front and center" to make it easier to know what you're viewing. One way to add a new camera is to choose the Camera tool from the Toolbox and click and drag briefly in the

Perspective window that most closely represents the angle you will be viewing from. Adding a new camera is a good way to experiment with different views. After you've repositioned the camera, select both it and the object you'll be pointing it at. Choose Arrange ➪ Point At, and your camera will face the object much as is shown in Figure 13-6.

Figure 13-5: The letters appear as blocks when viewed from above, but it's still apparent that they need to be moved.

Tip

If the objects on your screen appear only as boxes or outlines of shapes, make sure View ➪ Default Quality ➪ Bounding Box is not selected. It's best to work with Preview or Better Preview quality. (Unless you have a very fast computer, Better Preview is too time-consuming for rendering in between quick edits.) Also, if you load the file "Your Move" in order to work alongside this project, you may not have the required font on your computer. If the letters appear blank, double-click the outline of the letters and select a new font. You'll now be able to see the letters.

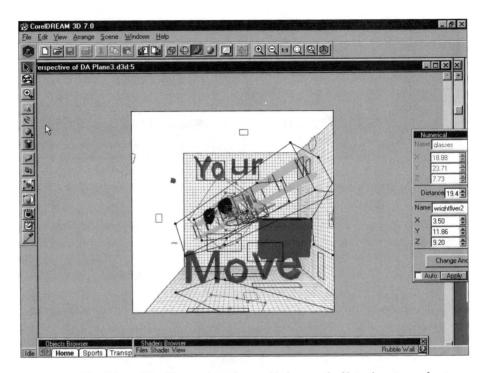

Figure 13-6: The "Chess Wars" letters have been added correctly. Note the camera front and center.

Coloring and Shading Text

Figure 13-7 shows the Shader Editor dialog box opened and one of the Glass shaders being selected. I could have instantly applied the preset color and texture to the text, but instead, I've double-clicked one of the Glass shaders, and the Shader Editor dialog box has opened. Dream 3D gives you control over many aspects of the surfaces you create for your objects. That's because surfaces have more than just *color* qualities. Glass has varying degrees of reflectivity, light absorption, and texture, depending on the type of glass shading you wish to simulate. For this texture, I chose to merely adjust the quality of shininess when I applied the texture to the text. (See Figure 13-8.) To do so, simply click the tab that represents the name of the texture feature you want to adjust. Turning up the Shininess slider causes a surface to reflect more of the light's color and brightness. Less of the object's innate color shows through.

Figure 13-7: The Shader Editor dialog box gives you control of surface qualities.

Figure 13-9 shows the process for applying a bitmap as your shader color. Once inside the Shader Editor, select Type ➪ Texture Map, and click the "floppy disk" icon. The Browse menu opens, enabling you to search your hard drive for a file to use as a bitmap. Dream 3D is capable of painlessly converting files of many types into color bitmaps for text objects.

You can make many more adjustments to shaders, such as controlling the surface texture or reflectivity of a surface with a bitmap image. (I explain some of these a bit later in this chapter.) As you close the program, you will be prompted to save the shader with its new adjustments as a separate file. You will then see the new shader in the dialog box with the preset sliders. Figure 13-10 shows the bespectacled airplane careening between the words "Your Move," which have now been changed to a Calligraphy font and shaded with customized Glass and Wood textures. As you may recall from the preceding chapter, the bitmap background that has been applied to this scene will not be visible until you render the scene.

Figure 13-8: Adjust the shininess with the Shader Editor.

Figure 13-9: Choose a bitmap to color a text object.

Figure 13-10: The "Chess Wars" image has text modified, ready to be rendered.

Backdrops

Your backdrop or background image is not just wallpaper. It's an integral part of the scene. When you add a bitmap to a shader, you select Type ⇨ Texture Map from the Shader Editor dialog box. Also, to create a backdrop for your scene from a picture in a different file format, you must select Scene ⇨ Backdrop and scroll down to the word "Map." That's because when rendering, Dream 3D precisely calculates how the chosen lighting setup will reflect on your backdrop or background. Light intensity, color, spread, elevation, and angle all interact with the objects to produce detailed lighting effects against your bitmap. Figure 13-11 shows the final "Chess Wars" rendered scene. The upper portion of the "Chess Wars" bitmap was removed in Photo-Paint and replaced with one of the Waterdrop Texture fills from Photo-Paint's presets. This edited backdrop creates a much more attractive image than the "jaggy" bitmap you get with a photograph.

Figure 13-11: The Final "Chess Wars" picture appears with text and chess pieces.

More Dream 3D Tools

Some helpful tools exist that you should know how to use to get the best results in Dream 3D. These tools include the Render Area tool and hot points. You'll also learn about the projections, which are the small rectangles you can see in the Reference window. Then there's the 3D Paint tool, which enables you to paint colors on an object, while maintaining the object's lighting, curve, shadow, and reflective qualities.

The Render Area tool

Whenever you make a change to an object in your scene — whether it's adding a new shader or changing the distance between objects — it's useful to render *just the area* you have changed. To do so, click the Render Area tool, found near the bottom of the toolbar, and drag a rectangle around the area you wish to render. See Figure 13-12.

Figure 13-12: The Render Area tool appears near the bottom of the toolbar.

Hot points

Every object in Dream 3D has a hot point. This is the small circle, usually in the middle of the object itself. The *hot point* is the point at which a light or a camera will face an object. It is also the reference point that the Numerical properties dialog box and the Alignment dialog box use to calculate distance measurements. The hot point is also the rotation axis. If you rotate an object 45 degrees, it will rotate around that point. If two objects are grouped, the hot point becomes the center of those two objects. You will always see the hot point as a small circle inside any object, as projected in your Perspective window.

You can move an object's hot point. For example, to simulate a batter swinging a baseball bat, the bat should appear to rotate at the point the batter's hands hold the bat, not at the exact center of the bat. You can drag an object's hot point anywhere you wish. If you want a light or a camera to shine somewhere other than the direct center of that object, simply drag the hot point to the desired location.

Secret

An object's hot point can even be located outside the object itself.

Projections

While looking at the main perspective window, you've seen how each object in your window has a projection on both walls, and on the floor, if available. These projections serve to locate your object in 3D space. You can move each projection of the object as if it were the object itself. For example, if you need to move an object along its Y axis only, this is hard to perform on the object itself in the main perspective window. But dragging the projection of that object along the appropriate wall moves the object itself along the corresponding axis. The object's projection includes its hot point. If you need to move an object's hot point, sometimes it's easier to move its projection instead.

The 3D Paint tools

The 3D Paint tools enable you to paint directly on 3D objects. Applying a 3D Paint tool does not alter the lighting effects (such as shininess or glow qualities) that have been created around your object. When you paint with 3D Paint, you select a shader and a brush size (the brush dialog box opens when you select the 3D Paint Brush tool) and begin applying paint to the chosen object. Dream 3D comes with Shape tools also, for applying paint in exact shapes. Because you are using shaders from the Shaders browser to select paint, you are not merely applying color, but all the qualities of the chosen shader become part of the brush, such as bump, reflection, and shininess. (You may also use the Eyedropper tool to pick up a shader from an object already in your scene.)

Tutorial #1: Alien Visitors

For this project, you'll build 3D objects from scratch, place them in 3D space (as well as outer space), and render them against a background bitmap, adding some lighting to show off a 3D object's reflective surfaces. The resulting picture appears on the back cover of this book.

Creating objects

Start with a new Dream 3D Empty Scene, and drag the Free Form tool (on the toolbar) into the Hierarchy window. Be sure you drag it into the Hierarchy window and not the main perspective window.

You'll be taken to the Modeling window, shown in Figure 13-13, and prompted to name the object you are about to create. Name it "Alien." After doing so, you'll see the empty Cross Section plane (the darker blue mesh near the front of the box) and the Sweep plane (the lighter blue mesh that makes up the remainder of the box). You will draw on the Cross Section plane. However, to adjust how deep your object is (in other words, how long its

Extrude path is), you'll be adjusting the pink line you see stretching halfway across the Sweep path. Notice that that pink line is actually visible on two sides of the model. That's because you can add different Extrusion paths for the different dimensions of your object. You can bend, curve, lengthen, or shorten those Sweep path description lines in order to make your object protrude or contort in various directions along its X and Y axes. The "Front" of your object, what you actually *draw,* is designed on the Cross Section plane, which is the "front part" of the Modeling window.

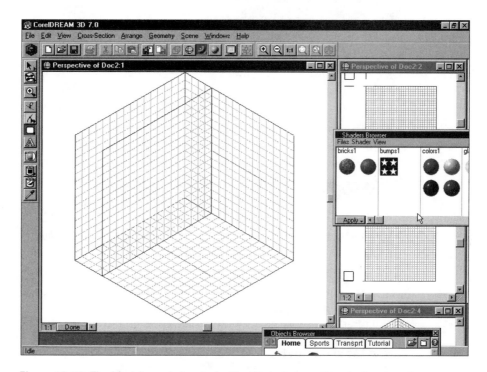

Figure 13-13: The Modeling window looks like this before anything is drawn on it.

Notice that the toolbar and the menu are different. The choices will revert to their original values when you leave the Modeling window (press Done at the lower left of the window).

Press and hold your mouse over the Rectangle tool (also on the toolbar), and select the Draw Rounded Corners Rectangle tool when it appears. Draw something similar to the shape that appears in Figure 13-14.

Figure 13-14: A shape is created with the Rounded Corners Rectangle tool.

Press and hold the Convert Point tool until other icons appear. Select the plus sign, which is the Add Node tool. What you are doing is creating points at which your new object can bend and be curved. Otherwise, your options are limited to simply making the pink Extrusion path lines shorter or longer. Using the Add Node tool, click the upper Extrusion path line to create new nodes, as shown in Figure 13-15.

Select Geometry ⇨ Extrusion ⇨ Symmetrical, and shape the lines as shown in Figure 13-16. This option enables you to create an object with two parallel paths while drawing only one, much as drawing half of a wine glass and holding it up to a mirror reproduces the other half of the glass. You'll need to select the Bézier tool, using it just as you would in CorelDraw, to bring curvature qualities to the lines. This gives the object (It's an alien ship! You'll see.) a more rounded, less boxy quality. Use the Selection tool, still found at the top of the toolbar, to move the nodes, and hence, to move the lines. Notice the object reflects every change you make to the lines. Don't worry if the lines you move appear to overlap with the object. They exist on two different planes, just like in science fiction stories.

Figure 13-15: New nodes are added to the Extrusion path line.

Figure 13-16: Adjust the extrusion lines with the symmetrical extrusion.

What about the other pink line at the lower part of the mesh box? This is the other Sweep Path Description line; it can be used to create protrusions and shape changes along the X coordinates, "moving away from or closer to" the front of the screen. Figure 13-17 shows how to adjust these lines to add a more snazzy, sports car appeal to our alien vehicle.

Figure 13-17: Move extrusion lines along a different plane.

Click Done to return to the Perspective windows.

Using the Numerical properties dialog box

Our alien ship looks a bit thick. Let's make it shorter; that is, let's decrease its Z axis size by using the Numerical properties dialog box. To open the Numerical properties dialog box, right-click an object while it's selected and select Numerical Properties. Figure 13-18 shows the Numerical properties dialog box next to the alien ship. When one object is selected, the Numerical properties dialog box displays the XYZ coordinates of the object, that is, where it is located in your scene. You'll also see the Yaw, Pitch, and Roll coordinates, which indicate the degree of rotation in any direction. At the bottom of the Numerical properties dialog box is the size of the object, again expressed in XYZ coordinates. Our job here is to decrease the Z parameter of the ship, meaning to make it shorter from top to bottom. To do this, we must uncheck the Keep Proportion check box, which is checked by default. (Look again at Figure 13-18, where the mouse pointer is.) Doing this makes the ship sleeker but keeps the width and depth the same.

Figure 13-18: Use the Numerical properties dialog box to change only the height of an object.

Creating shaders from scratch

We want to color our alien ship with something totally different. To do this, let's create our own shader. Select Shader Browser ➪ File ➪ New, and the dialog box shown in Figure 13-19 appears. You must name your shader before doing anything else. To make it easier to keep all the materials used for this project together, let's name the shader "Alien."

Figure 13-19: Give the shader a new name in the New Shader Name field of the Create Shader dialog box.

Select Shader Editor ➪ Type ➪ Texture Map, as shown in Figure 13-20, and open a picture file you'd like to use.

Figure 13-20: Create a new shader by using a bitmap.

Shader Editor channels

Having selected a bitmap for the shader color, we've only just begun. The Shader Editor contains many *channels*. If you are familiar with Pixar Typestry or RenderMan technology, then you'll know what I mean here. You can use colors or pictures to adjust many qualities of the shader. For example, if you drag any compatible bitmap (.BMP, .CPT, .TIF, and so forth) onto the Shader Editor's Bump channel (see Figure 13-21), that picture will be broken down into its *shades of gray,* and the information will only be used to create higher or lower bumps (in other words, raised or embossed areas) in your picture. Think of the process as resembling a Photo-Paint mask using a picture to create different levels of masking protection. Similarly, if you drag a picture and drop it onto the Shader Editor's Shininess channel, that picture will be used to determine how shiny certain areas of your surface will be. If you select a color, or a gradient, the color pixels involved will be converted to grayscale and applied accordingly. The tabs on the Shader Editor access channels for Color, Highlight, Shininess, Bump, Reflection, Transparency, Refraction, and Glow.

Figure 13-21: A bitmapped being is dragged into the Shade Editor's Bump channel.

Figure 13-22 shows the alien ship after applying a newly created shader. After you've created a shader, it is applied just as easily as the presets.

Figure 13-22: The new shader is applied to the alien ship.

Duplicating objects

No alien ship would go on a dangerous journey alone, so let's create some friendly company. While a ship is selected, click Edit ⇨ Duplicate, and use the Virtual Trackball in various Perspective windows to reposition the newly created ships in a pleasantly random pattern. (See Figure 13-23.)

Figure 13-23: Duplicate and rotate the alien ship.

Adding a new light

Let's add a new light near Camera 4. This is easiest to do by dragging the New Light tool onto the Hierarchy window and dropping it near your preferred position. (See Figure 13-24.) Because you are adding the light near a known camera, you should have less trouble finding where the light shines its beam. Look for the outline of a red rectangle on the wall opposite where the light is positioned. Or if the beam is directly hitting an object, you'll see the outline of a red rectangle on the object itself. Double-click the light to open the dialog box for changing the light's qualities, such as color, drop-off rate, and brightness.

Figure 13-24: Add a new light to enliven the alien ships.

Preparing to render the picture

Don't forget to set up your Production Frame to limit the scope of the rendered image to things you really want to see. Figure 13-25 shows the Production Frame centered snuggly around the three ships. Tightening up the field of vision will create an illusion of depth. I chose an "into the cave" backdrop bitmap to accent that effect further. Figure 13-26 shows the final rendered "Alien Visitors" image.

Figure 13-25: The Production Frame tightens its noose around the alien visitors.

Figure 13-26: "Alien Visitors" is complete.

Tutorial #2: "Beer and TV"

In this project, you'll use the Alignment dialog box to reposition objects and cameras to obtain the best viewing distance and angle for a scene.

The Alignment dialog box

The objects shown in the following figures are from the Objects browser. They are all found under the Home tab of the Objects browser. (If the Objects browser is not visible, select Windows ⇨ Objects Browser.) Included in this project are *TV*, *sodacan*, and *ajstlamp*.

Figure 13-27 shows the unfortunate results of placing a camera too close to some objects to be rendered. The large rectangle to the right of the "Beer and TV" is the camera. It's not supposed to be nearly that close. The upper screen shows a quick rendering of what that camera sees: just the TV screen, and not much else. How can we mathematically move the camera farther to the right (the Y axis) without changing the "up and down" (Z axis) angle?

Figure 13-27: "Beer and TV" has been rendered by a camera set up by someone who's probably had too much of both.

Select Arrange ⇨ Align Objects, and the dialog box shown in Figure 13-28 appears. With both the camera and the TV selected, choose the Y Axis, as shown, by using the downward arrow to select which plane to adjust. You'll see a checkbox for you to select the *type* of alignment to use, as well as a data box to input the distance involved. In Figure 13-28, "Space" was selected as the *type* of alignment, and 170 inches was selected for the distance. This method confines our movement to *only the chosen axis*, which is important when adjusting camera positions.

Figure 13-28: Adjust the Camera distance via the Alignment dialog box.

Figure 13-29 shows the use of the Alignment dialog box to place the can precisely on the television. Clicking the right-facing arrow expands the Alignment dialog box to show X, Y, and Z coordinates as completely adjustable, as they are shown here. By inputting distances in the data boxes for each coordinate, and putting a check in the checkbox indicating which type of alignment was required, you can place the can exactly where it should be on the television.

Figure 13-29: Use the expanded Alignment dialog box to position the can.

Figure 13-30 shows a lamp that will be positioned on the television also. But the way the lamp is angled now, it will face backward. We need to rotate it so that it faces at a nice, forward, casual angle. We will input a value in the Alignment dialog box to rotate the lamp on its "Y" axis, or Yaw.

Figure 13-31 shows the lamp rotated, and a new Yaw value of 120 degrees is shown in the data box. Although the results might not appear earth-shattering at the moment, we are trying to predict what the objects will look like when positioned on the TV.

Figure 13-30: The lamp is ready to rotate on its "Y" axis (Yaw) so that it faces appropriately.

Figure 13-31: The lamp has been rotated with a new Yaw value.

Locating objects with the Numerical properties dialog box

Figure 13-32 shows the TV being rendered at a very unflattering angle What we know is that the camera is quite far below the TV level. So this Camera 4 has a Z coordinate below zero, very far below zero.

Figure 13-32: The TV is rendered from far below ground level.

Figure 13-33 shows that the camera, once located, has a Z value of −184.21 inches. Note the Perspective window on the bottom right, labeled "Perspective of Doc5:3." This is the window that would most naturally provide a view of the missing camera. But as you can see, no camera icon appears in that Perspective window. The camera must indeed be quite far below the TV level. (To access the Numerical properties dialog box of any object, right-click it and select Numerical properties.)

Figure 13-33: The Numerical properties dialog box shows the rendering camera to have coordinates well below eye level.

Let's fix this problem. In this instance, we've grouped two objects and then selected Arrange ⇨ Align Objects. (Remember, all the objects' options will be unavailable unless two or more objects are selected and unless you've made some numerical change or checked one of the data boxes in the Alignment dialog box.)

Note that in Figure 13-34, the dialog box shows location coordinates for the TV, below which appear location coordinates for Camera 4. In between is the distance separating the two objects, measured from their hot points. Figure 13-34 shows Camera 4's new Z coordinate of –22 inches to be adequate, for the camera has come into view in Perspective window 3. In fact, now the camera's Z coordinate is the same as the TV's. Also, by looking at the distance measurement, we can see that almost all of the distance between the camera and the TV lies along the Y plane, meaning that the camera is *directly across* from the face of the TV.

Figure 13-34: Calculate the differences between the numbers in the Numerical properties dialog box to properly position the camera in relation to the TV.

Look again at the numbers in both data box groups: the numbers for the TV, and the numbers for Camera 4. You can see that, adding the TV's –29.64 inches along the Y coordinate with the Camera's 72.64, you'll come up with a distance value that matches the one in the Alignment dialog box. That means that the camera and the TV are in the same place, except for their position along the Y axis; they are "right across from each other," at a distance of 102 inches. This is a nice camera position, and it rendered the picture shown in Figure 13-35.

Duplicating with Symmetry

Now you're going to create text, and you'll use the Duplicate with Symmetry command to create a mirror effect in the bitmap surface beneath the text.

Select the Text tool from the toolbar and drag it onto the main Perspective window. The Text dialog box appears. Type a short text entry in all capitals, and give the text the default Bevel amount by putting a check in the appropriate checkbox.

Close the Text dialog box, and the text will appear in the main Perspective window. We need to push the text high on the Z Axis. To do this easily, create a new view. While the text is selected, click View ⇨ Type ⇨ Front, and position the text high on the wire mesh window. (See Figure 13-36.)

Figure 13-35: The rendered TV appears with ornaments.

Figure 13-36: Use the Front submenu item to create a new, front-facing view to reposition text.

Stretch the text so that it reaches the entire length of the front-facing Perspective window you are using, and select Edit ⇨ Duplicate with Symmetry. Your text will be mirrored a few inches beneath it. (See Figure 13-37.)

Figure 13-37: Stretch the text and select Duplicate with Symmetry.

Recolor the text using the Shaders browser. I used Stone from the Tutorial folder for the top text and Dark Wood from the Wood folder for the bottom. (See Figure 13-38.)

Doing a fast render with the bitmap background, I found that the text tilted slightly to the left and did not create a believable "horizon" effect when rendered. In this case, you should group both text instances together and select the Numerical properties dialog box. This enables you to rotate them together on their Y axis until it matches the horizon. (See Figure 13-39.)

Figure 13-38: Each text instance has been enriched with selections from the Shaders browser.

Figure 13-39: Rotate the grouped text instances so that they "sit" on the bitmap's horizon.

Now begins the arduous task of placing the text group *exactly* on the horizon. Figure 13-40 shows a quick rendering of the text against the bitmap. We're obviously way off, here. Luckily, the Numerical properties dialog box is on hand to input changes in the Z coordinates, so I can get a direct hit . . . after a few misses, of course.

Figure 13-40: The Numerical properties dialog box helps position the text group exactly on the horizon, but it takes trial and error.

It's time to angle the bottom text portion a bit forward so that it appears to sit on the ground below the horizon, closer to the screen. To do this, you must ungroup the two text instances, and thus the rotating operation can be performed on the bottom text object only. (See Figure 13-41.) A negative value must be entered into the Roll data box to project text forward on its X axis. You may have to move the text object's hot point in order to rotate the text object on a new rotation point. That's because, depending on how your text objects are positioned, rotating them on the default "center" rotation point may not properly adjust the letters.

Figure 13-42 shows the final image to demonstrate Duplicate with Symmetry. We've succeeded, no doubt?

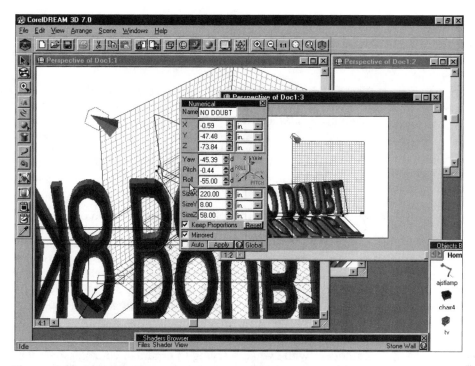

Figure 13-41: Rotate the bottom text on its "X" axis after ungrouping.

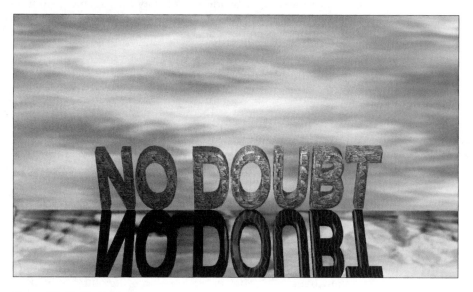

Figure 13-42: No Doubt.

Expert Advice

Here are some general tips to keep in mind as you're learning to use Dream 3D:

- **Using alpha channels.** When you save your rendered scene as a .CPT or TIFF file, the objects in your scene are saved as Alpha channels and will open in all "alpha-aware" programs as selected masks. That means you can apply layering, photoediting, and painting techniques to the objects alone, even after they are saved in non-3D formats. However, if you save your rendered 3D artwork as a TIFF file and then try to open that TIFF file in a program that doesn't support Alpha channels, such as Paint Shop Pro 3, the file will not open.

- **Check your scratch disk.** If you have more than one hard drive, and if one of your drives is either much faster or less cluttered than the others, pick the fastest and emptiest hard drive for your scratch disk. The temp files Dream 3D creates are enormous. Give the program lots of room. I have found Dream 3D to behave well even using compressed drives created with Microsoft Drive Space 3, a benefit that I was not expecting. So Dream 3D seems to just appreciate the room to stretch, anyway it can get it.

- **Use the Save Workspace feature.** I've spoken about the confusion that can occur while you are trying to organize your Perspective windows. Also, at times, the Hierarchy window, shader, and Objects browsers can get themselves stuck in a corner that's nearly impossible to reach. Once you've arranged your windows in a way that seems productive to you, click File ⇨ Save Workspace. From now on, any time you begin a new project or open an older one, the windows will open in the pattern you saved as a Workspace.

- **Use Show Axis Information.** If it's hard for you to remember the directions or dimensions represented by the XYZ coordinates, select File ⇨ Preferences ⇨ Show Axis Information. This causes a small XYZ diagram to be placed at the foot of the selected object. This diagram helps orient you as to which way is which.

- **Work with deformers.** Dream 3D includes tools that can twist, bend, and stretch 3D objects for some very interesting effects. Figure 13-43, "Earthquake Art," shows one of the basic Scene Wizards (Indoor Scene ⇨ Indoor Templates ⇨ Open Door) with a Bend and Twist deformer applied. To accomplish this, group all the objects you want to deform. Right-click the group and select Properties. Choose the Deformer tab, and change the drop-down menu that initially reads "none." Select Bend and Twist from the Deformer list. Choose which axis to deform, and adjust the sliders until you are happy with the results as shown in the preview panel. The Shatter option also brings interesting results when applied in small percentages with the slider.

Figure 13-43: "Earthquake Art" illustrates the effects of the Bend and Twist deformer on one of the basic scene wizards.

■ **Drag and drop vector-type files directly into Dream 3D.** Drag the Free Form tool from the toolbar into the Reference window and drag to create a small box. The window automatically changes to the Modeling window. You can then drag any vector file (.CDR, WMF, and so forth) onto the Modeling Box, to extrude and edit as you would any other Dream 3D file. Figure 13-44 shows a company logo created in CorelDraw. Figure 13-45 shows the same logo rendered as a 3D object and included in a Dream 3D scene.

Figure 13-44: A logo created in CorelDraw

Figure 13-45: The same logo has been rendered as a 3D object and included in a Dream 3D scene.

More Fun with Dream 3D

If you've enjoyed dabbling in this very basic introduction to Dream 3D, here's what I recommend to do next:

- Access the huge 3D clip-art selection that comes with the CorelDraw CD-ROM. Import your own bitmaps as backgrounds, and experiment with building scenes.

- Experiment with creating objects with various Extrusion methods. This chapter and the previous one have only touched on one such method, the Symmetrical Extrusion. There's much more to learn and apply.

- Learn to apply lights and cameras at interesting angles and with attractive color combinations.

- Import 3D modeling objects from other programs such as Ray Dream's Designer 4.2. Dream 3D allows importing standard .DXF modeled objects.

- Try the opening tutorial that comes with the CorelDraw 7 manual. It introduces many Dream 3D features in a short time.

Summary

In this chapter, you learned how to:

- ▶ Create text and add it to an existing scene
- ▶ Use hot points and object projections
- ▶ Use the Hierarchy window
- ▶ Model 3D objects from scratch
- ▶ Use the Numerical properties dialog box
- ▶ Edit shaders and create them from scratch
- ▶ Use the Alignment dialog box
- ▶ Duplicate objects with symmetry

Chapter 14

CorelDepth

In This Chapter

You'll learn about the CorelDepth application. This chapter covers:

▶ Recoloring text and other objects

▶ Ordering and grouping objects

▶ Editing text

▶ Importing and editing images

▶ Working with two-dimensional Shape and Node tools

▶ Getting the most out of CorelDepth

CorelDepth is like "Extrude-in-a-box." CorelDepth comes with presets of various logos, boilerplates, and simple art objects that are extruded and have a degree of dramatic lighting effects. CorelDepth is a simple program, enabling you to edit the included templates further, inputting your own text, importing .WMF files to extrude yourself, or create new objects on a 2D plane, using node tools and shapes.

You can open CorelDepth as you would any Corel application, by selecting Corel, and then CorelDepth from the Program icon on the Start menu. But you can also launch CorelDepth from within CorelDraw itself. See Figure 14-1. Because CorelDepth is not a memory hog, you could probably get away with having both programs open on your computer. In fact, CorelDepth files are usually less than one megabyte, which is relatively small, especially when compared with CorelDraw and Photo-Paint files.

As Figure 14-2 shows, four options are available when you launch CorelDepth:

■ Create a Blank New Document

■ Use the Template Wizard

■ Use the Step By Step Wizard

■ Cancel

Figure 14-1: An alternate way to start CorelDepth from within the CorelDraw program is to click the Application Launcher button.

Figure 14-2: You have four options when starting CorelDepth.

The Template Wizard is the best way for you to immediately start creating CorelDepth projects without having to figure out every last toolbar. The templates included in the Wizard section are predesigned projects that can build a finished product for you if you do as little as add a bit of text. If you understand something about the interface, and how to add and reposition objects, you can do more than simply recreate what is already on the screen with your words attached. Figure 14-3 shows the opening Template Wizard screen. The mouse pointer is shown ready to open the Wizard with a gear running around some text. You'll have to scroll down with the scroll bar on the right to see this template.

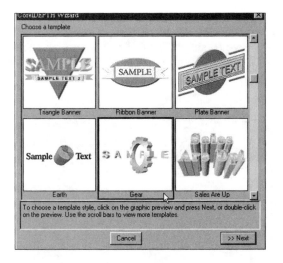

Figure 14-3: Using the Wizard for CorelDepth makes it easy to produce good-looking extrusions.

By selecting the Wizard, you can replace the existing text with your own. Clicking Next gives you the dialog box shown in Figure 14-4.

Figure 14-4: Replace the template's text with your own.

Click Done, and your image appears on the main working screen. Keep in mind that the resulting image may not fit on the page. If your printer is set to Portrait mode, you may have to select File ⇨ Print Setup, as shown in Figure 14-5, to change the display to landscape mode. (If your printer is already set to landscape mode, you won't have to do this.)

Figure 14-5: Changing to Landscape mode via the Print Setup option can help accommodate the objects on your screen.

The letters still need to be resized to fit on a standard 8½" × 11" sheet of paper set at the landscape orientation. Clicking once on the two objects — the gear and the letters — displays a single bounding box, which indicates that the objects are grouped. See Figure 14-6. If you just click on the objects and drag inward from the edges, you resize *both* the gear and the letters.

Figure 14-6: Clicking on the objects reveals a single bounding box because the objects are grouped.

However, you can resize the letters to fit on the page without shrinking the gear as well. Figure 14-7 shows that you can select Ungroup (Arrange ➪ Ungroup) to gain control over the size of the letters. Once an object is ungrouped, you can perform individual edits on size, color, and shading on each object. After ungrouping, select only the letters, and drag inward from a bounding box corner to shrink them. I also made them a bit higher, by dragging upward on the same bounding box corner. See Figure 14-8.

Figure 14-7: Ungroup the gear and the letters to perform individual edits on each.

Figure 14-8: Resize the letters and move them more toward the center of the page.

Looking again at Figure 14-8, notice the individual bounding boxes around each object. To center them on the page, you need to move them together. Rather than group them, you can press Shift and select each object by clicking on it. They can then be moved together.

CorelDepth does not facilitate selecting multiple objects by marquee selecting — that is, drawing an imaginary box around them. You must Shift-click.

You may want to change the preset lighting effect, which can cause the letters on the right to look blurry. Changing the light source creates interesting shadows and reveals more texture on correctly placed objects. To adjust lighting effects, make sure the object is selected, and then choose Arrange ⇨ Light Source, as shown in Figure 14-9.

Figure 14-9: Edit the Light Source from the Arrange menu.

The effect I preferred was placing the light at the bottom of the objects, shining up, as shown in Figure 14-10. Use your mouse to drag the light source circle (the small circle) in the direction from which you'd like the light to shine.

Figure 14-10: Use the mouse to drag and select a new source direction.

Figure 14-11 shows the letters with a new lighting effect. Notice that the letters are now moved a bit more to the front and to the right. CorelDepth includes a Virtual Trackball tool for freely rotating objects on any axis. The tool works the same as its counterpart in Dream 3D.

Figure 14-11: The lettering appears with a new lighting effect. The Virtual Trackball was used to reposition the text forward and to the right.

CorelDepth includes an Align and Distribute dialog box. (Select Arrange ➪ Align and Distribute.) This dialog box enables you to reposition objects with precision and is especially helpful for equally spacing several objects along a common border or object. The Align and Distribute dialog box has a preview area, and Figure 14-12 shows the results of checking new options on the Depth and Horizontal parameters. This dialog box works similarly to its CorelDraw counterpart.

Figure 14-12: Change the object alignment in the Align and Distribute dialog box.

The multiple text placement around the gear effect in Figure 14-13 was executed by copying and pasting the text around the gear, but then using the Virtual Trackball to obtain the random "coming and going" angles associated with each text object. Some of the text objects were recolored.

Recoloring Text and Other Objects

As you may have noticed, you seem to be limited to the color combinations included with the Styles dialog box that appears when you open the program. The Styles dialog box can become the Edit Styles library by selecting Edit ➪ Style Library from the menu. You'll then see the Edit Styles library buttons, as shown in Figure 14-14.

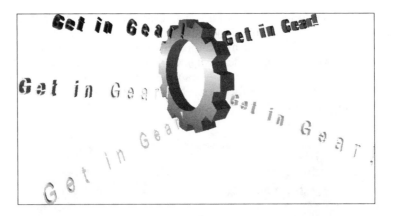

Figure 14-13: Using multiple text objects and the Virtual Trackball to position text produces interesting results.

Figure 14-14: The Edit Styles library is available from the Edit menu.

Selecting Edit from the Edit Styles library provides options for adding new colors to the Front Face, Front Bevel, Side Surface, Back Bevel, and Back Face. See Figure 14-15. Remember, because this is a 3D program, it's quite possible to view an object's back surfaces as well. Worth noting is the Grab option, which enables you to save the style of the selected object as a style for later use.

Figure 14-15: The Color Style editing screen gives you many options.

Ordering and Grouping Objects

How do you get the letters through the middle of the gear? Lest you drive yourself crazy trying to do it yourself, the gear is actually *two objects.* The back half of the gear was sent to the back using the Send to Back command from the Arrange menu. Then the letters were positioned in front of the back gear portion. Finally, the front gear portion was lined up with the back gear, but positioned *in front* of the letters. Figure 14-16 shows the object slightly separated for easy viewing.

Editing Text

While text is selected, Click Style from the Edit menu. The drop-down menu has options for how your text should be filled with color. One of those options is Decal. See Figure 14-17. Select Choose Decal and you'll be given a browse menu to import a .WMF file to use to fill your letters. As you can see from the same figure, you are given bounding boxes to stretch the decal to fill a larger area. (.WMF files resize well and keep their integrity.)

Figure 14-16: The magic trick of getting the text to run through the gear is exposed by showing the gear's two layers.

Figure 14-17: Decals added to a text selection are easy to stretch to fill a larger area.

Figure 14-18 shows the results of applying the decal effect to the word Scissors. I had to rotate the end of the text selection forward to prevent the white of the decal from blending with the white of the background.

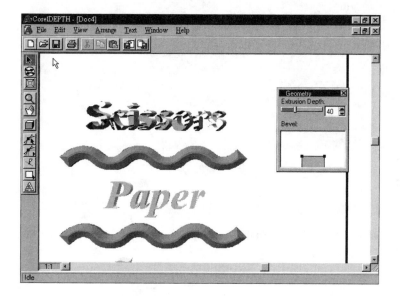

Figure 14-18: The word "Scissors" has a .WMF decal applied.

You can also apply a Gradation effect to a group of letters. Figure 14-19 shows the Gradation section of the Color Style dialog box, where you select starting and ending colors, as well as how gradual you want the gradation to be.

Figure 14-20 shows the word "Paper" with a gradation applied to the letter's front surface. I applied some rather extreme color and size effects to the bevels and middle surface of the letters. Right next to the word Paper in Figure 14-20, notice the Extrude dialog box. The number "58" refers to the extrude amount applied to the lettering. The preview window below the extrusion depth setting enables you to adjust the bevel depth by hand. This is good for making bevel adjustments "as you go," because a figure that might seem right numerically sometimes turns out to be a poor choice when you see the final result of the extrusion process.

Figure 14-19: The Color Style dialog box lets you choose colors for a gradation effect on text.

Figure 14-20: The word "Paper" sports a gradation effect. Note the extrusion dialog box nearby.

The Perspective tool (the third tool on the CorelDepth toolbar on the left side of the screen) was applied near the word "Stone." You can see that this causes the lighting and extrusion to pull the word to the right. See Figure 14-21.

Figure 14-21: The Perspective appears as a box. Here it is shown dragged near the word "Stone."

The Perspective tool appears as a "box-within-a-box" on your screen. Place it in an area where you'd like to exaggerate extrusion and distance effects. First click and drag the back box to actually move the area where perspective alteration will occur, and then click on a corner node (shown near the word "Stone") to change the depth of the perspective itself.

Completing the image "Scissors Paper Stone," which is simply an edited preset provided with CorelDepth, is a fairly easy process, as follows (see Figure 14-22):

■ All five objects on the screen were grouped.

■ The entire group was resized to fill the paper area. (It is better to enlarge an object at this point in the process rather than after you export it as a different file type.)

■ The Virtual Trackball and Perspective tool were used to tilt the image to provide a sense of movement and spontaneity.

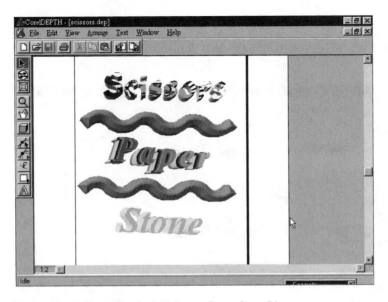

Figure 14-22: Here's the final "Scissors Paper Stone" image.

Importing and Editing Images

Figure 14-23 shows an image created from two pieces of clip art (.WMF files) imported into CorelDepth (Select File ➪ Import).

Figure 14-23: "I Don't Drink De-Calf."

Figure 14-24 shows how the image was originally imported, a rather flat common cup of coffee.

Figure 14-24: The coffee clip art looks a bit dull as it was originally imported.

To give clip art extruded qualities, select the existing clip art and chose File ➪ Import/Replace Outline, as shown in Figure 14-25. As its name implies, this command imports the clip art and replaces it with a depth-sensitive outline.

Figure 14-26 shows the converted coffee clip art, now with an Extrusion value of 18. As with other CorelDepth objects, you may extrude it as much as you like, apply Decals and Gradations, Bevels, and other 3D traits.

Figure 14-25: Use the Import/Replace Outline command to turn clip art into a 3D object.

Figure 14-26: The coffee cup is now a 3D object.

Secret

Lighting alterations affect the appearances of clip art extrusions, but the clip art itself won't look brighter or dimmer just because you've changed the light source.

Figure 14-27 shows the first calf imported and treated in the same manner. Text was created using the Text tool, also found on the toolbar. The calf was copied, pasted several times, and all of its little progenies were scattered willy-nilly around the canvas. Different Extrusion sizes were used for each calf. Perspective and Virtual Trackball were applied liberally to each object.

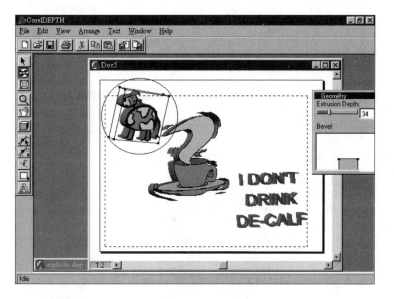

Figure 14-27: The two-dimensional calf and text join the cup of coffee on the 3D canvas.

Using the Two-Dimensional Shape and Node Tools

When you click the 2D Selection tool, the work surface becomes flat. You are now working in two-dimensional space. You may create shapes from a familiar set of shape tools and edit them by adding nodes, subtracting nodes, and curving them using the Bézier tool. These techniques will be familiar to you because you've worked through similar tools in other Corel Programs, including CorelDraw, Photo-Paint, and Dream 3D. Clicking the 3D cube returns you to 3D mode, and your tools will return to the 3D tools of Extrude, Virtual Trackball, and so on.

To create freeform shapes, you must start in 2D mode and click on your screen with the Bézier tool. You can then move nodes with the 2D tool, alter nodes with the Add and Delete Node tools, and change curvature qualities with the Bézier tool. If, for some reason, your 2D work in progress becomes unselected, you cannot just "click on it" to select it and drag the nodes again. You must use the 2D tool to drag a rectangle around the object. The nodes will again be available for editing.

You can edit the colors and line qualities of your 2D work as you would any other object. However, when you switch to 3D mode (which happens when you select any of the 3D tools), your 2D image does *not* retain your 2D color choices unless you select Import from the Style library. (The Style library is the floating dialog box covered with M's.) If you do not select the "M" labeled Import, your picture's colors will become whatever the default 3D colors are. The bunny rabbit shown in Figure 14-28 is a combination of rectangle, oval, and freeform objects created with the Bézier tool. Once a 3D tool was selected, I could apply 3D techniques to create a bunny only Picasso would love.

Figure 14-28: The Bézier tool helped create this pop-art bunny in CorelDepth.

Getting the Most out of CorelDepth

CorelDepth is a program that is easily overlooked, but if you need a fast 3D logo or a simple 3D composition, CorelDepth can fit your needs exactly. Here are some tips for getting the most out of CorelDepth:

■ **Work while you extrude.** The bad news is that extruding objects can sometimes take quite a while with CorelDepth. The good news is that you can move objects, open and edit other files, and work generally unmolested while your picture extrudes. This feature of being able to work while objects are extruding is fairly unique to CorelDepth and adds some practicality to the program. You can even drop additional artwork and lettering into your current project while it is extruding.

- **Use the Zoom tool.** To choose from various Zoom settings, you must click on the number at the lower left of the screen near the status bar that displays the current Zoom amount. Several Zoom options appear.

- **Keep your eye on the status bar.** The status bar tells you when objects are done extruding. This is important information that is not otherwise available. If the status bar is not present, right-click on any empty tool-bar space and place a check by Status Bar.

- **Import images.** From CorelDraw, you can import .WMF files, and use the Bézier and Node tools to edit them. You can get some really creative results using this technique.

After learning the program, you'll be able to create images in less than half an hour, and you'll actually have something ready to print or export. You can really get fast results on the fly. Experiment with editing the templates that are included. For example, you might try changing the lighting and font selections.

Tip

You can export CorelDepth art as Adobe Illustrator files, and as .EPS files. If you come up with something good here that just needs some more professional editing, consider these options.

Summary

▶ CorelDepth is a useful 3D utility that is much easier to get up and running with than its trickier cousins, such as Dream 3D.

▶ Some of the tools, such as the Virtual Trackball and 3D lighting effects, use the same principles as more elaborate 3D programs. If you've never used a 3D program, experimenting with CorelDepth is a good way to get your feet wet.

▶ You can import clip art from other programs and reposition objects on the screen to achieve compositions that are more pleasing.

▶ Use the Node tool to reshape objects. This is a great way to create art that's truly unique.

Part III

Utilities, Clip Art, and Templates

Chapter 15

Corel OCR-Trace

In This Chapter

You'll learn about:

▶ The OCR-Trace interface

▶ Tracing black-and-white bitmaps

▶ Tracing colored bitmaps

▶ Optical character recognition

The CorelDRAW 7 package contains virtually everything you need to work with all types of graphics, including the two major graphics formats — vector and bitmap. As you've seen in earlier chapters, the primary application in the package, CorelDraw, provides everything you need to create and edit vector images. And Photo-Paint lets you perform all kinds of magic on paint-program, bitmap images.

As Chapter 8 mentioned, vector and bitmapped graphics each have both benefits and limitations. For this reason, sometimes it's useful to convert bitmapped images to a vector graphics format. Bitmapped images, for example, are not easily resized without degrading image quality. And you can't always reshape and resize portions of bitmaps successfully. In addition, the lack of editable paths in paint-program images sometimes makes recoloring objects difficult.

Here's where the nifty utility OCR-Trace comes in handy. Basically, what OCR-Trace does is to trace — that is, create outlines, or paths — around objects in a bitmapped image. You can then make simple alterations to the paths (and their fills) in OCR-Trace, or you can import them into CorelDraw for a full range of vector image editing.

Sound too good to be true? Well, it's not. And this chapter shows you how to turn paint-program bitmap images into vector paths you can edit in CorelDraw. In addition to tracing bitmaps, OCR-Trace performs basic optical character recognition (OCR) functions. As you probably know, OCR is the process of turning scanned text pages into text that is editable by a word processor.

In this chapter we look at both tracing bitmaps and converting scanned text into editable text. Once you learn the secrets of this utility, OCR-Trace proves itself an extremely powerful tool to use along with your other business and graphic design applications.

The OCR-Trace Interface

In many respects, the OCR-Trace interface (shown in Figure 15-1) is virtually identical to that of CorelDraw and the other applications in the package. You can configure options and customize menus and toolbars the same way you do in CorelDraw. Many of the tools, including Zoom, Pan, and the Pick tool, work according to the same principles. Rather than rehashing material discussed elsewhere in this book, this chapter focuses on parts of the OCR-Trace interface that are different from the other CorelDRAW 7 applications. Those are the tools used specifically for bitmap-tracing and OCR.

Draw OCR Block

Draw Trace Block

Number Block

Node Reshape

Create Bézier

Rubber Band

Delete Nodes

Source Window   Output Window

Figure 15-1: The OCR-Trace interface has many features in common with other CorelDRAW 7 applications.

Here's an overview of the main features of the interface:

■ **The Source window** displays the image (or text, when performing OCR) to be traced.

■ **The Output window** displays the results of the trace or OCR procedure. You can also use this window to perform OCR-Trace's image editing functions, such as deleting paths, deleting notes, creating Béziers, erasing objects, and so on.

■ **The Draw Trace Block tool** enables you to define an area of a bitmap you want traced. This tool lets you pick and choose objects to be traced, eliminating the need to wait for the program to trace the entire image. This can be a big time saver, because large images can take quite some time to process. By selecting specific blocks to recognize, you don't have to edit portions of the scanned image you don't need. Figure 15-2 shows this tool in action.

Figure 15-2: Use the Draw Trace Block tool to define areas in a bitmap image to trace.

■ **The Node Reshape tool** lets you edit nodes and Béziers in the Output Window. It works similarly to CorelDraw's Shape tool, discussed in Chapter 2.

■ **The Create Bézier tool** lets you add Bézier curves to the image in the Output window. It works similarly to the Bézier tool in CorelDraw, discussed in Chapter 2.

■ **The Rubber Band tool** lets you manipulate nodes and paths in an elastic fashion.

■ **The Delete Nodes tool** lets you delete nodes on paths. For information on the benefits and uses of deleting nodes, refer to the discussion of the Shape tool in Chapter 2.

■ **The Draw OCR Block tool** enables you to define the area of text on a scanned page that you want recognized and converted to editable text. You can also use this option on a page where you want to perform OCR and trace bitmaps at the same time. By default, Draw OCR Block blocks are "Text & Graphic" mode. You can change them to recognize just text, ignoring graphics, by clicking the right mouse button in the block and then selecting Text Only. To define an area, simply draw a box around the text, as shown in Figure 15-3.

■ **The Number Block tool** enables you to number multiple blocks in the Source Window. This tool becomes available when you use Draw OCR Block and Draw Trace Block to define areas for processing. It lets you choose the order in which areas are processed. The procedure for using this tool is as follows: Draw multiple blocks in the Source Window. Select the Number Block tool. Click in the blocks in the order you want them numbered. If you don't number blocks, they are processed in the order in which you draw them.

Figure 15-3: You can use Draw OCR-Trace to define areas in scanned text to recognize.

Tracing Black-and-White Images

Tracing black-and-white bitmaps and editing the output is much easier by far than working with color and grayscale images. In most instances, OCR-Trace creates a vector image that requires little touch-up.

To trace a black-and-white bitmap, you must first, of course, bring a source image into the program. You can do this in a number of ways:

■ You can scan it directly into OCR-Trace, which works the same as scanning into Photo-Paint, discussed in Chapter 8.

■ You can use the Open command on the File menu.

■ You can drag and drop the image from another OLE-aware program, such as Photo-Paint. You can also drag and drop from Corel Multimedia Manager, Windows Explorer, or any of several other clip catalogs or file management programs.

■ You can cut or copy (Edit ➪ Cut) from another Windows application and paste (Edit ➪ Paste) into OCR-Trace.

No matter how you bring the source image into OCR-Trace, it is displayed in the Source Window. You can now choose to trace all or a portion of the image. To trace all of the image, choose OCR-Trace ➪ Perform Trace ➪ By Outline. (You can also click on the Outline Trace button on the toolbar.) To trace a portion of the image, use the Draw Trace Block to define the area, and then choose Perform Trace.

You really have several options for tracing, including Outline and Center Line. The other options on the Perform Trace flyout on the OCR-Trace menu — Sketch, Woodcut, Mosaic, and 3D Mosaic — are special effects, which are discussed later in this chapter in the section "Using Special Effects with OCR-Trace." For creating vector paths, you'll work primarily with two options, Outline trace and Center Line trace. Outline trace creates filled paths by tracing the black areas of the image and then filling them with a black solid fill, as shown in Figure 15-4. The Center Line trace option creates paths by tracing the outlines and filled areas without filling the closed paths, as shown in Figure 15-5.

Figure 15-4: An image has been traced with the Outline trace option. Use this method to recreate the image, complete with fills.

Figure 15-5: An image has been traced with the Center Line option. This method draws outlines around filled areas and traces lines.

As you can see from Figures 15-4 and 15-5, Outline trace recreates the image in vector format. Center Line, on the other hand, recreates only the outlines of the image. In either case, once the image is traced, you can use OCR-Trace's tools to edit the image, or you can import the image into CorelDraw and edit it there. Typical editing in OCR-Trace would include using the color palette in conjunction with the Pick tool to recolor closed paths, or to use the Bézier and other node editing to manipulate and close paths.

You can adjust several factors of how OCR-Trace performs a trace by adjusting the options in the Trace Settings dialog box. Mostly, these options are the same whether you trace a black-and-white image or a color one. Rather than going over them twice, I discuss the options in Trace Settings in the next section.

Tracing Color Images

The procedure for tracing a color bitmap in OCR-Trace is primarily the same as for black-and-white images as just described, but the results can be quite different. First, not all images can be successfully traced in OCR-Trace. Many photographs, for example, contain far too many colors and patterns for OCR-Trace to figure out how to create paths for all of them. When that's the case, you can increase your chances of success by first editing the image in Photo-Paint. Refer to Chapter 9 for a discussion of how to remove objects from images by turning paths into selections.

When you trace a color image in OCR-Trace, the program is capable of separating it into only 257 colors, for which it creates separate paths for each occurrence of a color and separate layers for each color. (Actually, the program supports 256 colors and creates a separate layer for plugging holes, or areas for containing colors for which it was unable to create a layer. Figure 15-6 shows OCR-Trace Document Information (Tools ➪ Layer Manager) after tracing a full-color image.

Figure 15-6: When you trace color images, OCR-Trace creates a separate layer for each color.

So as you can imagine, you'll have a rough time getting successful traces of images containing thousands or millions of colors. OCR-Trace works best on scanned drawings or artwork with white or solid backgrounds and less than 256 colors. Other types of images can cause you to perform far too much touch-up to make it worth your while.

Once the image is traced, you can edit each path by using the Layer Manager in Document Information to go to the layer containing the desired path. The Layers portion of the Document Information dialog box functions like the CorelDraw Layers roll-up, which is discussed in Chapter 3. You can turn the display of individual layers off, delete layers, and so on. Or you can bring the image into CorelDraw and edit layers with the Layers roll-up.

Improving your trace results

You can adjust several factors involved in the decisions OCR-Trace makes when it processes a trace from the Trace Settings dialog box (OCR-Trace ⇨ Trace Settings), shown in Figure 15-7. Each type of trace — Outline, Center Line, and the special effects — has its own sets of controls.

A   **B**

Figure 15-7: Use the Trace Settings dialog box to modify the way OCR-Trace traces bitmaps. The tab on the far left (A) enables you to adjust settings for Outline trace; the second tab from the left (B) can be used to adjust Center Line traces.

Let's look at the settings for Outline trace and Center Line trace and how they affect how the program performs:

- **Node Reduction:** If you've read much of this book, you already know what nodes are and the benefits of reducing the number of them on a path. Nodes, of course, mark a place in a path where it changes directions or joins. Using this method smoothes lines, taking many of the kinks out and eliminating small line segments. This option works the same whether you are using Outline or Center Line trace.

- **Color Tolerance:** Available only when performing an Outline trace, this option determines the accuracy for the color representation of the vector graphic. *Color tolerance* refers to how different (in hue) the source colors can be before the program can convert them to the same color in the vector graphic. The lower the color tolerance, the more unique colors will appear in the resulting graphic, and the more closely it will resemble the original image. Keep in mind that the more colors you allow, the more layers you will get in the resulting graphic. Editing an image with a couple of hundred layers is no picnic.

- **Hole Filling:** When you are working with color bitmaps, after an image has been traced, small holes are often left in the resulting vector graphic. Hole Filling creates a background layer of small rectangles of each area's average color. These rectangles fill the holes. By increasing the number in Hole Filling, you increase the number of rectangles, increasing the accuracy of the colors in the resulting traced image.

- **Noise Reduction:** When you are working with either Outline and Center Line trace, this option enables you to screen out small, unwanted, or not easily edited objects. Noise Reduction works by eliminating areas of color smaller in pixels than the value set in this field. Using this option can require some tradeoffs. If, for example, your bitmap contains fine details, they could be lost if Noise Reduction is set too high. If it is set too low, you could wind up with a lot of tiny paths that are difficult to fill and delete.

- **Iteration:** When processing a trace in Center Line mode, OCR-Trace eliminates the outline from the outside in, searching for the center of the line. Adjusting this value affects how quickly the trace processes and the thinness of the ensuing lines. The higher the setting, the thinner the resulting outlines.

Secret

While the settings in Trace Settings can greatly improve the quality of output from OCR-Trace, it's often difficult to predict how the program will analyze and trace your images. All images are different and have their own properties. It's often difficult to avoid a few trial-and-error traces before getting the best results. In these cases, the speed with which OCR-Trace traces can greatly affect how long you will have to work with an image to get it just right.

The physical size — in inches or pixels — plays less of a role in determining how long a trace takes than do image resolution and file size (remember that dpi and file size are closely related). You can reduce an image's file size in Photo-Paint with that program's Resample function (discussed in Chapter 8). There's really no reason to use images higher than about 200 dpi in OCR-Trace. And keep in mind, too, that once you make the conversion from bitmap to vector, the traced image is easily resized in CorelDraw — so the size of the source image is not all that critical during a trace.

Using special effects in OCR-Trace

OCR-Trace ships with four special-effects trace options. They are Woodcut, Sketch, Mosaic, and 3D Mosaic. Unlike Outline and Center Line trace, these options are for creating specialized artwork, rather than tracing bitmaps in order to edit them as vector graphics. Figures 15-8 through 15-11 show the four effects available in OCR-Trace.

Figure 15-8: An example of OCR-Trace's Woodcut tracing option

Figure 15-9: An example of OCR-Trace's Sketch tracing option

Figure 15-10: An example of OCR-Trace's Mosaic tracing option

Figure 15-11: An example of OCR-Trace's 3D Mosaic tracing option

You can control several aspects of each effect from the Trace Settings dialog box (OCR-Trace ➪ Trace Settings), such as the angles of the lines in a Woodcut, or the number and size of the pyramids, fans, or bricks in a 3D Mosaic pattern. Depending on the effect you choose, the options can be pretty extensive. To find out what each option does and how it affects the resulting output, you should experiment with different settings. To get a description of what each option does, right-click on the option in the dialog box, and then choose What Is? from the pop-up menu. This gives you a context-sensitive pop-up help caption explaining the option, as shown in Figure 15-12.

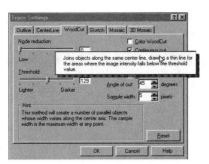

Figure 15-12: You can get explanations of the options in the Trace Settings dialog box by right-clicking on a specific option and then choosing What's This? from the pop-up.

Optical Character Recognition

If you've ever used optical character recognition for bringing hard copy text into your word processor, than you know how much time it can save. It's must faster and often more accurate than retyping. While OCR-Trace is not as powerful and feature-rich as most dedicated OCR programs, such as Caere's OmniPage, it works well enough for occasional text recognition tasks.

The most common way to get a text source page into OCR-Trace is to scan it. However, you can also import images from fax software, such as Delrina's WinFax — as long as the fax program has the capability of exporting to a format supported by OCR-Trace, such as TIFF.

As with Photo-Paint (discussed in Chapter 8), you can use the TWAIN-compliant software that came with your scanner to scan a text page, or you can use CorelScan, the scanning utility bundled in the CorelDRAW 7 package (discussed in Chapter 19). After you scan a page, it shows up in the Source Window. From here you can elect to either recognize the entire page or use Draw OCR Block in the toolbox to select specific portions of the page to recognize. Figures 15-13 and 15-14 show the two methods.

Figure 15-13: A full page of text is ready to recognize in OCR-Trace.

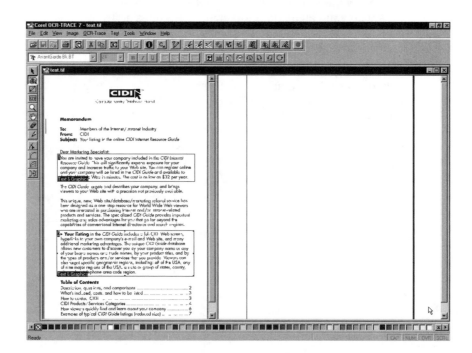

Figure 15-14: Draw OCR Blocks is used to recognize selected portions of a page.

To recognize the text, simply choose Perform OCR from the OCR-Trace menu, or click on the Recognize Text button on the tool bar. If the scan is clean — 200 dpi or higher, straight, and free of noise (including dirt and interference from colored paper or backgrounds) — the recognition should perform without a hitch. The recognized text displays in the Output Window. You can now export the text (File ⇨ Export Text) to an ASCII text file or to one of many supported word processor files. Or you can cut or copy (File ⇨ Copy) the text and paste (File ⇨ Paste) it into CorelDraw and edit it as Paragraph Text (discussed in Chapter 4).

When working in either the Source or Output windows, you can use the Zoom tool to magnify portions of the source or output, just as you would in any other CorelDraw application. This can make it easier to see which portions of the Source document you want to block for recognition. In the Output Window, zooming in enables you to better judge the results of a recognition session or edit portions of the output.

Secret

Don't forget that you can use the right mouse button. In the Source Window it provides options for changing views, adding pages, and several other useful functions. In the Output Window, the right-mouse pop-up provides quick access to several editing tools.

Changing OCR settings

OCR-Trace provides extensive options for modifying the settings the program uses while performing text recognition, including spell checking during recognition, special settings for pages that contain multiple columns or tables, and many, many other options. You control how OCR-Trace recognizes text from the OCR Settings dialog box (OCR-Trace ⇨ OCR Settings), shown in Figure 15-15.

Figure 15-15: Use the OCR Settings dialog box to control the decisions OCR-Trace makes while recognizing text.

As you can see, OCR Settings contains four categories for controlling how OCR-Trace recognizes text. Each option in each of the four sections has pop-up help via the What's This? command on the right-mouse pop-up, so I won't go over each setting individually. Instead, the following list provides an overview of the various options available in each section of the dialog box and what you can do with them.

- The **Language** section of the OCR Settings dialog box contains three options:

    - Whether OCR-Trace should recognize text using one of the many languages the CorelDRAW package supports

    - Whether the program should check spelling as it recognizes text

    - What level of confidence to operate at

    The first two options don't need explaining. *Confidence* controls how thoroughly OCR-Trace trusts its own judgment. Here's how it works: Each time OCR-Trace has trouble discerning a character, it inserts a reject character (a tilde ~ by default). A low confidence level decreases the number of rejects; a high confidence level increases the number of rejects. In other words, OCR-Trace guesses less often when you set a high confidence level.

- The **Content** section of OCR-Trace settings enables you to tell OCR-Trace whether it is scanning a page of single-column text, a page containing multiple columns, or a table. The program then tries to reformat the output accordingly.

- The **Source** section of OCR-Trace lets you provide information about the source page prior to recognition. This can not only speed up recognition but also improve the accuracy. From here you can tell the program whether the source is a normal scanned page, a dot-matrix page, or a fax. You can also set the page orientation at which you scanned the page, and you can adjust the skew level of the source page. *Skew*, in this case, refers to pages that are not set straight in the scanner or photocopies that did not print straight.

- The **Formatting** section controls the output from the recognition process. You can, for example, elect to keep all of the page formatting or to keep just the text formatting, such as bolds, indents, and so on. You can also choose the output font.

As I mentioned earlier, in most cases OCR-Trace does a fair job of recognizing text. However, if the results are not to your liking, you can use these options to tweak the final output. OCR does you little good if you have to spend much time editing the results.

Working with multiple-page documents

Many text recognition jobs entail processing several pages. The way traditional OCR programs handle this is to have you to scan several pages before executing the recognition. You can do this manually or via a scanner sheet feeder, which scans 20 or more pages in succession automatically.

Unfortunately, you can't scan multiple pages into OCR-Trace.

But you can open several scanned pages in the same OCR-Trace document and then process them all. You have several ways to do this: You can open them all at once with the Open command on the File menu; you can add them to an existing document with the Page Manager (Tools ➪ Page Manager); or you can drag and drop them into Page Manager from Windows Explorer or another OLE-aware application, such as Corel Multimedia Manager. Figure 15-16 shows Page Manager.

Figure 15-16: Use Page Manager to add and delete pages from the current document.

The most efficient way to get several scanned pages into OCR-Trace is through Open or Add Pages (also on the File menu). When you use the Open command, you can select all or some of the files in a directory either by Ctrl-clicking on each file or by Shift-clicking on the first file and then Shift-clicking again on the last file you want to import. When you click OK, OCR-Trace opens all of the files and places them in the same document or session.

You can now recognize all the pages at once by clicking Recognize Text, which opens OCR Multiple Pages, shown in Figure 15-17. From here you can select pages to recognize, or you can choose All Pages to recognize the text on them all. Red check marks inside the page icons in OCR Multiple Pages means that the page is selected to be recognized.

Figure 15-17: Page Manager lets you choose specific pages for recognition or recognize them all.

Secret

A further note on multiple-page documents: I should point out that you can go through and define blocks on each page for recognition with Draw OCR Block, as explained earlier in this chapter. OCR-Trace then ignores the other text on those pages. You should know, too, that you can also trace multiple pages of bitmapped images with the method I just described. You'll find that handy when you need to trace several images. You can just leave the computer working on it while you have lunch or work on something else.

Summary

▶ You can create vector images from bitmaps that can be edited in CorelDraw with OCR-Trace.

▶ When you trace black-and-white images in OCR-Trace, they are placed on one layer, on which you can then edit and fill paths either in OCR-Trace or in CorelDraw.

▶ When you trace colored bitmaps in OCR-Trace, each color is placed on a separate layer, on which you can edit paths or which import into CorelDraw.

▶ You can turn scanned text into text editable in a word processor (or CorelDraw) with OCR-Trace OCR capabilities.

Chapter 16

Customizing Clip Art, Textures, and Templates

In This Chapter

You'll learn lots of tips on working with:

▶ Clip art

▶ CorelTexture

▶ Templates

The CorelDRAW 7 package comes with many extras besides the applications: thousands of pieces of clip art, numerous templates, and a wonderful little program for creating your own textures that can be applied to CorelDraw, Photo-Paint, Dream 3D, and CorelDepth. In this chapter, you'll learn to customize clip art, changing it significantly, and giving it a far broader application than the usual window-dressing clip art gets relegated to. You'll also learn about CorelTexture, a program that allows you to create textures with so many variations that it's nearly impossible to make the same texture twice. Last, you'll learn how to customize Draw's templates so that, if you work with the same template often but find that you keep making the same changes each time, you can save those changes as part of the template — and even give it a new name. This chapter shows you how to maximize many of the extras that came on your CorelDRAW 7 CD-ROMs.

Customizing Clip Art

Figure 16-1 shows a rocket, a piece of clip art included with CorelDraw 7.

Most clip art objects are groups of smaller art objects. A typical piece of clip art, for example, often consists of a solid black background that frames the shape of the entire picture. First, though, let's look at what you can do with clip art without ungrouping it. Figure 16-2 shows an envelope applied to the rocket.

Figure 16-1: This rocket clip art object comes with CorelDraw.

Figure 16-2: The envelope effect is applied to the rocket.

As you can see from the envelope bounding box around the rocket, the envelope can be modified by manipulating the curve handles, giving the rocket a unique twist. You can do this without having to ungroup the rocket and deal with its individual components.

Figure 16-3 shows the rocket after the contour effect was applied to the wings on both sides. The contour effect has stretched and curved the wings according to the envelope that was applied. For this to be done, the wings must first be ungrouped but not moved away from the rocket itself. Before applying the contour effect, be sure to select only the wing and not the rest of the rocket.

Figure 16-3: The rocket looks like this after a contour effect was applied to the wings.

Figure 16-4 shows an unmodified clip art object, Little Red Riding Hood, available from the Fantasy folder of your clip art CD-ROM.

You can ungroup Little Red and then reposition the curves and lines on the hood. Figure 16-5 shows the beginnings of Little Red leaving her riding hood behind.

Figure 16-4: Little Red Riding Hood appears as clip art.

Figure 16-5: Little Red begins to lose her hood.

When you first ungroup this piece of clip art, select one of the objects, and switch to the Shape Tool. You'll notice dozens and dozens of nodes outlining Little Red's red hood. In order to manipulate the hood, the first thing you must do is delete about 95 percent of those nodes. One of the main rules in altering the shape of clip art is simplifying the curves. If you don't, you may end up with untraceable twists and turns, not knowing which node is affecting which line. To delete a node, right-click on it and press the D key, or scroll down the shortcut menu to the Delete command. To delete many nodes at once, particularly nodes that are redundant and not needed for the shape's integrity, use the Node Auto-Reduce option to simplify the shape and reduce the sheer number of nodes.

You can do a lot with Ms. Red — perhaps you'd like to give her a more modern hair style? Or something more drastic? Look at Figure 16-6. By rearrangement of the lines and nodes, a shadowy cave was created. Another piece of clip art was inserted and treated with the Interactive Transparency tool. This was to create the impression of Red emerging from a cave after passing by a mysterious lake.

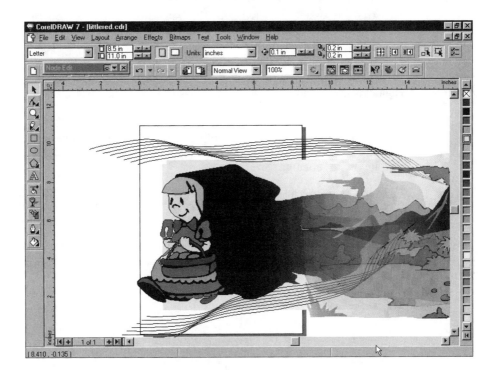

Figure 16-6: Little Red emerges from a dark Scottish loch . . . many miles away!

Recoloring clip art

Figure 16-7 shows a gazelle from the Animals folder of the clip art CD-ROM. One nice feature of Draw's clip art is that even the smallest shapes that make up the whole clip art object can be colored individually. The boundaries are firm. This quality is very helpful when you are using fills to recolor clip art. If the boundaries between the clip art individual pieces are solid, you don't need to spend lots of time closing gaps in order to keep the fill in the area you want.

Figure 16-7: A clip art gazelle includes shapes that can be manipulated individually.

Figure 16-8 shows that same gazelle treated with many blends of fountain fills and texture fills. The legs and flank were repositioned slightly to give the gazelle more "spring."

Figure 16-9 shows a clip art bird that was ungrouped; each piece has been treated with a unique fountain or texture fill. The background behind the bird was filled with a spiral pattern that draws your eyes to the bird.

Figure 16-8: This clip art gazelle has been treated with every type of fountain fill known to humankind.

Figure 16-9: This clip art bird has been filled with texture fills.

And finally, Figure 16-10, "Wings of Desire," is a study in contrasts using clip art. (This piece was developed in CorelDraw, exported to Photo-Paint, and then finalized in CorelDraw.) The girls walking at the lower right of the picture are clip art images converted to black and white only. The two women sitting in the middle are grayscale clip art pieces. The images behind and above them are clip art figures converted to masks and filled with sky and other textures. The woman in the very back talking with one of the "angels" is a clip art image converted to black only.

Figure 16-10: A study in contrasts has been created with clip art.

Clip art and composition

Sometimes placement makes all the difference. How you position simple clip art objects, perhaps lightening the color value to draw attention to text nearby, can breathe new life into a tired medium.

In Figure 16-11, you see one piece of artistic text and a man with a worried look on his face.

Figure 16-11: A clip art businessman is alone with his troubles.

Let's try to do some interesting repeating and arranging. Figure 16-12 shows the artistic text with a shadow added, duplicated four times, each time reduced in size.

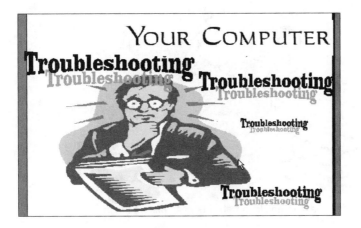

Figure 16-12: Duplicates of the text are gradually reduced in size and a shadow is added. More troubleshooting lies ahead.

But how to arrange it? In Figure 16-13, the text and clip art are arranged to create a sense of "trouble spiraling into a crisis."

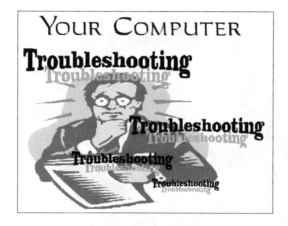

Figure 16-13: The clip art and artistic text are rearranged for a pleasing effect.

In Figure 16-14, you see some fairly blah clip art selections.

Figure 16-14: These three clip art objects don't inspire much.

But once we've rearranged, lightened the color, rotated, and added a frame, the clip art actually complements the text rather nicely. The results are shown in Figure 16-15.

Figure 16-15: Reducing the color value and moving the clip art increases its artistic effect.

CorelTexture

CorelTexture is accessed by choosing Graphic Utilities from the CorelDraw 7 menu and selecting CorelTexture. It can also be launched from within CorelDraw, using the Application Launcher. If you will be creating only small texture bitmaps or rendering to the application window, the program is not a memory hog and can render nicely in the background while you work in another CorelDraw application.

The opening screen of CorelTexture allows you to begin work entirely on your own, receiving guidance from a wizard (for example, "Do you want your texture to look like wood or stone?" "Do you want grainy wood or smooth wood?"). Or you can start with one of CorelTexture's presets and build from there. For now, let's choose the latter course.

Using layers in CorelTexture

CorelTexture builds textures based on layering elements of an object's surface. Think of building a texture as resembling making a sandwich. Each layer of a texture brings a different element to the whole. One layer determines the texture's simple physical properties: wood, stone, water, clouds. Another layer contributes lighting effects to the texture. A further layer influences how "bumpy" the overall texture effect is. Building a texture is simply a matter of manipulating these layers to your own satisfaction. Each of the layers is described next.

The Form & Geometry layer

When you begin layer editing, you'll see a preview screen with the layers one upon another, each contributing some feature to the whole, which changes as you manipulate the individual layers. At the very bottom is the Form &

Geometry layer, which is used to establish the texture's basic appearance and edge qualities, such as bevel and extrude amount. Think of this as the "bottom slice of bread."

The Lighting layer

The very top layer is the Lighting layer, where you add lights and move them, controlling their intensity and color. This is the "top slice of bread."

The Surface Properties layer

Right under the Lighting layer is the Surface Properties layer. This layer dictates how dramatically the lighting effects affect the texture. Four powerful slider controls are found here to change how the light plays on your texture's surface.

The Shader layers

"Sandwiched" in between these layers are various shaders. These shaders provide algorithms that further alter the texture's appearance. For example, you can mix a Marble appearance with an Aluminum Foil layer right underneath it. Each type of algorithm comes with its own shader controls. These controls affect characteristics such as the size of clouds, the depth of the marble's veins, how "crinkly" the aluminum foil looks, and so forth.

The final texture, then, is one big sandwich. With adroit and creative manipulation of the layers, you can create one-of-a-kind textures every time you use this application.

Saving layers

You can save any of the individual layers you've edited, as well as entire textures. You can then use saved layers later to make other textures. Figure 16-16 shows the mouse pointer accessing the Save Layer menu. Here, a new Form & Geometry is being saved. Looking at Figure 16-16, you can tell that the Form & Geometry layer is being saved because the white "broken-line box" appears on the bottom layer, which is always the Form & Geometry layer. The layer has been named "Bevel Frame" because beveling has been added and the form has been changed to resemble a picture frame.

This layer is being saved

Figure 16-16: Save a layer for later use.

Why not call the layer in Figure 16-16 "Cloud Frame"? After all, the preview box clearly shows a cloudy texture on the frame. But remember, just the *layer* is being saved, not an entire texture. This particular layer has nothing to do with the "cloudy" effect seen in the texture. The cloudy effect is a function of one of the Shader layers (one of the slices of meat in the sandwich). If I were particularly happy with the cloud effect and wished to save it, I would click whichever Shader layer has a Cloud algorithm and then save that layer.

Before saving to a file, you'll need to determine the image's size and resolution. First select File ⇨ Image Setup and input your parameters. Next select Texture ⇨ Render to File and choose your file type. When you select Save, you'll be prompted to name the bitmap, and after clicking OK, you'll see a blue "progress bar" that "fills up" as the bitmap is saved to file. When you are saving a very large texture, this progress bar is sometimes your only indication that your computer hasn't frozen up. Saving textures at resolutions higher than 150 dpi will not particularly improve the texture's appearance, but it will greatly increase file size.

After saving a layer, you can select it from one of the preset layers that you use in your textures.

Saving textures as bitmaps

Individual layers are saved in a particular resolution and size that you specify. They are saved as .TEX files, and as such, they cannot be imported into any other application. Before you can apply a texture elsewhere, you must convert the texture into a bitmap. You can save a texture to the application window or to a file. When you're ready to save a texture as a file, you'll find that most graphic file types are supported. To save one as a bitmap, make sure you're happy with the texture, and then select Texture ⇨ Render to Window or Texture ⇨ Render to File.

The Texture Editing screen

Figure 16-17 shows CorelTexture's Texture Editing screen.

Figure 16-17: The CorelTexture Editing screen gives you a number of useful options.

The Texture Editing screen sits inside the main screen, which contains all of the standard menu commands, such as File, Open, View, and Help. The Texture Editing screen is where the action is. The mouse pointer is seen selecting one of the Shader layers, one of the pieces of meat in this great sandwich of a texture. The layer's algorithm is Granite, and sliders can be used to adjust the amounts of magnification and rotation. At the bottom of the main screen are color controls for each layer. They are set up as a gradient, measured between two color pins at either side of the spectrum. In this case, the darker gradient of the granite is not allowing much granite effect to show through, as we can tell from the preview box, which seems to look much more like bumpy aluminum foil. To make the granite show through more, we must drag a color box of a lighter shade of gray to replace the darker gray color pin. Figure 16-18 shows the mouse pointer dragging a color box that is almost pure white (to replace the original gray color pin at the left).

Figure 16-18: Dragging a color box changes a layer's color value.

Figure 16-19 shows the new texture rendered to a window. Rendering to a window is the best way to check a texture's true characteristics before rendering it to a file. As you can see, some granite effect is mixed in with the "wrinkle" coming through from an underlying shader. To render to a window, select Texture ➪ Render to Window from the main screen.

Figure 16-19: A texture edited by the user is rendered to the Window.

The Lighting layer can be edited extensively. Figure 16-20 shows a color box being dropped onto one of the three lights. Notice the label Light #2 is now shown as a colored light, whereas the other two lights are still white. You can use the mouse pointer to move lights around the surface. Just click and drag the light you want to move.

Any changes you make cause the preview box to immediately refresh itself, showing the new texture.

CorelTexture's main menu

You could use CorelTexture's main menu only for rendering textures and setting file type, size, and resolution. However, you can use some additional controls on the main menu to make texture editing even easier.

Preview Selected Layer Only

Tip

Sometimes it's important to see the effect that one single layer is having on the texture. To see only one layer at a time, select a layer and choose Preview ➪ Preview Selected Layer Only.

Figure 16-20: A color box is added to Light #2.

Add Layer

You may add an additional layer to the sandwich. By default this is a Shader layer, and you may choose which type of algorithm you want to apply to the layer. The nine algorithm types include adding a bitmap as a layer, a simple color gradient layer, and various natural textures. To add a layer, select Texture ⇨ Add Layer.

Change Layer Orientation

You can alter your layer's positioning in the sandwich. It need not be straight and flat. You can rotate your layer and change its distance from the other layers along any axis. The closer layers are to each other, the more pronounced the effects are. The farther apart they are, the more subtle their interaction. If one layer is rotated, its overall effect on the whole texture will be "skewed" along the axis of the rotation. To change your layer's orientation, select Texture ⇨ Layer Orientation.

Generate Tiling Image

Secret

You can use CorelTexture to render any image as a set of tiles. To create a tiling image, select Texture ➪ Generate Tiling Image. To test the appearance of your tiling effect, select Preview ➪ Test Tiling.

A complete texture

Figure 16-21 shows a wood texture rendered at 150 dpi, image size 320 × 240 dpi. A small area light was added to the upper right to provide more of a "smoky" appearance. Total time in creation and rendering, approximately six minutes. After you've finished a texture, you may save it in any file format you wish and import into your CorelDraw or Photo-Paint projects.

Figure 16-21: An edited "wood" texture has been treated with a light in the upper right-hand corner.

Templates

Another great feature CorelDraw includes involves *templates*. Templates give you quick control over the look of text, lines, and other objects. Using a template, you begin typing on your page, and the text is automatically rendered in the Harrington font, 72p, for example. A template enables you to begin creating a line that will automatically be blue, with a width of ⅛ inch, for another example. Templates, therefore, store stylistic information about what goes on a page, so that you can simply start creating, without having to make formatting choices. Templates store information about text and paragraph alignment, number of columns, positioning of graphics on a page, headline and date placement. They are marked out with "placeholder" text and pictures. Typing over (or inserting a graphic in place of) one of these placeholders erases the placeholder, but your new object will retain the stylistic information of the placeholder.

The following templates are included with CorelDraw and are accessible by selecting File ➪ New from Template, rather than File ➪ New:

- Advertisement
- Business Card
- Brochure
- Calendar
- Card
- Certificate
- Envelope
- Fax Cover
- Invitation

- Invoice
- Label
- Letterhead
- Memo
- Menu
- Misc
- Newsletter
- Purchase Order
- Product Marketing

CorelDraw includes templates from a company called Paper Direct, which sells predesigned paper. You can use the Paper Direct templates included with CorelDraw to see how your work will appear when printed onto this special paper.

To understand how templates work, you first need to understand Draw's Style feature. When you enter text to your documents, CorelDraw keeps track of all the style elements involved in your creation. Style elements may include any outlines around the text, margin settings, the kinds of bullets you use, headings, and so on. You can the view the style of your document by selecting Layout ➪ Graphics and Text Styles. Right-click and select Properties. You'll see the Style Properties dialog box. Clicking on the appropriate tab reveals the information about the selected style. Refer to Figure 16-22, where you can see the Text tab of the Style Properties dialog box for the style Body Text 2.

Figure 16-22: The Style Properties dialog box reveals information about the selected style.

The tabs beneath the Text tab enable you to create Outline and Fill styles that can be applied to any object by right-clicking on the object and selecting the style. For example, to create a style that changes an object so that its outline width is ¼ inch and the object is filled with an exact color value that you've determined, simply create an object with the Outline Color and Fill values that you want to apply with a mouse-click to other objects. Right-click inside the Graphic and Text dialog box and select New. Choose Graphic Style. A box appears inside the dialog box entitled "New Graphic." You may rename this. Right-click on the box, and select Copy Properties From. Your cursor turns into an arrow, and you are prompted to select the object with the properties that you would like to save as a new style. Click the arrow on the object that you just created. The box representing the saved style now takes on the characteristics of the object you just clicked. The style is now saved under the name you selected in the Styles roll-up.

However, you need not open the Styles roll-up to apply this style to any other object. Simply create a new shape, right-click on it, and select Styles ⇨ Apply; you'll see the name of the new style you just created, as well as other default styles. The new shape you just created now bears the color and outline characteristics of your saved style.

Saving templates

By saving your document as a template, you are creating a convenient way to reproduce your work faster the next time — by automatically adding text or a particular graphic, without your having to worry about font selection, size, outline width, and so on. A document saved as a template enables you to open the template later, replace the "marker text" with new text, and just get to work. In the case of a newsletter, for example, you would need merely to replace the volume number and date, without having to format the text appropriately for volume number and date styles.

When you save a style as part of a template, CorelDraw remembers the placement of graphics on the page, as well as any other features on your page that exist in the current document. If you decide to save the current document as a template, select File ⇨ Save As, and instead of saving your file as a .CDR document, choose .CDT, which is the template file type.

Adding a template to the Template Wizard

One quick way to create a template is to open the Template Wizard (Select File ⇨ New from Template,) and select a template that approximates something you'd like to create. Reposition text and graphic objects on the page to your liking, and type in new text with any formatting changes you want. Choose Tools ⇨ Scripts ⇨ Script and Preset Manager. Scroll down to a script called "Temp Wiz." Click Temp Wiz, and follow the onscreen prompts for saving your document as a template.

After creating your template, you may load it by selecting File ⇨ Open and choosing the .CDT file you created, or by choosing File ⇨ Open from Template. Once your template is part of the Template Wizard menu, you'll get these results:

- You get a graphic preview of your template.

- You will see it in a list with all the other Wizards for easier selection.

- An option is provided to load the template without the contents. This option loads only the blank text and graphic boxes with styles attached.

To add a template you've created from scratch to the Template Wizard list, first make sure your current document is exactly the way you like it. Remove any features of the document that you do not want to be part of the template's formatting. Next, open Tools ⇨ Scripts ⇨ Script and Preset Manager and scroll down to the document called "Temp Wiz." You'll be prompted to provide information about the template you are saving that will be used in the Template Wizard preview, the next time you use it.

Later, you can load this template just as you would any other template by selecting File ⇨ Load from Template.

Summary

In this chapter, you learned:

▶ How to modify clip art to increase its artistic value and make it applicable to a wider variety of projects

▶ How to use clip art compositionally to your advantage

▶ How to use CorelTexture to create some new and unique texture effects that you can apply to your CorelDraw projects

▶ How to work with the templates included with CorelDraw

▶ How to create, work with, modify, and save custom templates

Chapter 17

Multimedia Manager and Font Management

In This Chapter

You'll learn some useful tips on how to organize your CorelDRAW 7 files and fonts. You'll learn about:

▶ File management for graphic artists

▶ Working with thumbnails

▶ Keywords

▶ Corel Multimedia Manager

▶ Font management

It turns out that the secret is to *not* store all your images and fonts on your system, but to keep catalogs and albums of these necessary files and put them back on your computer as needed.

File Management for the Graphic Artist

Many graphic file managers are available on the market. No computer graphic specialist should be without one. As a graphic artist or designer, you're forever grouping and regrouping your art files. You'll need quick access to them. However, Murphy's Law for computer artists and graphic designers dictates that the more you must find a particular file quickly, the less likely you are to find it where you thought it should be. You ought not be relegated to spending high-priority, creative time searching through endless folders and directories to find an important picture, sound file, or document.

Why not just move the files themselves in a tidy, systematic way? As simple as this may sound, it's not feasible to actually move all your art files around for the sake of organizational logic. Many of them are just too darn big. Computer artists need a system that can quickly display a visual collection of artwork even if all of those files are in different nooks and crannies on your hard drive.

Working with Thumbnails

In short, you should have a "thumbnail" system. A good thumbnail system can display 12 to 36 minipictures on your screen that represent a larger work of art. You should be able to search many folders; point, click, and add; and have each file you select available in the same visual collection, regardless of where the file itself resides. Click on the minipicture, or thumbnail, and you should be able to see that single picture blown up to full screen. These thumbnail collections are called *albums*. As a computer artist, you'll have many such albums of art files on your computer. (An album, as you probably already know, is a collection of multimedia files — for example, your own pictures, TIFFs, or GIFs for creating projects, or sound files for Web page augmentation.) Some albums will have pictures grouped according to client, by chronology, or as different "takes" on a single project, enabling you to view each approach and then determine which you like best.

An album itself should not take up much disk space. It should store a compressed "thumbnail" of a file in as small an amount of disk space as possible. That's because some albums are Clip Art collections and have thousands of entries. They need to be small, or you've defeated the purpose of storing your work in an album. For the album system to work, you need to be able to print, obtain information about, and perhaps "batch edit" your art files themselves without having to leave the album and go hunt for the file itself. After all, what good is an album of your collected works if, after grouping a collection of pieces together, all you can do is look at them?

Keywords

As you develop a large client base and produce an ever-larger body of work, you'll need to associate each picture with a keyword. You're probably used to using keywords to hunt down clip-art in huge collections. But when it comes to your own art, what if certain files you need to access are in different albums at a given moment? A good album system enables you to search through *all* the albums according to keyword and compile a collection based on your word search. For example, one picture's thumbnail in an album might be associated with the keywords "sky," "watercolor," "Fletcher Enterprises," "Fall 1996." If you've associated the keywords mentioned here with one picture, you could retrieve this picture according to its subject (sky), painting technique employed (watercolor), client (Fletcher Enterprises), or when you did the work (Fall 1996). A good album system enables you to search by keyword across *many* albums and retrieve pictures that meet the criteria.

Up until now, my terminology has been a little loose. I've been saying "picture." In today's world, graphic designers are called upon to deal with media of all kinds: animation, videos, sound files, and 3D objects, not to mention Java applets and Internet media files that require special players such as Shockwave. So a good album system must hold more than just visual files. In short, you'll need a full-blown Multimedia Manager.

Corel Multimedia Manager

Multimedia Manager is available by selecting Graphic Utilities from the Corel Group of your Windows Start ⇨ Programs button, or by launching within CorelDraw itself by using the Launcher button on the Standard toolbar.

Here are some ways you can use Multimedia Manager:

- To group your own work.

- To view all the files on a Photo CD without opening them one by one.

- To perform "batch edits" on many files at once. For example, to convert all the files in a particular collection to grayscale, or to print all your artwork over a given period of time.

- To save disk space.

Tip

When it's time to remove some older work from your hard drive, perhaps to a Zip disk, create a thumbnail collection and store that on your hard drive. Then if you ever do need quick access to the art on your Zip disk, you can view the thumbnail and, with the Zip disk in the drive, click on the thumbnail; the file will open in its native application, ready to edit.

The Multimedia Manager main screen

Pictured in Figure 17-1 is Multimedia Manager's main screen. It looks a bit like Windows Explorer. Your first task is to create an album. Then you'll need to hunt through the files on your hard drive to find files you want to store in it.

Select a directory where you'd like to store your albums. If you have a choice of hard drives, choose the drive with the most disk space. Albums can hold subalbums. They can get quite large. Figure 17-2 shows the results of selecting File ⇨ New, which is how you create a new album. Here, I opened a folder called Web Support Files and created a new album there. As in Windows Explorer, the larger window to the right shows the contents of the folder. Not much happens after selecting File ⇨ New. The mouse pointer in Figure 17-2 is pointing at the newly created album in the folder I opened. It holds nothing. Let's fix that.

Figure 17-1: The Multimedia Manager's main screen lists multimedia files by folder.

Figure 17-2: The mouse pointer shows where a new album has been created.

Adding items to an album

Double-clicking on the New Album icon causes it to move to the left side of the screen, and the right side now reveals the album's contents. Initially, nothing will appear there, as shown in Figure 17-3. The mouse pointer in this figure shows where the Album icon is. Now you're ready to add items to the empty album.

Figure 17-3: We're ready to add items to the empty album.

Secret

If you log onto a CD-ROM drive and select New ⇨ Album, your computer will do nothing. In fact, you may have to hit Alt+Ctrl+Delete to exit Multimedia Manager. When you create an album in Multimedia Manager, the first thing that happens is the album is saved to disk under the current directory. (And, of course, you can't save to a CD-ROM drive, so the program sits there, non-stop, trying to save to the CD-ROM disk.) This course of events is different than creating a new album with JASC's Media Center or Cerius's Thumbs Up. With either of these products, after indicating a new album is to be created, the first thing you do is find files to save in your album; you then select

File ➪ Save to make your album permanent. Not so with Multimedia Manager. A newly created album, and every further addition to it, is automatically saved to hard disk as soon as the file is added.

Select Edit ➪ Insert to see the submenu shown in Figure 17-4. After selecting Item, you'll be shown a Browse menu to search your hard drive for pictures, sound files, and all the kinds of media that Multimedia Manager can help you organize. Please note that one menu option is Sub-Album. You'd create an album within an album by clicking here.

Figure 17-4: Select Item from the New menu Insert submenu.

I've jumped ahead to show you an album populated by many different kinds of files. Multimedia Manager can keep track of and edit many file types. Pictured in Figure 17-5 are some .BMP files, some .DOC files, and a subalbum within the existing album.

Figure 17-5: An album's contents appear.

Secret

When you create an album in Multimedia Manager, you don't have to save it. Multimedia Manager automatically saves everything you add to the album. To name your album, right-click on it and select Rename, just as you would any file with Windows Explorer.

You can control the size of the thumbnails by selecting View ⇨ Large Icon Size. As shown in Figure 17-6, the default icon size is 32 by 32 pixels. In that figure, the mouse icon is shown getting ready to enlarge the icon.

Adding a subalbum

Figure 17-7 shows the benefits of increasing the size of the icons in your album. You can get a good idea of what a particular picture looks like just by looking at the thumbnail.

In Figure 17-8, the subalbum has been opened. The left side of the screen shows the directory structure where the subalbum is located. Note that albums can contain sounds, Photoshop files, and a variety of other items. To widen your file-searching potential to include all the albums you create on your computer, you should create subalbums below a single, top Main album. That way, when you search, Multimedia Manager will look through all the albums that meet your search criteria.

Figure 17-6: Increase the size of the album's icons.

Figure 17-7: Larger icons show the pictures more clearly.

Figure 17-8: The contents of a subalbum are displayed.

So far, what I've shown you probably looks something like glorified Windows Explorer with bigger icons. Keep in mind, though, that with what you've learned, you already have the skills necessary for the following steps, which you should now try:

STEPS

Creating an Album of Photos on a CD-ROM

Step 1. Put a Photo CD in your CD-ROM drive.

Step 2. Log on to a new directory on your hard drive and create a new album.

Step 3. Select Insert ⇨ Item.

Step 4. Log on to your CD-ROM drive. While pressing Shift, select all the Photos on the CD-ROM (or all those that interest you). After you click OK, all the photos you've selected will have thumbnails in your album. Remember, you don't have a Save Album command.

Step 5. When you are done, you can remove the CD-ROM, but you will still have an album of thumbnails of the CD-ROM's photographic contents on your hard drive.

Special features of Multimedia Manager

Multimedia Manager has some special features that set it apart from other thumbnail-album software. As shown in Figure 17-9, Multimedia Manager gives you direct access to Corel Color Manager. This enables you to quickly run a gamut check, to see which colors in a picture will not print. Multimedia Manager also enables color correction (under the View menu) and will Simulate Printer colors, if selected.

Figure 17-9: Multimedia Manager has a direct link to Color Manager.

Right-click on any thumbnail in your album to access one of Multimedia Manager's most powerful features. Select Properties, and you'll see four tabs. Under the Notes tab, you may type several lines of personal notes about the file. These notes will remain attached to the thumbnail even after you close the program. One of the tabs is entitled Keyword (see Figure 17-10). In the New Keyword space, type any word you'd like to be associated with the selected file. Select Add, and the keyword will now appear in two places.

- The new word will appear under Item Keywords. This means that if you run a Multimedia Manager search (Tools ➪ Search) with your new word as a keyword, the search will return with that particular item, as well as any others that got tagged with that word.

■ The new word will also appear under Album Keyword. This list keeps track of all keywords associated with any files in the entire album.

Figure 17-10: The Keywords tab of an item's Properties dialog box lets you add new keywords.

Powerful search tools are among the great advantages to using Multimedia Manager to keep track of your work. After you've made a few albums, including some keywords and descriptions of the work along with the thumbnail, you don't even have to open all your albums to find the item(s) you are searching for. If you have judiciously created subalbums below a single main album, just open Multimedia Manager and log on to the Main album, the one at the very top of the directory tree of albums you've created. Select Tools ➪ Search, and type in your search criteria. If Search Sub-Albums is selected, Multimedia Manager will return to you all the files that match your criteria, no matter what albums they are found in.

Figure 17-11 shows the General sheet of the Properties dialog box. (Remember, this Properties dialog box appears when you right-click on any item in an album.) Your artwork's Label (meaning the filename) is noted here, along with the drive and directory it is linked with and room to type a description of the file. Later, you may perform a search that can include any or all of the preceding criteria. As with all search engines, more specific keywords bring fewer matching files. And conversely, very general search criteria may return more files than are useful.

Figure 17-11: The General tab of the Properties dialog box lets you modify label information and view file attributes.

Figure 17-12 shows a search being initiated. One thing to keep in mind: unless you selected an album right before hitting the Search button (as shown in this figure, on the left side of the screen, notice that an album has been selected), no search will start. The program *doesn't* return an error message, such as "No Album Was Selected, Search Aborted." No, nothing happens at all. So make sure you have an album (or an item within the album) selected before selecting Tools ➪ Search.

Figure 17-13 shows an example of a keyword search. Notice the Item Search dialog box has drop-down menus for selecting qualifiers for using more than one keyword in a search. For example, if your album included two paintings of a woman in India, one was abstract, and you had another abstract painting of a still life, you could search for Keyword: Woman AND Keyword: Abstract to narrow the number of images that would return to you from your search. In the example in Figure 17-13, I used the "like" qualifier with my keyword. The picture I was looking for was a "Bird" in "South America." So in my search, I used "Bird" OR "like" "America." The Keyword "America" was "like" "South America," so the search returned the South American bird. The mouse pointer is pointing at it, below and to the right of the Item Search dialog box. Notice also that "Include Sub-Albums" is selected. This prompts the search engine to check all albums "under" the current album in the directory chain.

Figure 17-12: Initiate a search from the menu after an album is selected.

Figure 17-13: Use Keyword qualifiers such as "like" and "OR" to create search criteria.

This is why it's a good idea to group your albums under one main directory. Take a look at Figure 17-13 one more time: notice the small icons to the right of the "Objects found" box. After the search returns your items to you, you can Print, Cut, Paste, Delete, and examine the Properties of any file returned to you through your search.

Print Preview

One of Multimedia Manager's most distinctive features is its set of Printing Options. With a file selected, choose File ➪ Print Preview. You'll see a screen like the one shown in Figure 17-14.

Figure 17-14: The Print Preview screen appears like this.

You can use high-end printing options right from Multimedia Manager, without having to open the file in its native application. The Prepress Printing Bar enables you to print file information, registration marks, crop marks, and page numbers; you can also include a Color Calibration bar, include a

Densitometer scale, Print negative, and print with Emulation side up or side down. The Settings menu of the Print Preview screen includes Color Separation settings control, Layout options, and the printing of a Job Information sheet.

Managing Fonts

Managing fonts is an important concern for computer artists. It is imperative to have a wide selection of fonts available for your projects. It's hard to predict which typeface will look best for a particular job, and it's helpful to have many to choose from. However, if you have more than a couple hundred fonts loaded onto your computer at one time, your computer's performance suffers. But if your fonts are organized in *groups* — according to font style, client, or project — you can have many fonts *available* without having to load all of them through Windows. If you load only one or two groups of fonts at a time, you'll get much better performance from your computer.

Panose Font Matching

Have you ever opened a template in CorelDraw and received a warning that a particular font requested by the template was not found on your computer, along with a suggestion to substitute another font? If this has happened to you, then you've already become acquainted with the Panose Font Matching system.

Panose examines characteristics of the requested font — its name, x-height, midline, proportion, font weight, and so on — and finds one on your computer that most closely matches the one requested.

Panose doesn't automatically know about all the fonts on your computer, so if you're prepared to spend some time, you can customize the Panose list so that more intelligent font substitution choices can be made.

To open Panose in CorelDraw, create some text and right-click on the Font drop-down menu from Draw's Format toolbar. Click on Font Options, as shown in Figure 17-15.

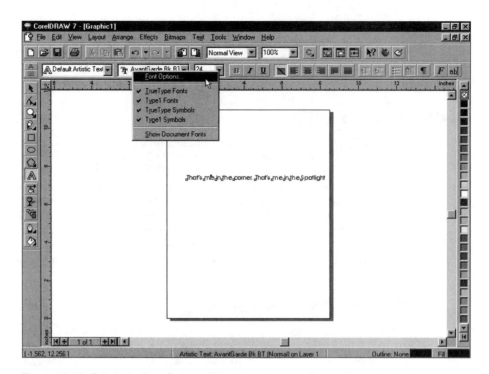

Figure 17-15: Select the Font Options dialog box to access Panose font substitution.

Now click on Panose Font Matching, as shown in Figure 17-16.

Click Panose Font Matching on the Font Options dialog box, and you'll see the Panose Font Matching Preferences dialog box. Keeping the Allow Font Matching box checked enables Panose to substitute fonts. Show Mapping Results instructs Panose to show you the font chosen to substitute for a font not found. If Show Mapping Results is not checked, CorelDraw will make the substitutions without checking with you first. The Substitutions Tolerance slider decides how picky CorelDraw will be in selecting a font substitute. Should it only suggest a font that very closely matches the missing font (the slider moves from Exact to Loose), or should it suggest fonts that only approximately match the missing font? The font at the bottom of the dialog box, in the Default Font drop-down menu, is the font that CorelDraw uses if it cannot find any font to substitute for the missing font.

Secret

Change the Default Font to a symbol font or something attention-getting. That way you will know right away if Panose has substituted the default font for a missing font. If the Default font choice is something that blends in, you may be slow to realize that you're working with a substitute font.

Figure 17-16: Open Panose Font Matching from the Font Options dialog box.

Because Macintosh versions of fonts are spelled differently than their PC counterparts, the Spellings option is included to permit you to indicate that a certain font may be used even if it is spelled slightly differently than the original. The Exceptions option is included so that you can manually create substitutions for missing fonts on the fly, as the need arises, rather than accept the substitution CorelDraw has provided.

Corel FontMaster

Although not included on the CorelDRAW 7 CD-ROM set, Corel FontMaster, Adobe Type Manager, and other programs such as Ceres Font Minder are essential to managing fonts on your system. Anybody who has made the error of "loading all the fonts" that come with a Corel Gallery CD-ROM or something similar understands the need to maintain a *slim* permanent font collection on your computer. Having more than a couple hundred fonts permanently installed on your system can slow down almost all Windows operations. The solution? Maintain a collection of fonts temporarily installed on your computer on a "per project" basis. Font managing systems enable you to search through an entire CD-ROM of fonts for "just the right ones" for a particular client. You can then install those temporarily on your system.

When the project is completed, an annotated file — a catalog — is created to help you automatically install those fonts again, later, should you need to bring up that project for revision. Then the temporary fonts are removed.

Figure 17-17 shows the Add Fonts tab from the Corel FontMaster screen. Notice the categories on the left of the screen. These are font groups. Opening a font group reveals a large collection of fonts, as shown on the left. The mouse pointer is shown choosing, font by font, which fonts should be temporarily added to the system. An option is included for adding them permanently, as well.

Figure 17-17: The Add Fonts tab is reached from the Corel FontMaster screen.

It must be noted that, when fonts are installed temporarily, they remain only until the computer is turned off. One way to make sure temporary fonts don't get buried in your system is to go ahead and install them permanently but then open Corel FontMaster, or a similar Font Manager program, and view the list of Most Recently Installed Fonts. You can then remove the fonts needed only for that one project.

Summary

▶ You can manage your art files on your computer with systems of thumbnails, enabling you to perform "batch edits" on many files at once.

▶ Perform powerful searches to locate files and save disk space by keeping art files themselves on Zip disks or Jaz drives, while maintaining the thumbnails on your computer.

▶ Corel Multimedia Manager provides a good tool to carry out both of these big jobs.

▶ Font management with the Panose Font Substitution system enables CorelDraw to substitute missing fonts with similar ones.

▶ You'll be able to keep fewer fonts permanently on your hard drive when you use Corel FontMaster.

Chapter 18

Corel Scripts

In This Chapter

You'll learn how to do the following:

▶ Open and save scripts

▶ Use preset scripts

▶ Record and edit scripts

▶ Compose scripts from scratch

▶ Run scripts

CorelDraw comes with a fully integrated scripting program, an application you use to create "scripts," which are a lot like the macros you may have used in word processing programs. They contain a set of instructions for carrying out tasks, such as opening files, filling polygons, extruding blends, or even creating multistep operations that require dialog boxes. Corel Script Editor also contains tools for creating dialog boxes. The basic scripting program, called Corel Script, loads right into CorelDraw (and Photo-Paint). The easiest way to use the scripting program is to use the preset scripts that come with CorelDraw and Photo-Paint. To do this, you need not enter any code yourself. Recording scripts is simply a matter of performing a CorelDraw task while Script Recorder is recording. However, if you know a little Visual Basic, you can develop complex scripts yourself with Corel Script Editor. Scripts you create in Script Editor can be used in other applications, such as Corel Ventura and CorelDraw 6.

Opening Scripts in CorelDraw

After you've started a new picture (or opened an existing one), select Tools ⇨ Scripts. You'll be presented with three options: Script and Preset Manager, Run Script, and Corel Script Editor. (See Figure 18-1.)

Figure 18-1: These Script options appear in CorelDraw.

Let's look first at Run Script, because it's easiest to understand. Run Script opens a Browse menu that enables you to select a script from any directory and run it as a program, right within CorelDraw.

The first option on the flyout, Script and Preset Manager, is a roll-up of icons representing two groups of scripts: those that come with CorelDraw as presets, and those that you create by yourself or by editing the presets. In this chapter, most of the discussion focuses on the Script and Preset Manager.

Also included is a path to Script Editor. Script Editor is a standalone application that enables you to create your own scripts and edit existing ones more to your liking. You may access it here in CorelDraw, in Photo-Paint, or from the Windows Program menu, by choosing Programs ⇨ CorelDraw 7 ⇨ Productivity Utilities ⇨ Corel Script Editor.

Saving Scripts

For all their power, CorelDraw scripts exist as simple text files until they are compiled into a language similar to Basic right before you run them.

Therefore, when you compose a script with Script Editor, you are actually working with a simple text editor.

CorelDraw installs some scripts in four locations on your computer:

- `C:\Corel\Draw70\Scripts`

- `C:\Corel\Draw70\Draw\Scripts`

- `C:\Corel\Draw70\Draw\Scripts\Presets6`

- `C:\Corel\Draw70\Draw\Scripts\Scripts`

In working with Script Editor, the locations of scripts as they are saved are particularly important, because you may be spending time recording scripts within CorelDraw and then editing them via the Script Editor as a text file. The preceding directory references will help you know where to find them. The first directory referenced is for scripts you compose using Corel Script Editor. The other directories are the default directories containing presets and scripts you record by simply performing tasks in CorelDraw. Once you open Script Manager in CorelDraw, you'll see them. Clicking on these directories provides access to scripts that you can immediately run in CorelDraw.

Working with Scripts

It's possible to work with scripts and never compose one yourself. You'll still find them marvelously convenient. Once you get the hang of working with scripts, you're likely to spend untold hours recording many of them. Here are four approaches to working with scripts:

- Using only preset scripts

- Recording your own scripts

- Editing existing scripts

- Composing scripts from scratch

Using only preset scripts

You can accomplish a lot using only the *preset scripts* that come with CorelDraw. To use these, select Tools ➪ Scripts ➪ Script and Preset Manager, and open one of the two folders (see Figure 18-2), each containing various preset scripts that you can instantly apply. These are explained in detail a little later in the chapter.

Figure 18-2: These two folders contain preset scripts for immediate application to your artwork.

Recording your own scripts

You can also record your own scripts and save them for later use. That way, you can have scripts at your disposal that are specifically suited to your own needs. After recording a script, you can apply it instantly to any appropriate situation. Figure 18-3 shows the row of buttons found at the bottom of the Script and Preset Manager. The farthest to the left is the Playback button, for playing scripts. Press this button to play any script, one of your own or a preset. The middle button is the Stop button, highlighted while a script is recording or while a script is playing. Pressing it while recording ends the recording of your script and prompts the Save Script screen (see Figure 18-4). Pressing Stop while a script is playing abandons playback. Stopping playback does not reverse any operations performed before Stop was pressed.

Figure 18-3: The Playback, Stop, and Record buttons appear at the bottom of the Script and Preset Manager.

Figure 18-4: The Save Recording dialog box is prompted by pressing the Stop button.

Editing scripts

After learning a bit about composing scripts by exploring Script Editor's very thorough Help files, you can open existing scripts and edit them. You can perhaps alter a script that turns an object red to turning the same object blue instead, or you can change the direction of an extrusion path. Learning to edit existing scripts is a marvelous introduction to learning to compose your own scripts from scratch.

Composing scripts from scratch

If you know even a small amount of Visual Basic, you can use Script Editor to compose scripts entirely by yourself.

Working with Preset Scripts

Open the Script and Preset Manager, and open the folder labeled "Presets 6." This folder holds more than 70 predefined scripts. Create a rectangle using the Rectangle tool in CorelDraw, with the default line width and no fill, as shown in Figure 18-5. Now select the preset "3dplaque." While the empty rectangle is selected, press the Play button on the Script and Preset Manager. After a minute or two, the empty rectangle looks like a filled and bordered rectangle, also shown in Figure 18-5 (but in color, of course). By the way, playing back scripts takes time. Sometimes is appears as if no disk activity is taking place. Your computer may appear to have "frozen up," but be patient. I've had scripts take as long as three minutes to complete.

Abandon the preceding rectangle. Now, on a new page, enter a string of artistic text, preferably with a 72-point font. Select the preset below "3dplaque." It's called "arches." While the text and the "arches" preset are selected, click the Playback button on the Script and Preset Manager. The results should resemble Figure 18-6.

Figure 18-5: Create a 3D plaque like this one with a preset.

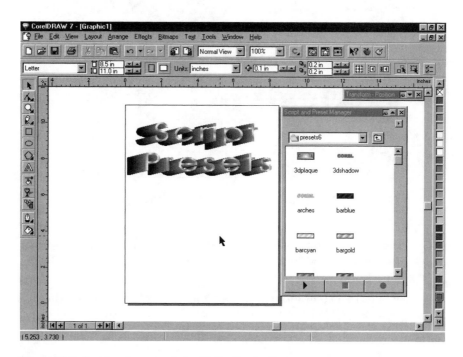

Figure 18-6: Text has been treated with the "arches" preset.

Figure 18-7 shows the "button" and "design01" preset applied. In this example, you can see that the small representative picture shown in the Script and Preset Manager gives you a pretty good idea of what the results will look like when applied to an object on screen. The large button was created as a simple circle with no fill. When I selected the circle, clicked the "button" icon in the Script and Preset Manager, and pressed Play, it transformed the large circle into an object that looked just like the icon. Similarly, as shown in this same figure, the phrase "design 1" was a simple, unembellished text object. After I clicked "design01" in the Script and Preset Manager, the text took on the same Fill and Extrude qualities as represented by the "design01" icon. To make it easier to see which script icon edited which object in this figure, I've positioned the button and text object in the same relative positions they occupy in the Script and Preset Manager menu.

Figure 18-7: The "button" and "design01" presets have been applied.

Remember

Figure 18-8 shows "design19" and "earthgld." Remember, the effects shown here are applied to simple text with no editing whatsoever. Only the effect was applied.

Figure 18-9 shows four worthwhile text effects; the words that have been used to demonstrate the effects are the same as the effects' names. In color, they are each eye-catching and unique.

Figure 18-8: The "design19" and "earthgld" effects have been applied to simple artistic text.

Figure 18-9: Four excellent preset text effects are demonstrated.

Secret

"Spectrl1" and "Spectrl2" should only be rendered on simple fonts with very few serifs. Otherwise, portions of your text will disappear when the effect is finished rendering.

One way to look at these presets is as jumping-off points for further creativity. You might try changing the perspective to "small back" or changing the colors of the extruded portion of the text to contrast more with the text face. Some are perfect right out of the box.

Click on the "up one folder" icon in the Script and Preset Manager, and select the folder called Scripts. This menu has a handful of quick special effects. One is called "accelcon" (for accelerated contour) because it creates a deeply contoured version of any object you select. Figure 18-10 shows two preset effects applied consecutively. These objects started as simple Bézier curves. The preset called "fillout" was applied first. This preset thickens the outline of the selected object and fills the outline with a color gradient of your choice. Next "replica" was applied, which duplicates or clones (your choice) the selected object as many times as you specify.

Remember

Remember, *cloned* objects retain their links to the master object, so most effects or editing applied to the master object will affect the cloned objects as well. A *duplicated* object is not linked to the master object.

Figure 18-10: Two preset scripts were applied to a simple Bézier curve to create this effect.

The "Template" scripts

Inside the Scripts folder (one of the folders you see in the Script and Preset Manager) are three hidden templates: one to create an instant calendar, one to set up grids on your page, and one to alter the templates included with CorelDraw. Pictured in Figure 18-11 is the Template Customization Wizard. You'll see this opening screen when you click the "template" icon in the "presets" folder of the Script and Preset Manager. Template customization is explained in more detail in Chapter 16.

Figure 18-11: The Template Customization Wizard opening screen welcomes you.

It took about five minutes for the "calendar" script to create the calendar shown in Figure 18-12. After clicking on the icon, you'll be prompted to provide year and month, page orientation, font selection, and an optional link to a picture. After a brief interval, the calendar will be finished.

Figure 18-12: This calendar was created by selecting the script labeled "calendar."

Other presets

Other presets are available on the bonus CD-ROMs that come with CorelDRAW 7. Without a doubt, CorelDraw users will be posting helpful scripts on Web sites for the public to download, providing features such as being able to open one of the last four pictures you were working on with a single mouse click or to change text to a particular font with one motion. Just by understanding how to use ready-made scripts, you can see that the Corel Script tool is quite helpful. Scripts need not be relegated to the cumbersome menu of folders in the Script and Preset Manager (and it will become cumbersome once you have more than a handful of scripts in one folder). Scripts can become icons on a toolbar, appear as items on a menu, or be launched with a hotkey combination. We'll learn to set these options later in the chapter.

Recording Your Own Scripts

Recording your own scripts is an intermediate step for somebody new to Corel scripts. By recording your own scripts, you need not learn any scripting language. By recording your own scripts, you'll learn a lot more about the possibilities (and limitations) of scripts. When recording you own scripts, you work right inside CorelDraw. You need not have Script Editor open. Your only interface with the script program is the Script and Preset Manager. Using the Manager, you can record, stop recording, and save your scripts to hard disk, and you can play back your scripts.

To prepare to record your own scripts, have the Script and Preset Manager open and moved to the upper right of your screen. Open and position conveniently any roll-ups and toolbars that you'll be using for your scripts.

After your screen is organized, press the red "record" button and begin your procedure. You'll be able to tell you are recording because the red button will then be "grayed out." When you are finished, press Stop. You'll be prompted to save your script. (Scripts are saved as .CSC files.) At the bottom of the save screen is an area to write a description of your script. As your scripts become more complicated and grow in number, you'll be thankful for this option.

Corel Script remembers any roll-up parameters you adjust and execute during your script recording. However, it helps to have all the roll-ups in place that you intend to use during the script. It's time to note one remarkable fact: in order to play back the script, you need not have any roll-ups that were required for the recording present on the screen. Your script will be carried out with a "clean screen."

Advice on scripting

Tip

Here are some scripting pointers to remember:

■ Contrary to what you may have learned using macros, Corel Script remembers only mouse-clicks. You cannot create a macro out of your favorite hotkey combinations. For example, you can't create a script to open the most recently used file by pressing Ctrl+O. Even though that is a valid hotkey combination, Corel Script will not record it as part of a macro. With the exception of remembering text you enter while a text tool is being used, Corel Script does not record keyboard commands. You cannot incorporate existing hotkey combinations into your recorded macro. However, after you've created a macro with mouse clicks and/or text, it can be *saved as* a hotkey combination, as explained later.

Note

■ When you record a script to perform a task on a selected object — for example, to execute a complex fountain fill on a rectangle or an ellipse you have selected — Corel Script performs the task on the selected object no matter where it is on the page. You need not position the object in the exact same portion of the page as you did when you recorded the script. Additionally, you don't need to reproduce the exact screen position of any roll-ups you used during recording in order to playback the script later. Corel Script is capable of locating the roll-up on the screen, even if it moved from a prior position.

■ Corel Script remembers where on the screen you created objects while recording your script. Upon playback, it recreates those objects in the exact same position where they were created during recording. This means that if you moved far off the page to record a script, perhaps because your page was getting crowded, Corel Script creates that object far off the page during playback. If, while you play back a script, nothing seems to be happening, wait a second or two, change your Zoom setting to 25 percent, and see if your script was carried out somewhere in the far reaches of the workspace.

■ If you create scripts to perform tasks that involve selected objects, such as blends between two objects, or Text to Path routines, make sure you have those two objects selected before you record your script. If you create a script that includes the need for Corel Script to select the objects first, two things might happen: first of all, it may select the two objects in the wrong order to perform your operation. Second, it may not select the two objects you have in mind, if more than two objects exist on the screen. So it's best to have the objects selected before you record your script.

■ Before you play back your script, make sure you've selected any objects involved. If you forget, you may sometimes get an error message. But at other times, you'll get no response at all after pressing the Playback button.

So far, you've seen how to record scripts to perform simple tasks that involve two or three steps. However, Corel Script is very competent at recording complex, lengthy procedures. The program does not appear to be a memory hog, which has marvelous implications.

For example, how many times have you developed a piece of work, looked back at it later, and wondered how you accomplished it? Trying to reproduce the same winning technique *exactly* can sometimes be frustrating. But with Corel Script, you can record *the process*. If, at a particular moment, you are feeling especially creative, just turn on Corel Script, start creating, and see what happens. No longer are your "magic moments" relegated only to the moment. Once you've recorded the script, you can play it back, watch what you did, and even stop the playback in the middle to examine the procedure a bit closer. With even a small amount of Script editing knowledge, you can alter a script you've created to use different colors or tool settings.

Examples of recorded scripts

Figure 18-13 shows the Script and Preset Manager with some personally created scripts in the viewing window. By default, any scripts you record will be stored in this folder for immediate viewing. If, for example, you use this window to explore scripts included on one of the extra CD-ROMs included with CorelDraw, this window will be filled with the contents of a different folder.

To find your way back here, note that the default folder for scripts you create is: C:\Corel\Draw70\Draw\Scripts. Use the "up one folder" browse tool to find your way back to this folder, and all the scripts you create should be here. If you edit scripts later using the Script Editor, take care to save them in this default location, or you'll have to go searching for your edited script.

Figure 18-13: The Script and Preset Manager viewing window shows scripts recorded by the user.

Figure 18-14 illustrates several principles. Notice the mouse pointer pointing at a recorded script called "Yellow-Blue." I recorded that script by creating a simple rectangle, pressing record, opening the Fill dialog box, choosing those two colors, and filling the object. Corel Script recorded my filling operations. Notice that, as part of saving the script, an icon is created showing the final product of the script. This makes it easy to remember what the script was for. In the example shown in Figure 18-14, I selected text rather than a shape before playing back the command. As you can see, the playback script worked just as well on the text as on a shape object.

Figure 18-15 shows the mouse pointer near the script labeled "Scale 150 percent." I recording this by selecting an object and adjusting the Scale Factor on the Property Bar accordingly. You can record and save as many scale-adjusting scripts as you like. These can be applied to any object.

Figure 18-14: The Script and Preset Manager main screen displays some text effects.

Figure 18-15: A user-made Scale Adjusting script is ready to run.

Secret

While recording a script, take your time. The script process will not remember time intervals between commands implemented. It is fine to pause and check a note you've written to yourself, or take a second to think carefully about the command you are about to execute. Your script will still commence at lightning speed.

Figure 18-16 shows the pointer near a script entitled "Rotate 45." Not surprisingly, this script rotates any object 45 degrees. Note that the icon saved with a script does not always reflect the script's purpose very well.

Figure 18-16: This user-created "Rotate 45" script rotates the selected object 45 degrees.

What Corel Script saves as an icon is the object that the command was performed on while recording. You can replace the icon with another chosen picture by right-clicking on the icon in the Script and Preset Manager, bringing up the Create Thumbnail command. This command replaces the existing thumbnail image with any image you have selected at the moment (see Figure 18-17). In this case, the image will be replaced with a picture that has more to do with rotating. Figure 18-18 shows the new image reproduced as the icon for the command.

Figure 18-17: Select Create Thumbnail to replace the current icon for the user-created Rotate command.

Figure 18-18: The new Thumbnail icon appears for the rotate command.

Figure 18-19 shows the mouse pointer about to execute a script to create a complex line object with many curves. Corel Script recorded the entire procedure of creating and adjusting the line until I was happy with it. The script was saved and can be played back to create the same image at any time. Why is this better than cutting and pasting? Because you can use the script in later sessions. This routine rather resembles Draw's capability of creating and saving Power Lines.

Figure 18-19: A user-created script helps create a complex, curved line object.

Figure 18-20 shows a remarkable script action. By pressing play, I can have these two objects blended in 60 steps. When I created this script, the Blend roll-up was on the screen. But I can play it back with the Blend roll-up off screen, and yet the procedure is carried out flawlessly. This example shows a major benefit to using scripts: you can carry out tasks that require roll-ups without their having to be present, cluttering up your screen!

Figure 18-20: These two objects will be blended using a "Blend in 60 Steps" command created by the user. Notice that the Blend roll-up is nowhere in sight.

Running Scripts with Buttons and Hotkeys

Here's how to create a button on a toolbar from one of your Corel scripts:

STEPS

Creating a Toolbar Button for a Script

Step 1. You must first relocate your scripts to the directory where CorelDraw's Customize Tools menu will be capable of seeing and working with them. To do this, open the Script and Preset Manager, and select one of the scripts you want to turn into a tool button.

Step 2. While pressing the Ctrl key, drag the script upward to the folder labeled "Scripts." Pressing Ctrl also leaves the script behind in the Script and Preset Manager viewing area.

Step 3. Now Select Tools ⇨ Customize from the CorelDraw menu.

Step 4. In the Commands area, open the folder that says "Application Scripts."

Step 5. Click on the icon for the script you want to create a button from. (See Figure 18-21.)

Figure 18-21: Select a Script from the Customize menu to create a button from.

Step 6. Move your mouse pointer to any of the buttons in the three rows set aside for you to choose from. (Again, see Figure 18-21.) Get ready to drag that button to any toolbar on the CorelDraw main screen.

Step 7. Drag the button of your choice up to a toolbar, as shown in Figure 18-22. This button is "loaded" with your script command and is now ready for service.

(continued)

STEPS *(continued)*

Creating a Toolbar Button for a Script

Figure 18-22: Drag a button loaded with your script up to an existing toolbar.

If you drag the button "out into the open" on the main CorelDraw screen, it will open as a free-floating toolbar and will adhere to the same rules that all CorelDraw toolbars operate under. If you intend to create buttons for many of your scripts, this step I just described, creating a free-floating button, would really be the first step in *creating an entire toolbar of your scripts.* Having created a free-floating button, make this into a full-fledged toolbar by opening other scripts you want to move and attaching them to this free-floating button. This new toolbar can be as large as you wish.

When you're finished, close the Customize Tools dialog box. No further "saving" is necessary.

To create a *hot-key combination* to activate your script, look again at Figure 18-21. That figure is of the Toolbars tab of the Customize dialog box. But instead of operating with the Toolbar tab, open the Keyboard tab. The same procedure applies as previously outlined, except instead of dragging a button to a toolbar, type in a hot-key combination that will execute your command.

You can also use this same dialog box to attach scripts to an existing roll-up.

Learning How to Compose Scripts

Even a light background in the Visual Basic language is enough to get started using Corel Script. If you don't know it, many excellent, user-friendly books are available on the subject. It is one of the easiest computer languages to learn. Corel Script is a cross between Visual Basic and simplified CorelDraw-specific command code.

The rest of this chapter provides hints on how to use the Corel Script online manual. After working with the online manual and learning a bit of Visual Basic, you'll be writing and editing scripts in no time.

Corel Script's online manual comes complete with example scripts. Every command is explained in detail with examples given, and ready-made scripts are offered to create custom dialog boxes that you can apply in any situation. The online manual also includes an organized compendium of commands used for CorelDraw and Corel Photo-Paint. It further includes instructions on how to use Corel Script to create scripts for other Corel applications such as Ventura 7.

Here are three quick tips to remember:

Secret

■ Because Corel Script is just text, you can literally copy an example script right out of a help file and paste it into Corel Script Editor. (You must place the proper application-specific headings, of course.)

■ Please note that many scripts in the online manual are application-specific. If it says it works only with CorelDraw 6, you can try adding the `.WITHOBJECT CorelDraw.Automation.7` command line and removing the one referring to CorelDraw 6, but the results are not predictable.

■ Corel Script supports drag and drop. Open CorelDraw with the Script and Preset Manager viewing window available. Now open Script Editor. Drag any icon of a script from the Script and Preset Manager, drop it onto Script Editor, and the script will open, ready for editing.

Using the Corel Script Online Manual

The only way to access the Corel Script online manual is from outside CorelDraw. Select Program from the Windows Start Menu, choose CorelDraw ➪ Productivity Tools ➪ Corel Script Editor, and select Help on the menu. Click the Contents tab, and open the Corel Script "book," which is shown in Figure 18-23. You may wish to browse the "Using the Corel Script Online Help" article, which is two items above the Corel Script online manual itself. This article contains a book-by-book breakdown of what is available in the manual. (See Figure 18-24.)

Figure 18-23: Open the Corel Script Online Help manual.

Using the Corel SCRIPT online Help

If you want to learn how to record and playback your actions with a Corel application (such as CorelDRAW 6*, PHOTO-PAINT 6, VENTURA 7, CAD 1 or FLOW 3), see the Reference topic in your application's online Help. You can also learn how to save your recordings as scripts (sometimes called macros) and find out how to assign scripts to keystrokes, menus, and toolbar buttons.

This online Help can provide all the information you need if you're ready to go beyond the features noted above. This information is intended for both novice and experienced script or macro writers and programmers. The information is broken into the following categories:

Corel SCRIPT Basics
This section provides an overview of what Corel SCRIPT is and how you can use it. It also provides information regarding the syntax and documentation conventions used in Corel SCRIPT.

Corel SCRIPT Concepts
This section introduces Corel SCRIPT programming language concepts. You should view this section if you are new to script writing. If you're an script writer or programmer, you may want to skip to the next section.

Corel SCRIPT application commands and functions &
Corel SCRIPT programming statements and functions
These two sections explain the syntax and purpose of all Corel SCRIPT application commands and programming statements.

Corel SCRIPT Editor
Explains the features of the Corel SCRIPT Editor and how it can be used to quickly create and edit your scripts. This section also explains about creating and editing custom dialog boxes.

Custom dialog boxes
This section explains how to use custom dialog boxes in your scripts.

How to
Provides procedural information for using the Corel SCRIPT Editor and creating and editing custom dialog boxes.

Advanced Corel SCRIPT features
Describes the advanced features available in Corel SCRIPT to develop and use DLLs and executables. This section is aimed at experienced Windows programmers and third-party developers.

Reference
Provides reference information such as error codes, warning messages, character map and a glossary.

Note

• *Corel DRAW 6 doesn't support recording commands and actions but you can write scripts for it.

▓ Related Topics

Figure 18-24: Here, access the "Using the Corel Script Online Help" article.

Figure 18-25 shows the articles included in the Corel Script Basics book. Of particular interest to beginners is the Sample Script article, the Corel Script Programming Language, and the Sample Scripts articles.

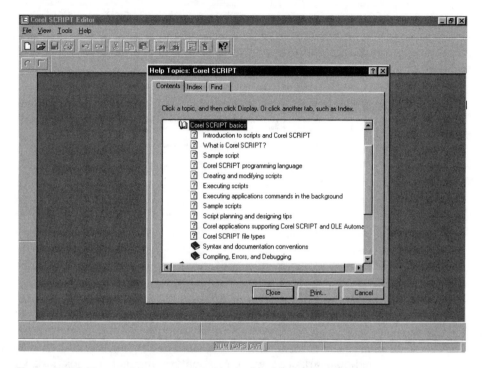

Figure 18-25: These articles are included in the Corel Script Basics book.

Figure 18-26 shows a sample script, available by clicking on the Sample Scripts article in the Corel Script Basics book. (You cannot see the entire script description in this picture.) Each parameter and each command are explained. Remember that this script can be copied and pasted right into Script Editor itself. You may then use the CorelDraw's Tools ⇨ Scripts ⇨ Run command to Run the script.

Figure 18-26: A sample script appears in the Corel Script Basics book.

It's very easy to lose your place while using these help files. Don't forget to create bookmarks as you go. As soon as you create a bookmark, you'll be able to open help to that exact location the next time you click on the bookmark tab, and scroll down. Help can store an unlimited number of bookmarks.

Understanding Corel Script programming statements

From within the Corel Script Basics book, click on the Corel Script Programming Language article. Scroll down to a right-facing arrow that reads "Click here for a listing of all programming statements and functions." They mean it. Click the right-facing arrow, and here's what you'll see (Figure 18-27):

Figure 18-27: All Corel Script's Programming statements and functions are listed.

In Figure 18-27, the mouse pointer is shown hovering over one of the programming statement examples. Clicking takes the reader to an example of the use of that programming statement, with descriptions of the syntax used.

Creating custom dialog boxes

This online manual also includes instructions for creating custom dialog boxes. With Corel Script, dialog boxes are just about as easy as dragging and drawing the features you want to include right onto the box. The Corel Script online manual contains many interactive dialog boxes that you can edit to suit your needs. The programming component (such as causing one box to close while another opens when the user clicks) has been taken care of. All you need to do is change the labels and link the dialog boxes to a script of commands for the boxes to control.

Summary

- ▶ You can simply use the preset scripts that come with CorelDraw.

- ▶ You can learn to record your own scripts from within the CorelDraw program.

- ▶ If you know even a small amount of the Visual Basic language, you can easily learn to edit recorded scripts by opening a recorded script in CorelDraw's Script Editor.

- ▶ By exploring the Corel Script online manual, you can combine your knowledge of Visual Basic with the information in the manual to create your own fully functional scripts from scratch.

Chapter 19

Other Utilities

It may be hard to believe that after all of the preceding chapters about CorelDraw's supporting applications, there's still more to talk about. But there is. Your understanding of the CorelDRAW 7 graphics suite isn't complete until you know at least the basics of two highly useful utilities — CorelCapture and CorelScan.

The first utility, CorelCapture, enables you to easily capture and save what people in the computer journalism business call *screen shots*. Screen shots (also called *screen captures*) are pictures of computer monitor screens. After you capture a screen, you can use it in a manual, on the Internet, or just about anywhere you want. As we move through the discussion on how to use this nifty little utility, I'm sure you'll think of lots of ways to use screen shots.

CorelScan simply makes scanning easier — whether into a CorelDRAW application or another TWAIN-compliant program (TWAIN stands for Technology Without An Interesting Name). It is a set of wizards designed to help you set up your scanner and then make the proper settings for the source image and the intended use, or application, for the final scanned artwork. CorelScan is designed to help novices scan more effectively, but if you've been using your scanner for a while, you too may find that it makes scanning easier.

CorelCapture

When friends and acquaintances look over my books, they usually ask, "How did you do all of these graphics?" Many of them I create in CorelDraw or Photo-Paint. But all of the screen captures (and partial screen captures) are done with CorelCapture. CorelCapture takes much of the work out of the capturing, saving, and organizing process. All I do is press a key. CorelCapture captures the screen I designate, converts it to grayscale, prints it, and then saves it with a filename in a predesignated sequence — all while I keep working.

Today, people have many uses for screen captures — as instruction sheets for employees, in software and hardware documentation, for Internet presentations, and in application help files, to name a few. CorelCapture can provide screen captures suited to just about any use you can think of, even multimedia presentations.

Creating a screen capture

One of the joys of CorelCapture is that it's so remarkably easy to use. It requires little (and sometimes no) setup, and then it just sits there, waiting in the wings to activate each time you need a screen shot. The CorelCapture interface, shown in Figure 19-1, is straightforward — no hidden menus or dialog boxes, and it's logically arranged. Setting up usually entails a quick and simple progression through the six sections of the CorelCapture dialog box, often in the order they appear.

![CorelCapture dialog box interface showing the Activation tab with Hot key, Timing options, and Help, Capture, Close buttons]

Figure 19-1: Use the CorelCapture interface for setting up screen captures.

Setting Activation options

Activation means "When do I take the screen shot?" In other words, here's where you tell CorelCapture when you press a key, or a combination of keys, to capture the screen. By default, CorelCapture executes a capture when you press F7. You can change that to any function key from the Hot Key dropdown list, or you can choose User Defined from the list and set just about any Ctrl, Alt, or Shift+keystroke combination.

You may be asking yourself, why not just leave it at F7? Here's why: when CorelCapture is active — in capture mode — even though it waits in the background, it overrides hotkeys in the active application. Say you're working in an application, Microsoft Word, for instance, and you normally use F7 to activate the spell checker. If CorelCapture is open and active, pressing F7 will instead take a screen shot. So changing the hotkey simply enables you to set a keystroke combination that won't interfere with the way you work.

Secret

When setting CorelCapture activation, consider how long you want the program to wait once you press the hotkey before it actually captures the contents of the screen. Does this seem like a no-brainer? Right away, right? I mean, why wait longer than you have to?

Here's why: Often, you'll want the screen shot to include an open menu or flyout, or you may want the mouse to display doing something or other. Giving yourself a little time to set up the screen before CorelCapture goes to work enables you to prepare for the screen shot. You can set a delay from 1 to 60 seconds with the Initial Delay Before First Capture option in the Timing portion of the Activation section of CorelCapture's Interface dialog box. The default is five seconds, which I find is usually long enough.

Telling CorelCapture what to capture

Sometimes you don't want to capture the contents of the entire screen. Occasionally, the active window or dialog box will do. You control which portion of the screen CorelCapture grabs with the Source section of the Corel Capture dialog box, shown in Figure 19-2.

Figure 19-2: Use the Source section of CorelCapture dialog box to tell the program what to capture.

The first three options in Source are self-explanatory. Besides, when you select one of them, the preview window on the left side of the dialog box shows you what will be captured. You may, however, wonder about the third option, Client/Animation Window. As you'll see in a moment, CorelCapture lets you create animated movies from your screen shots. The third option enables you to capture roll-ups and toolbars as active windows, which can be helpful when creating animation sequences.

The last three options — Rectangle Area, Elliptical Area, and Free-hand Area — let you select portions of the screen with your mouse. To use one of them, you select the desired shape option (Free-hand lets you capture oddly shaped objects), click Capture, and return to the application from which you want to capture a portion of the screen. Now press the hotkey to initiate the capture. While CorelCapture cycles through the duration pause you set in Activation, set up the screen objects as you want to capture them — open a menu, a fly-out, or whatever. When the mouse cursor turns into a butterfly net, drag a marquee around the portion of the screen you want to capture. When you release the mouse, CorelCapture will capture the area you selected.

Telling CorelCapture where to send the captured image

One of the really slick features of CorelCapture is that you can send the captured screen shot wherever you need it — a file, your printer, the clipboard, or an OLE-aware client. You can even send it to two destinations at once. While capturing screens for this book, for example, I sent each capture to a file *and* my desktop printer. This saves me the extra time of having to open them in another application to print them later on.

Where CorelCapture puts the image is controlled from the Destination portion of the application's dialog box, shown in Figure 19-3. Again, these options are for the most part self-explanatory. The File option saves the image to a filename you designate in the File section of the CorelCapture dialog box. You can name files individually or tell CorelCapture to name them sequentially, as you'll see in the later section, "Setting Up Automatic Naming."

Figure 19-3: Use the Destination section of CorelCapture to designate where to send the screen capture.

The two options that probably need explaining are Animation File and OLE Automated Application. The first, of course, designates an AVI movie file in which to save consecutive captures. I explain creating movies with

CorelCapture in the sidebar "Lights, Camera, Action!" OLE Automated Application sends the capture to an OLE-aware Corel application of your choice — either CorelDraw or Photo-Paint. When you select this option, after CorelCapture captures the screen, it launches the application you designate in the drop-down list and pastes the capture into a new document.

When you select the Printer option in Destination, the Select Printer option becomes available, enabling you to choose and set up a printer as you normally would from that particular printer's Print Setup dialog box.

Telling CorelCapture how to process the screen shot

Secret

I told you CorelCapture was full-featured and handy. In many screen capture utilities, you must open the captured image in a bitmap editor, such as Photo-Paint, to tailor it to your needs. But not in CorelCapture. Using the Image portion of the CorelCapture dialog box, shown in Figure 19-4, you can set the color depth, resolution, and physical size of the image on the fly — often eliminating the need to resample the image later.

Figure 19-4: Use the Image portion of the CorelCapture dialog box to set color depth, resolution, and image size on the fly.

When setting options in Image you first tell CorelCapture what kind of output you need — Screen, Printer, or Custom — in the Settings drop-down list. Depending on the choice you make in Settings, more options in the dialog box become available. The Screen setting provides no additional options. CorelCapture captures the screen as is, with your current Windows resolution and color depth. The Printer setting enables you to set the color depth in the Type drop-down list. You can use this option to change the image's color mode. For this book, for example, I set the Type to Grayscale. The options in Type are: Black and White, 16-bit Color, Grayscale, 256 Color, and 24-Bit Color.

Note

If you aren't familiar with color depth, you can learn more about it in Chapter 5.

The Custom setting provides the most extensive controls over how CorelCapture processes the image. It enables you to set not only color depth but two resolution options, dots per inch and pixels per inch. The first, of course, refers to printer, or hard copy, resolution, and the second pertains to screen, or monitor, resolution. Depending on how you plan to use your captures, these settings are important. They are covered extensively in a few places in this book. The importance of dots per inch resolution is covered in Chapter 7.

Secret

Here's a way to adjust screen shots on the fly. Resize can be used to resample. Set the Width to a different size than the capture and check Maintain Aspect Ratio. It will be captured at the new size and resolution. This feature is great for enlarging screen grabs for editing, or for capturing images at exactly the right size for a layout, such as a Web pages.

Naming and saving files

At the risk of seeming too enthusiastic, let me rave again about the thoroughness of the CorelCapture application, as this next discussion demonstrates. Not only does this utility let you control color depth and resolution, but you can also designate file format and filename from the File section of the CorelCapture dialog box (shown in Figure 19-5). The options here are extensive and not necessarily obvious. So let's look at them one at a time.

Figure 19-5: Use the File section of CorelCapture to designate filenames for your captures or to choose automatic file naming.

Designating a filename and format

Naming the current capture is easy. First you must make sure that the File option in the Destination section of CorelCapture is active. Then you name the file in the File Name field in the File Settings portion of File in CorelCapture. Keep in mind, though, that if you do more than one capture, CorelCapture names each capture with the name you type in File Name — unless you turn on Use Automatic Naming (which we look at in a moment). In other words, it overwrites the file each time you press the hotkey.

You can also designate which folder CorelCapture saves the file in by clicking the Select Capture Directory button and then going to the desired folder. You can even capture to a folder on another computer on a network by clicking the Network button in the Select Directory dialog box.

To designate the type of file (TIFF, JPEG, Adobe Photoshop, and so on), you choose the desired format from the Type of File drop-down list. Many formats also support compression schemes, such as LZW compression for TIFF images and RLE compression for JPEG and Photoshop formats, that you can control from the Type of Compression drop-down list. When you choose a file format, CorelCapture automatically tacks the format extension (.TIF, .JPG, .PSD, and so on) onto the end of the file. So do not include the extension in File Name, or you get the extension twice (IMAGE.TIF.TIF), which is annoying and nonsensical.

Setting up automatic naming

I keep referring to how I used CorelCapture for this book. But it's a perfect example of a typical application for this utility. When you need multiple sequential captures, automatic naming is a lifesaver. Here's the procedure for setting up automatic naming:

STEPS

Setting Up Automatic Naming for Screen Captures

Step 1. Type the first few characters for the naming scheme in File Name. Keep in mind here that CorelCapture adds zeros to the automatic name, depending on the number you start with. For example, if you start with *1*, the program tacks on two zeros, like this: *001*. The next will be *002*, and so on. So unless you plan to use the files only in a Windows 95 environment, where long filename conventions are observed, you should type no more than five characters in File Name. For this book, for instance, I typed *cds* to identify the book (*CorelDraw Secrets*) and then a number designating the chapter number (01, 02, 18, 19, and so on). When CorelCapture tacked on the automatic name, it added three characters (001,

002, 018, 019, and so on) and the extension. I'm not sure this is clear, so Figure 19-6 shows a list of files created with CorelCapture for Chapter 2 of this book.

Figure 19-6: Several files have been created with CorelCapture's automatic naming function.

Step 2. Select Automatic Naming, and then set the number with which you want the naming to begin in Start Naming At. Don't add zeros before the number, as CorelCapture adds them automatically.

Step 3. Click the Select Capture Directory and then, in the Select Directory dialog box, go to and open the folder in which you want your automatically named files to be saved. To save to a directory on another computer on your network, click the Network button in Select Directory, and then go to and open the shared folder on the network where you want to save the files.

That's it! Now, each time you press the hotkey, CorelCapture captures the screen, gives it the next name in the sequence, and saves it in the folder you designated. Voilà!

Capturing the cursor and placing borders around captured images

Often when capturing a screen, you'll also want to capture the cursor to help demonstrate your point (as I've done several places throughout this book). Sometimes too, you may want to place a colored border around your screen shots, sprucing them up a bit. You can control whether the cursor is captured and designate the size and color of a border from the Preferences section of CorelCapture, shown in Figure 19-7.

Figure 19-7: Use the Preferences section of CorelCapture to tell the program to capture the mouse cursor or to place a border around your screen shots.

To capture the cursor, simply check Capture Cursor. The next time you press a hotkey, the cursor will be included in the screen shot. This option works great for Current Window, Client/Animation Window, and Full Screen settings. However, because you use the mouse to capture partial screens with Rectangular Area, Elliptical Area, and Free-hand Area, you cannot capture the cursor when using these settings. To add a border, set the size (in pixels) in the Size field under border. To set the color of the border, click the Color button and choose a color.

Now get out there and capture some screen shots!

Lights, Camera, Action!

Secret

Talk about star wars! Did you know that you can create movies consisting of your mouse movements and other actions in Windows applications? What a great way to create training tools. Say, for example, that you are a systems administrator, and that you want to place files on the network (even the Internet) showing workers how to perform specific tasks on their computers. Can you think of a better way than having them launch a movie containing animated screen shots *demonstrating the task in action?* (And, if you're really energetic, you can even open the movies in a digital film-editing application, such as Adobe Premiere, and record narration to accompany the clips.)

Recording animated sequences in CorelCapture is relatively easy but slightly involved. The following steps show how:

STEPS

Recording Animated Sequences in CorelCapture

Step 1. In the File section of CorelCapture under Timing, select Regular Timing, and then select Repeat Captures (2–999 times). This option tells CorelCapture to perform several captures, one after the other, the number of times you designate in the field to the right. Each time you press the hotkey, CorelCapture captures the number of screens you set. To capture another set of screens, simply press the hotkey again, and again, until you've finished recording the procedure. Keep in mind though, that if you're working at high resolution (1024 × 780 or higher) and color depth (24-bit color), each capture may require close to half a megabyte or more of disk space. You'll have better luck setting your screen size to 640 × 480 and your color depth to 256 colors. Your movies won't take up nearly as much space, and they'll capture and run faster.

Step 2. In the File section of CorelCapture set the Interval between Captures. This option tells CorelCapture how many seconds to wait before performing the next capture, up to the number you designate in Repeat Captures. The lower you set this option, the smoother your movie will run, but the larger your movie file will be. Higher settings will cause jerky movies, but file sizes are smaller and more easily managed.

Step 3. In the File section of CorelCapture set the Animation Duration (sec).

Step 4. In the Destination section of CorelCapture select Animation File, and then choose the movie file format, Microsoft Video, QuickTime for Windows, or MPEG. Keep in mind that to run a movie format on a computer, the drivers for that format must be installed *on that computer.* To ensure that the movie will run on any Windows 95 or Windows 3.*x* machine, Microsoft Video (AVI) is a safe choice.

Step 5. In the Image section of CorelCapture set the image size in pixels and the color depth. To do so, you must use the Custom setting in the Settings drop-down list in the Image section of CorelCapture. The best method to use for movies is to set your screen resolution and color depth in the Windows Display control panel and then choose Screen from the Settings drop-down list in CorelCapture.

Step 6. In the File section of CorelCapture under Animation Settings, name the movie file in the Movie File Name field. Then set the Frame Rate (msec). This option determines how long each captured screen is displayed when you play the movie in a media viewer, such as Windows' Media Player. The rate is set in milliseconds. Each screen captured is treated as a movie frame, what you actually set with this option is frames per second (fps). The faster the frame rate, the smoother the movie and the larger the file. Be sure, too, to set the directory where you want the movie to be saved.

That's it. You are now ready to capture a movie of the actions you perform in an application (or in Windows in general). To capture the movie, return to the desired application, set up the screen as you want the movie to start, and press the hotkey. CorelCapture starts capturing screens based on the settings you made. For the best results, move the mouse slowly and deliberately and pause at points, such as when selecting menu commands or when setting options in dialog boxes, that you want to be sure to capture.

If you want to make sure your movie is well-designed and well-organized, write a script and practice it a few times before actually recording the captures.

One other thing before leaving this discussion of capturing movies: the procedure I just described is straightforward, but a number of variables, such as screen resolution, color depth, and even the rate at which you move the mouse and perform other functions on screen, can effect the final movie. I wish I could assure you that you won't have to perform some trial runs to perfect your technique and tweak CorelCapture settings. But that would be like trying to tell you that you don't have to practice to learn to play piano.

CorelScan

If you own a scanner, you probably already know how to use it. And, if you're like me, you probably like to use the interface software that came with your scanner, and you're probably thinking about skipping this section. Before you go on, let me assure you that electing to use CorelScan does not preclude you from also using the scanner software you already use.

If you are not wedded to your scanner software, be sure to check out CorelScan. It enables you to perform a wide range of procedures, such as color correction and setting up and saving scanner presets, that most built-in scanner front ends don't provide.

CorelScan is a new utility in Version 7. In this chapter, I'll go over some of its hidden intricacies and point out some of the benefits of using this feature-rich scanning front end.

Starting CorelScan for the first time

The first time you launch CorelScan, before using it, you'll need to set up the software to use your scanner. Like CorelCapture, CorelScan consists of a series of dialog boxes, rather than a full-blown application window. Unlike CorelCapture, CorelScan works more like a conventional Windows application wizard, providing a step-by-step approach to scanning and processing images. Let's take a look at the dialog box CorelScan greets you with when you first launch the utility. (See Figure 19-8.)

Figure 19-8: From this initial CorelScan screen, you set up CorelScan to work with your scanner.

The first time you use CorelScan, you must set it up to work with your scanner, which is why so few options are available. So if this is the first time you've fired up CorelScan, make sure the Setup Scanner and Processing options are correct and that Scan is selected. Then click the Next button. This brings up the screen shown in Figure 19-9. From here you choose whether to use the scanner interface that came with your scanner or the CorelScan interface for scanning. Which you should choose depends on how happy you are with the manufacturer's interface. In my case, my ScanJet uses DeskScan, which I happen to like very much. Either method you choose will work fine with CorelScan. If you choose to use your manufacturer's interface, at the end of the scanning process, the scan is dumped into CorelScan for further processing.

Figure 19-9: Choose whether to use your interface or the CorelScan interface to operate your scanner.

With either method you choose, if this is the first time you've set up a scanner, CorelScan will perform a TWAIN compatibility check to make sure your scanner conforms to the CorelScan specs. You can also use this routine to update CorelScan by clicking Force Compatibility Test. Use this option when you add a new scanner or upgrade the interface software. In addition, if you are using Corel Color Manager (discussed in Chapter 5), you should also check Use Color Calibration. When you've finished setting up this screen, click Next. CorelScan provides you with a dialog box showing you the specs for your scanner. If you haven't done so, you can also set up Corel Color Manager from here by clicking the Color Manager button.

Choose OK, and then click Next again. CorelScan runs your scanner interface and lets you make adjustments to the scan. After you've made these adjustments and made your final pass, the screen shown in Figure 19-10 is displayed, letting you choose the type of image or format you want CorelScan to process the image as. The program makes its best guess based on the information it receives from the scanner interface, but you can change it to whatever you like.

Figure 19-10: Use this screen to select the type of image you scanned. The type of image you select determines the next phases of using CorelScan.

Depending on the type of image you choose, after you click Next, CorelScan provides you with several processing options. For example, you might choose Color Photograph, which would open a particular dialog box for that option. From that point on, CorelScan is pretty straightforward, providing you with explanations for the processes the program suggests applying. For example, the next screen you would see in this process would offer to apply moiré removal, which my scan really needed. Take my word for it: if you let CorelScan make these decisions for you, you get better scans. At the end of the process, CorelScan provides a screen with options for saving your scan.

Summary

▶ CorelCapture enables you to capture screen shots, save, resample, and automatically rename them on the fly. And you can even capture a series of screens in an animation sequence (or movie).

▶ CorelScan is a wizard-like utility that enables you to use preset scanning configurations, apply color correction, and make numerous other adjustments to images as you scan them.

Patrick Lichty is an artist and writer, and a partner of Lichty Studios. His digital art and metal sculpture have been shown internationally, and he is an exhibitor at the 1996 New York Digital Salon. His commercial work has included multimedia titles, publication design, 3D animation, music videos, and Web design. Companies using his work include the Colin Riley group, IBM, Diebold, and MTV.

As a writer, Lichty has been published in computer art and academic circles. He has contributed most frequently to *Corel* and *3D Artist* magazines, and journals dealing with postmodern social theory. Lichty speaks frequently at academic conferences on cyberculture and the society of the Information Age. In his spare time, Lichty studies Asian flute music, martial arts, and popular culture.

Plate A-1: PowerLines were used to attain a variation in line necessary for facial expressions. Blends were also used to add realism to features such as eye glints.

Plate A-2: The source file contained over 2,500 discrete objects. To keep the machine from bogging down with excessive redraw times, I saved off the artwork in sections, and merged them to build the final piece.

Plate A-3: Blends were used heavily to produce soft, flowing fabric folds that were unattainable through the use of fountain fills. However, use of blends resulted in a high object count.

Plate A-4: In many areas where precision blends were not necessary, radial and custom fountain fills (such as those in the hair) added a pleasing effect.

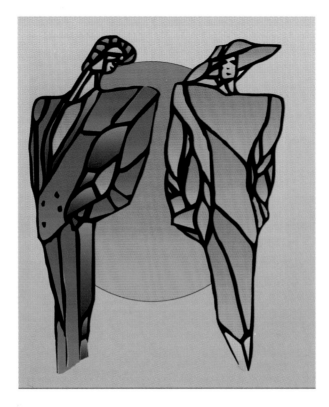

Sue Rodgers, an artist for 20 years, lives in Pittsburgh, Pennsylvania, with her husband, Randy, and their two children, Zachary and Tyler. She and her husband own two small businesses. They also do professional desktop publishing on the side.

Plate B-1:
The picture was originally scanned in using Corel Photo-Paint, and then saved.

Plate B-2:
The file was then imported into CorelTrace in order to separate each piece so most of the work could be done in CorelDraw.

Plate B-3:
The graphic was imported into CorelDraw and reduced in size.

Plate B-4:
A circle was drawn using the ellipse tool, beside the graphic so it could be used behind the two people. The circle was then highlighted and moved to the back using Arrange ⇨ Order ⇨ To Back.

Plate B-5:
A rectangle was drawn with the rectangle tool and the graphic was sized and placed within the rectangle.

Plate B-6:
The people's clothes were highlighted using the pick tool and then filled in using the fill tool. A similar effect was applied with the circle behind them.

Timothy J. Moran is a graphic artist who lives and works in Elyria, Ohio. He uses CorelDraw for marketing and advertising projects, including logos, brochures, catalogs, and presentations.

Plate C-1: The eagle in the checker was a clip art image. All fills were changed to none and it was made into a wireframe outline. Three copies of the image were staggered, each with a different color outline, to produce the embossed effect.

Plate C-2: The rainbow swirl is a conical fountain fill using a two-color, red-to-red blend with a clockwise path around the color wheel at a 90-degree angle.

Plate C-3: The embossed "VS" was the Swiss 721 Black Outline font converted to curves and edited into several pieces using the node edit tool. Black and white fills were then applied.

Plate C-4: The magnifying glass handle is a combination of objects with custom linear fountain fills. The rim is two circles of different yellow shades and line widths blended together.

Plate C-5: The loose tiles were resized squares that were extruded slightly using solid fills. From within the extrusion options window, the squares were rotated in 3D.

Edward Fitzgerald is a freelance graphic designer and photographer who lives in the Kansas City, Missouri area. He retired several years ago from a 30-year career with Hallmark Cards, where he was a retail designer.

He has adapted the design in his logo to business cards, stationery, and note paper.

Plate D-1:
The logo is made up of circles and rectangles with fountain fill blends applied to achieve a reflected look. All of the blends are linear. The first circle was drawn and centered on the page. The circle is composed of a linear blend and two colors. The lower rectangle was created by mirroring the existing rectangle horizontally and vertically and applying it as a duplicate.

Plate D-2:
A second circle is centered on the page and reduced in size allowing the first circle to appear as a band. The lower rectangle was duplicated as in the first step.

Plate D-3:
Another circle is centered on the page and reduced in size, allowing the first and second circles to appear as bands.

Plate D-4:
The final circle is a radial fill centered on the page. Three stripes were added at the top and bottom.

Anne Baker is a graphic designer who specializes in technical illustration. She lives in central Illinois. She uses CorelDraw on a daily basis, both at work and for fun projects, such as this illustration.

On a gray October day several years ago, she noticed a pair of antlers wired to a fence post, evidently forgotten by some hunter in a prior season. On the tip of one antler, a Monarch butterfly provided a splash of brilliant color. This illustration is an attempt to depict the subtle beauty of the scene.

Plate F-1:
The background is composed of two rectangular objects and one free-form object, all filled with gradient blends. These three objects were blended together to form one compound object.

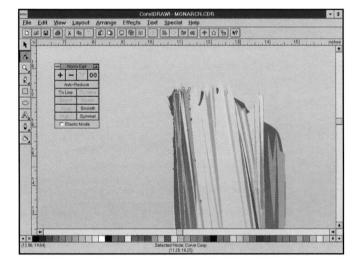

Plate F-2:
The fence post is a series of objects drawn freehand

Plate F-3:
Barbed wire was created entirely from power lines. After one section was completed, it was copied several times to form a continuous strand, and the colors were altered slightly. (Hint: Power lines can create large files. If you are limited on space, use the Separate and Ungroup features to convert power lines into smaller objects, and then reduce the number of nodes with the Autoreduce feature in the Shape menu.)

Plate F-4:
To create the antlers, the illustrator first drew some simple freehand shapes to serve as guides. The subtle shading and suggestion of different textures were accomplished by drawing lines of various widths and colors, which were then blended together.

Plate F-5:
The wireframe view demonstrates the pattern and technique used.

Plate F-6:
Vines were created by drawing freehand shapes. The Contour feature was used to create the gradient fills. Smaller vines were drawn using the power line feature.

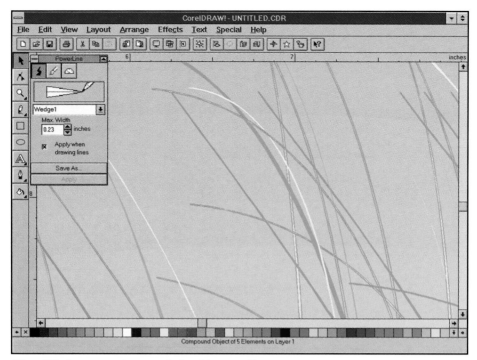

Plate F-7: Grass was drawn entirely with power lines.

Plate F-8: As a finishing touch, a butterfly was imported from CorelDraw's clip art.

Part IV

Electronic Media

Chapter 20

CorelDraw and the Web

In This Chapter

You'll learn use tips on:

▶ Preparing images for the Web

▶ Designing attractive Web pages

▶ Choosing software to help you with Web page design

▶ Using CorelDraw to create Web pages

▶ Testing a Web page

▶ Using CorelDraw and Java

Preparing Images for the Web

One unusual aspect of designing Web pages is how you can bring home an entire day's work on a single floppy disk. In this era of behemoth images weighing in at 60MB and more, it's strange to create an entire Web page and have enough room left on your floppy for a backup of all the .GIFs as well. In fact, that's one way you can tell you're doing a good job.

What should be in the back of your mind when designing a graphic for your Web page is an image of somebody surfing the Net, casually searching for a certain topic. He or she stumbles upon your Web page. This is your moment to shine. Someone has stumbled onto the page *you* designed. The viewer clicks, and waits . . . 20 seconds . . . 30 seconds . . . still loading. Boredom hits. Boom. Your chance is gone. Your potential new viewer is now following a link to somewhere else, where they remembered that on the Web, small is better.

CorelDraw creates beautiful images, with beautifully detailed fountain fills and sharp lines. But if the World Wide Web became instantly populated with CorelDraw images in their native format, the whole thing would come to a crashing halt. CorelDraw images are too big for the Web. They're too big, and they have too many colors. You do have tools at your disposal to make sure your images maintain their sharp, crisp "Corel look" while conforming to the norms of Web viewing.

To use CorelDraw or Photo-Paint images on the Web, you must convert the image to 256-color mode, shrink the size, change the resolution, and optimize the color palette for viewing on the Web. Before I explain how to export entire CorelDraw documents as Web pages, I want to show you how to prepare individual images for use on Web pages.

Converting images to 256 colors

Because we work most often in CorelDraw or Photo-Paint in 16.7 million colors, the trick is to reduce the image to use only 256 colors, and the question is, which 256 colors? When you elect to reduce an image from 16.7 million colors to 256, some severe choices must be made. The conversion process involves blending combinations of the new 256-color palette to simulate what the image looked like before. It is from these 256 "target" colors that the conversion process must choose. Corel applications enable you to choose from many 256-color pallets, so you do have some control over the process. How do you decide which pallet to choose? The choice is determined by who will be viewing your end product. At present, we are preparing a graphic for use on the Web, and consequently it's best to use colors favored by the two most popular browsers. To avoid having to convert your images to 256 colors, you can save them as .JPG files. Your Web page visitors will be able to view these files, but they will take longer to download.

CorelDraw's Internet-optimized palettes

Happily, Photo-Paint and CorelDraw provide a Netscape Navigator–optimized palette and an Internet Explorer–optimized palette. For the record, I prefer the Netscape palette, but either will do. Figure 20-1 shows the Photo-Paint Color Table menu with the Netscape Navigator palette chosen. To reach this menu, select Image ⇨ Convert To ⇨ 8 bit ⇨ Custom. Scroll through the drop-down palette menu to select a palette. Photo-Paint then converts your image to 256 colors. Remember to save your image as a .GIF or a .JPG for viewing on the Web. When converting a CorelDraw image to a .GIF (the preferred format for Web page viewing), choose File ⇨ Export and select .GIF. About halfway through the conversion process, you'll be prompted to select a color palette for your new .GIF image. Choose Custom, and then select either the Netscape or Internet Explorer palette.

Figure 20-1: Use the Photo-Paint Color Table dialog box to choose a color palette for your Web page.

Secret

When you are converting a CorelDraw image to a bitmap, the default size will be much too large for the Web. An individual image on the Web should have a compressed size of no more than 100K. You may save your image in .JPG format to escape this limitation. If your viewers don't mind the wait, a .JPG image compressed to 100K can have an uncompressed size of over a megabyte. The image quality will be higher.

Dithering

When converting an image to 256 colors, you may select Dithering and then choose a type of dithering. Selecting Dithering instructs Photo-Paint or CorelDraw to carefully blend colors to simulate the complicated color patterns found in your original image. If dithering is not selected, each spread of color in your image is quickly averaged and assigned a new value from one of the 256 choices. Of the two types of available dithering, Error Diffusion is the most accurate, but it takes longer to complete.

Image-format conversion

When converting an image for use on the Web, you have several choices to make. Let's go over those briefly now:

- Image resolution for a Web graphic should be set to 96 dpi.

- Saving as a .GIF allows for setting a transparency color and 89A interlacing.

- Saving as a .JPG allows a larger file size to be used, and the file will not need to be reduced to 256 colors. Complex images will look better at the larger file size.

- Selecting a transparency color allows you to save loading time by making the background color transparent. This is available as one of the .GIF options.

- Choosing 89A interlacing for your .GIF image allows Web viewers to see small portions of your image as it is loading up.

Secret

When exporting a CorelDraw or Photo-Paint image for use on the Web, don't forget to crop as much background area as possible from around your image. However, you don't have to go to the trouble of building a mask to remove the background entirely because, later, you can select a .GIF transparency option to eliminate the background color from your image. But trimming most of the background will make the file size smaller, which is important for images on the Web.

Web Page Design

Even if you've never tried to create one, you may have heard how notoriously easy it is to design a Web page. Using HTML (HyperText Markup Language), you can quickly create all the essentials of a good Web page: some text, complemented by pictures to accent what the text is saying and links to lead the viewer to other locations. HTML is called a "language," and that description may scare some people away from it. But HTML is really just a collection of short phrases (called *tags*) that you place before and after items you want to place on your Web page. For example, to instantly design a Web page that says "Hello World," you would type:

```
<HTML>
<HEAD>
<TITLE>My Web Page
</TITLE>
</HEAD>
<BODY>
<Hello, World.
</BODY>
</HTML>
```

If you were to type the preceding text, exactly, into Windows Notepad and, instead of saving it as a .TXT file, save it with the extension .HTM or .HTML, you would have composed a genuine Web document. Without going into more detail about HTML, let's just say that it works by enclosing each part of a document — for example, the body of the document — between two *tags*.

If you were to type the tag `<BODY>`, then type your text, and then finish with the tag `</BODY>`, every Web browser in the world would understand that the text you typed between `<BODY>` and `</BODY>` is the *main text* of your Web document. Those beginning and ending tags tell browsers how the text should be formatted (for example, that it should be formatted as the body of a paragraph, not as the heading of a paragraph). Many Web browsers have their own ways of formatting text and graphics for viewing, but HTML allows you to give a Web browser enough information about your text to make sure it appears the way you want it to, for example, as the main body of paragraph text. Many tags exist. For example, `<HEAD>` and `</HEAD>` are the beginning and ending tags for the heading in your document.

Learning HTML

Dozens of excellent books are available for teaching yourself HTML and getting started creating Web pages. However, more than a dozen software products have been marketed to shield you from the process of learning HTML yourself. Office 97, Microsoft Publisher, HoTMetaL, and Corel WordPerfect 7 are examples of the new wave of publishing and word processing products that let you design Web pages by typing text and inserting pictures anywhere you want. The program then converts your document to HTML. You can check your links, upload your documents to your server, and be done with it.

Some problems exist with this system of letting a software package do your HTML work for you. When your Web documents don't look like what you thought they would, you won't know why. Although the packages I mentioned previously, and others, each have some sort of "debugging" program to make sure the converted document is turned into "good HTML," the explanations they give and the suggestions they make for rearranging things won't make any sense if you don't know HTML.

Part of designing an HTML document is testing it and revising it to work in different circumstances. If you've designed your own HTML document and you find that under Netscape 2.0 you get an error but under Netscape 3.0 you don't, you may be able to insert a couple of *tags* in the right places to suit the older version of Netscape. But if you don't know HTML, you are dependent on the savvy of the HTML-conversion software that your program uses. And no matter how sophisticated such conversion programs are, if they are more than a month old, they are already out of date. If you are remotely interested in creating Web pages, I heartily recommend setting aside the two or three weeks it may take to learn HTML for yourself. Then you should be sure to keep up with the newest versions of HTML, learning new tags as they come into widespread use. That way, your knowledge of

HTML will grow along with the Web itself. The following Web sites can assist you in learning and staying on top of the latest developments in HTML:

- `http://www.ncsa.uiuc.edu/demoweb/thml-primer.html`

- `http://www.access.digex.net/~tilt/cgh/`

- `http://kuhttp.cc.ukans.edu/lynx_help/HTML_quick.html`

- `http://developer.netscape.com/platform/html_compilation/index.html`

Secret

Once you learn a little HTML, you can improve your skills by doing a little detective work. For example, if you see a Web page that has made very good use of *structure* (how the graphics are placed on the page, how the hyperlinks are arranged, where the tables are located, and so forth), you can download that page and view its HTML. (Simply download the Web page, and then open it in Windows Notepad.) The purpose is not to plagiarize the contents, but to see how the creator used the HTML tags and commands to create a good-looking document. If you know a little HTML, you'll be able to understand how the results were achieved.

For the Experts

For those of you more experienced in creating Web pages, I'm going to cut to the chase and tell you what you want to know: how CorelDraw (and Photo-Paint) can facilitate creating Web sites and pages.

Here it is in a nutshell:

- You can save a CorelDraw or Photo-Paint document as an .HTM file. What the program really creates is a large image map that takes up the entire size of the page, with Head, Body, Image SRC, and Title HTML tags attached. Your entire CorelDraw document — text, various images and all — is saved as a .GIF or .JPG file. The .GIF or .JPG file will be saved in the same directory as the .HTM file that CorelDraw creates. The picture file will have the same title as your .HTM file's name, and it is this .GIF or .JPG file that the .HTM document links itself with through Image SRC tags. When you save your CorelDraw document as an HTML document, CorelDraw does not pull out your text and surround it with `<BODY>` tags, nor does it attempt to map the sizes of the pictures on your CorelDraw document

and place and tag them appropriately throughout your page.

- CorelDraw excels at creating graphics for Java Class applets for Web pages. By exporting your CorelDraw document to a Barista.class file, you can use your CorelDraw documents to assist in the creation of Java applets. CorelDraw comes with several Barista Java applets, including ones that create scroll bars, pop-up menus, and toolbars.

- You can attach URLs to any CorelDraw or Photo-Paint object. The entire object will be "clickable" and activate the URL. In this sense, then, you can create a Web page with CorelDraw. After you've saved a CorelDraw or Photo-Paint document with hypertext links as an .HTM file, all text and objects that are not links will more or less be "part of the background," although no `<BACKGROUND>` tags are used, in the HTML sense. This picture will take up the same space on the Web page as all of its components did on the Corel document. The objects that had URLs attached to them will be recognized as separate image maps by the HTML document.

Designing attractive Web pages

Here are some tips to help novice Web page designers get started:

Change your units of measurement to pixels

Beginners tend to design a page as if it will be outputted to an 8¹/₂ by 11 sheet of paper, which it won't. Your Web page should be designed to fit into 640 pixels × 480 pixels, not a portrait-oriented paper size. The first thing you should do, therefore, when creating a Web page is to change Draw's system of measurements to pixels, and keep your eye on the ruler. If you work in an 800 × 600 or 1024 × 1248 pixel environment, this adjustment will seem disconcerting at first. If you design your Web page using those higher screen resolutions just mentioned, most of your viewers will have to use scroll bars just to see the first few lines.

Don't crowd your home page

The most common error of novice Web page designers is putting too much information on home pages. This is what you should do with your home page:

- Include an attractive logo. Put all your skills to work toward making this logo eye-catching and unique.

- Include a brief introduction to yourself, your company, and your services.

- Farm out everything else you want to say to a different page. Here on the home page, you should provide a link allowing the viewer to read about your past happy customers, another link to get details about your services, and another link to where people can find out more about you, something like a biography. Your front page, the home page, *has to load fast*. Think of your front page as an annotated business card.

- Provide unambiguous labels on the links to those other pages in your site. Checking out your links takes valuable time on the part of the viewer. The average Web surfer's attention span approaches that of a hyperactive third-grade boy. Make sure your link labels are legible and clearly indicate what people will find when they log on to that page.

- Provide helpful links to other sites offering relevant information, freebies, or services. These can go on the front page. Make sure you maintain the links regularly. (Are they still valid *this* month?) If you go to this trouble, people will come back to see what else you have to offer. Reputations for helpful, thoughtful work spread quickly on the Web. For example, thousands of people go to a Web site called "Linda's Home Page" to find genuinely helpful information, even though they have no idea who "Linda" is, because, whoever she is, she maintains her links.

- Place your hyperlinks across the bottom in neat rows. When you get really good at designing, you can play some attractive tricks that make putting them on the sides just as effective, but for beginners, hyperlinks on the bottom make the page look less cluttered.

Keep your Web pages simple

Although more and more Web sites are incorporating animation, sound effects, and complicated scripting, yours doesn't have to be like that to be good. Simple, informative Web pages with well-maintained links are still appreciated more than anything else. As large corporations set up flashy sites that are truly just commercials, we'll see more glitz and less content. But with a simple Web page, you can keep content on your side.

If you create a Web page with the following five components, you have already accomplished more than many of the other "megabucks" pages seen daily on the Web:

- Include a simple background graphic, composed of colors that don't interfere with the foreground text and graphics

- Deliver interesting, to-the-point text. If you have something unique to say or sell, people will respond.

- Feature a couple of tasteful .GIF or .JPG images. Lots of pictures are distracting and take too long to load.

- Provide a way for people to contact you, interact, and do business.

- Supply links to other informative sites. Creating a link in HTML takes about two minutes. But people always appreciate being told where they can find useful information. Make sure your links are current, and always be on the lookout for new ones, and your Web site can become surprisingly popular.

Provide thumbnails first, and then entire pictures on separate pages

When people log on to a page deeper in the site, they are ready to find out a bit more about you or your services. Provide a clickable thumbnail picture showing each *"thing,"* whatever that might be: artwork you are selling, car parts, samples of music, whatever. Providing a thumbnail is superior to just loading on a big .GIF or .JPG at the same time the page loads. By providing a thumbnail for people to click if they *choose* to see "the big picture," you are doing two things: first of all, you are letting them choose what they want to look at. (Viewers love it when you do that.) Second, you can fit lots of thumbnails on a page. This enables you to build a sort of "catalog" or index of your work into this page.

Include helpful Java applets

Java applets can create drop-down menus on your Web page. These look snazzy and save screen space. Java applets can also include checkboxes that viewers can click to reach to other choices or data boxes where people can input numbers. Other applets will compile these numbers for you in helpful ways. These little Java programs can help you create good-looking frames and tables and, of course, the all-important "hit counter," meaning the digits at the bottom of the screen that report how many people have visited your site to date.

Choosing software for your Web-page design

Earlier in this chapter, I recommended that you learn HTML and design your pages yourself. Although the day will surely come when that advice sounds like telling you to churn your own butter, in the meantime you're going to need the right tools to create your pages. What follows is a description of some of the best Web design software that is appropriate for users who are fairly new to the field.

All the following products provide "what you see is what you get" Web page creation tools. You type text on the screen where you want it to appear and drop pictures anyplace you think they should go. If your text has italics, various colors, and bolding, so be it. All of the HTML tagging is done for you. You can just click and create tables, and you can instantly apply frames to portions of your page. These programs all automate HTML heading and body text formatting. Background .GIFs (watermark pictures behind your text) and transparency issues are taken care of. All of these mentioned here will allow you to embed sound, animation, and videos instantly. Of course, adding hyperlinks is as easy as clicking and typing the URL. The programs also provide some form of page-testing mechanism, so you can see how your page will really look and run.

Corel WordPerfect Suite 7

Corel WordPerfect Suite 7 converts full-featured word processing documents into Web pages with ease. Tables in your WordPerfect document are converted into HTML tables, and headings and body text are converted to their appropriate HTML counterparts. Images will appear on your Web page pretty much where they do in your WordPerfect document. Images will be saved as separate .GIF or .JPG files in the same directory as the HTML document itself and referenced accordingly. If your document has more than one page, other pages are saved together with the first page, all in one directory. This makes it easy to upload your work all at once to a server while keeping the relative directories intact.

Claris Home Page

Claris Home Page excels at allowing you to include as many frames as you wish in your document. There's a generous clip-art library to begin with, and you may import any graphic and quickly convert it for Web use. Claris Home Page includes a nifty feature that estimates your page's download time for 28.8K or 14.4K modems.

HoTMetaL Pro 3.0

HoTMetaL Pro includes an extensive collection of ready-made Web page templates and over 400 multimedia files, including Java and Shockwave files. With HoTMetaL Pro 3.0, you can convert just about any word processing document into a Web page. The program includes an extensive spell-checker, a thesaurus, and a search-and-replace utility.

Macromedia's Backstage Designer

Macromedia, creator of Director and Shockwave, has designed a Web page creation kit that specializes in allowing you to create return forms, password authentication and logon setups, complex database searching capabilities, and other high-end content features that used to be the domain of "experts" only. Through the use of "Backstage Objects" rather than simple HTML objects, procedures such as searching through records online according to specialized criteria can now be built into your Web page as easily as inserting a graphic. Backstage also comes with a healthy assortment of Java applets, and of course using Shockwave is your key to making animation, video, and sound available on your Web site without making visitors wait forever for the files to download.

InContext Spider 1.2

This program has the best template layouts I've seen. These templates are full of attractive designs, multimedia content, even Java and Shockwave samples. Starting InContext Spider 1.2 with the Template dialog box begins an elaborate process for helping you choose the type of page you'd like to create. You can get results fast.

Microsoft Front Page

Microsoft Front Page provides the best word processing tools of any HTML authoring tool. There's even a drag-and-drop thesaurus. Lots of templates are also available, along with a multiple undo feature and a feature that automatically fixes hyperlinks that are no longer correct.

Netscape Navigator Gold

Not surprisingly, Netscape Navigator Gold's top feature is that you can tool around in the familiar Netscape environment while creating your page. Navigator Gold does not, however, include clip art libraries, support for instant frame creation, or word processing extras such as spell checking and thesaurus assistance. Those familiar with the Netscape interface will nonetheless have a very easy time creating Web pages with this program.

Creating a Web Page with CorelDraw

At the outset of this section, I should point out what CorelDraw cannot do:

When you export a document as an HTML file, bulleted lists and headings placed in your CorelDraw documents will not be converted to bullets and headings *in HTML*. They will *appear* as they did in your CorelDraw document, but in HTML text objects such as bulleted lists and headings are recognized as such only by the appropriate *tags*.

Every browser can recognize the HTML tags for bulleted lists and headings and treat such text objects accordingly. A particular Web browser might have its own unique way of displaying bulleted lists and headings, but the common use of HTML tags creates a standard for how Web pages look. As for what happens when your CorelDraw document is exported to HTML, the entire document is turned into one big .GIF or .JPG file. It can look very nice, and it will function out there on the Web, but it will not have the flexibility of a document created in HTML from scratch

Additionally, CorelDraw does not have the HTML or CGI tools to create a return form, meaning a place where people can type text and numbers and send it to your e-mail address. CorelDraw does have graphic tools to make such a form look quite attractive, however.

With CorelDraw and Photo-Paint, you can create hyperlinks. A CorelDraw object can be created and turned into an *image map,* that is, a clickable image that visitors to your site can click and be moved to a new location.

Figures 20-2 and 20-3 show two Web pages that were created using images from CorelDraw and Photo-Paint. The HTML was done in Windows Notepad.

Figure 20-2: The banner graphic "The Inside Track" was created in CorelDraw.

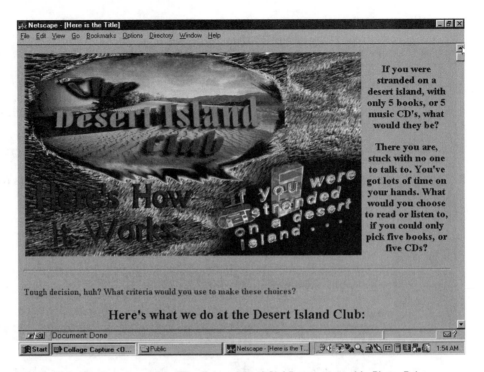

Figure 20-3: The banner graphic "The Desert Island Club" was created in Photo-Paint.

CorelDraw's Web-aware color palette options

When planning to create a Web document with CorelDraw, choose View ⇨ Color Palette, and you'll notice color palette choices that bear significance, including a color palette optimized for viewing with Netscape Navigator and one optimized for Microsoft Internet Explorer. Pick one of these before beginning your project, according to what you imagine your visitors' preferred browser will be.

Creating URLs in your CorelDraw document

A URL is a Universal Resource Locator. It is an address that you type into a "clickable" area of your document. When it is clicked, the user will be logged onto that address. URLs are typically used to link viewers of your Web site to other Web or FTP sites.

In any document, you have two steps for creating a "clickable" link that transports the viewer of your document to another "location on the Web."

■ Creating a "clickable" object, marking out its boundaries, and indicating its location on the page itself. This is typically done in HTML, through the use of USEMAP and IMAGE SCR tags. This process is very important because the clickable object must have very specific boundaries indicating where the clicking action will be effective. With its Internet Objects toolbox, CorelDraw takes care of this process for you. Any object you assign a URL will automatically be a "clickable object." As we'll see briefly, you'll have the choice to designate that the clickable area will extend as far as the object's bounding boxes, or only to the object itself.

■ Indicating an address clicking the object will log onto. In HTML, this must be done exactly as specified in relation to the clickable object itself. Again, CorelDraw has included tools to take care of this coding process. Of course, you need to make sure the URL you are typing is correct, but Draw's Internet Objects tools flawlessly create a connection with the URL and the clickable object.

Creating clickable objects in CorelDraw

Figure 20-4 shows a Web page in the making. A CorelDraw object with text has been designated for the viewer to click and then be transported to a page with a form to fill out, give credit card information, or initiate some other form of payment. The figure shows a drop-down menu that includes the Internet Objects toolbox. This menu was revealed by right-clicking any blank toolbar space. As already noted, this Internet Objects toolbox will not create a script for allowing people to order an item from you, but it will make this object "clickable" and cause the viewer to log onto the URL you supply, if it truly does exist.

Figure 20-4: Reveal the Internet Objects menu.

Figure 20-5 shows the Internet Objects toolbar open with a URL supplied. Let's look at each component of the toolbar.

Figure 20-5: The Internet Objects toolbar shows a URL.

- Starting from the left, the first data box is for typing the Location URL. Often this will begin with http://www. In this case the location URL sends the viewer to another HTML document on *the same* computer, specifically to an order form. Because it is a *local* address, only the filename itself is needed. In fact, it is advisable to keep all Web *pages* relating to a single Web Site (the home page, the order form, the "What's New" page, the "Send me e-mail page") in the same directory. That's because you can easily upload all your Web site–related files to your server, and the file locations *relative to each other* will all still be the same. That means your *local* URLs will still be accurate.

- Next is the Alternate Text data box. You should include text as an alternative to a graphic in case a particular viewer cannot view graphics or has set his browser preference to not view graphics. The text should reflect the same message as the missing graphic.

- The next button, with random small objects on it, is a toggle switch allowing you to highlight or not to highlight the Internet Objects on your page, *as Internet Objects*. Toggling this button to "off" does not hide the objects themselves, only the colored "wiremesh" that CorelDraw provides to indicate Internet Objects.

- The next button is titled "Use Object Shape to Define Hotspot." Toggling this button to "on" sets the object's exact shape to be clickable. When the document is exported as .HTML, it will include an image map of the object's exact boundaries to make it clickable. This feature works even with highly irregular objects.

- The following button, "Use Bounding Box to Define Hotspot," means that the entire rectangular bounding area associated with the Internet Object will be clickable. When the document is exported to HTML, the clickable image map created will extend to the full area of the object's bounding box. This option requires less accuracy on the part of the viewer. If the clickable area you have defined is a rather small button, it is advisable to use this "bounding box" option.

- The "Foreground Color of Hotspots" button allows you to choose what color you'd like the "wiremesh" Internet Object marker to use.

- The "Background Color of Hotspots" button lets you fill an Internet Object with a marker color, rather than use a "wiremesh" covering. This option is helpful if the Internet Object in question is rather small. In order to truly assess the clickable boundaries, you may need to fill the entire region with the marker color, rather than just apply a wiremesh.

After assigning URL and "clickable region" options to an Object, what happens? Nothing, until you save it as a CorelDraw .HTM file. This file will be in HTML and will contain an image map marking out the exact location and boundaries of every Internet object you've defined in your document. The HTML document will also include the URLs you specified and the alternate text to be displayed by graphics-deficient browsers. You have the choice of saving this document as a Barista.class Java object. This topic will be discussed later in the chapter.

Indicating an address for a link

To indicate an address for a link, you'll have to know the exact location of the file you want to reference. If the URL is going to link visitors to another page of your own Web site, be sure that the page is saved in the same directory as the current page. Next, when you type in the link, *include only the filename itself*. Because you've saved it in the same directory as the first page, you have no need to type "C:\Webdocs\Page2.htm" for example. You should type only "Page2.htm." If you include the entire address, including the root directory, the Web page will work when you test it on your computer, but when you upload it to your server, it will not work. So only type the *relative address* into the URL address data box of the Internet Objects menu (for example, "Signoff.htm"), not the entire address.

You can also provide visitors with links to other Web sites of interest. In fact, most good Web pages include links to other sites. Make sure you type in the entire address, and check the reference yourself by logging on to the site once or twice to make sure it is still good. Nobody likes Web sites with links to other sites that are no longer valid. If you include a link to another site as one of your hyperlinks, include a couple of sentences describing the new site referenced in your link. That way, your visitors will have a better idea that the site you are sending them to is something they'd truly be interested in.

Saving a document as an HTML file

This part's easy. Select File ➪ Publish to Internet. You'll be given the choice between Corel Image Map .HTM and Corel Barista .HTM. Up till now, we've only discussed saving your documents as Corel Image Map .HTM files, meaning documents with URLs and clickable objects placed on the page itself. We'll discuss Barista objects later.

Secret

Although CorelDraw 7 lets you to save your Web document with a long filename, it's best to conform to the standard eight-dot-three character norm. Ultimately, you will be uploading these Web files to your server. The server software and certain Web browsers may not be able to work with Windows 95 long filenames.

Selecting Publish to Internet does not affect the current CorelDraw document at all. In fact, you may go online and view your new HTML file while the CorelDraw document is still open. When you select Publish to Internet, two files are created. One is the .HTM file, and the other is the .GIF or .JPG file, whichever format you selected during the saving process. These two files should always be kept in the same directory. If you move them to a new directory, you have to move them both. They are no longer dependent on the CorelDraw document, which can be moved or deleted.

Selecting resolution and .GIF options for your Web page

What follows are the choices you will have to make from the various dialog boxes you'll see while publishing your CorelDraw document to the Internet.

After selecting Publish to Internet from the File menu and choosing "Corel Image Map .HTM" as your choice, you'll soon see the dialog box shown in Figure 20-6. You are to choose between saving your image as a .GIF file or a

.JPG file. Here are the issues to consider: saving as a .GIF allows you to specify a transparency color and interlacing option for your graphic. These important options will be discussed momentarily. Saving as a .JPG file will preserve a broader color range, which can be important if you used fountain fills and complex colors in your document. JPEG files will take longer to load than their .GIF counterparts.

Figure 20-6: The HTML Image Map Export dialog box permits a choice of file formats.

Next you'll see the Bitmap Export dialog box, as pictured in Figure 20-7.

Figure 20-7: The Bitmap Export dialog box permits choices of number of colors, size, and resolution.

If you export a file as shown, with its default options, you're in big trouble. Take a look at the number at the very bottom of the dialog box: "Projected Uncompressed File Size: 8,069,721." As a creator of Web pages, you should hear an alarm ring in your head. A projected uncompressed file size for a Web page should be no more than 700K. Even with a fast modem, transmitting data takes a long time over the Web. If you export your Web page as it is with these default options, it would be almost impossible for anyone to view it. Here's what you do:

STEPS

Adapting a Web Page for Export

Step 1. First move down to the Resolution area of the dialog box and set the Resolution drop-down menu to Custom. Now place a check by the Identical Values box. Make each number in the two data boxes 96. This is the resolution for most computer monitors, and this is the medium you are dealing with now, not printed output.

Anything higher than 96 dpi will increase loading time without improving results for most viewers.

Step 2.   Move on up to the Size area of the dialog box and set the Size drop-down menu to Custom. Sequence is important here, or you may end up with a Web page of uneven dimensions. This will activate the Maintain Aspect Ratio checkbox, in which you should put a check now.

Step 3.   Keeping your eye on the number at the bottom of the dialog box, the "Projected Uncompressed Size" number, input a number in one of the size data boxes that is about 1/3 the number there now. In this example, the current Width in Pixels is 2521. In order to make my Web page small enough for timely viewing, I'll eventually need to dial that number down to 740 pixels. To change the Height in Pixels dialog box to be in proportion with the Width, click once inside the Height numbers data box. The numbers will instantly change to a height in proper proportion to your new Width setting. Conversely, if you set the Height in Pixels first, clicking once in the Width numbers data box will automatically change those numbers appropriately. You may have to experiment with several numbers before finding the right size for the exported Web page. Keep in mind that your images should not be wider than 640 pixels or taller than 480 pixels. Otherwise, your Web page visitors will have to scroll to see the entire image. This 640 × 480 figure specifies the width and height of a typical screen, so your images should be even smaller than that, allowing for a browser's various menu bars and any text you have next to an image. Most Web images should not be larger than about 500 × 340 pixels. The figures I'm working with here relate to the most common screen resolution, which is 640 × 480. If your Web page visitors are working in 800 × 600 resolution mode, they can accommodate a wider image. However, it's a good idea to build your page for the lowest common denominator.

Step 4.   When you are finished, select OK.

Secret

One way to avoid having to set new size options for your exported HTML bitmap is to reset your ruler measurement system in CorelDraw to pixels and create your Web page within the constraints of a 640 × 480 pixel resolution. When building a Web page, always try to anticipate and avoid technical problems the viewer might encounter. That means building your document for viewers that are running at 640 × 480 pixels with 256 colors. Creating a Web page that asks for more than this from the viewer's system will mean locking out large portions of a potential audience. Create a page for the lowest common denominator.

If you elected to save your HTML bitmap as a .GIF, you'll see the dialog box shown in Figure 20-8.

Figure 20-8: The Gif89a Options dialog box appears.

I mentioned earlier that exporting your HTML image as a .GIF would afford you transparency and interlacing options. Here's what that means:

Looking at Figure 20-8, you'll notice a transparency option. You are prompted to select a color that will be rendered transparent when your Web page is viewed. Why assign a transparency color? Because transmitting any color data over the Web takes time, and if you can assign the background color as transparent, people visiting your site will be able to log on sooner, because the Web browser's default background color will show through. Most often this is gray, so avoid using very much gray in your Web design if you are planning to use this option.

For CorelDraw users, this transparent color will often be the default paper color, that is, white. In the dialog box shown here in Figure 20-8, you can see that the transparency color must be selected by its numerical *index* value. Pure white, of course, is 255, but the dialog box gives us color squares to check. Two hundred thirty-five is selected. These color squares are taken from the image itself. (You can, however, place your mouse cursor into any box and drag downward to see the rest of the colors in the palette.) When working on your own, you'll notice that the color of the clickable objects is *not included* as one of the choices for a transparency color. That's because if your clickable objects were transparent, the viewer could not see them to click them.

Down below is the Interlacing checkbox. Selecting interlacing allows the viewer to see a portion of your image a "little at a time" as it is loading. With the Interlacing option unchecked, the viewer will only see the alternate text you've provided until the image is completely finished loading.

Clicking OK will prompt CorelDraw to complete the process of exporting your CorelDraw document to HTML. You may now continue working with your CorelDraw document or test your Web page.

Testing Your Web Page

Contrary to the popular saying, you *do* want to try this at home! Two steps are necessary for testing your Web page. First, try it out on both Netscape and Internet Explorer without being online. Simply open the browser, and instead of logging on with your server, just open the local file, the HTML document you created with CorelDraw.

Figure 20-9 shows a Web home page designed exclusively in CorelDraw. The figure shows the page opened locally in Internet Explorer.

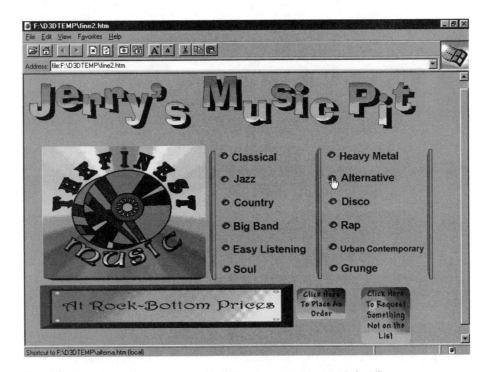

Figure 20-9: Test the operation of a Home Web page designed with CorelDraw.

The purpose of the test is to see if the size is correct for the computer screen, meaning no scrolling is necessary to see the whole page. It's important to make sure the transparency color selected affects only the background and doesn't degrade any of the images. As you can see, no background White color appears, and the images look fine. Finally, do the hyperlinks work? In this figure, the tester is shown placing his mouse over the word "Alternative." The mouse has turned into a pointing finger, so you can tell that a hyperlink was detected. If there were no hyperlink, the mouse pointer would not have become a pointing finger. Also notice that, at the lower left of the screen, the link's address is displayed. Because the page is being tested on the creator's own computer, no "http://www" and so on appears. We simply see a link to another local .HTM file called Alterna.HTM. Clicking here, the visitor will be logged onto a new Web page, presumably a list of records by alternative rock bands. Only by testing the link locally can the creator be sure it is really valid.

Some Web page features, such as Java applets, will not work on a local computer. If you've placed Java applets in your page (and this segues quite nicely into the final section of this chapter), you'll need to be online to test them. You can sometimes circumvent this limitation by logging on to your Internet Service Provider, opening a browser, and then checking out your own page locally, the page that is still on your own computer. You can see if the Java applets and other extra features work.

CorelDraw and Java

Java is a computer language similar to C++ that was developed to create miniprograms that can be plugged into your Web page. These miniprograms, called "applets," perform special functions such as creating an "Audio CD Panel interface" for visitors to select and listen to music you've made available. You can use Java applets to make interactive dialog boxes, "marquee-style" rolling text, information-gathering forms, and order forms. Here are some quick points about Java:

Java is not like HTML. It is not as easy to learn. To create in Java, you need interpreters, code compilers, and a working knowledge of languages similar to C++.

You do not need to know Java in order to use Java applets. You *do* need to know how to insert *Java tags* into your HTML document. These must include at least three *applet attributes* with these tags: the applet name; the applet's physical parameters, such as height, width, and alignment properties; and the alternative text to be displayed for non-Java-powered browsers. Some applets require more attributes to be specified with the applet tags in order to work correctly. In some cases, Java-specific language must be inserted *at the beginning* of the HTML document in order for the applet to work.

In many cases Java applets cannot be tested locally with the methods I've just described. You need to obtain a *Java applet viewer*, and these are available online or come with various software packages such as Microsoft Front Page and Macromedia's Backstage. In any event, the best site online to obtain Java help in time of need is probably still http://www.Java.sun.com.

CorelDraw can create Barista.class Java applets. This is done as easily as creating the Corel Image Map .HTM files that we discussed earlier in the chapter. However, what you are actually creating in CorelDraw is the Java applet's *graphic component*, together with its location on the page. It doesn't program the applet's actions. This is a bit like making the dialog box but deferring programming the script that makes the dialog box really do something.

CorelDraw does include Barista.class Java applets, but these will be installed on your computer only if you select custom installation and then make sure that Internet filters are selected as part of your installation. If installed, these Java applets will be stored in a folder called Barista under the CorelDraw folder.

Secret

To work with applets you create in CorelDraw and export to Barista, you must install your files in the Barista directory. The other .class files must be in the same directory as your created files. When you create a Barista.class document, a new directory of the same name is created under the Barista directory. It will contain HTML documents, one for every page you created in CorelDraw and then exported to Barista.HTM. If your document had three pages, you will find HTML documents p1.HTM, p2.HTM, and p3.HTM in that same directory.

Summary

- ▶ Preparing images for the World Wide Web includes converting images from their native CorelDraw or Photo-Paint format to formats and resolutions supported by the Web.

- ▶ Avoid crowding images and text on Web pages, and use thumbnails to guide people to pages below your home page.

- ▶ If you don't already know HTML, you should learn it. It's easy to use and universally accepted.

- ▶ With CorelDraw you can convert a document into a Web page.

- ▶ Some software programs complement CorelDraw by helping you create Web pages.

Chapter 21

Preparing Graphics for Multimedia

In This Chapter

You'll learn how to do the following:

▶ Work within the confines of 256-color mode

▶ Convert a 16.7 million color image into 256-color mode

▶ Use interesting color schemes in your presentations

You've probably seen multimedia products in action, such as PowerPoint or Macromedia Director presentations that have been optimized for a top-flight computer. They probably looked great on the Pentium 200 on which they were created. The animation came in on cue, the sound effects were heard at the appropriate moments, and one slide segued neatly into the next. Meanwhile, back at the ranch, trying to get the same presentation to run well on an average machine can be a real chore. There's a good thirty seconds of hard drive chattering in-between slides while the CPU tries to get all its ducks in a row. The animation that was supposed to hit the screen at a dramatic moment finally appears when the slide is about ready to close. So the creator who slaved all day trying to make a good presentation for the rest of the world to enjoy has to start almost from scratch.

These kinds of problems can be attributed to one cause: mistaken assumptions — about computer speed, available RAM, color depth, and video card quality. Of course, graphics specialists tend to have the best computer equipment they can possibly afford, but if you send your PowerPoint or Astound presentation to a client on a floppy disk, you shouldn't assume that the equipment will be of the same caliber. You should follow certain basic rules when you're not sure on what equipment your presentations will be run. These rules generally apply to presentations created with Premiere, Director, PowerPoint, and Astound, among others.

Gear your presentations to the lowest common denominator. Assume your stand-alone presentation will run on a 486-66 with 8MB of RAM, and an old Trident 8900 video card with 1MB of RAM. And sadly, and most distressingly, you ought to assume the show will be viewed in 256 colors.

Working in 256 Colors

You have wonderful images you've developed for multimedia presentations. And unless you're developing some *cinema noir* Raymond Chandler project, I'll bet they're all in 16.7 million colors. One way to work within the limitations of 256-color mode is to use few bitmaps in your presentation, and when creating fountain fills in CorelDraw, keep the number of steps around 20. CorelDraw's strength is its capability of creating good-looking art without using bitmaps. And converting quality bitmaps to 256 colors always hurts.

Secret

If you know you are going to be spending the day creating a presentation in CorelDraw for a system that may be set to display only 256 colors, before you start the project, Select View ➪ Color Palette ➪ Uniform. Similarly, to convert a bitmap to 256 colors, import it into CorelDraw, select Bitmap ➪ Convert To ➪ (Palleted) 8 Bit ➪ Uniform.

Smooth blends such as the ones displayed in Figure 21-1 should not be on your agenda for presentations that will be run on the typical computer. This image was created with Photo-Paint and Adobe Photoshop and rendered as a 300 dpi TIFF.

Figure 21-1: This image was created with Photo-Paint and Photoshop and rendered at 300 dpi.

Figure 21-2 is more like real life. This image was rendered to the screen (96 dpi), and it looks pretty good. As a 256-color image, the blends are not horrible. You can do some tricks to make smaller, low-resolution images appear punchy and dramatic on the screen.

Figure 21-2: The same image was created again on-screen at 96 dpi.

■ Make sure you employ Dithering ⇨ Error Diffusion when converting your image to 256 colors.

■ You will have to sacrifice accurate color value in an effort to at least put some zip back into the picture itself. First, import the image into Photo-Paint and adjust the Level Equalization. Choosing AutoLevels probably won't make much difference, but if you take the time to set the highs and lows yourself, you can do some good.

■ Try altering the Highlights a little using Photo-Paint's Color Balance tool. There's really no rule here, just keep your eye on the image and adjust the sliders until you see an improvement in the definition that was lost when the image was reduced to 256 colors.

■ Finally, I hate to say it, but a little bit of old fashioned Brightness-Contrast augmentation can also be helpful. These are tricks you can play that don't increase an image's loading time, or drag on your system resources during the presentation.

Secret

Many multimedia developers make the mistake of importing an oversized picture into the presentation and then using the presentation software's Resize tools to shrink the image to a size appropriate for the presentation. Even after resizing, you will end up using more CPU power to work with this imported picture than if you had reduced its size and resolution before importing it.

Working Around 256-Color Mode

Now, if you want to see what a 16.7 million color picture looks like when you open it in 256-color mode (which you shouldn't), take a look at Figure 21-3.

Figure 21-3: This is what a 16.7 million color image looks like opened in 256-color mode.

If the presenter were to convert the picture to 256-color mode by choosing a palette and employing dithering, the results would not be so bad.

The picture in Figure 21-3 was treated with the Photo-Paint techniques explained earlier, and also greatly profited from a trip to Photoshop's "Despeckle" filter. (In Photoshop, select Filter ⇨ Noise ⇨ Despeckle.) These extras help take the "dull layer" off the image that often results from the conversion process.

Secret

In the preceding example, I recommend using a Photoshop filter for treating an image. Because you've already converted your image to 256 colors, that filter will not be initially available. After opening your image in Photoshop, select Mode ⇨ RBG, and the filter should then be available. When you are finished, select Mode ⇨ Indexed Color. You can now save your image.

Opening a 16.7 million color picture while working in 256-color mode will severely deplete system resources of the computer that is trying to run your presentation, making the computer sound like the train in that children's story that says, "I think I can, I think I can." Actually it can't. I've had computers report General Protection Fault errors when opening 16.7 million color images in 256-color mode.

Windows machines default to 256-color mode. Unless you're an artist or designer, one would not have a reason to learn about changing color modes. When you open a bitmap in 256-color mode, the Windows system palette does a fair job of rendering the bitmap. (It's only when you open a bitmap that was previously saved in 16.7 million colors that you run into problems.) Changing a computer's color mode involves loading new drivers, going back and searching for the floppy disks that came with the video card, restarting your computer, and other chores that the average viewer of your presentation might not have an interest in. Additionally, standard consumer-grade computers that are more than two years old generally came equipped with video cards that could not comfortably handle high color modes. I'm afraid it's up to us as designers of multimedia titles to see to it that our presentations run well under less-than-optimal conditions.

Using Interesting Colors

The need to convert images to 256 colors often arises out of a dependence on using bitmaps and complex images in projects. Graphic artists operate on the principle that these complex images are more impressive. Sometimes, however, the use of complimentary and harmonious color arrangements can create a presentation that looks just as professional.

Let's briefly review some principles for combining colors in multimedia presentations.

As you know, the primary colors are Red, Blue, and Yellow; and complimentary colors are their opposites on the color wheel. Red compliments Green, Blue compliments Orange, and Yellow compliments Purple. Lots of Web pages out there have some form of lavender or purple backgrounds, with yellow text. This combination is an example of complimentary color usage. Mixing a blue-green background with a light orange text is another example of complimentary color usage.

Using Contrasts

In designing a presentation, the idea is to provide visually pleasing contrasts so that the viewers understand what they are supposed to focus on, and what is merely an aesthetic background. You have several ways to achieve good color contrast values in your work, and the examples mentioned previously are the most obvious.

You can compose a presentation that uses perhaps only two color hues, but with a large variation of the light and dark values of those hues. When objects are more lit up, our eye perceives them as being closer. Using this simple principle, one can create a multimedia presentation with fewer colors, tastefully varying the light and dark values of those colors, rather than switching to a new hue. When done correctly, these type of presentations can look quite professional and businesslike.

Similarly, you can build a presentation with *warm* and *cool* color contrasts. Using a landscape analogy, cool colors — green, blue, and purple, and, for multimedia use, brown — lend depth and visual weight to your project. They are generally used as background colors, just as in a landscape portrait. For example, a blue lake, green grass that goes on forever, and brown mountains provide depth and distance to a work of art. That's why blue, green, purple, and darker shades of brown are often called "receding colors." Conversely, warm colors, such as yellow, orange, and red (and their common shades), provide excitement, and appear closer to the eye than do the cooler colors. Red, yellow, and orange are often called "advancing colors."

You can also build subtle contrast into your work by using a "split harmony" color scheme. Have your foreground (text or main image) favor yellow and orange, for example. Now select complimentary colors just to the right or left on the color wheel as your primary color (yellow). In this case, these colors would be purple-blue and purple-red. The subtle alteration avoids the obvious "yellow-purple" combination, but still provides a workable color scheme for your presentation.

To understand how these principles work, take some time examining the color wheel in CorelDraw, and get a feel for which colors and shades are across, or complimentary, from one another. Or, familiarize yourself with selecting color values for your work by viewing some of the templates that come with some of the big multimedia presentation packages, such as Macromedia Director, WordPerfect Suite 7 Presentations, and Office 97 PowerPoint.

Keep in mind also, that adapting a color scheme does not mean that you can never deviate from that scheme in the presentation. In fact, including a graphic that totally stands out apart from the color scheme is one way to make the scheme work for you. But color schemes are good for determining text color, background color, borders, line art, and any objects that your viewers are going to have to view over and over again on each slide. And luckily, adapting a good color scheme can save you from having to spend hours converting images that worked well in high-color modes to something that will work in 256-color mode.

Summary

In this chapter, you learned:

▶ How to work around the 256-color limitation when working with high-quality bitmaps in your presentations

▶ How to use color schemes to diminish your reliance on photograph bitmaps when creating presentations

▶ Techniques that help make your presentations run smoothly and look good even on older computers, or computers running under less than optimal conditions

Chapter 22

Distribution Options

In This Chapter

▶ Portable data storage

▶ Recordable CDs

▶ PKZIP

Graphic designers spend a huge percentage of their time shuffling data around. Moving documents of Herculean file sizes to a service bureau can become a major task. Floppy disks, which have a small storage capacity, are often not a suitable medium for transporting your documents from place to place. As the size of your Draw files grows and grows, you might be wondering how in the world you are ever going to get them somewhere to print them out professionally.

Happily, you have several options. There are many media types that can hold the equivalent of hundreds of floppy disks, such as the following:

- **Iomega Zip Drives**, which come in SCSI internal or Parallel Port external models

- **SyQuest EZ Drives**, which come in SCSI internal or external models

- **Iomega Bernoulli Drives**, which are cartridge drives available in internal or external models

- **SyQuest Cartridge Drives**, another model of cartridge drive, available in internal and external models

- **Iomega Jaz Drives**, which are SCSI drives and available as an internal or external drive

- **The Olympus SYS 230 MO Drive**, which can be purchased as SCSI or Parallel port and runs with 230MB disks

Recordable CD drives are discussed later in this chapter.

Portable Data Storage

All of the names and brands mentioned previously and the technology they represent put you in the business of transporting between 100MB and 1GB of data in your hip pocket. Such is the stuff of true freedom and power. After reading this chapter, you may never use floppies again.

The discs required for any of these media types described previously weigh less than a pound. The smallest is the Zip disk, which looks like an overgrown floppy disk; the largest is the cartridge for the Bernoulli Drive, which is shaped like a CD caddy and is about as big as one of the pancakes they serve at Denny's restaurants. These devices vary greatly in storage capacity, reliability, and acceptance by service bureaus and print houses at large. The smallest storage device is the Zip Drive, weighing in at a disk capacity of 100MB. The largest storage device is the Jaz Drive, which can hold 1GB in a disk that is about as large as a beeper.

Now let's cut to the chase. As of this writing, your best buy per megabyte, dollar per dollar, is the Iomega Jaz drive. The cartridges cost between $89 and $100 and can hold 1GB of information.

When you're considering the various distribution options, however, it's important to understand the following terminology.

SCSI

SCSI (pronounced *scuzzy*) stands for Small Computer System Interface. SCSI devices on your computer employ a different technology than standard IDE or Enhanced IDE hard drives and CD-ROM drives. A bus card is placed in your computer, and information from the SCSI device is routed through this card, bypassing the normal channels. The SCSI technology "frees up" your CPU to do more computing chores, rather than managing peripheral devices like hard drives. SCSI adapters, which are a bit larger than sound cards, cost between $200 and $400, and are not hard to install. Adaptec is the most popular manufacture of SCSI cards for PCs. You may have only one SCSI device on your computer, perhaps a Jaz Drive, while your hard drive and CD-ROM drive are standard, non-SCSI. The following are the advantages of SCSI devices:

- They are extremely fast.

- You can quickly install up to seven devices, such as scanners, additional hard drives, and portable drives, without any denigration in performance.

- Since SCSI technology reduces utilization of the CPU for managing devices, you will notice an increase in overall computer performance.

- Because it is quite easy to link multiple SCSI devices, most of the movable media drives you'll see on the market are SCSI as well.

SCSI versus Parallel Port

One more bit of general information before we take a look at each device. A movable drive attached to your Parallel Port will inevitably be much slower than its SCSI counterpart. The Parallel Port is one of the oldest pieces of technology in your computer. It cannot transfer data nearly as fast as a standard hard drive, much less a SCSI hard drive. Newer computers have Enhanced Parallel Port performance, which improves the situation somewhat, but by and large, data transfer to and from a Parallel Port removable drive feels like you are saving data to one giant floppy disk.

Running programs

Today's portable drives and disks are faster than ever. Some are as fast as most hard drives. I was able to install Adobe Photoshop on a SCSI Zip disk and run it from there, noticing only a slight amount of speed loss. Some of the devices we'll discuss can function as actual hard drives, and are worth more to you than a data donkey. I wouldn't get into the habit of installing Windows software on movable media, however, because Windows may report errors if certain program files are not found because you've moved the files. But the fact is, you *can* use some of the better movable drives to actually run applications. Zip disks, however, are not as durable as Jaz Drive disks and can wear out, just like their ancestor, the floppy disk.

Before you buy

If you've already picked out the service bureau or printing house you intend to work with, your choices in purchasing a portable drive will be limited by what that company uses. Call them up and find out what sort of portable storage medium they support. Most services can facilitate more than one type of device. For example, many have Zip Drives and the older Bernoulli cartridge drives as well. If you haven't selected a service bureau yet, perhaps you ought to delay purchasing a portable hard drive until you do. One more general observation to make that is common between all the above devices: With the exception of the Zip Drive, the internal model of each of these drives will cost about one hundred dollars less than the external version.

Your portable storage options

Figure 22-1 shows some of the best options out there.

Figure 22-1: These are a few of the data storage options available.

Now, here are the specifics of each product.

The Iomega Zip Drive

The Iomega Zip Drive is the most popular portable drive with home computer users and is gaining popularity rapidly with service bureaus. The drives themselves cost between $150 and $250 and are very small. They are available in internal SCSI and external Parallel Port models. The Zip disks themselves cost between $15 and $20 each and can hold 100MB of information. Buying the Zip disks in bulk greatly reduces the cost. The external Parallel Port model, slow as it is, can be a lifesaver for laptop users who need to transport data from a laptop to a home or office desktop computer. Zip disks also have a low failure rate. I have never known one to present a problem when it was reading back data.

The SyQuest EZ Drive

SyQuest's EZ Drive is similar to the Iomega Zip Drive; however, it holds 135MB of data, rather than 100MB. The EZ Drive comes in external and internal SCSI models. The unit itself costs slightly more than the Zip Drive. The disks are 15 to 25 percent more expensive than Iomega Zip disks, and it's hard to find a vendor that can keep them in stock. They are, however, faster than a Zip Drive, and many EZ Drive owners run applications from them, interchangeably with their hard drive.

The external unit is not as thin and sleek as the Zip Drive. While the Zip Drives are becoming a fashion statement on Silicon Valley coffee tables, EZ Drives are tireless workhorses. Just like Apple computer owners vehemently insist that theirs is the better mousetrap, EZ Drive owners claim that this product performs head over heels above the Zip Drive.

The Iomega Bernoulli Cartridge Drive

It would be hard to find a service bureau in the United States that doesn't have a Bernoulli cartridge drive. These drives represent the older "cartridge" technology that has enjoyed many years of popularity with graphic designers and others who must print their work. The standard Bernoulli Drive available today works with a 230MB cartridge and is capable of running the older Bernoulli formats, which featured cartridges that carried between 150 and 35MB of data.

The SyQuest Drive

As the phrase is used in service bureau lingo, "Yes, we have a SyQuest Drive." The reference might not be to a literal driver produced by the SyQuest Corporation, but to the longstanding technology that SyQuest first developed. If there is a portable media "standard" recognized between graphic designers and service bureaus, it is the SyQuest Drive. The drives support 44, 88, 200, and 270MB disks. There are both internal and external SyQuest Drives. Surprisingly, given their acceptance in the field, disk failure rates can be high, especially when storing data for more than a year.

The Jaz Drive

The Jaz Drive is currently the fastest and highest capacity portable drive on the market at this time. The drive itself sells for $400 for the internal model and $500 for the external model, both SCSI. Disks cost in the neighborhood of $100, making it by far the best "dollar per megabyte" deal. The Jaz Drive is one of the newest on the market, certainly the newest of all the drives mentioned previously. Therefore, it is hard to say how the drive will rate as far as "permanent" storage capabilities. However, all signs indicate that they function with all the speed and reliability of any 1MB hard drive that just happens to be portable. Since Jaz Drives are new, one should not assume that your favorite service bureau supports them. However, they are quickly gaining in popularity.

Secret

When transferring large amounts of data within various directories from one drive to another, it's easy to forget what got transferred and what didn't. If you just did an archive two weeks ago, and then went on to begin an important project, you might want to archive those new files as well. What do you do, transfer *all* the files again just because you can't remember where all the new ones are? Not necessarily. There are many new file management programs that will synchronize files between two groups of directories, scanning both and updating the archived files with anything new. This process is much faster than copying all of the recently archived files over again. For example, on the Internet, search for a shareware program called "Drag and File." This product synchronizes data transfers so that only new files are added.

Recordable CD Technology

Recordable CD drives have now dropped to the price that standard CD drives were at when they first entered the market six years ago. And if history is any indicator, today's luxury will become tomorrow's necessity. But CD-Recorders still have their drawbacks. For starters, the amount of free hard drive space on your computer must exceed the amount of data you want to archive on your CD-Recorder. You cannot use your computer while you are saving data to the CD. At this time, most CD-Recorders will save data at a rate equaling a double-speed CD drive. (Although many of the newer CD-Recorders will play CD-ROMs at the quad-speed rate.) Therefore, saving "an entire CD worth" of data will take about 45 minutes. And if there are problems, you'll have to throw the CD out and record again on a new one. Because the recording process actually "burns" the data into the CD via a laser, you cannot use the CD again once a session has gone awry. (At that point, it starts to matter that Recordable CDs cost about $8 each.)

One more considerable limitation: When working with Jaz Drives or other movable media, you can save some data today, leave the rest blank, and come back tomorrow and add some more. The way CD-Recorder technology works, one session becomes a hard drive. As far as File Manager is concerned, when you are done recording CD-ROM data to disk, you have created a hard drive. Yes, you can come back later and record more data on your disk. But it will be archived and read later as yet another hard drive. Before long, you're going to have to change the "Last Drive=" line in your Config.sys file to equal drive "Z." And all of this just for one CD! Not a good thing. And there is one potential situation that has led to more than one "oops" around our household: What happens when you are using data you cleverly archived on your recordable CD, but then want to use your CD-ROM for a CD-ROM-based program? If you take out the recorded CD while you are utilizing data from it, your computer will most likely crash.

In spite of all these complaints and caveats, nothing can beat the convenience of popping in a CD and retrieving last month's work you did for a client, or having all of your best artwork archived on one CD-ROM. The following are some of the advantages of CD-Recorders in graphic design work:

- CDs are 100 percent archival. Unless they are scratched, they won't fail a year from now just when you need them most.

- You can distribute your work to clients and potential customers on a CD, which is a medium anyone with a desktop computer is almost sure to have access to.

- The "dollar per megabyte" value exceeds even the Jaz Drive. If all goes well with your session, you can save 640MB of data on a disk that costs $8, as opposed to a 1GB Jaz disk that costs $100.

There is a large variety of CD-Recorder software available to choose from. Not all packages are created equal. The most desirable feature in a CD-Recording Software is reliability of data transfer, followed closely by the product utilizing a simple interface that shows the directories and files on one side of the screen being neatly transferred over to synchronized directories on the other. The most usable and well-rounded CD-recording software I have seen is Corel's CD Creator.

PKZIP

Sometimes a floppy disk isn't enough. What are you going to do if the file you need to send to somebody is 1.6MB? Send the information on a $20 Zip disk because the file exceeds a floppy disk's capacity by 200K? No! You use PKZIP.

PKZIP is a universally available program that compresses data to an infinitesimal portion of its previous size. It can shrink certain kinds of TIFF files down from 5MB to 112K. Using PKZIP, a 10MB Microsoft Publisher file will end up requiring only 590K of disk space. You "zip" your files using a simple command line in DOS or pointing and clicking your way in Windows. When you want to use the file, it is "unzipped" using a similar command line.

That being said, the actual executable files that comprise PKZIP are less than 100K total. If you place these two executable files in your DOS or Windows directory, you can run a PKZIP session from any directory or drive on your computer.

Although there are elaborate versions of PKZIP available for Windows and Windows 95, PKZIP itself works with a very simple command line. It works well through DOS or Windows, or in a DOS window. In five years of using PKZIP to shrink files and save them to floppy disks, I have never had PKZIP fail to recover a file due to an error in the program. You may locate a Windows version of PKZIP by logging on to your favorite Web search engine and typing "WinZip." Retrieve the DOS version similarly by searching for a file called "PKZIP."

One "spin" on the familiar PKZIP program that deserves special mention is Zip Folders, by Mijenix (download the 30-day, fully functional demo from www.mijenix.com). Although your files are zipped, you'd never know it. All your zipped files are fully functional in DOS or Windows. They appear in Windows Explorer in an unzipped state, and can be opened, edited, and saved just as if they were not zipped. But in reality, the files are fully zipped and thus use very little disk space. With Mijenix Zip Folders, you can enjoy the functionality of having all of your files handy, with the disk storage savings of zipped files.

You can use PKZIP to archive data across several floppy disks. When it comes time to unzip the data, the program prompts you to insert another floppy at the appropriate time. This is one of those simple programs that always works. What follows are two instances of using PKZIP command lines from DOS to zip a file:

- To zip a file called "Myart.tif" you log on to the directory where the file you want to zip is located and type: **pkzip myfile.zip myfile.tif** (watch the spaces!).

- To zip a large file across several floppy disks you would type: **pkzip -& a:\myfile.zip myfile.tif**

- PKZIP will work with any standard wildcard. For example, you can type **pkzip mytif.zip *.tif.** This would create one zipped file of every TIF file in the current directory.

- The nice thing is you need not remember any of this. If you have the pkzip executable file in your DOS or Windows directory, type **pkzip /h** and you'll receive a menu of switches that qualify the pkzip command, and their explanations.

- For those DOS-deprived, the various Windows versions of PKZIP work just as well with the same results.

PKZIP is a proprietary product distributed on the World Wide Web and is included with various software packages. If you use PKZIP without registering it and sending the company a little bit of money, "nag lines" will appear on the screen every time you open or close the Windows-based version of the program.

Summary

▶ It is imperative for the graphic artist to be adept at managing large files. If managed poorly, the simple chore of moving large art files from place to place, as well as minimizing disk space loss, can take up more time than creating art!

▶ There are many movable storage options available, ranging from Zip Disk Drives that contain 100MB of data, to Jaz Drives that can store 1GB of data, allowing you to access it as if it were a fully functional hard drive. Increasingly, recordable CD-ROM drives are becoming more popular and user-friendly.

▶ For smaller jobs, the PKZIP program, which compresses files down to their smallest possible storage space, provides a way to store and transport art files in convenient, small chunks. PKZIP is especially helpful when the need arises to move documents that are larger than a floppy disk's capacity, but not large enough to require a movable hard drive.

Appendix

What's On the CD-ROM?

Deciding what to put on the CD-ROM that comes with this book was no easy task! The CorelDRAW suite already ships with so many applications and utilities and plug-ins and fonts and clip art and . . . well, you get the idea. So, I looked around for some unique and useful utilities you don't get with the CorelDRAW package. I hope these goodies make your work with CorelDRAW more productive.

So, here's what's on the CD-ROM. The following is a description of the CD-ROM's various subdirectories (in alphabetical order) and what's in them:

Artshow

This is a collection of the images showcased in this book's second color insert. Many thanks to the artists who contributed. You can open these images in CorelDraw and check them out, but you can't reproduce them for any reason. They belong to the artists. But do study these images, as they can teach you a lot, especially if you examine the details. These files are in the Corel Presentation Exchange (CPX) fromat. You'll have to use File ⇨ Import rather than File ⇨ Open to bring them into CorelDraw.

Bills_art

This collection of artwork, created by one of this book's authors, appears in the first color insert. You can open this artwork in CorelDraw and Photo-Paint to see how it was created, but please don't use it in any of your layouts. Much of it belongs to William Harrel's clients and is used with their permission.

Chapter 9

These are the supporting files for Chapter 9. You'll find instructions in the chapter for using these files, and also please see this chapter's readme file on the CD-ROM.

Chapter10

These are the supporting files for Chapter 10. You'll find instructions in the chapter for using these files, and also please see this chapter's readme file on the CD-ROM.

Chapter12

These are the supporting files for Chapter 12. You'll find instructions in the chapter for using these files, and also please see this chapter's readme file on the CD-ROM.

Chapter13

These are the supporting files for Chapter 13. You'll find instructions in the chapter for using these files, and also please see this chapter's readme file on the CD-ROM.

CorelMag

This is the contents of the *Corel Magazine* sampler, containing several scripts you can run to automate tasks in CorelDRAW applications. Instructions for using them appear in the various readme files in the CorelMag directory.

ImageClb

This is a collection of sample images from Image Club. Feel free to use these in your work. And if you like them, check out the readme.txt file to find out how to get more. These are EPS, PCT, and TIFF files. You should use Import when bringing them into CorelDraw. You should use Open when bringing them into Photo-Paint.

MetTools

MetaTools provided this nifty collection of plug-in demos, including the popular Kai's Power Tools, a Photoshop plug-in that also works with Photo-Paint. Information for obtaining the full version of Kai's Power Tools and the other demos in the MetTools directory appears in the Acrobat files in the Acrobat subdirectory. Keep in mind that these are marketing demos, and are "crippled" in one way or another. Some, for example, won't let you save files. To get full use of the programs in this directory, you should contact MetaTools for the full versions.

Enjoy!

INDEX

C

P

10/31/95

The Internet For Macs® For Dummies® 2nd Edition	by Charles Seiter	ISBN: 1-56884-371-2	$19.99 USA/$26.99 Canada
The Internet For Macs® For Dummies® Starter Kit	by Charles Seiter	ISBN: 1-56884-244-9	$29.99 USA/$39.99 Canada
The Internet For Macs® For Dummies® Starter Kit Bestseller Edition	by Charles Seiter	ISBN: 1-56884-245-7	$39.99 USA/$54.99 Canada
The Internet For Windows® For Dummies® Starter Kit	by John R. Levine & Margaret Levine Young	ISBN: 1-56884-237-6	$34.99 USA/$44.99 Canada
The Internet For Windows® For Dummies® Starter Kit, Bestseller Edition	by John R. Levine & Margaret Levine Young	ISBN: 1-56884-246-5	$39.99 USA/$54.99 Canada

MACINTOSH

Mac® Programming For Dummies®	by Dan Parks Sydow	ISBN: 1-56884-173-6	$19.95 USA/$26.95 Canada
Macintosh® System 7.5 For Dummies®	by Bob LeVitus	ISBN: 1-56884-197-3	$19.95 USA/$26.95 Canada
MORE Macs® For Dummies®	by David Pogue	ISBN: 1-56884-087-X	$19.95 USA/$26.95 Canada
PageMaker 5 For Macs® For Dummies®	by Galen Gruman & Deke McClelland	ISBN: 1-56884-178-7	$19.95 USA/$26.95 Canada
QuarkXPress 3.3 For Dummies®	by Galen Gruman & Barbara Assadi	ISBN: 1-56884-217-1	$19.99 USA/$26.99 Canada
Upgrading and Fixing Macs® For Dummies®	by Kearney Rietmann & Frank Higgins	ISBN: 1-56884-189-2	$19.95 USA/$26.95 Canada

MULTIMEDIA

Multimedia & CD-ROMs For Dummies® 2nd Edition	by Andy Rathbone	ISBN: 1-56884-907-9	$19.99 USA/$26.99 Canada
Multimedia & CD-ROMs For Dummies® Interactive Multimedia Value Pack, 2nd Edition	by Andy Rathbone	ISBN: 1-56884-909-5	$29.99 USA/$39.99 Canada

OPERATING SYSTEMS:

DOS

MORE DOS For Dummies®	by Dan Gookin	ISBN: 1-56884-046-2	$19.95 USA/$26.95 Canada
OS/2® Warp For Dummies® 2nd Edition	by Andy Rathbone	ISBN: 1-56884-205-8	$19.99 USA/$26.99 Canada

UNIX

MORE UNIX® For Dummies®	by John R. Levine & Margaret Levine Young	ISBN: 1-56884-361-5	$19.99 USA/$26.99 Canada
UNIX® For Dummies®	by John R. Levine & Margaret Levine Young	ISBN: 1-878058-58-4	$19.95 USA/$26.95 Canada

WINDOWS

MORE Windows® For Dummies® 2nd Edition	by Andy Rathbone	ISBN: 1-56884-048-9	$19.95 USA/$26.95 Canada
Windows® 95 For Dummies®	by Andy Rathbone	ISBN: 1-56884-240-6	$19.99 USA/$26.99 Canada

PCS/HARDWARE

Illustrated Computer Dictionary For Dummies® 2nd Edition	by Dan Gookin & Wallace Wang	ISBN: 1-56884-218-X	$12.95 USA/$16.95 Canada
Upgrading and Fixing PCs For Dummies® 2nd Edition	by Andy Rathbone	ISBN: 1-56884-903-6	$19.99 USA/$26.99 Canada

PRESENTATION/AUTOCAD

AutoCAD For Dummies®	by Bud Smith	ISBN: 1-56884-191-4	$19.95 USA/$26.95 Canada
PowerPoint 4 For Windows® For Dummies®	by Doug Lowe	ISBN: 1-56884-161-2	$16.99 USA/$22.99 Canada

PROGRAMMING

Borland C++ For Dummies®	by Michael Hyman	ISBN: 1-56884-162-0	$19.95 USA/$26.95 Canada
C For Dummies® Volume 1	by Dan Gookin	ISBN: 1-878058-78-9	$19.95 USA/$26.95 Canada
C++ For Dummies®	by Stephen R. Davis	ISBN: 1-56884-163-9	$19.95 USA/$26.95 Canada
Delphi Programming For Dummies®	by Neil Rubenking	ISBN: 1-56884-200-7	$19.99 USA/$26.99 Canada
Mac® Programming For Dummies®	by Dan Parks Sydow	ISBN: 1-56884-173-6	$19.95 USA/$26.95 Canada
PowerBuilder 4 Programming For Dummies®	by Ted Coombs & Jason Coombs	ISBN: 1-56884-325-9	$19.99 USA/$26.99 Canada
QBasic Programming For Dummies®	by Douglas Hergert	ISBN: 1-56884-093-4	$19.95 USA/$26.95 Canada
Visual Basic 3 For Dummies®	by Wallace Wang	ISBN: 1-56884-076-4	$19.95 USA/$26.95 Canada
Visual Basic "X" For Dummies®	by Wallace Wang	ISBN: 1-56884-230-9	$19.99 USA/$26.99 Canada
Visual C++ 2 For Dummies®	by Michael Hyman & Bob Arnson	ISBN: 1-56884-328-3	$19.99 USA/$26.99 Canada
Windows® 95 Programming For Dummies®	by S. Randy Davis	ISBN: 1-56884-327-5	$19.99 USA/$26.99 Canada

SPREADSHEET

1-2-3 For Dummies®	by Greg Harvey	ISBN: 1-878058-60-6	$16.95 USA/$22.95 Canada
1-2-3 For Windows® 5 For Dummies® 2nd Edition	by John Walkenbach	ISBN: 1-56884-216-3	$16.95 USA/$22.95 Canada
Excel 5 For Macs® For Dummies®	by Greg Harvey	ISBN: 1-56884-186-8	$19.95 USA/$26.95 Canada
Excel For Dummies® 2nd Edition	by Greg Harvey	ISBN: 1-56884-050-0	$16.95 USA/$22.95 Canada
MORE 1-2-3 For DOS For Dummies®	by John Weingarten	ISBN: 1-56884-224-4	$19.99 USA/$26.99 Canada
MORE Excel 5 For Windows® For Dummies®	by Greg Harvey	ISBN: 1-56884-207-4	$19.95 USA/$26.95 Canada
Quattro Pro 6 For Windows® For Dummies®	by John Walkenbach	ISBN: 1-56884-174-4	$19.95 USA/$26.95 Canada
Quattro Pro For DOS For Dummies®	by John Walkenbach	ISBN: 1-56884-023-3	$16.95 USA/$22.95 Canada

UTILITIES

Norton Utilities 8 For Dummies®	by Beth Slick	ISBN: 1-56884-166-3	$19.95 USA/$26.95 Canada

VCRS/CAMCORDERS

VCRs & Camcorders For Dummies™	by Gordon McComb & Andy Rathbone	ISBN: 1-56884-229-5	$14.99 USA/$20.99 Canada

WORD PROCESSING

Ami Pro For Dummies®	by Jim Meade	ISBN: 1-56884-049-7	$19.95 USA/$26.95 Canada
MORE Word For Windows® 6 For Dummies®	by Doug Lowe	ISBN: 1-56884-165-5	$19.95 USA/$26.95 Canada
MORE WordPerfect® 6 For Windows® For Dummies®	by Margaret Levine Young & David C. Kay	ISBN: 1-56884-206-6	$19.95 USA/$26.95 Canada
MORE WordPerfect® 6 For DOS For Dummies®	by Wallace Wang, edited by Dan Gookin	ISBN: 1-56884-047-0	$19.95 USA/$26.95 Canada
Word 6 For Macs® For Dummies®	by Dan Gookin	ISBN: 1-56884-190-4	$19.95 USA/$26.95 Canada
Word For Windows® 6 For Dummies®	by Dan Gookin	ISBN: 1-56884-075-6	$16.95 USA/$22.95 Canada
Word For Windows® For Dummies®	by Dan Gookin & Ray Werner	ISBN: 1-878058-86-X	$16.95 USA/$22.95 Canada
WordPerfect® 6 For DOS For Dummies®	by Dan Gookin	ISBN: 1-878058-77-0	$16.95 USA/$22.95 Canada
WordPerfect® 6.1 For Windows® For Dummies® 2nd Edition	by Margaret Levine Young & David Kay	ISBN: 1-56884-243-0	$16.95 USA/$22.95 Canada
WordPerfect® For Dummies®	by Dan Gookin	ISBN: 1-878058-52-5	$16.95 USA/$22.95 Canada

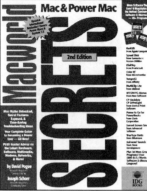

Macworld® Mac® & Power Mac SECRETS™, 2nd Edition
by David Pogue & Joseph Schorr

This is the definitive Mac reference for those who want to become power users! Includes three disks with 9MB of software!

ISBN: 1-56884-175-2
$39.95 USA/$54.95 Canada

Includes 3 disks chock full of software.

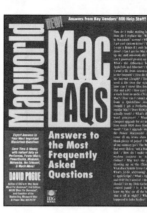

Macworld® Mac® FAQs™
by David Pogue

Written by the hottest Macintosh author around, David Pogue, *Macworld Mac FAQs* gives users the ultimate Mac reference. Hundreds of Mac questions and answers side-by-side, right at your fingertips, and organized into six easy-to-reference sections with lots of sidebars and diagrams.

ISBN: 1-56884-480-8
$19.99 USA/$26.99 Canada

Macworld® System 7.5 Bible, 3rd Edition
by Lon Poole

ISBN: 1-56884-098-5
$29.95 USA/$39.95 Canada

Macworld® ClarisWorks 3.0 Companion, 3rd Edition
by Steven A. Schwartz

ISBN: 1-56884-481-6
$24.99 USA/$34.99 Canada

Macworld® Complete Mac® Handbook Plus Interactive CD, 3rd Edition
by Jim Heid

ISBN: 1-56884-192-2
$39.95 USA/$54.95 Canada

Includes an interactive CD-ROM.

Macworld® Ultimate Mac® CD-ROM
by Jim Heid

ISBN: 1-56884-477-8
$19.99 USA/$26.99 Canada

CD-ROM includes version 2.0 of QuickTime, and over 65 MB of the best shareware, freeware, fonts, sounds, and more!

Macworld® Networking Bible, 2nd Edition
by Dave Kosiur & Joel M. Snyder

ISBN: 1-56884-194-9
$29.95 USA/$39.95 Canada

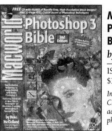

Macworld® Photoshop 3 Bible, 2nd Edition
by Deke McClelland

ISBN: 1-56884-158-2
$39.95 USA/$54.95 Canada

Includes stunning CD-ROM with add-ons, digitized photos and more.

Macworld® Photoshop 2.5 Bible
by Deke McClelland

ISBN: 1-56884-022-5
$29.95 USA/$39.95 Canada

Macworld® FreeHand 4 Bible
by Deke McClelland

ISBN: 1-56884-170-1
$29.95 USA/$39.95 Canada

Macworld® Illustrator 5.0/5.5 Bible
by Ted Alspach

ISBN: 1-56884-097-7
$39.95 USA/$54.95 Canada

Includes CD-ROM with QuickTime tutorials.

Mac is a registered trademark of Apple Computer. Macworld is a registered trademark of International Data Group, Inc. ----SECRETS, and ----FAQs are trademarks under exclusive license to IDG Books Worldwide, Inc., from International Data Group, Inc.

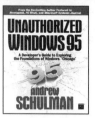

Unauthorized Windows® 95: A Developer's Guide to Exploring the Foundations of Windows "Chicago"
by Andrew Schulman

ISBN: 1-56884-169-8
$29.99 USA/$39.99 Canada

Unauthorized Windows® 95 Developer's Resource Kit
by Andrew Schulman

ISBN: 1-56884-305-4
$39.99 USA/$54.99 Canada

Best of the Net
by Seth Godin

ISBN: 1-56884-313-5
$22.99 USA/$32.99 Canada

Detour: The Truth About the Information Superhighway
by Michael Sullivan-Trainor

ISBN: 1-56884-307-0
$22.99 USA/$32.99 Canada

PowerPC Programming For Intel Programmers
by Kip McClanahan

ISBN: 1-56884-306-2
$49.99 USA/$64.99 Canada

Foundations™ of Visual C++ Programming For Windows® 95
by Paul Yao & Joseph Yao

ISBN: 1-56884-321-6
$39.99 USA/$54.99 Canada

Heavy Metal™ Visual C++ Programming
by Steve Holzner

ISBN: 1-56884-196-5
$39.95 USA/$54.95 Canada

Heavy Metal™ OLE 2.0 Programming
by Steve Holzner

ISBN: 1-56884-301-1
$39.95 USA/$54.95 Canada

Lotus Notes Application Development Handbook
by Erica Kerwien

ISBN: 1-56884-308-9
$39.99 USA/$54.99 Canada

The Internet Direct Connect Kit
by Peter John Harrison

ISBN: 1-56884-135-3
$29.95 USA/$39.95 Canada

Macworld® Ultimate Mac® Programming
by Dave Mark

ISBN: 1-56884-195-7
$39.95 USA/$54.95 Canada

The UNIX®-Haters Handbook
by Simson Garfinkel, Daniel Weise, & Steven Strassmann

ISBN: 1-56884-203-1
$16.95 USA/$22.95 Canada

Learn C++ Today!
by Martin Rinehart

ISBN: 1-56884-310-0
34.99 USA/$44.99 Canada

Type & Learn™ C
by Tom Swan

ISBN: 1-56884-073-X
34.95 USA/$44.95 Canada

Type & Learn™ Windows® Programming
by Tom Swan

ISBN: 1-56884-071-3
34.95 USA/$44.95 Canada

For scholastic requests & educational orders please call Educational Sales, at 1. 800. 434. 2086

FOR MORE INFO OR TO ORDER, PLEASE CALL ▶ 800. 762. 2974

For volume discounts & special orders please call Tony Real, Special Sales, at 415. 655. 3048

Official Hayes Modem Communications Companion
by Caroline M. Halliday
ISBN: 1-56884-072-1
$29.95 USA/$39.95 Canada
Includes software.

1,001 Komputer Answers from Kim Komando
by Kim Komando
ISBN: 1-56884-460-3
$29.99 USA/$39.99 Canada
Includes software.

PC World Excel 5 For Windows® Handbook, 2nd Edition
by John Walkenbach & Dave Maguiness
ISBN: 1-56884-056-X
$34.95 USA/$44.95 Canada
Includes software

PC World WordPerfect® 6 Handbook
by Greg Harvey
ISBN: 1-878058-80-0
$34.95 USA/$44.95 Canada
Includes software.

PC World DOS 6 Command Reference and Problem Solver
by John Socha & Devra Hall
ISBN: 1-56884-055-1
$24.95 USA/$32.95 Canada
NATIONAL BESTSELLER!

Client/Server Strategies™: A Survival Guide for Corporate Reengineers
by David Vaskevitch
SUPER STAR
ISBN: 1-56884-064-0
$29.95 USA/$39.95 Canada

Internet SECRETS™
by John Levine & Carol Baroudi
ISBN: 1-56884-452-2
$39.99 USA/$54.99 Canada
Includes software.

Network Security SECRETS™
by David Stang & Sylvia Moon
ISBN: 1-56884-021-7
Int'l. ISBN: 1-56884-151-5
$49.95 USA/$64.95 Canada
Includes software.

PC SECRETS™
by Caroline M. Halliday
ISBN: 1-878058-49-5
$39.95 USA/$52.95 Canada
Includes software.

IDG BOOKS WORLDWIDE

Here's a complete listing of PC Press Titles

Title	Author	ISBN	Price
BBS SECRETS™	by Ray Werner	ISBN: 1-56884-491-3	$39.99 USA/$54.99 Canada
Creating Cool Web Pages with HTML	by Dave Taylor	ISBN: 1-56884-454-9	$19.99 USA/$26.99 Canada
DOS 6 SECRETS™	by Robert D. Ainsbury	ISBN: 1-878058-70-3	$39.95 USA/$52.95 Canada
Excel 5 For Windows® Power Programming Techniques	by John Walkenbach	ISBN: 1-56884-303-8	$39.95 USA/$52.95 Canada
Hard Disk SECRETS™	by John M. Goodman, Ph.D.	ISBN: 1-878058-64-9	$39.95 USA/$52.95 Canada
Internet GIZMOS™ For Windows®	by Joel Diamond, Howard Sobel, & Valda Hilley	ISBN: 1-56884-451-4	$39.99 USA/$54.99 Canada
Making Multimedia Work	by Michael Goodwin	ISBN: 1-56884-468-9	$19.99 USA/$26.99 Canada
MORE Windows® 3.1 SECRETS™	by Brian Livingston	ISBN: 1-56884-019-5	$39.95 USA/$52.95 Canada
Official XTree Companion 3rd Edition	by Beth Slick	ISBN: 1-878058-57-6	$19.95 USA/$26.95 Canada
Paradox 4 Power Programming SECRETS™, 2nd Edition	by Gregory B. Salcedo & Martin W. Rudy	ISBN: 1-878058-54-1	$44.95 USA/$59.95 Canada
Paradox 5 For Windows® Power Programming SECRETS™	by Gregory B. Salcedo & Martin W. Rudy	ISBN: 1-56884-085-3	$44.95 USA/$59.95 Canada
PC World DOS 6 Handbook, 2nd Edition	by John Socha, Clint Hicks & Devra Hall	ISBN: 1-878058-79-7	$34.95 USA/$44.95 Canada
PC World Microsoft® Access 2 Bible, 2nd Edition	by Cary N. Prague & Michael R. Irwin	ISBN: 1-56884-086-1	$39.95 USA/$52.95 Canada
PC World Word For Windows® 6 Handbook	by Brent Heslop & David Angell	ISBN: 1-56884-054-3	$34.95 USA/$44.95 Canada
QuarkXPress For Windows® Designer Handbook	by Barbara Assadi & Galen Gruman	ISBN: 1-878058-45-2	$29.95 USA/$39.95 Canada
Windows® 3.1 Configuration SECRETS™	by Valda Hilley & James Blakely	ISBN: 1-56884-026-8	$49.95 USA/$64.95 Canada
Windows® 3.1 Connectivity SECRETS™	by Runnoe Connally, David Rorabaugh & Sheldon Hall	ISBN: 1-56884-030-6	$49.95 USA/$64.95 Canada
Windows® 3.1 SECRETS™	by Brian Livingston	ISBN: 1-878058-43-6	$39.95 USA/$52.95 Canada
Windows® 95 A.S.A.P.	by Dan Gookin	ISBN: 1-56884-483-2	$24.99 USA/$34.99 Canada
Windows® 95 Bible	by Alan Simpson	ISBN: 1-56884-074-8	$29.99 USA/$39.99 Canada
Windows® 95 SECRETS™	by Brian Livingston	ISBN: 1-56884-453-0	$39.99 USA/$54.99 Canada
Windows® GIZMOS™	by Brian Livingston & Margie Livingston	ISBN: 1-878058-66-5	$39.95 USA/$52.95 Canada
WordPerfect® 6 For Windows® Tips & Techniques Revealed	by David A. Holzgang & Roger C. Parker	ISBN: 1-56884-202-3	$39.95 USA/$52.95 Canada
WordPerfect® 6 SECRETS™	by Roger C. Parker & David A. Holzgang	ISBN: 1-56884-040-3	$39.95 USA/$52.95 Canada

For scholastic requests & educational orders please call Educational Sales, at 1. 800. 434. 2086

FOR MORE INFO OR TO ORDER, PLEASE CALL ▶ 800. 762. 2974

For volume discounts & special orders please call Tony Real, Special Sales, at 415. 655. 3048

ORDER FORM

Order Center: **(800) 762-2974** *(8 a.m.–6 p.m., EST, weekdays)*

3/26/96

Quantity	ISBN	Title	Price	Total

Shipping & Handling Charges

	Description	First book	Each additional book	Total
Domestic	Normal	$4.50	$1.50	$
	Two Day Air	$8.50	$2.50	$
	Overnight	$18.00	$3.00	$
International	Surface	$8.00	$8.00	$
	Airmail	$16.00	$16.00	$
	DHL Air	$17.00	$17.00	$

*For large quantities call for shipping & handling charges.
**Prices are subject to change without notice.

Ship to:

Name _____

Company _____

Address _____

City/State/Zip _____

Daytime Phone _____

Payment: ☐ Check to IDG Books Worldwide (US Funds Only)

☐ VISA   ☐ MasterCard   ☐ American Express

Card # _____ Expires _____

Signature _____

Subtotal _____

CA residents add
applicable sales tax _____

IN, MA, and MD
residents add
5% sales tax _____

IL residents add
6.25% sales tax _____

RI residents add
7% sales tax _____

TX residents add
8.25% sales tax _____

Shipping _____

Total _____

Please send this order form to:

**IDG Books Worldwide, Inc.
Attn: Order Entry Dept.
7260 Shadeland Station, Suite 100
Indianapolis, IN 46256**

*Allow up to 3 weeks for delivery.
Thank you!*

Credits

**Senior Vice President
and Group Publisher**
Brenda McLaughlin

Director of Publishing
Walt Bruce

Acquisitions Manager
John Osborn

Acquisitions Editor
Ellen Camm

Marketing Manager
Melisa M. Duffy

Executive Managing Editor
Terry Somerson

Development Editor
Ron Hull

Copy Editors
Michael D. Welch
Bob Campbell

Technical Editor
David Farkas

Editorial Assistant
Sharon Eames

Production Director
Andrew Walker

Project Coordinator
Katy German

Production Staff
Mario F. Amador
Laura Carpenter
Tom Debolski
Renée Dunn
Jude Levinson
Stephen Noetzel
Ed Penslien
Andreas F. Schueller
Mark Schumann

Quality Control Specialist
Mick Arellano

Proofreader
Christine Sabooni

Indexer
Lori Lathrop

Production Administration
Tony Augsburger
Todd Klemme
Jason Marcuson
Christopher Pimentel
Leslie Popplewell
Theresa Sánchez-Baker
Melissa Stauffer

Cover Design
Liew Design

About the Authors

William Harrel is a freelance writer and graphics designer based in Southern California. He has written 17 books on computer graphics-related topics, including coauthoring the *Macworld PageMaker 6.5 Bible*, *Lotus Freelance Graphics 97 For Dummies*, and *Adobe Acrobat 3.0 For Dummies*. In addition, he has written hundreds of articles for computer magazines, including *PC World*, *Publish*, and *Windows Magazine*. When not writing, he spends the rest of his waking hours "geeking" around with his new Internet company.

Winston Steward is a musician, and he and his wife Barbara homeschool their children on computers. He is the author of *Every Family's Guide to Computers*, *The Comprehensive Guide to WordPerfect Suite 7*, and coauthor of *The Guide to Macromedia Backstage Designer* and the *Word For Windows 97 Bible*.

IDG BOOKS WORLDWIDE LICENSE AGREEMENT

replace the defective software media. IDG's entire liability and your exclusive remedy shall be limited to replacement of the Software, which is returned to IDG with a copy of your receipt. This Limited Warranty is void if failure of the Software has resulted from accident, abuse, or misapplication. Any replacement Software will be warranted for the remainder of the original warranty period or thirty (30) days, whichever is longer.

5. <u>No Other Warranties</u>. To the maximum extent permitted by applicable law, IDG and the author disclaim all other warranties, express or implied, including but not limited to implied warranties of merchantability and fitness for a particular purpose, with respect to the Software, the programs, the source code contained therein and/or the techniques described in this Book. This limited warranty gives you specific legal rights. You may have others that vary from state/jurisdiction to state/jurisdiction.

6. <u>No Liability For Consequential Damages</u>. To the extent permitted by applicable law, in no event shall IDG or the author be liable for any damages whatsoever (including without limitation, damages for loss of business profits, business interruption, loss of business information, or any other pecuniary loss) arising out of the use of or inability to use the Book or the Software, even if IDG has been advised of the possibility of such damages. Because some states/jurisdictions do not allow the exclusion or limitation of liability for consequential or incidental damages, the above limitation may not apply to you.

7. <u>U.S. Government Restricted Rights</u>. Use, duplication, or disclosure of the Software by the U.S. Government is subject to restrictions stated in paragraph (c) (1) (ii) of the Rights in Technical Data and Computer Software clause of DFARS 252.227-7013, and in subparagraphs (a) through (d) of the Commercial Computer — Restricted Rights clause at FAR 52.227-19, and in similar clauses in the NASA FAR supplement, when applicable.

Replacement Software Media. If you need replacement software media, please write to the following address: IDG Books Software Media Fulfillment Center, Attn: *CorelDRAW 7 SECRETS*, IDG Books Worldwide, 7260 Shadeland Station, Indianapolis, IN 46256, or call 800-762-2974.

IDG BOOKS WORLDWIDE REGISTRATION CARD

RETURN THIS REGISTRATION CARD FOR FREE CATALOG

Title of this book: **CorelDRAW™ 7 SECRETS®**

My overall rating of this book: ❏ Very good [1] ❏ Good [2] ❏ Satisfactory [3] ❏ Fair [4] ❏ Poor [5]

How I first heard about this book:

❏ Found in bookstore; name: [6]

❏ Advertisement: [8]

❏ Word of mouth; heard about book from friend, co-worker, etc.: [10]

❏ Book review: [7]

❏ Catalog: [9]

❏ Other: [11]

What I liked most about this book:

What I would change, add, delete, etc., in future editions of this book:

Other comments:

Number of computer books I purchase in a year: ❏ 1 [12] ❏ 2-5 [13] ❏ 6-10 [14] ❏ More than 10 [15]

I would characterize my computer skills as: ❏ Beginner [16] ❏ Intermediate [17] ❏ Advanced [18] ❏ Professional [19]

I use ❏ DOS [20] ❏ Windows [21] ❏ OS/2 [22] ❏ Unix [23] ❏ Macintosh [24] ❏ Other: [25]_____
(please specify)

I would be interested in new books on the following subjects:
(please check all that apply, and use the spaces provided to identify specific software)

❏ Word processing: [26]

❏ Data bases: [28]

❏ File Utilities: [30]

❏ Networking: [32]

❏ Other: [34]

❏ Spreadsheets: [27]

❏ Desktop publishing: [29]

❏ Money management: [31]

❏ Programming languages: [33]

I use a PC at (please check all that apply): ❏ home [35] ❏ work [36] ❏ school [37] ❏ other: [38] _____

The disks I prefer to use are ❏ 5.25 [39] ❏ 3.5 [40] ❏ other: [41]_____

I have a CD ROM: ❏ yes [42] ❏ no [43]

I plan to buy or upgrade computer hardware this year: ❏ yes [44] ❏ no [45]

I plan to buy or upgrade computer software this year: ❏ yes [46] ❏ no [47]

Name: _____ Business title: [48] _____ Type of Business: [49] _____

Address (❏ home [50] ❏ work [51]/Company name: _____)

Street/Suite# _____

City [52]/State [53]/Zipcode [54]: _____ Country [55] _____

❏ **I liked this book!** You may quote me by name in future
IDG Books Worldwide promotional materials.

My daytime phone number is _____

IDG BOOKS

®

THE WORLD OF
COMPUTER
KNOWLEDGE

❏ YES!

Please keep me informed about IDG's World of Computer Knowledge.
Send me the latest IDG Books catalog.

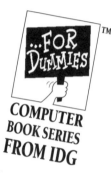

COMPUTER
BOOK SERIES
FROM IDG

BUSINESS REPLY MAIL

FIRST CLASS MAIL   PERMIT NO. 2605   FOSTER CITY, CALIFORNIA

IDG Books Worldwide
919 E Hillsdale Blvd, STE 400
Foster City, CA 94404-9691

NO POSTAGE
NECESSARY
IF MAILED
IN THE
UNITED STATES